Marketing
Research
In Practice
David Ashley
The George Washington University

Revised Printing

Kendall Hunt
publishing company

Kendall Hunt
publishing company

www.kendallhunt.com
Send all inquiries to:
4050 Westmark Drive
Dubuque, IA 52004-1840

Copyright © 2011 by David Ashley

Revised printing 2013

ISBN 978-1-4652-2292-3

Printed in the United States of America
10 9 8 7 6 5

BRIEF CONTENTS

BRIEF CONTENTS

TABLE OF CONTENTS

9 Questionnaire Design   149

10 Sampling Methods   171

PREFACE

Overview

Academic study and practical application meet in *Marketing Research in Practice,* an examination of the essential components of marketing research. Marketing research is a critical part of nearly every industry. From end users to practitioners, the marketing research profession is extremely varied and offers many exciting career paths that will position students for great opportunities in many industries such as entertainment, automotive, real estate, fashion, publishing, airline, travel, advertising, telecommunications, and pharmaceuticals, to name a few. Marketing research is a key driver in all of these industries. Marketing researchers also work in politics, sports, academia, and government. A firm understanding of marketing research, and its applications, will put today's students at an advantage in the business marketplace by opening doors to many job opportunities in a wide array of industries. Marketing researchers include focus group moderators and facility owners, interviewers, data analysts, data collectors, project managers, among many others. Knowing how to conduct a focus group, run an experiment, do observation research, conduct effective interviews, execute a survey, perform data analysis, and assemble a written report will position students for success in many professions.

This book presents marketing research in a practical, application based manner resulting in a clear understanding of the most important components of marketing research. This book covers the entire marketing research process from the initial research design to the final research report. Its fourteen chapters detail the marketing research process and examine the skills needed to become a marketing researcher. The *Issues in the Spotlight* features written by a diverse group of industry professionals provide students with real-world insight to the marketing research profession. These industry leaders detail their experiences as marketing research practitioners and put a practical face on marketing research as they discuss its implementation within their respective companies.

Marketing Research in Practice provides a comprehensive introduction to marketing research that will give students an effective foundation for future study and will provide them with knowledge they can leverage in the workplace.

Materials

This textbook includes sample Microsoft Excel data for data analysis drills as well as a Microsoft PowerPoint slide deck for instructor use both available through the publisher. In addition, there are three complete case studies in the appendix from the *Journal of Marketing Research* for examination and discussion and well as a guide on how to conduct a case analysis.

ACKNOWLEDGMENTS

Writing this textbook has been a challenging and rewarding experience in which I have tried to combine my years of academic study, university teaching, and professional work experience to produce a practical, application-based approach to marketing research. I could not have written this book without contributions and guidance from a number of people who, despite their hectic schedules, graciously offered their time, expertise, and advice in various ways for which I am most grateful. Special thanks go to Lara Sanders and Traci Vaske of Kendall Hunt Publishing who collectively provided critical guidance while navigating my work style graciously and without complaint. I am particularly grateful to long-time friend and colleague Michael Mermelstein who not only reviewed the text and provided detailed feedback, but also wrote an insightful marketing research vignette for this book on qualitative research. I am also greatly indebted to Professor Catherine Roster of the University of New Mexico who reviewed large parts of the text and whose substantive feedback and thoughtful insight was invaluable to this project. I would also like to thank Professors Jason Riis of Harvard University and Marian Moore of the University of Virginia for their support and guidance during this process.

I am especially appreciative of Jim Clifton, Chairman and CEO of Gallup, for taking the time from his busy schedule to provide the Foreword, and David Almy, CEO of the Marketing Research Association, for his contribution introducing us to the mission of the MRA. I would also like to express my deepest appreciation to the marketing research professionals and thought leaders who shared their expertise, insight, and wisdom by writing the *Issues in the Spotlight* vignettes. Students will benefit from their contributions which have added enormous practical value to the material. Finally, I must thank both my graduate assistant Sandhya Sivasankaran who has provided me invaluable assistance, and the many students I have had the pleasure of teaching over the years who unknowingly provided me the inspiration to write this book and who have left me with confidence about our future. My heartfelt thanks and continued best wishes go to them all.

Reviewers

Michael Mermelstein
President
G2 & Associates, LLC
www.g2associates.us

Professor Marian Moore
Darden School of Business
The University of Virginia

Professor Jason Riis
Harvard Business School
Harvard University

Professor Catherine Roster
Anderson School of Business
The University of New Mexico

Simone Smith
Community and Marketing Manager
HubPages.com—Star Student Emeritus

Industry Contributors

David Almy
Chief Executive Officer
The Marketing Research Association
www.marketingresearch.org

Jim Clifton
Chairman and Chief Executive Officer
Gallup
www.gallup.com

Seth Goldman
President
Honest Tea
www.honesttea.com

David Helfert
Adjunct Professor
The Johns Hopkins University
American University
Former Senior Advisor
Governor Neil Abercrombie (HI)

Lori Kaplan
Director, Audience Insight & Research
National Public Radio
www.npr.org

Jon Last
President
Sports & Leisure Research Group
www.sportsandleisureresearch.com

Jackie Lorch
Vice President, Global Knowledge Management
Survey Sampling International
www.surveysampling.com

Charles MacKay
General Director
The Santa Fe Opera
www.santafeopera.org

Michael Mermelstein
President
G2 & Associates, LLC
www.g2associates.us

Ed Sugar
Vice President
OLC Global
http://olcglobal.com

Timothy Triplett
Senior Survey Methodologist
Urban Institute
www.urban.org

Peter Van Brunt
President
ReData Inc.
www.redatainc.com

Jay White
President
Baltimore Research
www.baltimoreresearch.com

Case Contributions

Christopher Bartone
Managing Editor, Journals
The American Marketing Association
The Journal of Marketing Research

Brian Thompson
Acquisition Manager, Journals
The American Marketing Association
The Journal of Marketing Research

FOREWORD

Successful leaders collect and capitalize on data which come in multiple forms. Such data include secondary data, interviews, focus groups, questionnaires, observation, and experimental design. They are all critical tools that connect business leaders to their customers while also helping them to better understand the business challenges of the marketplace.

Gallup has used a variety of marketing research tools to study human nature and behavior for more than 75 years. Gallup's reputation for delivering relevant, timely, and visionary research on what people around the world think and feel is the cornerstone of the organization. Gallup employs many of the world's leading researchers and scientists in management, economics, psychology, and sociology.

As part of our research suite, Gallup Daily News provides leaders and decision makers worldwide with empirical evidence about how the world's seven billion citizens think and behave. Using many of the data collection and analysis tools detailed in this textbook, Gallup Daily News provides unique, unrivaled insight into the political, economic, and social issues of the moment.

Gallup further moves these sciences forward through Gallup University, a leading provider of degree and non-degree programs in management education and leadership development. Gallup University offers a complete curriculum to help leaders better leverage employee and customer assets to drive individual and organizational performance.

In *Marketing Research in Practice,* Professor Ashley examines the key facets of marketing research from research design to report writing and all the critical elements in between. He also couples practical examples with insight from industry experts to make this textbook a solid foundation in the study of marketing research. It is through these tools and the breakthroughs they bring that leaders discover the information they need to be successful.

Jim Clifton
Chairman and
Chief Executive Officer
Gallup
www.gallup.com

THE MARKETING RESEARCH ASSOCIATION

The Marketing Research Association (MRA) is the leading and largest professional society and trade association representing research professionals in the USA and the world. Founded in 1957, MRA's membership consists of corporate researchers, research service providers, research-related companies, and government researchers, as well as research professors and students. The Association's mission is to vigorously support and advocate for its members' professional growth and success.

MRA meets the challenges faced by a diverse community of research professionals by:

- Providing professional development services including broad-based business and technical education, as well as supporting Professional Researcher Certification (PRC)
- Facilitating a lively community for members with in-person networking events and dynamic social media environments
- Setting and enforcing standards of practice and ethical obligations for researchers
- Advocating on behalf of research to government officials and other stakeholders
- Monitoring new technologies and trends, then helping researchers to implement new methods of practice based on those developments

The recent popularity of user-generated online content is at the leading edge of the research profession. In addition to traditional modes of data collection (*e.g., telephone or Internet surveys, traditional in-person or online focus groups, or ethnographies*), researchers are harnessing information about consumers through observation of their public online communications. Blogs, micro-blogs, social networks, comment sections, and other social media offer powerful clues about how information spreads among the public as well as important trending information about brands, products, and market opportunities.

The full scope of uses for social media by research professionals continues to grow. In order to explore the potential of user-generated online content, MRA members are engaged in exploratory studies. Members have also developed questions and proposed answers regarding important ethical responsibilities to the public. These actions have begun to unify marketing researchers in the practice of social media research.

As the research profession tends to be very fluid in the development and adoption of new technologies and techniques, it is important for researchers to work together in order to understand the meaning and application of these developments on the practice of research. MRA functions, in large part, to provide for that future.

To learn more about MRA, its members, and the future of marketing research, please visit us at www.marketingresearch.org.

David Almy
Chief Executive Officer
The Marketing Research Association
www.marketingresearch.org

For the past ten years David Ashley has been teaching marketing research in Washington, D.C. His marketing research teaching includes Georgetown University, the George Washington University, and the Johns Hopkins University in Baltimore. He is also an adjunct professor and *Executive in Residence* at the University of Maryland (UMD) where he teaches project management, cross cultural research methods, and team building as part of the Quality Enhancement Systems and Teams (QUEST) program at the Smith School of Business. Professor Ashley has also taught marketing research for UMD and has led student study abroad trips to Italy, Tunisia, Brazil, and China.

Professor Ashley's other teaching includes faculty positions at the University of New Mexico and the France Business School in Tours, France as well as a visiting professor at the American University of Paris. He holds an undergraduate degree from the University of North Carolina and an MBA from the University of New Mexico. He has also successfully completed the *Hansard Scholars Programme in Parliamentary Government* at the University of London.

From 2008 to 2010 Professor Ashley served on the national board of the Marketing Research Association (MRA), as the Mid-Atlantic States Marketing Research Association chapter president for two terms, and in 2009 as board president of the *Marketing Research Institute International,* an educational consortium though the University of Georgia. Professor Ashley has also been certified at the expert researcher level by the MRA and has been published in *QUIRKS Marketing Research Review.*

He currently works for the Department of Homeland Security and has overseen various U.S. government research projects such as managing a review of the U.S. Fire Academy and anchoring a number of research studies for the U.S. Border Patrol Chief. He has also created a statistical model to assist the Federal Emergency Management Agency in determining its appropriate force structure size based on the number and severity of potential disaster-related events and has served as project manager on a number of projects aimed at building community and national resilience in times of emergency. Previously, Professor Ashley managed a number of national research projects as a marketing research lead while at the U.S. Small Business Administration. His other research work has included overseeing various U.S. government program review projects, conducting budget formulation and execution analysis, and leading a government contractor source selection team reviewing dozens of business proposals. Finally, he has been accepted into the President's Management Council Interagency Rotation Program which aims to increase participant exposure to other federal agencies though rotational assignments.

Before moving to Washington, Professor Ashley served as the director of the Small Business Development Center at the University of New Mexico where he led a staff charged with assisting area businesses with marketing research, business plan development, and financing packages designed to grow their businesses.

The Role of Marketing Research

Image © Yuri Arcurs, 2011. Used under license from Shutterstock, Inc.

Learning Objectives:

- Understand how marketing research is used in decision making
- Learn about common uses of marketing research
- Gain an appreciation for the main customers and users of marketing research
- Tie the marketing mix to marketing research
- Look at some common marketing research mistakes
- Learn some key reasons to conduct or not conduct marketing research
- Understand some common types of marketing research studies
- Appreciate how learning marketing research can aid your career
- Review careers in marketing research

Chapter One

arketing research informs business leaders about many aspects of the business and marketing environment in which they operate. Without solid information, business leaders will be unable to manage their businesses efficiently and effectively. Given that competition in many industries is intense, businesses need information that will put them at a competitive advantage. Turning data into actionable information is the foundation of marketing research. When students study marketing, they might not yet realize how business and marketing decisions are made. In fact, even everyday decisions are based on turning data into information. Consider something as routine as getting to the other side of the street. The next time you cross a busy street presumably you will "look both ways" before proceeding. Based on that information, you decide whether to cross the street. How about selecting the university you are attending or the courses you are taking? Did you do some research first? Have you ever asked a fellow student about a course he or she has taken before deciding which section to add? Marketing research is ultimately about making substantive and complex business decisions based on data collection, synthesis, and analysis. The point here is that even simple everyday decisions are based on data that is processed into information. Imagine entering complex and varied industries such as automotive, hotel chains, entertainment, telecommunication, publishing, or real estate without extensive research. Any product or service you buy or use is typically the result of some form of marketing research. The vast array of products and brand extensions are not created by happenstance. In many cases, years of research and a great deal of money are required to position a product or service for marketplace success. Although marketing research does not guarantee business success, trial and error is a well-known path to failure. Business leaders do not wing their way to wealth. The evidence is quite clear—well-run organizations rely on qualitative and quantitative information to make sound business decisions. Marketing research is about collecting, synthesizing, and analyzing data that become the foundation of decision making. This book covers the key aspects and steps of conducting a marketing research study. Its goal is to provide a practical application that will result in a lasting understanding of marketing research and its role in business decision making.

Organizations conduct research for many reasons. Developing a competitive edge in the marketplace is often a motivation for conducting marketing research. Perhaps a business has seen a decline in sales due to degradation in product or service quality or as the result of increased competition. Either way, businesses are ill-advised to ignore competitive forces in the marketplace. Figure 1.1 shows some common uses of marketing research.

Businesses might need to determine how much their customers know about their product or service and rate their relative satisfaction of the product or service. In many cases, businesses need to know how, when, and how often customers use their products. Perhaps you have been asked your ZIP code the last time you went to the grocery store. Supermarkets use this information to determine patterns of buyer behavior based on location. Companies that sell name-brand products, as opposed to the generic alternative, gauge the value of their branded product versus the generic offering and price their products accordingly. This dollar difference between what people will pay for a branded product as opposed to a generic version is brand equity, a quantifiable figure derived from marketing research. Measuring advertising effectiveness is also done through marketing research. One may wonder how the network carrying the Super Bowl (www.nfl.com/superbowl) can command millions of dollars for commercial airtime. Some products are made or broken as a result of this advertising outlay. After an advertisement is aired, marketing researchers can measure how effective

the advertisement was in increasing product sales, generating new business, raising customer awareness, changing customer perceptions, or whatever the goal is of the advertisement.

There are several general consumers, or buyers, of marketing research. Their motivations vary but ultimately these consumers are after the same thing: information that they can use to some advantage. Figure 1.2 shows the majors customers of marketing research.

Governments and universities often use grant money (www.grants.gov) to conduct marketing research studies for the general public good or for academic research purposes such as to expand the horizons of knowledge on a particular issue. Nonprofit organizations often conduct marketing research to better understand and serve their members or to generate more information they can use to support their respective causes. In some cases, nonprofit organizations might also get grant money. Typically businesses conduct marketing research to support the bottom line, to bolster sales, to increase their customer base, to expand to other market segments, and the like.

Today's marketing research involves both traditional qualitative and quantitative methods, which we will discuss in detail, coupled with Internet-driven methods such as blogs, Twitter, Facebook, e-mail, texting, and the list grows. More and more researchers are using mixed mode methods, which is a combination of several methods. The challenge for marketing researchers is to dovetail traditional marketing research methods with current technologies to detail the marketplace with the proven accuracy and quality that business managers and the public have come to expect from professional level research.

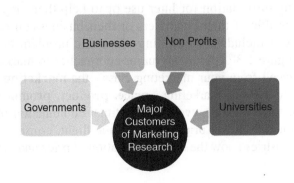

■ FIGURE 1.2

Major Customers of
Marketing Research

It is important to mention the difference between a product and a service and their respective relation to marketing research. Products are tangible—toys, food, furniture, and electronics—that might or might not have a limited lifespan. Services such as plumbing, accounting, lawn care, and teaching are often intangible and once the service experience is over, it's over. Conducting marketing research is critical to both products and services. Many products and services which you have enjoyed were likely the result of marketing research.

- **Marketing Research:**
  - *The process of collecting data and, through analysis, turning it into information used to address a marketing or business problem or issue.*
  - *Good sources for identifying marketing research services include:*
    - *www.marketingresearch.org—The Marketing Research Association*
    - *www.quirks.com*
    - *www.greenbook.org*
    - *www.marketresearch.com*
    - The American Marketing Association (AMA) defines marketing research:
      - *Marketing research is the function that links the consumer, customer, and public to the marketer through information—information used to identify and define marketing opportunities and problems; generate, refine, and evaluate marketing actions; monitor marketing performance; and improve understanding of marketing as a process. Marketing research specifies the information required to address these issues, designs the method for collecting information, manages and implements the data collection process, analyzes the results, and communicates the findings and their implications*
      - For more about the AMA visit - www.marketingpower.com

Not all research is intended to solve a problem. A marketing research study might be designed to answer certain specific or broad research questions such as "what are the demographics of my customer base?" Marketing research is information that might be used in an organization's strategic plan—or might just be information an organization wants to gather for a future purpose. Such information might include quantitative research such as a survey, or qualitative research such as focus groups, interviews, or an observational study of customers to gauge their opinions and/or behaviors about some aspect of the business. A business problem might include declining sales, product defects, or how to best introduce a new product or service. A marketing problem might be negative customer perceptions of your business or slippage in a particular market segment. Many highly successful and profitable companies conduct ongoing research despite the lack of a marketing or business problem—perhaps they are just gathering information for later use or to help their organization build a "big picture" profile of their customers or their business climate. Marketing research goals can include investigating a specific problem or researching a general issue. Figure 1.3 depicts two major approaches to marketing research.

You might recall from your marketing class—the **marketing mix:** the *combination* of the four Ps of marketing—**price, product, promotion,** and **place**. Well-done marketing research reveals the optimal combination of the fours Ps. Why are there multiple ticket prices on the same flight, cruise ship, or concert? How do those industries know the best combination of price and product? How do

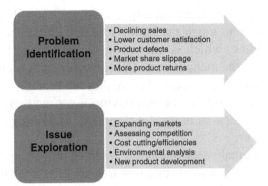

grocery stores decide what products to stock, how to price them, where to place them in the store, and how to advertise them? All these business decisions are driven by data that was transformed into actionable marketing information through various marketing research techniques. Figure 1.4 brings together the notion that the marketing mix involves the combination of the 4 Ps of marketing. Marketing research helps to inform the discussion as to the best marketing mix for a given situation.

Marketing Concept's Connection to Marketing Research

When stuck in traffic, or just on the highway, what do these cars represent? Each car, each article of clothing, each item on a restaurant menu is generally geared towards some part of a market, the so-called **market segment**. The market segment is a subset of the larger market to which marketing researchers target their marketing efforts in order to capture that part of a given market. Now to be sure, not all businesses are that sophisticated in their product development, but many are in fact very detailed and precise in their market segmentation strategies—strategies supported by marketing research. And there are varying amounts of research that go into these decisions—from none to extensive data collection and analysis. Of course, a restaurant might simply try new dishes weekly to see what people like without much marketing research on the front end. And then, based on sales volume, which is marketing research data, the restaurant will either keep or change the menu items. High-involvement products, such as cars, necessitate much marketing research before they are brought to market. Customers conduct marketing research before buying a car, and car manufactures do extensive marketing research in car development. Marketing research positions businesses for success.

This book will formalize the marketing research process and provide the tools to understand what types of marketing research are effective for given situations. We all use some form of research in our lives. By collecting, processing, and building on the knowledge derived from data, we learn and make better decisions. The challenge is determining the most effective way to collect data and making good use of it.

Marketing courses also cover the difference between a **product** and **marketing orientation**. The product orientation preceded the marketing orientation. Increasingly sophisticated marketing research techniques have enabled business leaders to maximize their business investments to produce the best products and services.

- **Product Orientation:** The business focus is primarily on the product and its features.
- **Marketing Orientation:** Products and services are researched first and then, to the extent possible, produced to meet to needs, wants, and desires of the marketplace and consumers.

Remember that the product orientation approach matured shortly after the industrial revolution when manufacturing products on a large scale became possible. The notion of first determining customers' preferences—then producing what they want *(the marketing orientation)*—had not yet been substantively developed partly because modifying products to customers needs and wants was not easy or inexpensive to do. Today, product modifications through manufacturing flexibility are often quite efficient.

Marketing Research Mistakes and Key Concepts

Marketing research can be both expensive and time consuming. And it's quite possible that marketing research might not reveal a solution—or even yield particularly useful information. Many businesses, both large and small, have made business mistakes resulting from a lack of, or poorly executed, marketing research. Here are a few common marketing research mistakes to avoid:

- *Failing to conduct research in the first place by relying on your "expertise";*
- *Using only secondary data to make a business decision when more research is needed;*
- *Conducting the wrong type of research, such as using focus groups when interviews are better;*
- *Researcher inexperience and biases that result in high levels of research error;*
- *Spending too much time and money on the wrong type of research;*
- *Unknowingly using the wrong or a non-representative sample of respondents;*

- *Relying too much on the Internet—not vetting information for accuracy and relevance;*
- *Conducting research with a predisposition to its outcome—you already know what you want to find.*

The role of marketing research extends internationally—which we will discuss. The challenges of data collection, regulations, cultural barriers, and access to populations have provided many challenges to conducting marketing research internationally. Many international business ventures that fail to conduct proper marketing research can result in costly business mistakes. Below are a few commonly reported international marketing mistakes major companies have made. Effective marketing research would have likely prevented these blunders.

1. Clairol introduced the curling iron "Mist Stick" in Germany. In German *mist* is slang for *manure*.
2. When Gerber began selling baby food in Africa the small baby food jars featured a baby on the label. In Africa, marketers often put pictures on the label of what's inside the product. Customers were subsequently alarmed by the packaging.
3. A Scandinavian vacuum manufacturer's foray into the American market began with its slogan: *"Nothing sucks like an Electrolux."*
4. Coors translated its slogan "Turn It Loose" into Spanish which translates to "Suffers from Diarrhea."
5. Colgate introduced a toothpaste in France called *Cue*—which is also the name of an indiscrete magazine.
6. The Coca-Cola name in China was first read as "Ke-kou-ke-la" which was mistranslated to a *female horse stuffed with wax.*
7. British sports manufacturer Umbro withdrew its sneakers called Zyklon when it realized Zyklon was the name of the gas used by Nazis in concentration camps.
8. Reed Business New's ill-conceived slogan—" If it's news to you, it's news to us" did not last.
9. An American T-shirt maker in Miami printed shirts in Spanish to welcome the Pope to the city. Instead of "I saw the Pope" (el papa), sadly the shirts read "I saw the potato" (la papa).
10. Pepsi's "Come Alive" slogan in Chinese translates to "brings your ancestors back from the grave."

Overall, the role of marketing research includes these concepts—which we will detail in this book:

- Research Design
  - *The Analytical Model*
  - *Problem Definition*
  - *Applied and Basic Research*
  - *Exploratory, Descriptive, and Causal Research*
- Qualitative vs. Quantitative Data
- Primary vs. Secondary Data
- Observation Methods
- Experimental Design
- The Sampling Plan
  - *Probability vs. Non-Probability*
  - *Determining the Sample Size*
- Data Analysis Techniques
- Presenting and Communicating the Data

Deciding Whether to Conduct Marketing Research

Although marketing research is often invaluable to business success, conducting marketing research is not always the best course of action. There are many situations when you probably should not conduct marketing research—or at least you should proceed cautiously. Some of these situations include:

- **The decision has already been made:**
  - *Suppose the university has already decided to change the class schedule, or a company has already decided to change the packaging of its products, why would marketing research be necessary to determine if they should embark on that course of action? Sometimes organizational leadership wants to validate a decision, rather than use research as a tool in decision making. This use of marketing research is not terribly valuable and likely not worth the cost as the research will not likely change the organization's leadership decision.*
- **A lack of resources:**
  - *An inadvisable type of research is research that is underfunded or understaffed. If an organization lacks the resources to do the research correctly, it should not be done. Decision making based on faulty research is risky. If an organization has limited resources, it might be best to conduct small-scale research first. Another resource is time. Ensure that there is time to execute the research in a way that will make it useful.*
- **The usefulness of the research is in question:**
  - *It might be that the opportunity to use the research has—or will have—passed by the time the research is done. This scenario can occur in fast-moving industries such as fashion, politics, or electronics. Organizations need to have a rapid research apparatus in place to gather data in a timely way.*
- **The information is already available:**
  - *Some organizations conduct marketing research when the information is already available. Perhaps management does not know where to find the existing research, or perhaps they are not aware it exists.*

■ **FIGURE 1.5**

Business Decisions Rely on Information Provided by Marketing Research

Image © Dmitriy Shironosov, 2011. Used under license from Shutterstock, Inc.

- **The cost/benefit analysis is negative:**
  - *Suppose marketing research determined that the computer manufacturer could save a million dollars by restructuring its process. However, it's ultimately not cost effective if the research costs two million dollars. Spending two million dollars to save one million is an ill-advised endeavor. Sometimes it's not clear how much the research will cost—or its cost can escalate during the project. Enlisting a project manager to monitor the project execution is critical.*
- **A lack of a clear focus:**
  - *If the research objectives are not agreed upon and supported by management and/or the research company provider, much time and money will be wasted. It is imperative that the research scope, goals, objectives, deliverables, and time table are thoroughly understood by all parties and are revisited on a regular basis to prevent costly surprises.*

If marketing research is so valuable, why do some organizations fail to conduct research and why are there business failures when research is conducted? Despite many quantifiable aspects of marketing research, it's not an exact science. Marketing research tries to link the customer and the business/organization to the marketplace. Remember that marketing research takes time and resources (chiefly money). During that time, there might well have been changes in organizational leadership, customers, and the marketplace. These three factors are often fast moving, making it difficult to always keep abreast of them. Add to the mix the research execution. It's certainly not a given that organizations execute the right type of research or even execute the right research well. Although many variables exist that threaten the effectiveness of marketing research, organizations that conduct effective and correct marketing research are in the best position for success.

Types of Marketing Research Studies

Marketing research is of great use to management through three important approaches: **descriptive, diagnostic,** and **predictive.** Suppose a hotel wants to know what its customers think about the hotel and its services even though there are no clear problems. Management might conduct a **descriptive study.** Now assume that

■ FIGURE 1.6
Marketing Research can Help Business Leaders with the Bottom Line

Image © StockLite, 2011. Used under license from Shutterstock, Inc.

room bookings have declined. Then management might expand the research to include a **diagnostic study.** Finally, to determine what needs to be changed at the hotel in order to increase bookings, management might conduct a **predictive study.**

Descriptive

- *Research designed to answer who, what, where, and how related questions. Descriptive research "describes" what it "sees" in the marketplace.*

Diagnostic

- *Diagnostic research attempts to explain what might be going on in the marketplace by answering the "why" related questions. Why are customers unhappy, why have sales declined, why are customers returning purchased products? This type of research requires more in-depth questions to determine customer motivations.*

Predictive

- *Predictive research helps management in deciding what to do. This type of research is useful to management by explaining: if management does X then Y will happen. If management decreases price, sales will rise. This type of research is complicated because its aim is to determine customer actions before they happen.*

These three types of research approaches can be used together to build marketplace profiles, conduct program evaluations, measure customer satisfaction, determine whether and where to expand, among many other uses. The best managed organizations use various levels of and approaches to marketing research before major decisions are made.

Why Should I Learn Marketing Research?

Students who are not interested in a career in marketing research might wonder why learning about marketing research might help their career. Most career-oriented people are interested in career advancement—the prospect of moving to successively more senior roles in an organization. Or perhaps you want to start your own business enterprise. In the former objective, rising in an organization requires intelligence, experience, hard work, and perhaps some form of serendipity. As you embark on a career, take note of how senior leaders rose. You will likely notice that they are relatively well-rounded academically and understand many aspects of their respective businesses. Let's look at an example of how understanding marketing research would be helpful. Suppose you are a middle manager for a large grocery store and that you advise the company marketing director. The marketing director wants a customer survey conducted to determine if the product mix meets their needs. You are tasked with leading this project. You decide to hire a marketing research firm to conduct the survey which ultimately yields valuable and actionable information. The marketing director is pleased with your leadership in getting this project completed but is stunned at the final project cost and asks you go to her office to review the invoice. While the pair is sorting out the project costs in the marketing director's corner office, Brian, the summer college intern, is invited to the meeting so that he might learn more about the business. Initially shy, Brian chimes-in questioning the survey sample size. Brian had taken marketing research and knew something about sampling. Intrigued at the neophyte's ostensibly solid analysis, the marketing director turns to you for an explanation as to why you did not question the excessive sample size, which was the key cost driver. At a loss for words, you cast a disapproving glare at the intern while you promise to "get back" to the marketing director after you do a little research into the matter. In this oversimplified case, you can see that, although you might not want a career in marketing research, understanding its broad concepts might well be useful. Although you are not conducting the research yourself, you are in a position to oversee and manage the project including screening the marketing research vendors who provided the work. Had you known something about marketing research, you would have caught the inflated sample size and simultaneously demonstrated your value to the marketing director. As for starting your own business, a failure to understand the marketing environment which includes your potential customers and the competition, as well as the economic, regulatory, and demographic environment will likely result in an unsuccessful business venture. Research takes time and money which can dissuade entrepreneurs from embarking on research before a business is started. This approach is ill-advised. Starting a business is difficult, and can be far more complicated than was originally expected. Research is essential to success at every level. If you do not agree, the next time you buy a computer, take a job, register for classes, or go on vacation, do so without any research. These choices require a trivial, practically immeasurably low, amount of research compared to starting or running a business.

Careers in Marketing Research

As with many professions, marketing research offers diverse career paths. Many company presidents come from the marketing department. The marketing department is a common path into marketing research. At the start of a marketing research career, perhaps you were hired as an entry-level analyst or data collector working for a project manager. Professor Naresh Malhotra in his text *Marketing Research an Applied Orientation* outlined ten common job descriptions in marketing research.

■ **FIGURE 1.7**

Take Your Business to the Next Level with Marketing Research Information

1. **Vice President of Marketing Research:**
   - A senior position with an organization, the VP of marketing research manages the entire marketing research efforts of an organization and reports to the organization president.
2. **Research Director:**
   - Also a senior position, the research director manages the execution of research projects and would also advise the VP of marketing research on strategic objectives.
3. **Assistant (or Associate) Director of Research:**
   - This mid-level manager assists the research director in many logistical aspects of executing a marketing research study. This person would likely manage a staff of research analysts.
4. **Project or Senior Project Manager:**
   - Again, a mid-level position, the person in this role is assigned specific projects to oversee.
5. **Statistics/Data Expert:**
   - A more junior role, this specialized position demands statistical expertise in managing the quantitative aspects of projects. This person serves as a statistics SME (Subject Matter Expert).
6. **Senior Analyst:**
   - This position is perhaps the broadest. You will find all levels of expertise at the senior analyst level. This person prepares the final report and is typically assigned to marketing research projects within his or her portfolio of project expertise. This person manages analysts and junior analysts in executing a marketing research project and ensures that the project is on cost and schedule.
7. **Analyst:**
   - A relatively junior role, this person manages various details of the project including overseeing questionnaire development and focus group design. This person might conduct some preliminary data analysis as well.
8. **Junior Analyst:**
   - An entry-level position, an analyst is assigned to a number of aspects of a research project. This person might do questionnaire coding, data entry, editing, secondary data collection, and basic statistical analysis.
9. **Fieldwork Director:**
   - This person selects, trains, evaluates, and executes the marketing research fieldwork and might also supervise other fieldworkers in executing the marketing research project.
10. **Operational Supervisor:**
    - The operational supervisor manages the overall fieldwork execution of the marketing research project.

This list is a general guide. In many marketing research departments, particularly smaller ones, you will find variations of this list. Some roles are combined or expanded to cover other areas. In large firms, roles might be more precisely defined as there are more people in the marketing research department, and each person has a specific role.

Research in Practice

Case:

- Place yourself in the role of the new marketing manager for Amtrak (www .amtrak.com). You are responsible for increasing ridership throughout the Amtrak system. You decide to hire a marketing research company to anchor the study that will determine why ridership has declined and how it can be increased. The marketing research company provides you a report detailing how the research will be done. As marketing manager, you review the proposal and concur that a marketing research study is needed despite the cost—which is greater than what you had anticipated. You are concerned because the head of Amtrak is not well versed on marketing research techniques or on the true value of or need to conduct marketing research, although she is open to hearing your proposal.

Assignment:

- Create a White Paper (http://www.stelzner.com/copy-HowTo-white papers.php) to convince the Amtrak president of the need to conduct marketing research by demonstrating its value and role in decision making.

Chapter Summary

Marketing research is the process of transforming data into information used to support the management decision-making process. Marketing research offers insight as to how the four Ps of marketing—price, product, promotion, and place—can be best used to maximize market potential. Several membership driven organizations such as the Marketing Research Association (www.marketingresearch.org) provide a professional component, networking events, and educational opportunities for marketing research practitioners. Marketing research is an anchor to understanding and formalizing the marketing orientation: determining customers' needs and wants. Business leadership might not want to conduct a marketing research study for several reasons, such as when the business decisions have already been made, or there is a lack of resources, or the utility of the research is in question, or there is a lack of resources to conduct the research. Marketing research studies can be descriptive *(describing issues),* diagnostic *(explaining issues),* or predictive *(predicting what might happen).* A wide range of careers is available in marketing research from entry-level data collectors to project managers to directors of marketing research departments. Many of these career areas become increasingly specialized as their relative responsibility grows.

ISSUE IN THE SPOTLIGHT   Understanding Our Audience

Charles MacKay, General Director
The Santa Fe Opera
www.santafeopera.org

The Santa Fe Opera has attracted audiences to its summer festival for over 50 years. High production standards and a unique open-air setting of natural beauty draw opera aficionados and neophytes alike. As a nonprofit arts organization, we depend on our ticket buyers and donors to make each season viable. Deepening our relationships and experiences with them, therefore, is integral to our success, and, indeed, survival.

The most important factor in developing our audiences has been to first spend time clarifying who we are in the relationship. Although our Mission Statement has not changed significantly over the years, we recently expanded it to express our organizational vision as well as our core values. This clarity of purpose provides a useful filter in defining what we offer, as well as how it is reflected back to us by our constituents.

The blending of popular standards with neglected masterpieces and exciting premieres is what attracts the opera aficionado. All five productions may be sampled in three of our full repertory weeks. Repertory and scheduling are given exhaustive scrutiny to ensure we remain high on the list for those who travel to fulfill their operatic appetite.

It is exceptional that a world-class festival thrives in a State capital with a population of just over 75,000 (in city proper). Our audience comes from all 50 states and about 24 foreign countries each summer. Surprisingly, approximately 40 percent are customers new to us each year, a testament to the consistent appeal of the locale, and, we think, our repertory offerings. Recognizing that the passionate operagoer is a minority in the general population, word-of-mouth remains our strongest factor for first-time buyers. Local perceptions are therefore quite important, and we invest significant resources to ensure that even those who do not choose to attend have pride in their resident opera company and recommend it as a "must-see" to summer visitors.

To increase the chances for a return visit, we are mindful that opera can present a number of barriers to the neophyte. Enjoying the art form in the open air often helps put visitors at ease. Customer service is paramount. Along with singers, orchestra and technicians, the parking crew, box office, ushers, bartenders, gift shop and maintenance staff must take their roles as hosts seriously to ensure a high level of perceived value in the experience. Free pre-performance lectures and access to informal dining enhance the evening.

Ticket prices usually reflect the fact that Opera is one of the most expensive art forms to produce. As entertainment options proliferate, we find ourselves in competition not only with other opera companies, but with Netflix and simulcasts. Having a broad range of ticket prices helps keep our product viable for most, and our 50+ year tradition of Opera for Youth access to dress rehearsals (which is how I first attended opera) helps adults encourage younger audiences. This year we are adding reduced-price Family Night packages at three performances to further this mentorship.

Ticket revenues provide just over half of our annual budget. Revenues have not kept pace with rising expenses, while increased prices overall inhibit total attendance. We are currently collaborating with The Pricing Institute to examine our pricing structures, and implementing RMA (Revenue Management Application—a new tool from the Tessitura Network, our CRM software application provider). By monitoring sales trends for each performance, we will apply dynamic pricing principles ("selling the right product to the right customer at the right time and the right price") to help increase revenues from those constituents who are price inelastic, and maximize attendance throughout the summer.

Having a primary repository for all constituent information allows us to view all aspects of our interactions— tickets, contributions, attendance at events, what materials are sent and which were responded to. Comments offered are captured as Customer Service Issues for individual follow up. Although we market by many factors including frequency of attendance, most recent visit, geographic location—we are mindful that each constituent is an individual and deserves specific interactions.

Our particular weaknesses often correlate to a lack of financial and/or human resources. Although we have had some experience with audience surveys and focus groups, we would value more information about our audiences—both their demographics and psychographics. Time and money are needed to develop this area, and we are working hard at finding both.

Social media have brought some of our younger constituents into a closer and more immediate interaction. A core advisory group on our staff has been thoughtfully developing our presence on Facebook, Twitter and other social media, and it has added an important dynamic in how we communicate with our audiences. We are launching a YouTube contest this spring for independent video set to arias from our contemporary repertory offering. I can't wait to see how this segment of our audience will respond. I know it will help inform who we are and will further our relationship in a new and meaningful way.

The Marketing Research Process

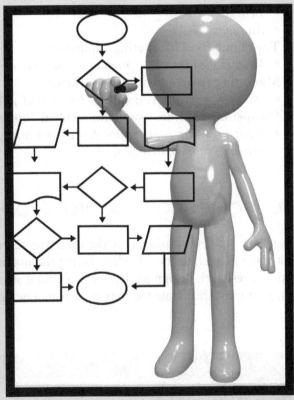

Learning Objectives:

- Understand some common reasons for conducting a marketing research study
- Learn the eleven steps in the marketing research process
- Know the key components of a marketing research design
- Understand the role and importance of the analytical model

- Know the difference between a Request for Proposal and a Request for Quote
- Appreciate the role of marketing research in the market growth matrix
- Understand the importance and difference between research method and approach
- See the difference between full service and syndicated marketing research suppliers

- Learn five key considerations when selecting a marketing research provider
- Appreciate the main components of ethics in marketing research
- Understand exploratory, descriptive, and causal research approaches
- Review the key components of a Marketing Decision Support System

Chapter Two

Reasons to Conduct Marketing Research

Conducting marketing research and the process by which you execute the research varies for many reasons such as time, budget, other resources, organizational issues, corporate culture, and the like. The objectives of research projects vary greatly. Possible (certainly not an exhaustive list) research topics might be to gauge:

- **Customer, employee, or stakeholder:**
  - *Satisfaction*
  - *Knowledge*
  - *Behaviors*
  - *Beliefs*
  - *Attitudes*
- **The "Four Ps of Marketing" analysis:**
  - *What is the best price, product, promotion, or place mix?*
- **Marketing environmental assessment:**
  - *What are relevant economic, technological, political, and regulatory issues?*
- **Competitor analysis—sometimes called "opposition research":**
  - *What are your competitors doing, and how can you best respond to the demands of the marketplace?*

The Marketing Research Process

Before any research project is undertaken, the researcher must first understand what research path to take. Understanding the **marketing research process** and writing a **research design** are two critical initial steps to marketing research success. Don't underestimate the impact of planning the research. Although there is

■ FIGURE 2.1

Managing Many Pieces of the Process Puzzle Maximizes the Impact of Marketing Research

Image © James Thew, 2011. Used under license from Shutterstock, Inc.

overlap, the *process* differs from the *design* in that the process details the *steps necessary* to conduct marketing research in general, whereas the design details how the specific research will be executed. Figure 2.2 is a broad overview of the marketing process.

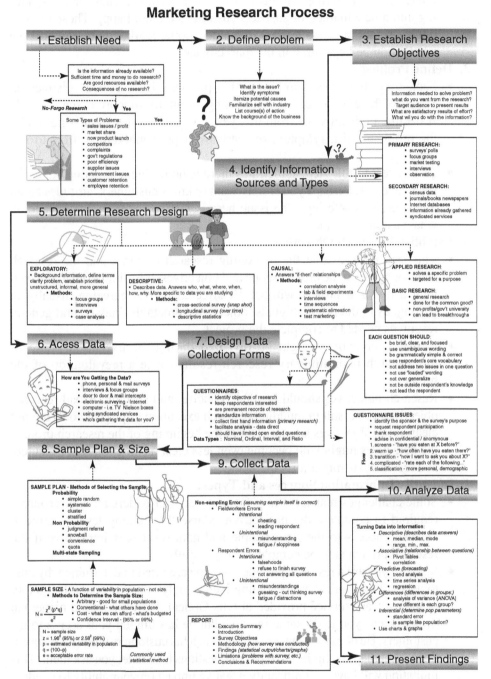

■ FIGURE 2.2
Marketing Research
Process

- **The Marketing Research Process:**
  - *The entire process from idea inception, to data collection and analysis, to report writing.*
  - *The marketing research process has a number of steps—here we break them into eleven steps. However, other textbooks or sources might well have fewer or more steps. The number of steps is not the key, as long as these concepts are addressed in a sequential manner.*

The Eleven Marketing Research Steps

1. **Establish Need:**
   - Here the research sponsor determines if research is warranted, whether the information already exists, and if there are negative conse-quences for not doing research. Perhaps a business has had declining sales, or is expanding into a new market, or suspects customers are not happy. These reasons might prompt business leaders to conduct some marketing research to see what might be happening in the marketplace.

2. **Define Problem:**
   - Separating the *symptoms* from the problem is a critical distinction. Suppose there is a school fundraising event to support a school club. A decline in ticket sales from this year compared to last year is not really the problem but a symptom of, perhaps, a poor marketing effort to sell tickets.
   - As a caveat to this step, sometimes there is no problem to define but an is-sue to address. Perhaps you simply want to know customers' attitudes about a new product offering. The issue here is just *information*, understanding what customers think.

3. **Establish Research Objectives:**
   - This step requires that the marketing research provider and the research sponsor agree on the project scope and objectives. It is ill-advised to proceed with a research project without all affected parties agreeing, usually in writing, as to the research goals, objectives, timetable, budget, and general resources needed to complete the project.
   - Research objectives might be revisited during the execution phase of the research if preliminary research results cause a reevaluation of the project.
   - Research objectives should be clear, concise, and specific. Broad research objectives can result in muddled research execution as project goals are not clear. If the objectives are not clear at the beginning of the research project, the objectives might well become even less clear as the project is executed, and the analysis might miss the mark.

4. **Indentify Information Sources and Types:**
   - Some challenges managers face from research providers are the resources required to complete the project. Of course the funding level is critical; however, access to the right people and data sources is imperative if the research project is to be completed successfully.
   - Suppose you are a research provider and you are hired to determine why customers at Otis Optical are becoming increasingly unhappy about the quality of the eye care service provided at Otis Optical. Otis, the rotund namesake owner, wants you to do some research but he has limited your access to his customers. He does not want you to approach his customers with survey questions, or perhaps he limits the types of questions he will let you ask them. This limitation will have a significantly negative impact on your ability to conduct the research. These information requirement parameters must be agreed to between the research provider and the client before the research is initiated.
   - Knowing where and how you will be able to get the needed information can be the difference between project success and failure.

5. **Determine Research Design:**
   - Broadly, the research design is the step-by-step guide by which the research is executed. This document enables research repeatability and traceability as needed.

- The research design helps the researcher to adhere to the cost and schedule of each phase of the research and enables the client to monitor project progress and provide feedback on its execution.

6. **Access Data:**
   - Deciding on how the data will be accessed plays a pivotal role in the marketing researcher's cost and schedule.
   - Accessing the data refers to how the primary and secondary data will be collected. Will the data be collected through interviews, focus groups, observation, experiments, or surveys? Will you use telephone, Internet, mail, or in-person data collection? These questions are answered in this phase of the marketing research process.

7. **Design Data Collection Forms:**
   - Data collection forms are questionnaires. Writing a good questionnaire requires a significant amount of time and expertise. The questionnaire length and complexity are driven by the project's research objectives, costs, timetables, and execution methods (telephone, Internet, in person, or mail).

8. **Sample Plan and Size:**
   - The major issues here are how to define the right audience, how to will select the respondents, and how many respondents to target for the data collection. How the respondents are selected involves whether they will be selected randomly or not.
   - The sample size refers to the number of people needed to complete the survey, be in the focus group, be observed, and so forth. Typically researchers need to recruit more respondents than are truly required because of some people who decline to be in the research or who do not participate when the research is conducted.

9. **Collect Data:**
   - This phase is where the marketing research execution is done in earnest. This part of the process involves executing the data collection such as running the focus group, doing the observation, conducting the experiment, or executing a survey.

■ **FIGURE 2.3**

Successful Research Projects Adhere to a Progression of Steps Building from Each Previous Research Step

Image © Sergej Khakimullin, 2011. Used under license from Shutterstock, Inc.

10. **Analyze Data:**
    - Analyzing the data involves merging the secondary and primary research data collection results into a comprehensive report. In this phase, researchers produce both descriptive and analytic results.
11. **Present Findings:**
    - In this final research phase, marketing researchers produce a written report, and perhaps a PowerPoint slide deck, as part of the final deliverable(s) to the research sponsor.
    - It is important that the research providers receive clear guidance from the research sponsor on the format and content of the research report.

Marketing Research Design

- **Marketing Research Design:**
  - *The research blueprint which includes the research statement and objectives followed by a detailed description of the qualitative and quantitative methods that will be used to collect, analyze, and report the research findings.*

Figure 2.4 depicts a general research design process flow from which marketing researchers can tailor their specific research projects. Research design requires much planning. The buildings on campus, or around town, required more time to plan than to build—they don't just start digging. The building planning would include various studies: economic viability, environmental impact, building utility, cost, contract selection, location, legal and regulatory issues, building design and layout—and the list goes on. Once construction begins, builders are simply following a well-developed plan while making adjustments during the process. A building that is completed in two years might have seen 10 years of planning. City planning can have a 30-year time horizon before the building is complete, or even begun. Even students taking university classes plan. How do you know that you will graduate in four years? You lay out all the classes you need and when they are offered to ensure you are on track to graduate. Marketing research planning is no different in the sense that successful research requires planning. In fact many products were heavily researched and never brought to market because doing so

■ **FIGURE 2.4**

Time, Budget, and Management in the Research Design Process

was not supported by the research. Or in other cases, adequate research was not done and the product failed when brought to market.

Research design is the planning part of the overall marketing research process. The research design can be modified—and in most cases will be changed—during the execution phase of the research. Remember, the research design is the initial plan on how to execute the research. As the research unfolds, many facts will affect whether you need to revamp the research design. The **analytical model** will also help you to understand the key research variables. A good understanding of those variables and how they are related, will enable researchers to target the research to the right aspects of the issue under study.

The Analytical Model

The **analytical model** is an important step in the research design process. The analytical model helps researchers understand, or visualize, the interrelationships between and among the key parts (also called variables) relevant to the research issue. Figure 2.5 is a notional analytical model which can quite often be significantly more complicated than this depiction – although it provides a useful framework from which to build.

- *The analytical model details the cause-and-effect relationships among research variables.*

For example, suppose you own a restaurant and you want to determine what causes sales to rise and fall. First we need to define the key variables associated with a restaurant. "Sales" is a **dependent variable** because its change is *dependent* on the manipulation of an independent variable(s). In other words, you cannot increase sales directly; you have to *do something to cause* sales to increase. Such action might be to lower prices, increase the hours of operation, add more product

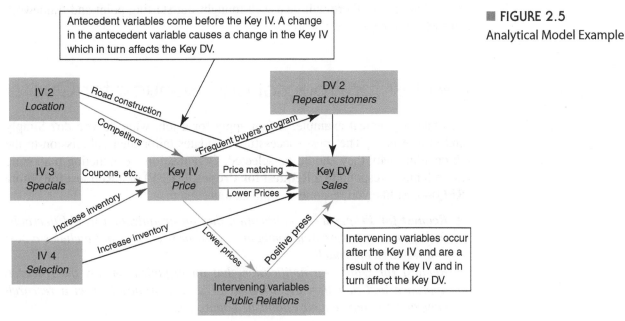

■ **FIGURE 2.5**
Analytical Model Example

IV – Independent Variables
DV – Dependent Variables

selection, improve product quality, change the store layout, etc. All of these variables are **independent variables.** The key variable types, which form the basis for experimental design, are defined below.

- *Dependent Variable—a variable changed through manipulating independent variables.*
- *Independent Variable—a variable that can be changed directly with the purpose of affecting the dependent variable.*
- *Extraneous Variable—a variable researchers have no direct control over but can be "managed to" such as the weather, government regulations, competition, and the economy.*

It is important to mention the key variables at this point in the marketing research plan development because understanding the major issues at play will provide the researcher with a starting point from which to begin the research. In our restaurant example we would try to determine what combination of independent variables affects the dependent variable (sales). In other words, what *combination* of the four Ps of marketing—price, product, promotion, or place—drives sales? Restaurant sales might well be driven 50 percent by price, 10 percent by promotion, 20 percent by product, and 20 percent by place. The analytical model provides an *estimation* of what might be going on with sales based on prior knowledge or background work (secondary data) that has been done and can be the basis for regression analysis. Executing the marketing research will reveal what the relationship actually is and help to quantify the elasticity of demand. There can be multiple dependent variables such as customer satisfaction or repeat buyers.

Researchers might jump right into the research execution phase and skip the analytical model and research design development. That approach risks missing key variable relationships that will surely surface. It is best to understand those variables in the planning phase rather than learning about them in the throes of the research execution.

Once there is an analytical model developed, research planning can revolve around a more informed understanding of the research topic. Of course this understanding will change—perhaps dramatically—during the execution of the research, but at least there will be a well thought-out starting point and framework from which to begin the research.

Request for Proposal and Request for Quote

Let's take a practical example. If you apply for a job, what do you do? Simply send in a résumé? The most successful candidates tailor their submission to the job detailing why they should be selected. Organization's conducting marketing research might respond to a **Request for Proposal (RFP)** or a **Request for Quote (RFQ)**—just like you respond to a job announcement.

- *Request for Proposal—a notification that an organization would like bids, from prospective research companies, on a project. This bid includes a cost and research approach.*
- *Request for Quote—a notification that an organization has the research approach and that they are looking for a cost proposal, from a research company, to execute their established approach.*

Now let's assume you are the university chancellor and you need to plan a big fundraising event. If you have little idea about what the event should look like, you might issue an **RFP** prompting party planning companies to propose to you what the gathering should entail and its costs. Now suppose you already know what you want for the event. Now you might issue an **RFQ** that has your requirements—you are just looking for the most cost-effective provider. Marketing research companies respond to RFPs and RFQs on a regular basis. So who issues RFPs or RFQs? Public and private organizations that need work done and are not able to do the work in-house. Many large companies have marketing research departments so they might do all or part of the work in-house. However, most medium to small companies contract with marketing research companies to provide various marketing research services.

In many cases, these organizations issue RFPs or RFQs to grow their business. These organizations might also want to know more about the marketplace before proceeding with a business decision. Some organizations issue RFPs or RFQs for non-marketing related reasons. For example, perhaps a company needs help with a building expansion, needs cleaning services, wants assistance with business consulting, or needs administrative support help. For our purposes, we reference the RFP and RFQ issuance in support of a marketing related need.

- To get an idea of RFP formats, take a look at www.fedbizopps.gov, the central location for the U.S. Federal Government Requests for Proposals.

The Market Growth Matrix and Marketing Research

Now consider a fine wine producer that advertises that they want to hire a research company to help them determine how to expand to new markets. You should recall the four marketing strategies as depicted in Figure 2.6—the **Market Growth Matrix** from your marketing class:

- *Market Penetration—selling existing products in existing markets.*
- *Product Development—selling new products in existing markets.*
- *Market Development—selling existing products in new markets.*
- *Market Diversification—selling new products in new markets.*

Marketing research can help to determine the best approach to meeting the goals of the market growth matrix. Successful research companies will submit a proposal which is their respective case as to why they should be hired to conduct the research. It's not enough to simply state you *will* determine; you must show *how* and *why* you will determine which markets to expand to.

A good starting point is to demonstrate an understanding of the problem. **Problem definition** is more complicated than it might appear.

- **Problem Definition:**
  - *The process of determining the root causes of a situation through an understanding of the link between symptoms and the problem.*

Consider the restaurant example from our earlier discussion. If restaurant sales are declining, is that the problem? Not really, the real problem might be that food quality is low or the service is substandard. The *symptom* of lower sales might be

Market Growth Matrix

Existing Products   New Products

Existing Markets

Market Penetration

Product Development

New Markets

Market Development

Diversification

caused by poor food quality or bad service. Often we use the symptom as the problem. Marketing research can uncover problems before symptoms arise.

Research Approach vs. Research Method

Creating a research design involves determining the entire process by which you will execute the study. Clearly stating the research approach and the methods by which you will accomplish the research goals and objectives is critical. Remember that many readers of your research proposal will not be as informed as you are; thus, you need to ensure that the reader is informed as to precisely what you are proposing.

- **Research Approach:**
  - *The overall scope of the marketing research study.*
- **Research Method:**
  - *The steps undertaken to accomplish the marketing research objectives.*

When creating a research design, the overall research approach—**basic research** or **applied research** (or some combination)—must be clearly conveyed as well as the proposed primary and secondary data collection methods.

Research Approaches

- **Basic Research**—*research conducted to expand general knowledge.*
  - *Exploratory:*
    - *Secondary Research—internal and external sources*
    - *Primary Research—interviews, focus groups, and observation.*
- **Applied Research**—*research conducted for a specific purpose—to solve a particular problem or address a certain issue.*
  - *Descriptive:*
    - *Primary Research—expanded interviews, experience surveys, focus groups, observation, and questionnaires.*
    - *Secondary Research—news articles, internal records, and background research on the key figures of interest.*

- **Causal:**
  - *Primary Research—experiments designed to map cause-and-effect relationships between and among the key variables.*
  - *Secondary Research—develops causal linkages such as by conducting a content analysis from news articles.*

Research Methods

- **Primary Research**—*research collected directly from the population of interest such as through focus groups, interviews, questionnaires, experiments, and observations.*
- **Secondary Research**—*existing research resulting in learning from through newspapers, the Internet, news programs, professional journals, etc.*

Typically, though not always, private-sector RFPs are applied research requests as they often want to solve a particular problem. Public-sector (i.e., some universities or governments) RFPs can be applied or basic research, or a combination of research approaches. For example, a potato chip company might want to know why its market share in Seattle has slipped (applied research—a specific issued or problem is researched,). Conversely a government or university might want to know general economic or demographic data that *might in general* be useful, or that might lead them to ask other questions. Private-sector basic research is sometimes done as well. For example, pharmaceutical companies spend millions of dollars on general research that often leads to more specific research. This basic research can help uncover issues that might well warrant more investigation.

Large organizations often have their own in-house marketing research department. If resources are scarce it is not unusual for these departments to hire outside research firms. Smaller organizations wanting to conduct marketing research might hire a research firm. Many types of marketing research firms offer varying levels of services. This link lists the top fifty marketing research firms for 2009 as defined by Jack Honomichl:

- http://www.marketingpower.com/ResourceLibrary/Marketing News/Pages/2009/43/6-30-09percent20pages/Honomichl_Top_50_Report. aspx

■ FIGURE 2.7

Marketing Researchers Use Many Qualitative and Quantitative Research Tools to Develop and Execute a Research Study

Image © Christos Georghiou, 2011. Used under license from Shutterstock, Inc.

Types of Marketing Research Providers

Generally there are two broad types of marketing research organizations usually called suppliers, firms, or providers: **full service** and **syndicated service**. Basically, full-service marketing research firms execute all aspects of marketing research including qualitative, quantitative, primary, and secondary, from project design to execution and data analysis. Syndicated marketing research firms offer a more limited, or targeted, set of marketing research services and might offer a limited combination of the services below, whereas a full-service marketing research company might offer the entire suite of services. Figure 2.8 shows the two major types of marketing research providers from which many sub classes of services are derived.

Possible Suite of Marketing Research Services

- Field Service or Data Collection
  - *The actual work of collecting the data—telephone calls, in-person interviews, Internet, etc.*
- Secondary Data
  - *Providing sources and analysis of secondary data*
- Data Tabulation
  - *Only the data computation phase—not analysis*
- Data Analysis
- Data Entry and Coding
  - *Entering the data into a spreadsheet and adding codes to represent answers*
- Questionnaire Writing
- Depth Interviews
- Experiments
  - *Which might include product testing*
- Focus Groups
- Observation
- Report Writing
- Niche Marketing
  - *A company specializing in one type of issue such as the travel industry*

Choosing a Marketing Research Provider

What should be considered when choosing a research supplier? In addition to a supplier's capabilities, key issues are time and budget availability, quality level desired, reputation sought, and relevant expertise. Surplus time and money are rare luxuries, thus clients must decide an approach for selecting a research provider. Often management needs data quickly in order to make a decision given the pressures of a fast-paced marketplace. Both consumers and competitors have little patience for dawdling. Large research firms have the resources to deliver a product

■ **FIGURE 2.8**

Types of Research Providers

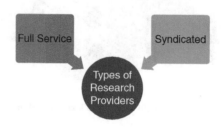

quickly; however, paying for this speed might be costly. Perhaps the most important consideration is the marketing research firm's reputation, work quality, and expertise. Often reputation is a subset of quality, but not always. Be sure to examine closely a firm's expertise to ensure its core competencies dovetail with your research topic. Many marketing research companies do not necessarily specialize as they might conduct general research in all types of fields. However, if your research topic is specific, such as those related to medical, technological, or esoteric issues, it is advisable to select a supplier with the relevant level of expertise. A general-practice doctor is all that is required for a basic physical. However, if you need foot surgery it's the surgeon you call. Before hiring a marketing research firm, do *your* research so you can select the most appropriate supplier. There are many considerations to weigh when choosing a marketing research provider as Figure 2.9 identifies.

It might be helpful to consult various marketing research associations. Below is a general, not comprehensive, list of some major marketing research related organizations. Search the Internet for other national or for local organizations.

- AAPOR—The American Association for Public Opinion Research—www.aapor.org
- AMA—The American Marketing Association—www.marketingpower.com
- ARF—The Advertising Research Foundation—www.thearf.org
- CASRO—The Council of American Survey Research Organizations—www.casro.org
- ESOMAR—The European Society for Opinion and Marketing Research—www.esomar.org
- MRS—The Marketing Research Society—www.mrs.org.uk
- MRA—The Marketing Research Association—www.marketingresearch.org
- QRCA—Qualitative Research Consultants Association—www.qrca.org
- CMOR—The Council for Marketing and Opinion Research—www.cmore.org

Marketing Research Ethics

Ethics should be considered before launching a research project. Ethical issues relating to marketing research suppliers, clients, and respondents are important to know. Figure 2.10 shows the major categories of ethical issues that need to be addressed when conducting marketing research.

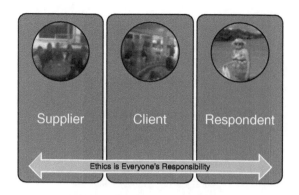

Marketing Research Suppliers Should Not

- *Misrepresent* his or her expertise or the cost of doing a research project in order to secure business. Sometimes research firms overpromise assuming that they can "figure it out" if and when the time comes to do the work. Overpromising on expertise, price, or time are the typical reasons vendors will say they can deliver a product more cheaply or quickly than they really can.

- *Abuse respondents* by pressuring them into biased responses or promising incentives that are not delivered. Also **Sugging** or **Frugging** (selling or fundraising under the guise of research) is considered unethical. Finally, respondents should be able to leave the research study if they want to and should not be pressured to remain in the study.

- *Inflate costs* by proposing too much research, inflating the sample size requirements, or by overcharging for other aspects of the research.

- *Falsify data* either through the data analysis or data collection research phases. Demonstrating unethical behavior, perhaps a research firm might "fudge" the research results if the results are overly negative. Perhaps the research provider does not want to offend his or her client for fearing the client will not retain the research services or might not recommend him or her to other organizations for business. Other falsification might include outright cheating. Suppose a research provider is required to make 1,000 phones calls—also known as **completes**—in order to meet his client's needs. Suppose the research provider only completes 990 on the day the research is due. Might the researcher simply "make up" the other respondents, reasoning that ten fake respondents' answers will not materially change the results (particularly if the ten are given "neutral" responses)? In fact, statistically the wayward researcher is probably correct, but this practice is still unethical. The researcher can either ask for more time to get the remaining ten completes or submit the research with 990 completes and adjust the margin of error accordingly.

- *Recommend additional research when it's not needed.* Research firms should not drag-out the research or propose additional research if the current research results are conclusive or otherwise adequate. Remember that many clients will not have the researcher's level of expertise and thus they rely on the researcher to be honest about what, if any, additional research is truly warranted. Think of a doctor, lawyer, or auto mechanic who proposes additional work just to extend his or her billing opportunity. This practice is unethical.

- *Divulge inappropriate or otherwise personal information about the participants.* Maintaining the privacy of individual information is an important ethical component for the research profession, and in some places is the law.

The Client Should Not

- *Issue false RFPs or RFQs* in an attempt to get free insight from would-be marketing research providers. Many research suppliers take great pains to provide a substantive response to project solicitations that are assumed to have been made in good faith. It is not ethical for an organization to knowingly issue RFPs or RFQs that they have no intention of executing just to see what research approach the firms would take. In some cases, organizations do this so they can then use the proposed research approach with their in-house research team.
- *Withhold valuable information* from the marketing research provider. The client should offer the appropriate support to the marketing research provider.
- *Materially change the research purpose* after the agreed-upon purpose has been established—unless not doing so would result in research failure. In some cases, organizations that issue RFPs or RFQs don't have a clear enough understanding of what research they are really asking for. Perhaps they presume they will "figure it out" along the way. This lack of direction is not fair to a research provider who might not be able to comply with the new objectives and might not have bid on the project in the first place had the true research objectives been clearly conveyed.

The Respondent Should Not

- *Intentionally provide false answers* to questions or otherwise try to "game" the research. If someone agrees to be a respondent, he or she should be an honest broker and provide the best possible answers to the research questions. Legitimate marketing research companies don't have a vested interest in the results as such; they are more concerned with providing sound research since their livelihood depends on the quality of their work.
- *Become a professional respondent* by trying to wangle oneself into multiple research studies, or otherwise be untruthful, for the purpose of collecting a monetary or otherwise valuable incentive by virtue of being in the research.

Exploratory, Descriptive, and Causal Research

There are three broad types of research—**exploratory, descriptive,** and **causal**. Exploratory is the simplest, then descriptive, and then causal. By the way, it's causal—not casual. Often one research type will lead to another type until the research objectives are met. Generally when little is known about the issue at hand, exploratory research is a good starting point. Think of your college major. Some majors you dismiss as unviable knowing only a little about the subject. Exploratory, or basic, data is enough in some cases to make a decision to pursue or not to pursue a particular course of action. However, if you are interested in the medical profession, you will have to do more research, descriptive or even causal, to determine which medical path to take.

Exploratory Research

Exploratory Research—*research designed to gain a general understanding of the issue at hand. Because it is more general, typically qualitative research methods are used. These methods include:*

- *Secondary Data Analysis—to learn what has been written about the topic.*
- *Focus Groups and Depth Interviews—to understand broadly the issues directly from respondents gauging, for example, their attitudes, perceptions, and beliefs.*
- *Observation—to gain information into behaviors in natural or contrived settings.*
- *Case Studies—examining similar or related events to draw general comparative conclusions to the research topic.*
- *Pilot Studies—a limited experiment to test the variables of the research topic.*
- *Experience Surveys—a small-scale survey of experts to determine the key issues from which an expanded understanding of the topic occurs.*

Descriptive Research

Descriptive Research—*research designed to quantify the understanding of the research topic. Descriptive research answers who, what, where, and how related questions. Once the researcher has a basic understanding of the marketplace through exploratory research, descriptive research will add a more sophisticated level of data. Descriptive methods include:*

- *Secondary Data Analysis—to learn what has been written about the topic.*
- *Statistically Representative Surveys—*
  - *Table 2-1 Cross Sectional Surveys—asking questions of various respondents, but not re-surveying the same group. Cross-sectional surveys ask one set of respondents questions at one point in time.*
  - *For example, a thousand people were asked once—to rate their **top** vacation destination.*

The analysis is quite simple—170 respondents said London was their top vacation destination preference, 88 named Moscow as their preference, and so on.

■ TABLE 2–1
Top Vacation
Destination

Cross Sectional Survey	Vacation Preference
London	170
Moscow	88
Paris	210
Beijing	155
Buenos Aries	175
Cape Town	202
Total Respondents	**1,000**

- *Table 2-2 Longitudinal Surveys—asking the same questions of the same respondents over time. Longitudinal surveys enable researchers to track trends and movement between and among preferences.*
- *For example, a thousand people were asked the same question twice at different points in time to rate their **top** vacation destination.*

■ **TABLE 2–2** Longitudinal Survey–Vacation Preference

	London	Moscow	Paris	Beijing	Buenos Aires	Cape Town	Totals	
London	40	25	15	44	36	10	170	
Moscow	15	15	10	18	12	18	88	
Paris	57	33	20	23	27	50	210	Survey 1
Beijing	30	20	25	25	27	28	155	
Buenos Aires	35	15	30	35	37	23	175	
Cape Town	45	22	37	28	41	29	202	
Totals:	222	130	137	173	180	158	1,000	

Survey 2

How to Read a Longitudinal Survey—Focus on Four Concepts

1. **Survey Totals:**
   - The key to understanding longitudinal surveys is to realize that the same respondents are asked the same question twice—perhaps after a few months or so. Let's look at Buenos Aries in Table 2-2. In survey 1, 175 rated it as their top travel destination and in survey 2 that number had grown to 180 people.

2. **The Intersection:**
   - The boxed "20" above is the *intersection* of like variables: Paris. This intersection represents the same response from a particular respondent in both surveys. In other words, the *same* 20 people ranked Paris as their top travel destination in both surveys.

3. **Horizontal Analysis:**
   - Let's look at Paris. In survey 1, 210 people rated Paris as their top choice. In Survey 2, 137 rated it as their top choice. As mentioned above, the intersection analysis reveals that only 20 people (the same people) rated Paris as their top choice in both surveys. However we must understand the source of the change. How did we get from 210 to 137? Where did the 73 respondents go? Perhaps we lost more than 73 but we gained some respondents to get us "back up" to 210. Well, *the losses are measured across*. Start with the intersection, 20, and go from there. To the left we see Moscow at 33 and London at 57 respectively. This data means that 33 of the people who responded Paris in the first survey said Moscow in the second survey and 57 switched from Paris to a London preference from survey 1 to survey 2, respectively. Fifty former Paris survey 1 folks switched to Cape Town in survey 2. *Again, the market losses are measured across.*

4. **Vertical Analysis:**
   - The vertical analysis represents the market gains. Yes, Paris lost a lot of folks—but they gained some respondents as well—for example, 10 from Moscow and 25 Beijing supporters, respectively, switched to Paris for survey 2.

Causal Research

Causal Research—*research designed to answer the "why" questions. Causal research requires that three principles are met:*

- *Concomitant Variation—a statistically predictable pattern between responses/variables.*
  - *If we lower price by 10 percent, sales will increase 5 percent.*
  - *If students study more, their grades will increase.*
  - *The more miles we drive, the less gas we have in the tank.*
- *Time Order of Occurrence—"A" must precede "B" if "A" is the cause of "B."*
  - *The pen will fall when I drop it—it will not fall before I drop it.*
- *Systematic Elimination—all other possible causes have been eliminated.*
  - *Sir Arthur Conan Doyle's famous sleuth often used this technique when pursuing, among others, the dastardly Professor Moriarty when he would proclaim: "If you eliminate the impossible, whatever remains, however improbable, must be the truth."—Sherlock Holmes*
- It's rare to have one variable as the **only** cause of the change in another variable. Often variables A, B, and C, etc., affect variables D, E, and F, etc. As you can see, causal analysis can quickly become complicated. For example, the cause in the change of sales might be due to price, location, selection, and quality.

The Internet Impact

What has been the impact of the Internet on marketing research? Has the impact been all positive? Are there any negative aspects to what the Internet has brought to the research table? To be sure, the Internet has revolutionized marketing research in many key ways.

- **Cost Reduction and Speed:**
  - *Much research can be done quickly and cheaply by using the Internet. Online surveys are a quick and inexpensive way to collect data—as opposed to in-person interviews or telephone surveys.*
  - *Access to secondary data is immediate. Suppose researchers want to learn about the fast-food industry. Collecting information on that industry is a few clicks away. Because secondary data are data that have already been collected, data quality is partly a function of the time delay of its collection. Traditional secondary data in journals, magazines, and books, is likely to be less current than what is online.*
- **Access to Respondents:**
  - *The Internet enables researchers to reach respondents through online or e-mail-based surveys. In some cases these respondents are otherwise difficult to reach.*
- **Immediate Analysis:**
  - *Online surveys enable researchers, and the client, to run continuing analysis of the survey results. This advantage is of particular use in fast-moving industries or when the sample size is large.*
- **Generally Higher Response Rates:**
  - *Although this advantage has been eroded by the onslaught of e-mails and online pleas, still, response rates are somewhat higher for Internet surveys than for many data collection methods partly because researchers can re-solicit respondents at little or no cost.*
- **Data Analysis:**
  - *The data collection will culminate with qualitative and quantitative analysis to include descriptive statistics, histograms, multivariate cross tabulations, correlation analysis, hypothesis testing, regression, Chi square, ANOVA, and other analyses as driven by the requirements of the research sponsor.*

- **Report Generation:**
  - *The report can be created in multiple formats.*
  - *Software enables quick changes and updates to the research report.*

Marketing Research Decision Support System

Organizations have a wide array of marketing research capabilities. In many cases marketing research is done on an ad hoc basis whereby someone within an organization is tapped as the marketing research "expert." Larger organizations will incorporate marketing research into a **Marketing Decision Support System** (MDSS). These systems are designed to provide organizational leadership with the marketing information they need to run the organization effectively. These systems blend primary, secondary, qualitative, and quantitative data to provide an information foundation from which organizational leadership can best manage the business affairs of an organization. Marketing research decision support systems can be complex. Figure 2.11 highlights the relationships in such a system.

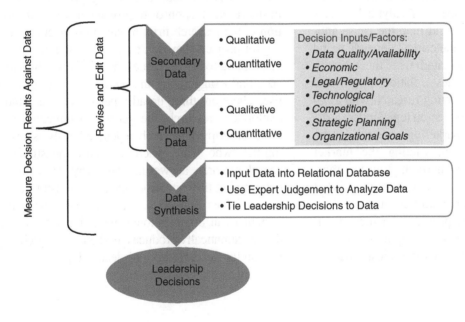

■ **FIGURE 2.11**
Marketing Research Decision Support System

Research in Practice

Case:
- Starbucks decides that it wants to create a customer profile. This profile will help Starbucks to solidify its market presence among existing customers while simultaneously providing valuable insight for its market expansion plans. Starbucks issues a Request for Proposal for the project and your marketing research company decides it will respond to this RFP.

Assignment:
- Write a research design that encapsulates the key objectives, research approach, and execution strategy to successfully accomplish the project goals. What key questions would you want to ask Starbucks' leadership that will help you in crafting your research design?

Chapter Summary

The marketing research process involves eleven key steps: establishing the need, defining the problem, establishing the research objectives, identifying the resources and types, determining the research design, accessing the data, designing the data collection forms, determining the sampling plan, collecting the data, analyzing the data, and presenting the findings. The research design, the detailed blueprint of the research execution, is perhaps the most critical piece of the research puzzle. When responding to a Request for Proposal, the process whereby an organization solicits proposals for projects, or a Request for Quote, when organizations ask for a price quote to conduct a project, the research design will detail how the researcher will accomplish the research project. The quality and thoroughness of the research design will have a significant impact on who will be selected to conduct the research. Analytical models help researchers to identify and map the cause-and-effect relationships among the critical dependent and independent variables associated with the research project at hand. Knowing these relationships enable researchers to conduct marketing research with a basis of knowledge about the research topic under study. A useful application of marketing research in the business world is in deconstructing the market growth matrix. This matrix charts the four key market growth opportunities: market penetration, market development, diversification, and product development. Marketing research provides business leaders with valuable insight as to the optimal business growth strategy. Two marketing research approaches are applied research, addressing a specific problem or issue, and basic research, more general marketing research. The major research methods are secondary research, research from existing sources, and primary research, research created by the marketing researcher specifically to meet the objectives of a given project. Many factors, in addition to a firm's capabilities, should be considered when choosing a research provider such as time, budget, and expertise desired. Syndicated research providers offer specialized marketing research services whereas full-service providers offer a full range of marketing research services including project development, execution, analysis, and presentation techniques. Marketing research ethics include standards of conduct for the research provider, the subject of the research, and the research sponsor. Some ethical issues include overpricing projects, a failure of the research sponsor to provide adequate information to the research firm, research providers advertising for projects they don't intend to fund, dishonestly responding to research questions, inflating the sample size, and exaggerating the researcher level of expertise. There are three broad types of research studies: exploratory research, the general examination of an issue, descriptive research, a detailed analysis answering the "who, what, where, and how" questions, and causal research answering the "why" questions by determining the cause-and-effect relationships among key variables. Finally, a marketing decision support system is an organizational marketing infrastructure that systematically produces marketing research information for the organization's leadership.

ISSUE IN THE
SPOTLIGHT   Research Measures in Sports Marketing

Jon Last, President
Sports & Leisure Research Group
www.sportsandleisureresearch.com

Sports marketing today is a multi-billion dollar industry. Brands align with teams, leagues and players to showcase their products and services. Difficult to reach target audiences, compete vigorously to stand out and differentiate themselves. Attend any sporting event and you are sure to see the implementation of these sponsorship affiliations. From the more static signage that lines the playing fields, venue concourses and even restrooms, to promotional giveaways and interactive events within the events, games, sponsoring brands and a variety of specialty marketing agencies deploy significant resources with the goal of creating breakthrough in-game marketing experiences that resonate with sports fans.

The cost of entry can be significant for marketers, and the revenue generated for the teams is critical in funding operations as player salaries and other costs continue to skyrocket. It is imperative that both sponsoring companies and the teams and venues that create and sell in game advertising and promotion partner effectively and can measure and evaluate the return on the sports marketing investment. This is not always easily accomplished. With more traditional advertising vehicles entrenched in the minds of brand managers and their advertising agencies, sports marketing can be a tough sell. With that has come a need for well-constructed marketing research programs to measure and evaluate the impact of venue-based activation. Brands seek to quantify the media equivalency value of their exposures and gauge its impact in changing brand perceptions and purchase intent among the target audience to justify their expenditures and plan more efficiently for future campaigns. On the seller side, the teams and venues seek to demonstrate the impact of their marketing opportunity so as to continue to grow sports marketing revenue. But in today's marketplace, simply equating exposure to a media equivalency dollar amount, is often not enough. Both sports marketers and activating brands want to understand how effective their sports promotions are at moving the needle in changing fan attitudes and behaviors.

Research firms like Sports and Leisure Research Group (SLRG) specialize in helping sports marketers on both the brand and property side to better and more objectively evaluate the impact of event-based sports marketing. As a custom marketing research firm, SLRG works closely with its clients to gather a holistic understanding of the impact of sports marketing activation. Rather than simply measuring exposure time and

assigning a traditional media equivalency valuation to it, SLRG subscribes to the belief that good sports marketing is iterative and is better evaluated by measuring the actual impact of activation on a consumer's awareness and perceptions of a brand. But that in its own right can be challenging to measure. Within a media and advertising world where consumers are consistently barraged with marketing messages in a variety of both traditional and out of home forms, it is improper to simply associate return on investment to the last marketing message that a consumer was exposed to before making a purchase. Brand perceptions and awareness grow over time and over multiple marketing exposures. Similarly, to ask a consumer directly, whether a particular advertisement or marketing initiative led to a purchase behavior is unrealistic. The human mind cannot cognitively attribute a particular behavior's impetus to a singular marketing activity. More realistically, the measurement opportunity lies in the ability of a sound research study to gauge changing perceptions of a sponsoring brand through experimental design.

In the late fall of 2010, a leading consumer products brand invested in a multi-tiered sports marketing program in partnership with an NFL team and one of their sports marketing agencies. The program included a series of in-game promotional messages that included an interactive, fan participation component on the main video scoreboards during the game. In addition, supplemental marketing messaging was delivered to a variety of auxiliary scoreboards that lined the bowl of the stadium. As a final component, sample product was distributed to one of the stadium seating sections as a result of the interactive promotion and this was announced over the public address system. Both the sponsoring brand and the property sought to better understand the impact of their specific onsite activation in transforming the target audience's brand perceptions within the client's relevant competitive set of products. By understanding these brand associations across a wide array of desired brand triggers and within the proper competitive context, the research would become not only about determining how a program worked, but also about understanding which message points were resonating and which need greater amplification. Hence, this symbiotic partnership between the property and client could ideally be enhanced and future activation efforts could be refined, accordingly. In essence, the research would become as much a springboard for future activation as it was an ROI scorecard. All parties could benefit.

Sports and Leisure Research Group deployed a field team of interviewers on-site, at the above referenced NFL game. A sufficient number of survey interviews were conducted both with a control group, of "unexposed" attending fans, prior to the in venue marketing activation and after the game with an identical number of fans "post-exposure." This research sampling methodology allowed for statistically valid respondent cells that enabled SLRG to analyze differences in brand recall, awareness, association with key brand attributes and perceived favorability across those in the market who were exposed to the brand activation both before (pre game interviews) and after (post-game interviews) exposure.

Respondents were randomly selected and both the pre- and post game surveys were similar in design, eliciting open and close-ended awareness and perceptions of the sponsor under study and its competitive set across a variety of brand attributes and message points. In the post phase, a series of open and close-ended awareness and recall questions were also included. To protect against brand bias, survey questions were posed in a blind/brand agnostic way. Where appropriate, broad "Likert" scales to evaluate agreement with various attitudinal statements were deployed and multiple versions of each survey were used to rotate questions and brand, thus eliminating potential order bias. The study's areas of inquiry included

- *Overall demographics and fan characteristics.*
- *Aided and unaided brand awareness within the sponsor brand's category.*
- *Overall awareness and association of the competitive set brand's activation at the event.*
- *Usage, perceptions and contextual evaluations of the test brand category and the actual competitive set.*
- *Overall awareness and association of the test brand's marketing positioning and key brand attributes within the space.*

- *Purchase behaviors within the sponsor brand's category.*
- *Fan experience with and perceptions of the test brand's products and services in comparison with those of competitors across key brand attributes.*
- *Use of brand identity agreement scale statements across the competitive set, to include relative rankings of each brand's ability to deliver a wide range of "brand personality" traits derived directly from desired positioning.*

The study results were quite compelling. By comparing the pre-exposure and post-exposure findings, the research team and clients were able to evaluate and quantify the direct impact of the in venue activation in lifting sponsoring brand awareness and proper perceptual associations. Of course, not all of the key message points were as resonant as others, and the results also varied across certain key demographic subgroups attending the game. Armed with this insight, all parties involved were able to objectively measure the ability of sports marketing to create a positive lift in attitudes and understanding. Further, the research findings were also impactful in enabling all parties to make necessary adjustments to subsequent game specific promotions.

This case study is just one of many similar projects that firms like Sports and Leisure Research Group engage in. By adding a thorough and appropriate layer of measurement onto sports marketing programs, teams, brands and their agencies can become more effective in leveraging the opportunities present in an increasingly fragmented marketing environment. Smart marketing research can be the engine that informs these critical decisions and maximizes return on sports marketing investment.

Qualitative vs. Quantitative Data and Secondary Data Methods

Image © Beboy, 2011. Used under license from Shutterstock, Inc.

Learning Objectives:

- Understand the difference between qualitative and quantitative research
- Appreciate the role of analytic research in tying together other research methods
- See the differences in the characteristics of qualitative and quantitative research
- Learn about the data collection analysis flow

- Understand the difference between external and internal secondary data sources
- Review the advantages and disadvantages of secondary research
- Learn techniques for assessing the quality of secondary data
- Learn some common marketing research mistakes

- Review some tips in developing a marketing research strategy
- See how Venn Diagrams can be used to determine the interrelation among variables
- Appreciate the impact of the Freedom of Information Act

Chapter Three

Qualitative vs. Quantitative Research

The marketing research process involves extensive planning based on the goals and objectives set forth by the research sponsor. This chapter lays the foundation for the marketing research process. Marketing research can be broadly categorized as primary or secondary and each type can be **qualitative** or **quantitative**. Marketing research efforts that emphasize both qualitative and quantitative methods are typically more comprehensive than simply a qualitative or a quantitative approach. Combining both qualitative and quantitative methods enables the researcher to provide more **analytic analysis** that addresses the "why" type questions.

- *Qualitative Data:*
  - *Data whose analysis relies of non-numeric conclusions. Often this type of analysis involves preliminary observations about research subjects.*
- *Quantitative Data:*
  - *Data whose analysis results in numeric findings such as percentages, correlations, sums and counts, and many other statistical applications.*
- *Analytic Analysis:*
  - *Analysis that answers the "why" questions or otherwise explains what the data might mean instead of simply what the data says.*

Researchers should focus their research on the goals of the research sponsor. In some cases, a simple descriptive analysis—what has happened—is all that is warranted. However, more complex marketing research requires describing what has happened and interpreting what the data might mean and how the data can be used by business leaders. Oftentimes marketing research starts with **qualitative** data collection (interviews, secondary data, and focus groups), then becomes more **quantitative** (statistically representative large scale surveys), and finally more **analytic** (the interpretation or analysis of what was found). Each research phase builds on the previous phase. Some research reports stop at the quantitative descriptive phase—perhaps because business leadership only wants to know what was found as a result of the research. The so-called "just the facts" position. Managers might prefer to interpret the research results themselves. Additionally, sometimes research companies are reluctant to provide too much interpretation or opinions as to what the research results mean for fear of misleading leadership. There are many approaches to writing a research report. Figure 3.1 offers one type of approach.

Most research involves a combination of qualitative and quantitative data. Often the preliminary qualitative research findings are used as the foundation of a larger-scale quantitative research approach, such as a full-scale survey. Secondary research—analyzing data that someone else collected—can be qualitative or quantitative. When researching traffic statistics, that information is usually quantitative—the word "statistics" should be the clue. If it's reported that 1,000 cars cross a given bridge during an hour, or that the average speed in a particular stretch of road is 65 MPH, or that there is an average of five accidents in a given intersection each year, then these findings are quantitative secondary data. Now consider a news article where they had interviewed various drivers who talked about traffic congestion during rush hour. Their observations are qualitative secondary data because someone else collected the data and the data are fairly "general." Primary research can be qualitative—such as depth interviews, or it can be quantitative in the case of a statistically representative survey with scaled questions—more on this technique later. Both qualitative and quantitative data can be collected through various methods; online, by telephone, by mail, and/or in-person.

■ **FIGURE 3.1**

Research Report
Approach

■ **FIGURE 3.2**

Quantitative Data should
be Used to Augment
Qualitative Data to Add
Depth to the Research

Image © Andreser, 2011. Used
under license from Shutterstock, Inc.

Key Differences in Qualitative and Quantitative Research

Various characteristics typify both qualitative and quantitative data. Figure 3.3 compares qualitative and quantitative methods based on a common issue.

- **Question Depth:**
  - Qualitative data, such as interviews, generally yield in-depth responses because the interviewer can ask follow-up questions. Quantitative research—such as surveys—typically involves a set list of scaled questions thus limiting the respondent to selecting a choice. However, some surveys have open-ended questions, the use of which is best limited to large scale surveys because of the time, cost, and subjectivity to analyze those types of questions.

■ FIGURE 3.3
Qualitative and
Quantitative Data

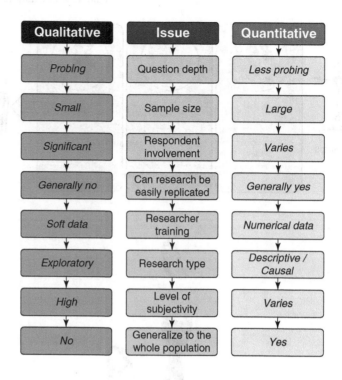

Qualitative	Issue	Quantitative
Probing	Question depth	Less probing
Small	Sample size	Large
Significant	Respondent involvement	Varies
Generally no	Can research be easily replicated	Generally yes
Soft data	Researcher training	Numerical data
Exploratory	Research type	Descriptive / Causal
High	Level of subjectivity	Varies
No	Generalize to the whole population	Yes

- **Sample Size:**
  - Most qualitative research methods (depth interviews, focus groups, and observation) involve smaller samples. Imagine trying to interview 1,000 people for a 30-minute depth interview. Conducting dozens of focus groups is also not a good use of research time. Quantitative research involves large samples, such as those used in a survey. Surveys generally take less time than interviews and can be done through the mail, Internet, in person, or over the telephone. Questionnaires are designed to tell the researcher something about the opinions of the population at large. Minimum sample sizes are required to meet the statistics requirements associated with using a sample to represent the population. Using more than one technique on the same project is called **mixed mode** data collection.
- **Respondent Involvement:**
  - Qualitative methods often require the respondent to have more involvement in the process. Quantitative methods—like surveys—might only take a respondent few minutes to complete, whereas an interview can take an hour and a focus group two hours.
- **Can the Research be Replicated:**
  - A questionnaire distributed to 1,000 people can be replicated by distributing the same questionnaire again. However, focus groups and depth interviews are difficult to replicate due to the differences between interviewers and moderators as well as the people in the focus group or interview. Replicating observation research is also not easily done. A big difference between these methods is the sample that is used. Most large-scale, and thus typically quantitative projects, use a sample frame that can be replicated, whereas qualitative interviews (which represent a small sample) are too small to have a sample that can be used to represent the population within a reasonable margin of error.

- **Researcher Training:**
  - It is incorrect to assume that quantitative research training is necessarily more difficult than qualitative skills due to the math component of quantitative research. Both qualitative and quantitative research training is complicated. An understanding of statistics is a critical skill quantitative researchers must have. Qualitative analysts must be able to make good analytic sense of more open-ended type data. Whether you are a qualitative or quantitative researcher, extensive training is necessary which results in most researchers building expertise in one area or the other.
- **Research Type:**
  - Remember that exploratory research is more general and often is the preliminary phase of research. Qualitative research provides less specific data that is usually associated with quantitative research which lends itself to more descriptive or causal research.
- **Level of Subjectivity:**
  - Think of a recent interview, or a presidential speech perhaps. If you are asked to summarize the speech, focus group, or interview, what might you say? In addition to a transcript, you will provide your analysis about what was meant by what was said. Your analysis might be insightful, biased, off the mark, etc. If we had five people watch the same speech and provide an analysis, we will get five different–perhaps very different— accounts of the same event. However, ask five people to provide a certain statistical output from a 1,000 respondent survey and all five should get the same answer. Quantitative calculations are generally not subjective. However, the analysis of what the numbers "mean" is subjective.

Comparing Qualitative and Quantitative Research Approaches

Typically the most thorough marketing research reports combine qualitative and quantitative research methods. Qualitative research should lead to quantitative research, which is then analyzed using both qualitative and quantitative methods. For example, suppose the president of Ford Motor Company wants to know what his customers think of a new vehicle. Before asking a large-scale sample in a questionnaire (quantitative research) Ford might first conduct qualitative research such as interviews and focus groups to understand what *types of issues* to cover on a questionnaire. Remember that when a questionnaire is administered to a large sample it's too late to "fix" the questions; thus, the researcher has to be certain to ask the right questions from the beginning. Unless researchers first test questions and concepts with smaller groups such as during a focus group or through interviews, they will not know the *best* questions to ask. Finally, the questionnaire analysis involves both quantitative work (descriptive statistics, correlation analysis, hypothesis testing, etc.) and qualitative analysis (interpreting the open-ended questions and gaining insight from what was not said—or reading between the lines of the survey results). Many researchers conclude their projects with quantitative descriptive analysis because analytic analysis (drawing various conclusions from the research) can be risky for the researcher. For example, suppose the Ford research reveals dissatisfaction with various vehicle design and styling elements. Although the researcher did not specifically ask a question about the car's length, he might *extrapolate* that finding from the research. Based on this analytic work, the researcher decides to recommend the car length be increased, which Ford does. Sales now drop and we learn that customers did not in fact want the car length increased; the researcher only *derived* that from the questionnaire based on their dissatisfaction with the car styling. Concluding a research project with analytics can be challenging, whereas descriptive analysis simply "describes" what was *actually* said, not what researchers are *extrapolating* from the data. Analytic research can be quite lucrative if the researcher is expert enough to execute such research correctly.

Data Collection to Analysis Flow

As we have learned, there is a connection between qualitative and quantitative research. Marketing researchers tie together both research types to form a comprehensive picture of the research topic. It is important to remember that the qualitative research foundation leads to the quantitative aspect of research projects. Figure 3.4 depicts a data analysis flow common in marketing research reports.

It can be difficult to strike the right balance between quantitative and qualitative analysis. There can be a tendency to shortchange the quantitative analysis by failing to use the right statistical analysis—or by oversimplifying the analysis with less sophisticated statistical tools. Conversely, researchers can overanalyze data by making sweeping or over-generalized observations not fully supported by a more sophisticated data analysis approach often yielded by quantitative methods. Fostering a balanced analysis approach to melding qualitative and quantitative research will yield the most robust marketing research. Figure 3.5 illustrates the balancing act between qualitative and quantitative marketing research.

■ **FIGURE 3.4**
Analysis Flow

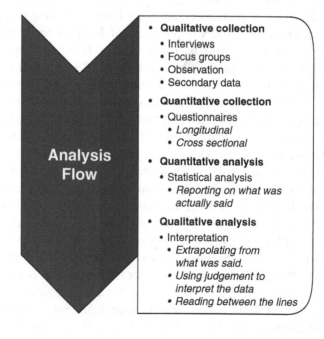

Secondary Data Sources

Often secondary data is a first step in the data collection process. The researcher might discover that the answer to the research question might be found in secondary data, thus negating the need for primary data collection. Or, this secondary data can help in formulating the issues and questions researchers ask on the survey. There are advantages and disadvantages to secondary data collection. There are also several ways to determine the quality of the secondary data before its use. Remember that secondary data serves as a foundational piece of research from which is built the total research effort. If the secondary data findings are incorrect or inaccurate, the rest of the research will be faulty. It is critical to get a firm grasp on the secondary data before collecting the primary data. Of course, the primary data findings might either support or be in conflict with the secondary data—either of which is an acceptable research outcome. Sometimes researchers use primary data collection to either verify or refute their secondary findings. And, this data might comprise part of the final report as a citation to support the findings. Many sources of **external secondary data** are reviewed below. There are many different sources of secondary research as depicted in Figure 3.7. Each type brings various pros and cons into the mix.

■ FIGURE 3.5

Striking a Balance between Qualitative and Quantitative Analysis

■ FIGURE 3.6

Professional Journals are Key Sources of Secondary Data. Peer-Reviewed Journals Add Credibility to Your Research

Image © Africa Studio, 2011. Used under license from Shutterstock, Inc.

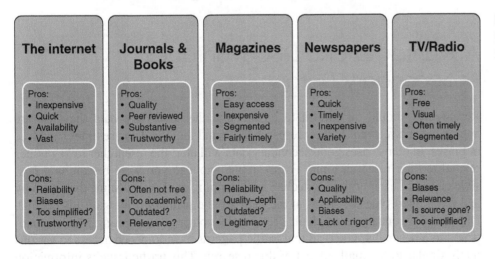

■ FIGURE 3.7

External Secondary Data Sources—Pros and Cons

The internet	Journals & Books	Magazines	Newspapers	TV/Radio
Pros: • Inexpensive • Quick • Availability • Vast	Pros: • Quality • Peer reviewed • Substantive • Trustworthy	Pros: • Easy access • Inexpensive • Segmented • Fairly timely	Pros: • Quick • Timely • Inexpensive • Variety	Pros: • Free • Visual • Often timely • Segmented
Cons: • Reliability • Biases • Too simplified? • Trustworthy?	Cons: • Often not free • Too academic? • Outdated? • Relevance?	Cons: • Reliability • Quality–depth • Outdated? • Legitimacy	Cons: • Quality • Applicability • Biases • Lack of rigor?	Cons: • Biases • Relevance • Is source gone? • Too simplified?

Internal Secondary Data Sources

Internal secondary data sources are sources gathered from existing records within an organization. These data can be most useful in understanding a research topic as the sources are often directly related and applicable to a given research topic. A drawback to secondary data is that the data might not be applicable to the given situation, but you *might think* it is related. Suppose you are studying what students at your university think about student housing. As part of your research you read about student housing opinions at other universities and you assume their opinions are relatable to the opinions of the students at your university. However, you ultimately realize that the students at other universities do not have the same reference point as your university students have, thus perhaps their respective opinions are not truly comparable to the opinions and experiences of your students.

Internal Sources Include:

- *Sales Receipts*
- *Income Statements*
- *Balance Sheets*
- *Cash Flow Reports*
- *Ratios Reports*
- *Accounts Payable and Receivable*
- *Various Other Financial Documents*
- *Shipping and Receiving Invoices*
- *Performance Reports*
- *Contract Documents*
- *Personnel Records*
- *Any Number of Other Internal Records*

When clients receive a research project they might question aspects of the primary and secondary data collection as well as the analysis of those data. Once the researcher includes secondary data in the report the client assumes that the researcher "owns" that secondary data. If the client catches errors in the secondary data, the researcher would be ill-advised to "blame" the quality of the secondary data on its originators. The client essentially assumes that the secondary data has been screened for quality by the researcher. If the client questions the secondary data, he will then likely look more skeptically on the entire research report. There are several ways the researcher should measure the credibility of the secondary data before it is introduced as part of the research project.

Advantages and Disadvantages of Secondary Data

Researchers should be careful to ensure that the secondary data they use are applicable and relevant to their research topic and that the data are timely and free of biases. In many cases good secondary data will alert the researcher to key issues related to their research topic. For example, suppose you were researching possible causes of a general sales decline at a shopping mall. You assume the economy and the limited types of stores at the mall are the primary drivers of this decline. During the secondary research phase, whereby you are investigating what has happened to other malls, you read that traffic patterns have impeded access to various malls similar to the mall subject of this research. This traffic issue is information

■ **FIGURE 3.9**

Advantages and Disadvantages of Secondary Research

Advantages
- Can clarify problems
- Can identify key issues
- Is inexpensive to gather
- Multiple sources are available
- Might identify other problems
- Can be gathered quickly

Disadvantages
- Can be misunderstood
- Not always applicable
- Might be outdated
- Might not be enough relevant data
- Sources might be biased
- Analysis can be over generalized

heretofore unknown to you, yet it now becomes a focal point of the research. Secondary research might well yield information critical to the research or it might result in a need to redirect the research. Once the researcher has collected the secondary data it must be **screened for quality**. There are several considerations when determining if the researcher should use, and by extension trust, the secondary data. Figure 3.9 summarizes the advantages and disadvantages of secondary research.

Assessing the Quality of Secondary Data

Before a researcher trusts and then uses secondary data, it must be screened for quality. When researchers put secondary data in a research report (and cite the sources), it helps to form the basis for the next phase (primary data collection) of the research. If the secondary data are flawed, the rest of the research is suspect. There are six major ways to screen secondary data to ensure it is good information. Figure 3.10 provides some guidelines on how to assess the quality of the secondary research.

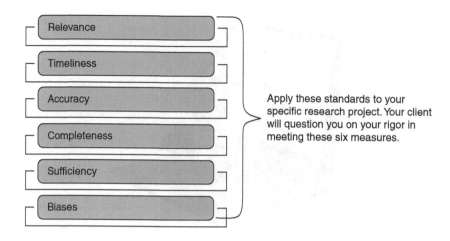

Relevance

Timeliness

Accuracy

Completeness

Sufficiency

Biases

Apply these standards to your
specific research project. Your client
will question you on your rigor in
meeting these six measures.

- **Relevance:**
  - *Are the data relevant to the research situation, or just a more general situation?*
  - *Is it appropriate to apply the secondary data to your research topic and objectives?*
- **Timeliness:**
  - *Are the data current enough to be useful?*
  - *Can the data be gathered in time to be useful?*
- **Accuracy:**
  - *How did the originator collect the data? Did they have good quality standards?*
  - *What research methods were used in collecting the original data?*
- **Completeness:**
  - *Does the data tell the whole story?*
  - *Is there too much reliance on article abstracts and summary information?*
- **Sufficiency:**
  - *Is there enough data to make an informed decision?*
  - *Is there enough of the "right kind" of data to be useful in the research?*
- **Biases:**
  - *Are the data biased in some way?*
  - *Did the originator of the data have a "hidden agenda" in collecting the data?*
  - *What were the objectives of the originator of the data?*

Once the data are determined to be of quality, researchers use these data to build the case for the primary data collection phase. It is ill-advised to skip the secondary data research phase by "jumping" right into the primary data collection. Many errors in the primary data collection can be avoided through rigorous and thorough secondary data analysis.

Finding Good Secondary Data

A number of government secondary data sources are free to the public and have generally been screened for quality. As you know, websites can lead to more sites ad infinitum. Some useful sites:

- **USA Government Web Portal:**
  - www.usa.gov and www.data.gov
    - *This site links to other useful government websites.*

- **The Bureau of Labor Statistics:**
  - www.bls.gov
    - *Offers enormous amounts of information on the labor market and economics data in general. This site enables researchers to create various tables and graphs for inclusion in report writing.*
- **The Small Business Administration:**
  - www.sba.gov
    - *The SBA provides comprehensive business, economic, and demographic data. There are also links to other resources from this page.*
- **The Census Bureau:**
  - www.census.gov
    - *The definitive source of U.S. demographic and economic related data.*

Additionally, many news sites offer a wealth of secondary data free. Here is a small sample:

- www.abcnews.com
- www.cnn.com
- www.msnbc.com
- www.foxnews.com
- www.cbsnews.com
- www.newsweek.com
- www.nytimes.com
- www.time.com
- www.latimes.com
- www.washingtonpost.com
- www.usatoday.com
- www.usnews.com
- www.bbc.co.uk
- www.suntimes.com
- www.reuters.com
- www.ap.org
- www.c-span.org
- www.global.nytimes.com/?iht
- www.spiegel.de/international
- www.consumerreports.org (subscription)

Other good sources of secondary data include various **syndicated sources**. Syndicated sources are customized data from research providers on specifics topics. For example, to learn more about market share, economic trends, the travel industry, etc. researchers can turn to providers who specialize in those research topics. Typically these special reports are not free. However, if done correctly, these sources are often unbiased and of great use. If the researcher wants to learn about a car manufacturer, he can go to that manufacture's website for information. However, although much of the information on that site might well be accurate and useful, it will likely not be without some biases. Thus the researcher might want to turn to a syndicated source specializing in the car industry to get "a second opinion" about what was learned on the website.

Of course more recent sources of secondary data are blogs, the ubiquitous expression of experts, pseudo experts, and sadly non-experts.

- **Blog:** *An online personal journal with reflections, comments, and often hyperlinks provided by the writer; also: the contents of such a site.*

Source: Merriam-Webster Dictionary

Forbes Magazine (www.forbes.com), an established and generally accepted authority on a number of business matters, publishes a list of its top-rated blogs. A search of its website will reveal Forbes' list of the best blogs which is segmented thusly:

- Political
- Photo
- Medical
- Travel
- Movies
- Sports
- Media
- War *(sadly)*
- Celebrity
- Technology
- Food *(the best for last)*

Common Marketing Research Mistakes

All Business*, a Dunn and Bradstreet company, recently released its list of the top ten marketing research mistakes. Many of these mistakes are easily avoidable. However, shortcuts in the research process often result in one or more of these mistakes being made.

1. **Overspending:**
   - The false assumption that you can "spend your way to success." Much money is wasted on poorly designed research. And what's worse is making business decisions based on that faulty research.
2. **Not knowing what you are looking for:**
   - The researcher should have a firm idea of what he is researching. Too much time dillydallying will yield unfocused data of marginal use.
3. **Poor choice of reference materials:**
   - Here the importance of solid secondary data is critical. Remember that the secondary data used in your research will be assumed to be of quality by your boss, client, general reader, etc.
4. **Not thoroughly researching the competition:**
   - Many businesses falter for a lack of understanding their competition. Don't assume that your restaurant is better simply because you *think* it's better.
5. **Not researching price information:**
   - Not necessarily a relevant issue for some research projects, understanding price is critical when financial factors are important to success.
6. **Researching the wrong group:**
   - If researchers need to know what medical doctors think, don't survey dentists. More subtlety, ensure you have the right demographic when researching an issue, product, service, or concept.
7. **Not using the right research instrument:**
   - For example, using interviews when focus groups are more appropriate. Or administering a long and poorly worded questionnaire.
8. **Not being aggressive enough in the research efforts:**
   - Don't skimp on spending, hoping to get more out of the research than you are willing to invest. Although good research can be expensive, its result can save money, reduce error, increase market share, etc.

9. **Relying on one set of data:**
   - Good research requires data collection and analysis from multiple perspectives and sources.
10. **Ignoring the marketing research:**
    - Failure to act on solid research often results in predictable and preventable business and marketing mistakes from which recovery could be costly.

Key source: http://www.allbusiness.com/marketing/market-research/3970-1.html

Developing a Marketing Research Strategy

In developing a research project, the researcher must also choose between a research statement and a research hypothesis. It is important that the research strategy link the research project's objectives, resources, and methods.

Key Considerations of a Research Strategy

Marketing researchers need to consider the objectives, resources, and methods of the proposed research project. Researchers should always keep the research sponsor—perhaps a company or other organization—informed as to the impact on the project these three issues will have if not properly addressed. Marketing researchers need to develop an overall research strategy to convey to clients. Figure 3.11 offers potential strategies. Key strategies include research:

- **Objectives**:
  - The project objectives will have an impact on how the researcher will plan and execute a research study. Suppose a key objective is to "understand customer needs." How the researcher will frame the project around that objective will affect the proposed budget and research methods—or approach—to collecting the data.
- **Resources**:
  - Marketing researchers and the research project sponsor must agree to the resources, chiefly money budgeted for the study, *before* the project starts. Marketing researchers should be candid with the research sponsor about the costs required to meet the objectives stated by the research sponsor. In many cases the research sponsor knows what information is sought, but might not have a clear, or realistic, understanding of the costs of getting that information.
- **Methods**:
  - The research methods refer to how the researcher will accomplish the research project objectives. The research steps required to meet the objectives

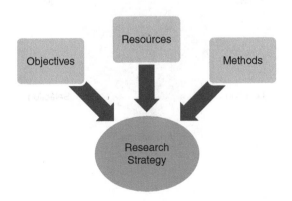

■ FIGURE 3.11
Research Strategy

should be clearly communicated to, and approved by, the research sponsor. It's possible that the research methods might be objectionable to the research sponsors. Suppose the researcher decides to conduct a sample of customers to determine customer satisfaction, yet the research sponsor wants the researcher to ask all 5,000 customers about their respective satisfaction as opposed to a sample of customers. There will be a major impact on time and budget if the researcher asks all customers as opposed to a sample.

Main Components of a Research Strategy

- **Research Statement:**
  - A declaration of the issue under study without a theory of cause.
    - *Examining the facts and circumstances around an event or issue.*
- **Hypothesis Testing:**
  - The systematic process of testing the possible causes of phenomena.
  - **Parameter vs. Sample Statistic:**
    - *Parameter—the actual value of a variable in the population learned from collecting data from the entire population.*
    - *A sample statistic—a sample of a variable in the population from which observations about the whole population can be theorized.*
- **Research Hypothesis:**
  - An argument the researcher hopes to prove:
    - *Higher prices have caused sales to decline.*
  - **Null Hypothesis:**
    - Stating there is no relationship between variables.
      - *There **is no** connection between price and sales.*
  - **Alternative Hypothesis:**
    - Stating that there is a relationship between variables.
      - *There **is a** connection between price and sales.*

Research Strategies—Determining the Interrelation Among Variables

Another method to conceptualize or visualize what might be occurring, and what variables might be affecting other variables, is by using a **Venn Diagram** as depicted in Figure 3.12.

■ FIGURE 3.12

Possible Independent Variable Relationships in Restaurant Sales

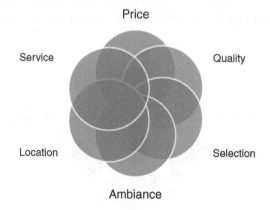

- **Venn Diagram:**
  - *A depiction of overlapping circles representing relationships among variables.*

As shown by this Venn Diagram, there are many possible connections or relationships among variables. There might well be other variables not yet known that the research will reveal. Here is the challenge—sorting out all the possible relationships—and *how and why* they relate. As we can see, the relationships can get very complicated, very fast.

Another useful form of research is a consumer panel. Consumer panels can be both primary research, if the researcher collects the data himself directly from the respondent, or secondary research if the researcher is using someone else's consumer panel results in his research. Often consumer panel research results are available for sale through a syndicated service. The researcher can also pay panel members to sit on the panel and respond to questions over time.

- **Consumer Panels:**
  - *Large samples of respondents, often households, who regularly supply information on purchase habits, or buyer behavior, over a long period of time. Consumer panels identity consumer behavior patterns over time.*

Although difficult to conduct and analyze, **content analysis** can produce a level of insight unattainable from one article, news story, or report.

- ***Content Analysis*** *is a secondary research technique that involves reading articles, Internet stories, newspapers, books, information,* etc. while searching for a pattern of data that might not be readily apparent in one article. Sometimes content analysis is called **synthesizing secondary data.** Here synthesis refers to compiling the secondary data to tell a story, the story of what the totality of the secondary data reveals.

The Freedom of Information Act

Finally, when doing secondary research researchers might want to get information from the U.S. government. Much information is attainable through a **Freedom of Information Act** request. This Act makes available to the public information on various government activities which can be most helpful in a number of research projects. Be aware of the time it can take to get this information.

- The U.S. **Freedom of Information Act**, 5 U.S.C. § 552—As Amended By Public Law No. 110–175, 121 Stat. 2524:

  In the interest of transparency, this act essentially states that the public can, with some exceptions, request government documentation on its activities.

- The full act can be found, along with other U.S. laws, through the U.S. Library of Congress (literally the library of U.S. documents formerly reserved only members of Congress) at http://thomas.loc.gov.

- And yes, it was named to honor Thomas Jefferson, chief writer of the U.S. Declaration of Independence, third U.S. president, and founder of the University of Virginia.

Research in Practice

Case:
- Your boss just received a marketing research report about the economics, environmental, and political situation in Phoenix, a city where your boss wants to expand her restaurant business. When the data are presented to the company board, several questions arise as to the source and quality of the secondary data. Many members of the board want assurances that the secondary data is quality data.

Assignment:
- Discuss how you would determine whether the secondary data should be considered trustworthy. What questions need to be answered to determine that the secondary data is quality information?

Chapter Summary

Marketing research can be conducted using qualitative and/or quantitative techniques. Qualitative research involves making judgments that are less mathematical or statistical than the conclusions typically made from quantitative research. There are key differences between qualitative and quantitative research such as the relative sample sizes required, the degree of repeatability, question depth, respondent involvement, and representativeness of the general population. The most effective and comprehensive marketing research reports tend to have both qualitative and quantitative research components usually starting with qualitative research such as secondary data, focus groups, and interviews and ending with quantitative analysis typified by statistically representative surveys. Secondary research, background data someone else collected, can be internal (such as company reports) or external such as from the Internet, magazines, newspapers, journals, or TV programs. When using secondary data, it is important that the researcher screen this secondary data for quality. Key quality measures include testing the secondary data for relevance, timeliness, accuracy (the quality of the method by which the originator collected the source data), completeness, sufficiency, and lack of biases. Several good sources of secondary data provided by the U.S. government include the Census Bureau, the Bureau of Labor Statistics, and the Small Business Administration. In addition many major news sources provide substantial secondary data. There are also paid secondary research resources available. There are many common mistakes in marketing research to be avoided such as overspending, not using the right research instrument/method, relying too much on the research results or not enough on the results, researching the wrong group, or relying on one set of data to represent the population at large. Key strategies in initiating a marketing research proposal include developing the objectives, marshalling the resources, and executing a research plan. Marketing research proposals can include a research hypothesis, presenting a theory and proposed causes, or a research statement that will be examined during the research execution. Venn Diagrams can help researchers determine what possible variables overlap and affect each other. These variables and their supposed interrelations can then be tested in a research project. Finally, consumer panels provide researchers with valuable qualitative and quantitative primary research whereby researchers tap subject matter experts, or otherwise interested parties, to respond to research questions over a predetermined period of time.

ISSUE IN THE
SPOTLIGHT　Honest Tea Honestly

Seth Goldman, President & CEO
Honest Tea
www.honesttea.com

My co-founder Barry Nalebuff and I launched Honest Tea in 1998 because we were thirsty. We felt there were too many sweet bottled teas on the market, and none with just enough sweetness to enhance the flavor. Our sample of two may not have qualified as scientific market research, but it was enough to give us the conviction that there was an opportunity to launch a line of low-sugar beverages where none existed.

Our view of market research is that the market provides the research. We can bring a real product to market and see the reaction. We also get immediate feedback from retail buyers as to their interest in bringing the product to their customers. And we can generally do all this in less time and for less money than a traditional market research test.

For many of the larger brands, the way they do market research means they won't ever come up with a product like Honest Tea. For example, one beverage giant uses the following test: Any new product has to beat an existing product 60:40 in a market research test. They take their test product and it has to beat the incumbent for at least 60 percent of consumers in a blind test. Sounds good on paper. But if you are thinking about bringing Honest Tea to the market, what is the product we are supposed to beat 60 percent of the time? Snapple? Water? Diet soda? There wasn't an obvious product for us to go against. We were looking to serve customers that weren't happy with the products in the market.

Henry Ford once said, "If I'd asked customers what they wanted, they would have said 'a faster horse'." Similarly, I'd bet that if customers in 1998 were asked whether they prefer the taste of a 17-calorie Honest Tea or a sweeter drink, many would have opted for the higher calorie offering. The fact that our brand has grown to more than $100 million in retail sales suggests that Honest Tea has tapped into a market opportunity that the big beverage players missed. A contrived situation, such as a focus group, where people taste one small sample of a drink against another, doesn't address how a thirsty consumer thinks when he or she is at a beverage cooler, and is seeking an entire bottle of refreshment.

Asking people which product tastes better may also be the wrong question. What people like when they take just a sip is different than what they like when they drink a whole bottle. And taste isn't the only dimension that matters. We think customers might be willing to trade off a tiny amount of taste in order to have a greatly reduced number of calories. The goal is to maximize the customer's utility level, which include dimensions other than taste as represented in Figure 3.13.

That's not to say we don't value the opinions and reactions of our consumers. It's just that our method for gathering that information is more informal. Our company talks to our consumers hundreds of times a day when we perform product tastings in stores and at outdoor events. We correspond with them daily through dozens of letters, and phone calls that we receive at our office and through our email address SethandBarry@Honesttea.com. Their daily feedback has helped guide our decision making on dozens of product and packaging changes.

As distribution for Honest Tea expands across the country, I can foresee a day when more formal market research gives us an understanding of the buying patterns of our consumers and helps us develop better marketing and promotional strategies. But I also hope that as an organization, we never get so far removed from our consumers that we can't anticipate how they will respond to what we do. Our business was founded on an instinctual sense that people would welcome a less-sweet alternative, not to mention one that seeks to embody our concerns about the health of the planet and our consumers. We know that our authentic approach resonates with our consumers, and we don't need market research to tell us that.

It doesn't take an econ Ph.D. to brew tea — but Barry has one and sometimes it actually helps. Here's how: sugar, like most goods, has a declining marginal utility. One teaspoon takes away the tea's bitterness. Another adds a nice sweetness. That's where we stop. More sugar adds calories but not much more taste. By the time you've got six teaspoons per serving, it's liquid candy.

Honestly yours,

P.S. The antioxidants in Green Dragon Tea can play an important role in a healthy diet. To find out more, visit the American Institute for Cancer Research at www.aicr.org.

■ FIGURE 3.13

4

Individual Depth Interviews, Focus Groups, and Perceptual Mapping

Image © Franz Pfluegl, 2011. Used under license from Shutterstock, Inc.

Learning Objectives:

- Understand what Individual Depth Interviews (IDIs) are and how they are used
- Learn the key components of Individual Depth Interviews
- Learn the pros and cons of IDIs and of focus groups
- See how focus groups are used in marketing research
- Learn the key steps in running a focus group
- Learn about projective techniques
- See how perceptual mapping is used to augment other research methods

Much marketing research begins with qualitative methods. Generally these qualitative methods help to focus the research objectives in preparation for the quantitative (often a full-scale survey) part of the research. Remember that qualitative methods involve smaller samples which are not intended to tell the researcher what the population at large thinks. Qualitative methods provide the researcher insight as to what the whole population "might" be thinking. This "might" theory can be tested on a large-scale statistically representative sample in the form of a survey designed to represent the population. Think of political polls. When a news organization talks to a handful of voters on the street and over 80 percent of them say they will support the mayor in his reelection quest, this 80 percent cannot be taken mean to that 80 percent of the population will vote to re-elect the entrenched mayor. The percent margin of victory prediction heralded when watching election news coverage refers to a sample of voters who statistically represent that population of voters. Interviews and focus groups are not randomly selected nor are their sample sizes large enough to extrapolate population means. In other words, would you trust a dozen people in a focus group to be an accurate representation of a large population? The focus group might well provide invaluable insight as to what people in general might think, but it is not precise enough to make broad conclusions about the population.

Marketing researchers use **individual depth interviews, focus groups**, and/or **perceptual maps** to gain insight on the population of interest's attitudes, beliefs knowledge, etc. on a particular topic. These initial qualitative research steps are invaluable parts of marketing research as this research might well answer the research question, or at least serve as a key part of the entire research project. Individual depth interviews and focus groups can be conducted in person and/or online.

Individual Depth Interviews (IDI)

- *Are lengthy interviews, typically between 30 minutes and an hour, of knowledgeable participants designed to get detailed information, including facts and opinions, on the research topic. Interviewee's attitudes, perceptions, beliefs, emotions, and motivations are often a focal point of the interview.*
- *Provide respondent quotes that enable the research sponsor to hear the "voice" of those taking part in the research project.*
- *Allow for the use of projective techniques to delve more deeply into a respondent's initial response to a question.*
- *Allow for subject matter experts (SME) to be chosen as interviewees to provide a level of expertise sought by the researcher.*
- *Provide valuable data for the onward parts of the marketing research project.*
- *Require much training and expertise to execute successfully.*

Keys to Conducting IDIs

1. **Plan the interview carefully:**
   - It is inadvisable to "wing" an interview falsely believing that your skill alone will yield a successful interview. Remember that in some cases the interviewee will be smarter than you (the interviewer) and that the interviewee will most certainly be more knowledgeable about the research topic than is the interviewer. Smart interviewees will quickly assess the interviewer's preparedness. A failure to prepare for the topics that will be

Image © Stocklite, 2011. Used under license from Shutterstock, Inc.

■ FIGURE 4.1

In-Depth Interviews Provide Researchers with Detailed Qualitative Data that can be Expanded on During the Next Phase of the Research Project

covered and how the interviewer will proceed including clear, precise follow-up questions, will likely result in an unproductive interview. Develop a detailed interview discussion guide and be prepared to ask questions beyond the guide to more deeply understand the respondent's opinions and attitudes.

- Learn the research topic well and understand the interviewee's history, point of view, and knowledge of the research topic.

2. **Interviewer Skills Required:**
   - Good interviewers can be hard to find because of the specialized skills required. Anyone can ask questions, but can you ask the *right questions* with the best *follow-up questions*?
   - Good interviewers are great listeners.
   - The interviewer must do his homework on the research topic and on the interviewee. It's not sufficient to simply ask a set list of questions. The interviewer must be prepared to challenge and draw-out the interviewee by demonstrating knowledge and understanding of the research topic.
   - Interviewer neutrality will yield the best results. The interviewer should not be biased or overly aggressive nor be too easy with the interviewee. The balance is quite difficult. Top interviewers command large salaries due to well-honed interview skills not readily available to the average person.

3. **Dealing with Challenging Interviewees:**
   - In some cases the interviewee is hostile, unforthcoming, or incoherent. The interviewee might intentionally try to obfuscate the issue at hand through misdirection, falsehoods, or by withholding key information. Conversely, the interviewee might simply be a "bad interview" by an unintentional inability to answer questions clearly and thus leaving the interviewer floundering for a coherent response. Resolution of these issues speaks to point 2 above—the interviewer's skill in handling difficult and often unpredictable situations.

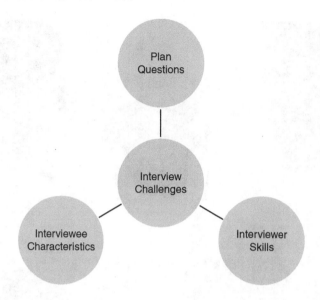

- The interviewee motivations must be thoroughly researched and understood before proceeding with an interview.
- Figure 4.2 identifies three key challenges in conducting interviews.

Oftentimes conducting an IDI will result in an expanding understanding of the research topic. This by-product can be leveraged to the next phase of the research: the focus group. Effective focus groups result from extensive planning and expert execution. Having done IDIs will enable the researcher to add depth to the focus group session. There are many advantages and disadvantages to conducting IDIs.

- **Advantages:**
  - Direct access to experts;
  - It can be conducted anywhere;
    - *Some effectiveness can be lost by not conducting the interview in person.*
  - The length of time of the interview can yield more insight than a survey, focus group, or abbreviated interview;
  - The lack of a group dynamic means that the interviewee can't use a large group to diffuse his answers. Also, the lack of a group prevents **"group-think,"** whereby the interviewee molds his responses to the ostensible group consensus;
  - Probing follow-up questions can result in a depth of understanding not fully attainable through other research methods.
- **Disadvantages:**
  - Cost—is dependent on set up costs and the fee for the interviewer;
  - Time—it can take a significant amount of time to recruit the interviewee and schedule/conduct the interview;
  - Access to high-level, professional, etc. people is often limited;
  - The results should not be presumed to statistically represent the general population;
  - A lack of a group setting can prevent other issues, spawned from a group dynamic, from surfacing given that only one interviewer and one interviewee are present.

Figure 4.3 details the major steps in conducting an Individual Depth Interview.

Select Interviewer:
• Some key skills include: insightful, deft, smart, prepared, good listener, and engaging.

Research the Topic:
• Interviewer should be knowledgeable about the research objectives and on the key issues related to the research topic.

Develop Question List:
• Key points to raise and follow-up questions should be readily available.

Screening Process:
• Verify the right people are going to be interviewed and that any interviewee substitutions are acceptable.

Execute:
• Interview the subject according to the research plan but deviate from the plan as needed based on interviewee responses and interviewer skill.

Analysis:
• Provide a written report on descriptive and analytic findings.

■ **FIGURE 4.3**
Steps to Conducting an IDI

Focus Groups

- *A moderator-led, structured brainstorming discussion among 8 to 12 participants designed to add insight, such as motivations, perceptions, beliefs, emotions, and attitudes, on a research topic that might be further explored through a questionnaire.*
- *www.focusgroups.com—a source to find focus group facilities and moderators.*
- *www.focusgrouptips.com—a helpful site to start your focus group research process.*

An invaluable primary research qualitative tool, often used to build on IDIs, secondary research, and as a precursor to a questionnaire, is a **focus group**. Focus groups help researchers in many ways. Remember that focus groups often precede a survey and the data gathering in the focus group usually helps the researcher better understand the critical issues that should be raised on a questionnaire. The researcher might also test various questions or concepts with focus groups as a measure of what might or might not work on a questionnaire. Consider a sensitive question such as religion. What is the best way to ask questions related to religion on a questionnaire? Before the researcher launches a large-scale questionnaire, she might benefit from the insights of focus group participants as to the best way to approach difficult, complex, or sensitive topics. In addition to testing questions or concepts, focus groups can be used to aid in message development or advertisements. Figure 4.5 provides an overview of the steps to conducting a focus group.

■ **FIGURE 4.4**

Focus Groups are an
Effective Research Tool
to Reveal Attitudes,
Perceptions, and Beliefs
About an Issue

Image © Yuri Arcurs, 2011. Used under license from Shutterstock, Inc.

- **Select Participants:**
  - Focus group participants should not be randomly selected—random selection is appropriate for the quantitative (questionnaire) phase of the research. The researcher should recruit focus group participants who are *knowledgeable* about the topic at hand, meet predetermined screening criteria, and can communicate well in a group setting. Remember the purpose of a focus group is to get brainstorming related information that might then be further explored during the questionnaire research phase. This round-robin discussion is qualitative. The researcher is trying to learn as much as he can from the participants in order to further the research.
- **Select a Moderator:**
  - The moderator must be a clear communicator and an effective discussion referee. The moderator should be able to draw-out quiet participants while simultaneously reining-in more domineering focus group participants. It is important for the moderator to ensure the group is a group, not a few participants dominating the discussion. Although the moderator will learn much from the participants, she should be knowledgeable about and informed on the research topics to avoid appearing unprepared. An unprepared moderator will not build trust with the group and will likely fail to get participants to be fully engaged and forthright.
- **Create a Moderator Guide:**
  - A **moderator guide,** the discussion roadmap, is critical to running a successful focus group. The moderator should not begin a two-hour focus group session without a clear sense of what will be covered. The moderator guide is typically a couple of pages outlining the key issues, themes, and questions the moderator wants to cover. If projective techniques are to be used they should be detailed in the moderator guide. Other aspects of a moderator guide are below:
    - The guide should contain timed thematic sections with up to a dozen sub-questions that are used to spur the discussion. For example, suppose a restaurant owner wants to know what patrons think of the restaurant.

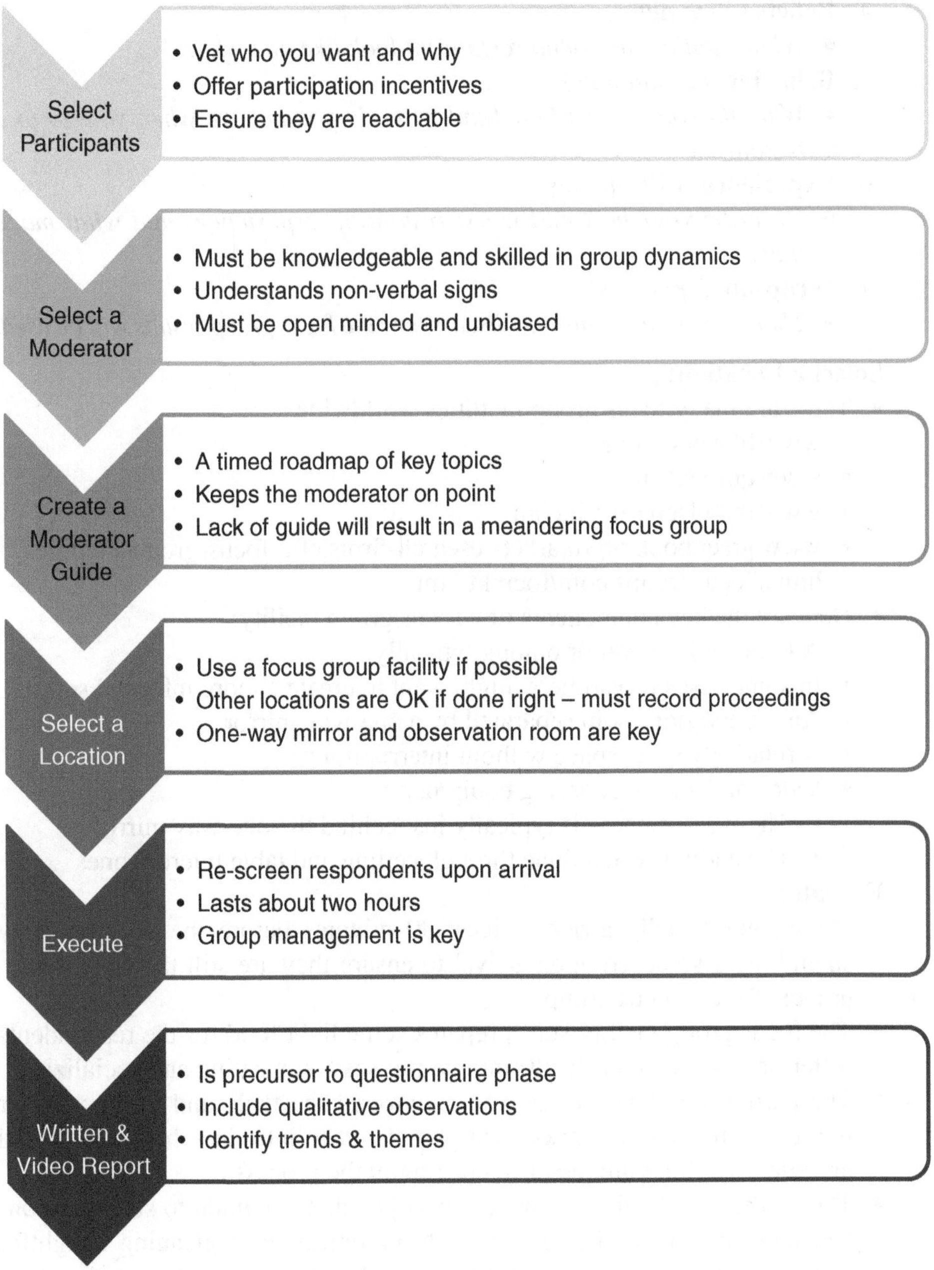

Select Participants	• Vet who you want and why • Offer participation incentives • Ensure they are reachable
Select a Moderator	• Must be knowledgeable and skilled in group dynamics • Understands non-verbal signs • Must be open minded and unbiased
Create a Moderator Guide	• A timed roadmap of key topics • Keeps the moderator on point • Lack of guide will result in a meandering focus group
Select a Location	• Use a focus group facility if possible • Other locations are OK if done right – must record proceedings • One-way mirror and observation room are key
Execute	• Re-screen respondents upon arrival • Lasts about two hours • Group management is key
Written & Video Report	• Is precursor to questionnaire phase • Include qualitative observations • Identify trends & themes

■ FIGURE 4.5

Six Steps to Conducting a Focus Group

Before the launch a full-scale survey the restaurateur might want to run a focus group or two in order to determine which key issues should be addressed on the large-scale, quantitative, and statistically representative survey.

Moderator Guide Sample Structure

1. **Introductions** *(5 minutes)*
   - *Discuss the focus group purpose, introduce yourself, and have the others do so.*
2. **Attitudes** *(15 minutes)*
   - *Describe your reaction(s) when you entered the restaurant.*
3. **Perceptions** *(20 minutes)*
   - *What do you think a restaurant in that part of town is like and why?*

4. **Beliefs** *(20 minutes)*
   * *What should a high-end restaurant look like and why?*
5. **Behaviors** *(15 minutes)*
   * *What do you do and how (and why) do you behave when you go to a restaurant?*
6. **Experiences** *(30 minutes)*
   * *Describe your best and worst restaurant experiences and what made them so.*
7. **Wrap-up** *(5 minutes)*
   * *Thank the participants and discuss how the focus group results will be used.*

* **Select a Location:**
  * There are many focus group facilities worldwide.
    * www.bluebook.org
    * www.quirks.com
    * www.impulseresearch.com
    * www.greenbook.org/market-research-firms.cfm/focus-group-facilities
    * http://focusgroups.com/focmkt.htm
  * Here are the key components of a focus group facility:
    * A large table—oval or oblong typically
    * In some cases researchers might want to create a more informal setting
    * An observation room separated by a one-way mirror
    * A relatively quiet space without interruptions
    * Video and audio recording equipment:
      * The video camera is typically just behind the one-way mirror
      * The audio is often done through ceiling and table microphones

* **Execute:**
  * Participants usually arrive at least 30 minutes before the session. They should be re-screened upon arrival to ensure they are still the right demographic for the focus group.
  * The focus group facility staff prepares some light food for the respondents (often sandwiches) for the 30-minute pre-session meeting and socializing.
  * The participants take random places around the table and the moderator introduces himself and asks each participant to introduce him/herself and provide something unique or interesting in the process.
  * The moderator should use the guide as just that—a guide to steer the conversation in a focused direction with the objective of gleaning insightful and substantive information that will be refined and quantified in the questionnaire phase of the research. The moderator should probe beyond the moderator guide questions and follow the discussion as the group dynamic dictates.
  * Group dynamic issues to avoid:
    * **Groupthink:**
      * *Allowing a few participants to dominate the discussion, leading the remaining participants to a collective opinion not otherwise in evidence.*
    * **Disruptions:**
      * *Participants who are too loud, aggressive, argumentative (with the moderator or other focus group members), or domineering should be reined-in by the moderator.*
      * *Participants who have some disruptive condition—fidgety, coughing, sneezing, etc. should be asked nicely to step out of the meeting and return composed.*

- **Failure to Participate:**
  - *In some cases participants will be shy or otherwise disengaged from the discussion. Sometimes participants feel they should listen to others' opinions rather than be heard. The moderator should avoid defaulting to the most talkative participants. If the moderator finds a few of the participants to be particularly helpful, she should make a note to contact those participants later for an in-depth interview.*
- **Projective Techniques:**
  - **Projective Techniques** are methods moderators use to spur group discussion. Sometimes participants find if difficult, particularly in the beginning of the focus group session, to be vocal and engaged. Projective techniques draw them out.
  - Projective techniques are used in many settings—not just focus groups—but they are a useful tool in spurring focus group participation.
  - Projective methods are depicted in Figure 4.6:
- **Word Association:**
  - The moderator quickly moves from participant to participant asking word association, reaction, based questions. For example, what word or phrase comes to mind when you hear:
    - *Summer, Winston Churchill, or yogurt?*
  - The focus group participants should quickly provide a gut response—not overly thought out—as this technique is used to get initial and unfiltered reactions. It is important that the moderator first sets expectations by telling the participants that he is looking for quick impressions, not facts. For example, if the moderator says "Winston Churchill", the participants should not say that he was a former British prime minister since we know that. Facts are not useful as they are known. Participants should provide more emotional answers such as leader, decisive, witty, etc.
  - The moderator should take notice of participant body language and expand on issues that one participant says if it resonated with the whole group. For example, the moderator might say, "I noticed that Sarah's remarks caused a reaction—tell me what you were thinking when Sarah said that the amusement park was not fun."

■ FIGURE 4.6
Projective Technique Methods

- **Sentence Completion:**
  - Similar to word association, sentence completion is geared towards understanding underlying issues. However with sentence completion, the lead-in question is more complex than for the word association technique. The moderator might say, "The president's policy towards social security is _____."
  - These questions are often more thought provoking as they are centered on a construct as opposed to a one-dimensional issue.
- **Third Party & Storytelling:**
  - A useful technique for more experienced moderators and participants. This technique involves delving into sensitive or controversial issues using a third person as cover. The moderator might explain a scenario and ask the participants about what Mr. Jones *should* have done in a given situation. What the moderator is really determining is what the focus group participants would have done in that situation but who might feel uncomfortable admitting to engaging in a particular behavior.
- **Photo/Card Sorts:**
  - Photo sorts are effectively used for advertising campaign–related focus groups. Participants can be given a list of photos (or an ad or website) and asked to sort them in a particular order. For example, they might put the photos in order from most to least appealing, best value, most upscale, most understandable, best use of color, most effective in conveying the core message, and so forth.
  - Photo sorts can also jog the memory or spur the thought process for participants who might then add more substance to the discussion.
- **Role-Playing:**
  - Also best used with experienced participants, and typically towards the latter part of a focus group session as participants will be more comfortable acting-out if they have had some time to get acquainted with the other focus group members and with the issue at hand.
- **Things to observe during a focus group:**
  - Moderators look for many things during a focus group session. Although what was actually said is the key driver, be mindful of other important aspects of monitoring a focus group. For example:
    - Verbalizations—what they are saying and what they actually mean
    - Use of language, vocabulary, and jargon
    - Level of discussion/understanding
    - Body language
    - Omissions—what people are not saying
    - New concepts
    - Values and principles
    - Fundamental beliefs
    - Relationships—interpersonal, conceptual, logical, emotional, and cause and effect
    - Emotional reactions
    - Changes in emotional tone
    - Prejudices and attitudes
    - Roles and responsiblities and what people do with them
    - Degree of consensus or dissension
    - Different points of view
    - Opinion shifts
    - Persuasion flow

- **Written Report:**
  - The focus group written report (which accompanies the video recording) includes both a descriptive (what was said) and analytic (what was meant by what was said) analysis. The written report should include:
    - The focus group purpose
    - How participants were screened and recruited
    - Where the session was held and how long it lasted
    - Who moderated the session and what projective techniques were used
    - The demographic mix of the participants
    - A summary of responses—discuss key patterns that were observed
    - Analysis of what the results mean
    - How the results can be used for the next phase of the research
    - An account of any issues or problems that surfaced

Focus Group Mapping

- A **focus group map** can be created and used to chart interactions among focus groups participants. This map is a detailed process flow of who talked to whom and on what subjects. This information can be used to determine if behavior patterns are present. The moderator can also number the amount of interactions between participants on a given subject to see if patterns develop. The map, drawn after reviewing the recording, should not be overcomplicated. Its purpose is to broadly identify opinion patterns such as topics that were discussed more often and between which participants. A sample focus group map is depicted in Figure 4.7:

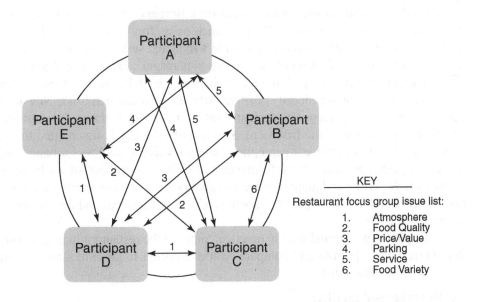

■ **FIGURE 4.7**

A Focus Group Map

Perceptual Mapping

Remember that one of the functions of marketing research is to understand what actually *is*, not what someone *thinks* is, the case. Marketing research can quantify the axiom that "perception is reality" through perceptual mapping.

Image © Lightspring, 2011. Used under license from Shutterstock, Inc.

- **Perceptual Mapping:**
  - *The process of producing a visual representation of perceptions about a product or service through questions of key constructs as anchor points.*
  - *Although perceptual mapping can have quantitative applications, it is important to address perceptual mapping during our review of qualitative methods as it is a very useful qualitative tool.*

Consider a fictitious local eatery—Buster's Burgers—and two potential key constructs, or issues, relevant to Buster's such as its food and service. The restaurant manager's thoughts on the restaurant's food and service might differ from those of her customers' perceptions. Buster's manager acknowledged some of the restaurant's shortcomings but said on balance she felt that her view of her customers' attitudes was generally positive. After all, business was brisk. Now let's compare customers' perceptions against what the manager *thinks* are her customers' perceptions. One of the first steps is to identify the key issues related to the topic at hand. For example, car perceptions might revolve around performance and quality, or price and value, or performance and safety. Perceptions of a television might include picture and glare or price and quality. This process works well when researchers develop *paired* qualities about products and services and then measure those paired issues.

Let's put the perceptual map in practice. Suppose the restaurant managers survey 100 restaurant patrons and compare customer ratings to those of management using the following rating:

- **Rate the food quality:**
  - 1=Poor, 2=Fair, 3=Average, 4=Good, 5=Excellent
- **Rate the service quality:**
  - 1=Poor, 2=Fair, 3=Average, 4=Good, 5=Excellent

The manager at Buster's assumed customers rated the food and the quality highly and predicated many perceptual map participants responded in the bottom-right

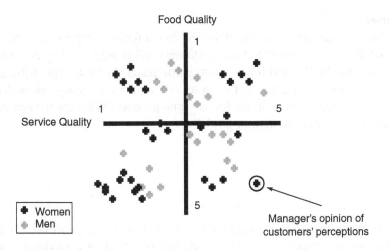

quadrant of Figure 4.9. However, the data reveal different customer perceptions. Figure 4.9 shows a perceptual map with demographic markers.

When using a perceptual map in a focus group or interview setting (a common qualitative application) researchers might not give the participants a scale. The researcher might simply provide a blank diagram and have the respondents mark the relevant area. The scaled approach, as depicted above, is more useful when collecting a large number of responses as it is not practical to have 100 people manually place dots on a diagram.

Perceptual mapping will bridge the gap between the manager's perceptions and the customers' reality. After the perceptual mapping is done, managers can add demographic markers to further quantify what is happening in the marketplace. Perceptual mapping can also be used more qualitatively in a focus group. Focus group members would be presented with individual blank focus group maps, or there might be one perceptual map posted at the front of the room and then the focus group participants would each mark the map. The results would then be useful for the groups' discussion.

Although there are many collection methods such as focus groups, individual depth interviews, and Internet methods (chats, blogs, bulletin boards, social media, online focus groups), focus groups and individual depth interviews still represent a significant amount of all qualitative data collection methods employed by marketing research firms. The tangibility of direct human interaction with respondents still remains a desirable method to collect information.

Research in Practice

Case:

• As a manager of a local hair salon, you are concerned that customers appear to be less satisfied than they have been. In fact you notice that there has been a decline in the number of clients over the past six months. Conducting a survey is too time consuming and expensive at this point. And without good qualitative information, you are not entirely sure what to ask on a questionnaire were you to conduct one.

Assignment:

- Create a research plan to use IDIs and then a focus group to indentify the key issues that are important to your customers. What are some key considerations in selecting the IDI and focus group participants? What are the different types of information you might get from an IDI vs. a focus group? How does conducting an IDI help you in the focus group process? What are the key elements of the focus group moderator guide?

Chapter Summary

Individual depth interviews (IDI), focus groups, and perceptual mapping are useful and common primary data collection tools. Individual depth interviews help researchers probe experts of the research topic for information useful to the next phases of the research project. Marketing researchers use secondary data as a foundational piece of IDIs. Several keys to conducting a successful IDI include adequate preparation, a detailed moderator/discussion guide, a knowledgeable interviewer, and a strategy for dealing with difficult interviewees. Some advantages to IDIs include: the ability to probe experts, the level of detail attainable, and the flexibility in that they can be conducted anywhere. Some disadvantages include time, cost, a lack of a group dynamic, and access to the right level people. Several steps typify the IDI process including: selecting the interviewee, researching the topic, developing the question list, screening the participants, executing the plan, and conducting the analysis. Focus groups, a directed, semi-structured brainstorming session of 8 to 12 participants, are used to gain insight on a topic or issue that can then be used during the primary data collection questionnaire process. A moderator should have a guide that keeps the moderator focused on the key issues that need to be discussed. There are six

major steps in the focus group process including: selecting participants, selecting a moderator, creating a moderator guide, selecting a location, executing the session, conducting the analysis, and reporting the results. Projective techniques such as word association, sentence completion, role-playing, third-person technique, and photo sorts are used in focus groups to stimulate the conversation and increase the insightfulness of the observations and findings. A focus group map enables researchers to see the patterns of who talks to whom and on what topics during the focus group. Marketing researchers might be able to determine useful information from these patterns that can be further explored in the questionnaire phase of a research project. Perceptual mapping is a technique that details customer's perceptions about a topic or issue that can be compared to what an organization's leadership *thinks* are its customers' perceptions. This technique takes two critical elements associated with a research topic and asks respondents to rate each element. These elements are then plotted to determine the perceptions that the combination of the two elements reveals. Qualitative research methods often form a foundational piece of a marketing research project from which quantitative data collection is built.

ISSUE IN THE SPOTLIGHT Moderating a Focus Group

Michael Mermelstein, President
G2 & Associates, LLC
www.g2associates.us

When leading a focus group discussion or conducting a one-on-one interview you never know what someone might say or do. For that matter, you don't know what your client may say or do. To be successful, a moderator needs to be an active listener, have flexibility and think quickly.

Leading focus groups means you are asking questions based on your discussion guide and asking appropriate, probing follow-up questions all within the time frame for each question that you've laid out in the discussion guide all the while making sure each person is involved in the discussion, moderators also deal with issues that arise during the session, sometimes dealing with client requests coming to you as a moderator while managing all of these components of a focus group at one time. This is all true whether the groups are being conducted in-person or online.

To be successful the moderator needs to make sure the right people are taking part in the research. Screen questions written by the moderator and agreed to by the client are used by the facility to recruit participants. It is always a good idea to re-screen (re-ask the screen questions) when participants arrive at the facility to make sure there are no surprises once the group has started. Otherwise, you can have people who know nothing about the topic or do not have the appropriate experience not only providing made-up information, but also impacting the flow and tenor of the discussion. You may have participants sitting next to each other in a focus group who turn out to be friends or otherwise know each other. Then, there are those participants who do not like a particular exercise that is part of the discussion guide and refuse to do it, usually refusing for the whole group by loudly saying we are not doing something this dumb. There are those who criticize or ridicule other participants and those who simply refuse to let others talk and dominate the discussion. All of these issues arise at one time or another and the moderator has to quickly manage them or risk losing the group and getting no useful information. And then there are clients sending notes to you during the group instructing the moderator to ask this or that—usually when something in the discussion guide is not going as anticipated.

All told, moderating is fun. Focus groups and in-depth interviews can provide great information that is very useful. Being prepared, flexible, and professional are important elements of success.

5

Observation Research

Image © Lori Skelton, 2011. Used under license from Shutterstock, Inc.

Learning Objectives:

- Understand types and uses of observation research
- Understand the conditions necessary for effective observation research
- Appreciate the impact of the Internet on observation research

- See how content analysis and forensic observation are used
- Understand key considerations when deciding whether to conduct observation research

- Learn about Mystery Shopping and how it is used in marketing research
- Learn some key advantages and disadvantages of observation research

Suppose you are perched on a bench in front of a department store patiently waiting for a friend. Your friend's tardiness habit becomes increasingly irritating. You have determined his being to be a "habit" as you have observed his actions enough times to establish a "pattern" of behavior from which you can predict that he will be late. However, his poor timekeeping skills provide you an opportunity to observe passersby, which you do with relish. As people walk past, you make judgments about people that might be positive, negative, correct, or incorrect. However, if you watch long enough, many emerging behavior patterns eventually become somewhat predictable, or at least measureable in some fashion.

Marketing researchers use observation research to see what people *actually do*, as opposed to what they *say they do*. Observation research can be both qualitative and quantitative and is a useful tool to augment other research methods by validating or refuting research findings, or by serving as the basis for the research objectives themselves.

Observation Research:

- *The primary research process of drawing conclusions based on observed behavior patterns of research subjects whether they are aware or unaware of the observation taking place.*

Ethnographic Research:

- *Observation research in a natural setting geared towards understanding human behavior and decision-making processes through the lens of social norms, traditions, and culture.*

Many observable behaviors have been documented. For example, marketing researchers have discovered that most Americans, when given equal opportunity of movement, turn to the right upon entering a store—perhaps a by-product of driving protocol. Although, observation research can provide a level of insight that can be quite useful, marketing researchers should seek to validate observation conclusions with additional research methods such as through focus groups, surveys, or experiments.

Several conditions, as shown in Figure 5.1, must be present in order for observation research to be successful.

Conditions Needed for Observation Research

- **Observable:**
  - The actions are observable—remember that opinions, attitudes, and perceptions are best measured through interviews, focus groups, and surveys.
- **Short Duration:**
  - The longer the observation occurs, the greater the chance that extraneous variables enter and thus the less control the researcher has over the situation.
- **Detectable Patterns:**
  - An inability to observe behavior patterns will prevent the researcher from drawing conclusions that are notionally transferable to the population of interest. Without these patterns, the researcher will only have a hodgepodge of data that will not yield solid actionable information.

■ **FIGURE 5.1**

Conditions Needed for Observation Research

For example: We make observations and draw conclusions from observations in many situations.

- *Don't you know when traffic will be the worst*
- *Or when the lines at Starbucks will be the shortest*
- *Or whether you feel that the audience liked the movie*
- *Or whether the fruit is fresh—the list is endless.*

We continually make observations and base our decisions on those observations. In many cases, our initial observations are incorrect due to inadequate observation opportunities, insufficient time, a misinterpretation of the observation data, or a positive/negative predisposition about the observation subjects. For example, many racial or ethnic stereotypes are based on suspect observation data influenced by the observer's predispositions, prejudices, or biases.

Observation research can be either qualitative or quantitative. Researchers can quantify the observation results by saying, for example, that 60 percent of the restaurant patrons ordered within 10 minutes. However, be careful when quantifying this type of data. Remember, one of the uses of quantifying data is to say that the results are statistically projectable to the population. Often qualitative observations turned quantitative are not a statistically representative sample of the population. Good qualitative observation research can augment other research methods and can then be tested in a larger-scale quantitative observation study. Some quantitative methods of observation are mechanical observation such as traffic counts, lie detector tests, grocery store scanners, and airport metal detectors.

Types of Observation Research

Figure 5.3 provides an overview of the major observation methods.

Direct/Indirect

- **Direct observation** occurs when the researcher observes the behavior firsthand. For example, *watching* someone make a purchase. **Indirect observation** results when, for example, the researcher is outside the department store and observes a woman with two children emerge with the adult holding a shopping

■ **FIGURE 5.3**
Observation Methods

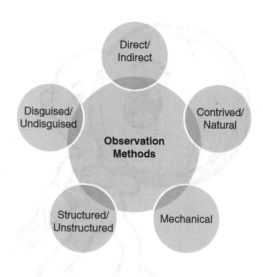

bag. The researcher might assume the adult made the purchase, although she does not have firsthand knowledge of having watched her make the purchase. The researcher might also assume that the two children are her children—although again she has no *direct* evidence supporting that indirect observation.

- You might have heard the term **circumstantial evidence**. Some defendants are convicted of crimes based solely, or mostly, on circumstantial evidence. Without witnesses, video, or forensic evidence, cases rely on gathering a critical mass of circumstantial evidence. Circumstantial evidence is similar to indirect observation in that the evidence gathered is not directly observed or positively linked to the crime but yet conclusions of guilt or innocence are deduced based on a "reasonable" interpretation of the data. Some defendants have even been found guilty of murder absent a body.

Contrived/Natural

- **Contrived observation** was the goal of *Candid Camera,* a show once hosted by TV icon emeritus Alan Funt who has been followed by other hosts of similar shows. There have been more modern iterations of that show. The show's premise it that poor unsuspecting souls are lured into situations created by the TV producers for the purpose of observing, for maximum TV entertainment value, how the subjects respond to contrived situations. The situations were harmless (except to egos) and generally quite silly but the observations yielded interesting data. How would someone respond if the ATM swallowed their card and returned a department store card instead? Marketing research uses contrived observations to test products immediately in ways that might take the marketplace some period of time to produce.
- **Natural observation** is simply when the researcher observes the subject in his or her "natural" setting. Such as watching people on the street, or in a store, or in traffic, or at a sporting match, or even in their home. The researcher, unknowingly to the subject, can glean valuable insight into how people behave based on observing them during their normal routine.

Mechanical

- **Mechanical observation** is when a machine records observation data in a quantitative manner. An advantage of mechanical observation is the lack of research biases. Non-mechanical observations can be compromised by the researcher's taking too much liberty in the analysis or by intentionally or unintentionally misinterpreting the results. Machines don't have biases, although machines can be poorly calibrated or can be faulty.

- There are many examples of machine observation methods: airplane "black boxes," cash registers that track sales, turnstiles at concerts, credit card transaction monitors medical monitoring equipment, truck stop weighing stations, grocery store scanners, tracking Internet click rates, and so on.

Structured/Unstructured

- **Structured observation** involves making observations while looking for specific aspects of the observation. For example, perhaps researchers are observing baseball fans and are specifically looking for their reaction when their star pitcher strikes-out an opponent.
- **Unstructured observation** occurs when the researcher observes actions without a list of specific behaviors they are looking for. In the baseball example, an unstructured observation study would be a researcher simply watching the game and then making a list of behavior patterns that might be the focus of future research. Often unstructured observation is more exploratory in nature whereby the researcher is there to see what he can learn from an overall vantage point.

Disguised/Undisguised

- **Disguised observation** occurs when the subject being observed is unaware of being observed or perhaps the true purpose of the observation is obfuscated. Suppose you are brought into a room to try a new bottled water brand. You are given three bottles and asked to taste each and determine which is the best tasting. Perhaps you are unaware you are being observed, or maybe you are unaware of the purpose of the research as its purpose is disguised. As it turns out, the three bottles all contain regular tap water. What the research is really measuring is whether package, product placement (the bottle order), ease of access (perhaps one has a more difficult cap, etc.), or the name of the water is the basis for the subjects' rating one better than the other. To be sure, many will likely say they cannot tell a difference among the bottled water choices (which makes sense as they are all the same). However, there will be some subjects, perhaps many, who pick one over the other. If the three water bottles are picked relatively equally among the subjects, the researcher might conclude the package, names, etc. have little impact on quality perceptions. However, it is quite notable if there is a pattern of subjects liking brand "X" when they are in fact all the same. The question that result would generate is why? If research subjects are told researchers are measuring the impact of package on quality perceptions, they would likely react differently to the research.
- **Undisguised observation** results when the research subject is aware that they are being observed. Perhaps store customers notice surveillance cameras or see a sign stating that they are recording activities in the store for security reasons.

Mystery Shopping

- **Mystery shopping** is when a researcher pretends to be a customer. This person might be a competitor looking for information on the competition or perhaps

Mystery Shopping
Enables Researchers to
Learn Consumer Behavior
in a Natural Setting

Image © Broudis Maria, 2011. Used under license from Shutterstock, Inc.

he is a company employee hired to see if employees follow certain protocols. Sometimes mystery shopping is broken into four levels. The levels are not truly critical; the important takeaway is to understand that there is a progression of involvement from one level to the next.

Level I:

- The mystery shopper might walk through the store, not interacting with employees or customers, to simply unobtrusively observe. He might be looking for competitor information or might be checking to see if the store is following company policies. Perhaps a phone call to the business would be all the research required to see how long it takes to have the phone answered, and whether the customer/employee exchange mirrors the company training. Again, the person's motive and purpose in doing the research will determine the objectives.

Level II:

- The mystery shopper might make a purchase or ask basic questions of the staff. At this level, there is minor interaction on a routine matter.

Level III:

- At this point the mystery shopper will interact with the staff, often with a complicated situation in mind, to see how well the staff handles the situation. Do they follow the rules, are they giving correct information, or can they handle pressure are often measured at this level.

Level IV:

- Here the mystery shopper will fully engage the staff in a situation that might require manager intervention. At this level, the researcher is looking to see how the staff handles crises, difficult customers, or unusual situations.

Determining the Best Observation Method

- How might the researcher determine the best observation method to use? Many factors must be weighed when selecting an observation method. Some key considerations are:
  - Time and budget available
  - The level of observation and analysis complexity—is it too hard to gather?
  - Level of accuracy desired related to the number of observable subjects
  - Determining the level of detail desired—will general observations be sufficient?
  - The usefulness of the observation in dovetailing with the other research methods used
  - The availability of enough observable subjects or opportunities

Content Analysis and Forensic Observation

Other types of observation research are notable and quite useful. Suppose you work for the CEO of a local furniture manufacturing company and sales have been declining. The CEO commissions a customer satisfaction survey to uncover the potential sources of the sales decline. The survey research reveals that customer perceptions of the company have declined, particularly in the area of product quality. The CEO does not understand this perception change because the furniture manufacturing process has not materially changed. Over the past year, the company has been in the print news quite often given its prominence in the community. Let's have another look at **content analysis**, but this time with observation in mind.

- **Content Analysis:**
  - *Identifying broad information patterns by combining individual data elements. Audits, a form of secondary data, are a content analysis approach.*

    After reviewing the data, the researcher determines that the furniture company has appeared in the local newspaper fifty times over the past year. Taken individually, these articles do not yield much information. However, when considering all fifty articles and their respective content together, we notice, for example that 30 articles are generally negative, 10 are generally positive, and 10 are neutral informational

Image © Andresr, 2011. Used under license from Shutterstock, Inc.

■ FIGURE 5.5

Content Analysis Involves Gleaning Observational Data from Patterns in Writings

articles. In other words, content analysis reveals that the critical mass and overtime impact of a majority of negative articles has gradually caused the reading public to view the company more negatively despite the fact that the furniture product has not changed. Content analysis helps the researcher to understand what the "content" of the articles reveals in their totality.

We have all seen various crime drama shows and movies, or real-life police cases in the news, or have read an Agatha Christie mystery novel. These cases are often solved through some form of **forensic observation** research that is accepted as evidence.

- **Forensic Evidence:**
  - *Tangible, sometimes physical, scientific evidence often positively linkable to the subject of interest.*

Forensic evidence is an invaluable tool in solving many types of mysteries. For example, in trying to determine if someone committed a crime, investigators might have fingerprint evidence, or credit card transactions traceable to the user through ATM videos, or information gleaned from someone's garbage. The clues that are left behind are the keys to forensic evidence.

- **Case studies** are a form of content analysis in that they involve gleaning information from the totality of written qualitative data. Cases tell the story of a particular issue, problem, or topic. Marketing researchers attempt to observe patterns within a given case—or across various cases—to make general conclusions about the issue, problem, or topic being researched. Case study research involves an in-depth analysis of an issue using a case, or an example, as a guide. Under this method, the researcher would study many facets of an issue using a case as a backdrop. An ostensibly similar or at least highly relatable case to your research topic should be used to ensure relative applicability parity. Case studies analysis can be used as part of a content analysis effort. Oftentimes case analyses are exploratory and provide the basis for more in-depth descriptive analysis. Careful vetting of cases can yield quality data as cases from professional journals have been peer reviewed and are assumed to be of quality. Marketing researchers must analyze the source before using case studies. Cases found on the Internet should be examined carefully to ensure they are reputable and worth analyzing.

The Internet and Growing Forms of Observation

The explosion of the Internet has yielded new forms of observation research methods. Internet research observation is a critical tool in determining the effectiveness of Web pages which leads to increased advertising revenue and more use of a respective website. Many companies are moving toward conducting business on the Internet to save money and facilitate quick ordering. This growth has led to changing variations of information collection, sharing, and analyzing. Marketing researchers are increasingly using Internet research techniques to study markets, buyer behavior, and general business trends to gain an advantage in the fast-paced marketplace.

- **Netnography:**
  - Netnography is essentially the Internet version of ethnography whereby observations of online patterns are mapped. Click rates, length of time to find a search item, time spent on various websites, which sites are visited, and the like, are all methods of creating an Internet usage profile based on online observations.

- The continued growth of social networking and other online activities has become a source of tremendous information for marketing researchers. Many people probably don't fully realize the Internet "fingerprint" that they leave when chatting, tweeting, texting, shopping, e-mailing, or "Facebooking."
- The Internet equivalent of ethnography—netnography is the analysis of online behaviors though observation.
- Check out: www.netnography.com

Some key types of netnography research are shown in Figure 5.6:

- Media ratings, such as Nielsen ratings, are common methods of observation research.
- **Eye tracking** continues to grown in sophistication. Researchers have developed programs that make it easy to track eye movement on Web pages to test which parts of the Web page are most appealing—or at least get the most attention. Researchers can then focus-group the results to determine why people lingered on particular parts of a Web page or fail to notice other parts. The key behavioral drivers might be color, movement, graphics, or text/headlines. This information is valuable to businesses that are trying to get and capture the customers' attention. This information can also be used to create TV, radio, and static advertisements such as magazines, newspapers, or billboard displays. Once the business knows what gets the customers' attention, it can duplicate that strategy in other marketing efforts.
- Visit: http://www.smivision.com—Eye-tracking companies use technology to track where people look and what part of the website attracts the most attention. This research is useful in assessing the most effective advisement placement on Web pages, in addition to the best layout for the website itself.
- **Brain wave tracking** analysis sounds more *Star Trek* than marketing research. However new technologies seek to map brain wave patterns to track the brain's reaction to various stimuli. This information can help marketers understand what messages resonate, positively or negatively, with respondents.
- **Click rate** analysis is useful when determining how long it takes customers to get to a given part of a Web page. Take the Web page of your university. If you were told to find a given course, how long and how many clicks might it take? With hundreds of university Web pages, you might think that someone would have developed the optimal path, yet universities have different Web page layouts, even though they might be in the same academic system. Which layout is best? It depends on the goal. In some cases, the amount of information is the key driver and in other cases perhaps navigation ease is the goal. Many universities will likely state that both objectives are their Web

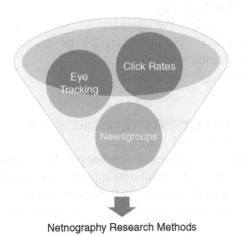

Netnography Research Methods

■ **FIGURE 5.6**
Netnography Research
Methods

page planning goals. Click rates help Web page designers determine how long it takes to get to the most pertinent information. This information is most useful among competitive businesses. Suppose it takes 10 minutes to find airfare on one airline's page and two minutes on another, customers will likely learn that starting a travel search should begin with the latter's page.

- Visit: www.google.com/doubleclick—DoubleClick by Google is an advertisement management and tracking system that is widely used to determine the advertising value of space on various websites based on the research of how much the respective site is visited. This tool aids marketing researchers in gauging Web page effectiveness.
- **Newsgroups** are evolving information sources in that they have grown in many directions. Subscribers are members of these groups to remain informed on a particular issue(s). **Listservs** and **Blogs** provide researchers with insight into people's behaviors, likes, and opinions. This site might be useful: www.newsgroupreviews.com
- Social media outlets such as **Twitter** and **Facebook** have been used to drive **word-of-mouth** marketing. Take a look at: http://womma.org/main and www.snama.org/SNAMA/SNAMA/Home
- Other methods include blog analysis whereby researchers conduct content and trend analysis.
- NBC News reported the extent to which Facebook gleans detailed information on how and when subscribers use their sites. Details such as how often you use the site, whether you use pictures, your profile details, the extent of your friend network, and usage changes (more or less) are all data Facebook collects and processes to better understand its users' behavior.
- Finally "Goggle Analytics" is a good source for social research.

Observation Research Advantages and Disadvantages

It is important to recognize the uses and limitations of observation research. When done well, observation research can add value, depth, and insight to other qualitative and quantitative research methods. Observation research should not be relied on as the sole research tool supporting decision making.

Advantages

- Enables the researcher to see research subjects in their natural setting;
- Offers the opportunity to create scenarios to test behavioral theories;
- Is useful in product testing or taste tests;
- Can often be gathered quickly;
- Acts as a building block to the research;
- Can be interactive producing more tangible results;
- Is interesting and engaging to execute;
- Allows for measuring actual behavior.

Disadvantages

- Should not be used as a statistical representation of the general population;
- Can be time consuming and costly;
- The researcher might misinterpret or misapply the results;
- Observation focus might be uninteresting, yet the researcher needs the data;
- It is not always clear that extraneous factors are not in play.
- It is very difficult to clearly assess motives, attitudes, or beliefs.

Research in Practice

Case:

- As the manager at a local Home Depot, you have noticed a decline in your customer base. After having conducted a few focus groups you learned that customers found the newly redesigned store to be confusing to both them and some of the staff. You also discovered that customers tend not to spend as much time browsing as they did before the store redesign.

Assignment:

- How might you use several observation methods to determine customer behavior? Create an outline of the techniques you will use along with the rationale for that technique and the presumed information you will learn from that technique. What questions might the observation research raise that should be examined through a customer survey?

Chapter Summary

Observation research is the primary research process of drawing conclusions based on observed behavior patterns of research subjects whether they are aware or unaware of the observation taking place. Ethnographic research is observation research in a natural setting geared towards understanding human behavior and decision processes through the lens of social norms, traditions, and culture. Effective observation research requires that three elements are present: that the event can be observed, that the observed event is relatively short in duration, and that behavioral patterns can be established. There are qualitative observation research methods such as direct/indirect (the observant is or is not being observed directly engaging in a certain behavior.), contrived observation (creating a scenario and observing reactions), natural observation (observing people in their natural setting without intervention), structured observation (the researcher is looking for specific behaviors), unstructured observation (the researcher is observing all aspects of behavior), mechanical observation (some quantitative observation methods include traffic counters, tests observing respondents' physiological changes, and grocery store scanners), and disguised/undisguised observation (the observant either knows or does not know that they are being observed.). Mystery shopping is a form of ethnographic research where researchers pose as customers of a given business and engage in various levels of interaction among the staff to observe their behaviors, actions, and reactions. Mystery shopping

is used by competitors, to see how the competition operates, or by a given organization's management to see if the staff is adhering to the organization's rules and policies. This latter category often dovetails with some staff training effort. There are several considerations to be weighed when deciding whether to conduct observation research such as time and budget (observation research can be time consuming and expensive), usefulness of the research (are the observation results actionable to management?), and the complexity of what the research is trying to accomplish (the research goals might be too complex for observation methods). Other forms of observation research include content analysis and forensic observation. Content analysis involves identifying broad information patterns by combining individual data elements by, for example, culling many newspaper articles in search of a pattern of information about an issue or topic. Forensic observation refers to tangible scientific evidence often positively linkable to the subject of interest. Forensic evidence is typified by the clues people leave behind, much like investigators who find evidence at a crime scene. The Internet has spawned many forms of observation research such as tracking click rates, Web page traffic, and eye-tracking devices to see what parts of Web pages get the most attention. Researchers can follow patterns of information from blogs, newsgroups, Twitter, and Facebook. Finally, there are a number of advantages and disadvantages to observation research. On the pro side, observation research is data collected directly from the people of interest, it can often be gathered quickly, is often a building block to other research, can be interesting and engaging to execute, enables researchers to interact with observants, and offers the opportunity for researchers to create scenarios.

A few disadvantages of observation research are cost and sometimes time, a lack of statistical representativeness of the general population, and an inability to fully account for extraneous variables that might have a deleterious effect on the observation experience.

ISSUE IN THE SPOTLIGHT   Marginals—A Must-Know in Marketing Research

Ed Sugar, PRC, Vice President
OLC Global
http://olcglobal.com

In my opinion, the key to being a successful marketing researcher is being able to read and comprehend a project's marginals. According to Decision Analyst's marketing research glossary, marginals are "a computer-generated frequency count of the number of people giving each answer to the questions in a questionnaire. They are also called an 80-Column Dump or a Flash Report." For each question on a survey, the marginal is how many people responded to a particular question. It becomes the parameter for responses on each question. The marginal is generally computer-generated and is used to monitor panel and/or respondent integrity.

Within these columns of numbers lie the stories behind the numbers and the truth. Unsure of a skip pattern; check the marginals. Need to know why are there so many don't know/no answers in question 12; check the

marginals. Does this data run include the over sample; check the marginals. Marginals are the road map for every quantitative study. Understand them and you will have a secure foundation for every research project.

For any research project that relies on digital data methodology, the marginals serve as the road map to the stories behind the numbers as well as double check on data quality. For the programmer, they are used as double-check to make sure the correct questions are asked based on the respondent's previous responses. For data processing they are used primarily to double-check the results in cross-tabulations. For the analyst it provides a pathway to verify any unsuspected trends or responses and allows for further "drill down" scrutiny.

When I started my career in the marketing research industry, I began as a tab writer for a full-service research company in Los Angeles. The people who mentored and instructed me during these early years always reinforced how important an understanding of the marginals were. "When in doubt, check the marginals" I was always reminded.

6 Research Error and Data Collection Methods

Image © Reji, 2011. Used under license from Shutterstock, Inc.

Learning Objectives:

- Understand the types of error in survey research
- Learn about the major data collection methods
- Learn how respondent rates can be increased

- Appreciate the importance of non-response error
- Learn about ways to handle non-response error
- Understand the key considerations when deciding on the data collection method

- Learn the major considerations when executing a survey
- Understand the elements of respondent access

Survey Research Error

Do you trust pre-election polls or do you believe they are either rigged or flawed? Reputable marketing research firms are unconcerned with who gets elected, they are more interested in staying in business by means of correctly predicting election races and thus becoming a trusted research source. If CNN trusts a research firm to do its polling and that firm intentionally skews the polling results towards its preferred candidate, that firm will not be in business long. But the question still lingers, do pollsters always get it right? The question is rhetorical really, pollsters do get the election results wrong sometimes. Let's examine the polling concept with a situation often faced in a university environment. Let's suppose the university is changing its parking policy to allow students access to better parking. Perhaps the faculty supports the policy by 65 percent plus or minus 3 percent. What that statistic means is that 65 percent of the sampled faculty supported the policy. When we project that figure to the population of all faculty, thus a census, between 62 percent and 68 percent of all faculty would support the policy assuming a 3 percent margin of error. That result, plus or minus a 3 percent error range, represents the statistical reality of going from a sample to a population. Remember that the real advantage to asking a sample is that we don't have to ask the entire population—which would be a census. The 3 percent error includes all error—random and systematic. Most surveys assume no systematic (execution or design) error. In professionally executed surveys, survey error usually refers to the non-correctable statistical error of going from a sample to a population (random sampling).

A very informative site that tracks political polling is Real Clear Politics (www.realclearpolitics.com). In addition to providing comprehensive political polling coverage, Real Clear Politics provides many links to articles on major news stories from the top news organizations. This site also reports on a variety of polls and tracks local and national races throughout the country every year. In the years and months before a national election we are inundated by polls and, in the days preceding the election, we are presented with the "very latest" poll and sometimes even, the "absolute very latest" as the hyperbole-prone media often advertise. Sometimes (particularly closer to the election) three-day tracking polls, whereby poll results are averaged or smoothed out over a three-day period, are conducted. These tracking polls produce a more stable assessment of where the voter trends lie as they account for one-day variations. Every year debates arise as to polling accuracy. Pollsters are often disparaged as purveyors of "junk science." However, done right, polling is quite accurate and is based on statistical modeling. Real Clear Politics provided a post-election analysis of the predictions versus the actual results of the 2008 U.S. presidential election. As shown in Figure 6.1, the pollsters were generally correct in their respective prediction. Of fifteen prominently quoted polls, all predicted Barak Obama would be elected president. In fact the average of the polls predicted Mr. Obama would win by 7.6 percent and the actual result was 7.3 percent. A remarkable level of accuracy was achieved given the relatively low sample sizes (*take note of the respective samples sizes*). Those who were polled were selected in a random manner through fairly precise and sophisticated sampling techniques. Public data collected by Real Clear Politics are shown in Figure 6.1 that highlight polling accuracy.

Although many elements of marketing research are scientific in nature, marketing research is not without various types of errors. Many errors can be avoided through a careful and thorough research design and through research execution controls. Determining where, when, why, and how the error occurred, and how to correct for the error, is a complicated undertaking. The researcher has to determine several things

Poll	Date	Sample	MoE	Obama (D)	McCain (R)	Spread
			Polling Data			
Final Results	--	--	--	52.9	45.6	Obama +7.3
RCP Average	10/29 - 11/03	--	--	52.1	44.5	Obama +7.6
Marist	11/03 - 11/03	804 LV	4.0	52	43	Obama +9
Battleground (Lake)*	11/02 - 11/03	800 LV	3.5	52	47	Obama +5
Battleground (Tarrance)*	11/02 - 11/03	800 LV	3.5	50	48	Obama +2
Rasmussen Reports	11/01 - 11/03	3000 LV	2.0	52	46	Obama +6
Reuters/C-SPAN/Zogby	11/01 - 11/03	1201 LV	2.9	54	43	Obama +11
IBD/TIPP	11/01 - 11/03	981 LV	3.2	52	44	Obama +8
FOX News	11/01 - 11/02	971 LV	3.0	50	43	Obama +7
NBC News/Wall St. Jrnl	11/01 - 11/02	1011 LV	3.1	51	43	Obama +8
Gallup	10/31 - 11/02	2472 LV	2.0	55	44	Obama +11
Diageo/Hotline	10/31 - 11/02	887 LV	3.3	50	45	Obama +5
CBS News	10/31 - 11/02	714 LV	--	51	42	Obama +9
ABC News/Wash Post	10/30 - 11/02	2470 LV	2.5	53	44	Obama +9
Ipsos/McClatchy	10/30 - 11/02	760 LV	3.6	53	46	Obama +7
CNN/Opinion Research	10/30 - 11/01	714 LV	3.5	53	46	Obama +7
Pew Research	10/29 - 11/01	2587 LV	2.0	52	46	Obama +6

See All General Election: McCain vs. Obama Polling Data

*Battleground's (Tarrance Projection) and (Lake Projection) are weighted at 50%, so that the survey only counts once in the RCP National Average.

■ **FIGURE 6.1**
Real Clear Politics
Polling Data

about the error before deciding how to correct for, or mitigate, the error. Figure 6.2 captures the key issues that should be addressed when assessing error and its impact.

- **Sampling vs. Non-Sampling *or Systematic Errors*:**
  - **Sampling Error (or random sampling error)** is simply a statistical reality and is the error associated with chance variations that typify samples. In other words, with a sample of 1,000 people that represent, perhaps 100M people, there are statistical variations that occur between the 1,000 sample to its representing 100M. Having 1,000 respondents represent 100M takes great precision. Think of all the people who were not asked. What of their options? Although a correctly selected 1,000 people can statistically represent the 100M, it's unlikely that they will do so without any error attributed to the math of the process—as opposed to human error such as research design and execution error.
  - **Non-Sampling or Systematic Error** occurs from some flaw in the research design or its subsequent execution. In this case the researcher or respondent caused the error.
    - **Auspices Bias:**
      - *Unintentional respondent bias. The respondent might be influenced in her response based on who is sponsoring the research. Perhaps a respondent gives a disproportionaly positive response to a survey because she is unintentionally swayed by the Red Cross who is conducting the survey.*
    - **Extremity and Central Tendency Bias:**
      - *Unintentional respondent bias. The respondent might be predisposed to respond to the extreme endpoints of a scale. For example, "rate the service from 1 (poor) to 10 (excellent)" whereby a respondent demonstrating an extremity bias responds to the top or bottom of the scale in order to provide a stronger opinion than he might normally have.*

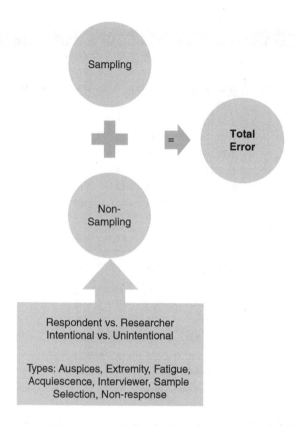

- *In some cases **central tendency bias,** a tendency to respond on the center of the scale, might be culturally driven. In highly collective cultures, respondents are often less likely to respond on the extremes of a large scale. Perhaps a smaller scale will help to reduce this type of bias.*
- **Fatigue:**
  - *Unintentional respondent bias. The respondent might be tired and not fully engaged in the survey process, which can result in incorrect answers.*
- **Acquiescence Bias:**
  - *Unintentional respondent bias. The respondent might provide answers she thinks the respondent wants to hear but the respondent is not intentionally trying to skew the results. The respondent might simply feel she is trying to be helpful.*
- **Interviewer Bias:**
  - *Perhaps the interviewer intentionally or unintentionally causes the respondent to respond in a certain way. Maybe the respondent was intimidated by the interviewer or perhaps the interviewer leads the respondent towards a particular answer by the way he phrases a question. Rigorous interviewer training is imperative to ensure this bias is avoided.*
- **Sample Selection Error:**
  - *This unintentional researcher error occurs when the researcher simply has the wrong sample—or partially wrong sample. Let's suppose we are surveying people who have been to France to gauge their travel experience. Suppose that 20 percent of the sample had never been to France. This 20 percent should not be in the sample. Marketing researchers must be vigilant to ensure they have the correct sample before initiating a survey. In this case the sampling frame—the subset of the target sample—is incorrect.*

- **Non-Response Errors (as it relates to not responding to the entire survey):**
  - *What is better—a 60 percent response rate or a 20 percent response rate? All things being equal, a 60 percent response rate is likely better. Although there might be no statistically significant difference in the responses of each, thus the higher response rate simply means more work to analyze the data. However assuming the sample is representative, more responses might be useful. Assuming the number of people who responded is statistically adequate, the real question is not the response rate but the **non-response** rate. In the example above, researchers might prefer a 20 percent response rate over the 60 percent response rate if:*
    - *In case A—the 80 percent who did not respond are statistically **no different** from the 20 percent who did respond and;*
    - *In case B—the 40 percent of those who did not respond **are statistically different from** the 60 percent who did respond. Suppose no women over 25 years old are among the 60% who responded (even though there are women over 25 in the target segment) then the 60 percent who did respond to the survey are not statistically representative of the entire population.*
  - Other error types include: Non-Response, cutoff (sometimes called "break-offs"), refusal, undeliverable respondents, and unreachable respondents;
    - *Non-response—(question specific) respondents might answer some of the questions but not all of the questions. Also, respondents might not respond to the entire survey for various reasons: refusal to participate or forgetting to participate (mail/e-mail/Internet).*
    - *Cutoff—respondents answer part of the survey but then quit part way through the survey. Possible causes: the survey is too long or the respondents get frustrated and no longer want to take the survey.*
    - *Refusal—this type of respondent is reached by the marketing researcher but refuses to participate in the survey process.*
    - *Undeliverable respondents—the location of these respondents is known but they are not, or do not, accept unsolicited correspondences. Perhaps the researcher was trying to reach a high-level corporate executive who will not accept the marketing researcher's correspondence.*
    - *Unreachable respondents—these respondents are people who are not reachable due to a bad address or unlisted phone number/e-mail/ postal address, etc.*
    - *Remember that the response rate is not that critical as long as the non-response error is low and that the actual number of respondents is an acceptable sample size.*
- **Intentional vs. Unintentional:**
  - Somewhat self-explanatory, **intentional error** is an error that the researcher or the respondent causes on purpose. If a respondent is asked about age or weight—the respondent might balk altogether or perhaps fudge the response. Respondents might intentionally provide incorrect responses to sensitive questions. Unscrupulous researchers might intentionally skew survey results in order to placate their client. **Unintentional error** occurs, for example, when a researcher incorrectly tabulates data, asks bad questions, or takes too long to finalize the analysis. Perhaps a respondent does not understand the survey questions, or becomes distracted during the questioning and provides incorrect answers, or is confused by the question scale. The respondent and researcher are not trying to skew the results; they simply are causing error unintentionally for a variety of reasons.

- **Respondent vs. Researcher:**
  - In determining where error occurs, we must understand who caused the error. It might have been caused by the respondent or by the marketing researcher whether intentionally or unintentionally.

It is important for researchers to understand the possible causes of error in conducting surveys to facilitate correcting for, or compensating for, those errors. In many cases multiple errors might occur. Some errors are easier to detect and correct, whereas many sources of error are difficult to determine. Suppose a survey shows that 80 percent of the respondents prefer the product color to be blue. As a result the product color is changed to blue and sales subsequently decline. How can researchers determine where the error and flaw in the research lies? Perhaps the interviewer was abrupt with some of the respondents who gave the interviewer answers they thought the interviewer wanted. Compound that error with some respondents' perception that although they don't like blue themselves, they assume that most people do in fact like blue; thus, they recommend blue for the benefit of others. All of these errors quietly combine to cause growing error. Revealing the source, or even the existence, of these errors is difficult.

In some cases political polling ahead of an election incorrectly predicts the winner, or related margin. Critics who dismiss political polling results as an unreliable measure are oversimplifying what happened. In fact the math is the math and statistically polling works. If surveys are wrong the culprit is likely the non-sampling error part of the equation as the sampling part of total error is accounted for in the plus or minus error estimation assuming the correct sample frame. In other words, somewhere the researcher or respondent created flaws, intentionally or unintentionally, in the research.

Handling Non-Response

Researchers can handle non-response biases in survey research in several ways. Remember that it is important to determine if the proportion of those who did respond is different from those who *did not*. The response rate itself is not the only important factor. Researchers must ensure that those who did not respond are not biasing the research. For example, suppose the population is 50 percent men and 50 percent women yet only 40 percent of the respondents are women. A key question to ask is whether the 10 percent of women who did not respond are statistically different from the 40 percent of women who did respond. So what can researchers do given the scenario below?

Scenario

- A population of 10,000 employees (half male/half female) are surveyed:
- 2,000 surveys are sent out and 1,000 are returned (50 percent response rate and an acceptable sample size)
- Of the 1,000 respondents, 600 were women and 400 were men.
- Problem: Actual male/female population ratio is 50/50 yet survey response ratio was 60/40.
- There are four reasonable solutions:
- Figure 6.3 offers four strategies for handling non-response issues.

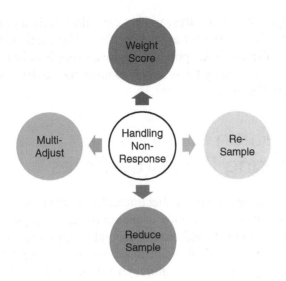

Weight Score

Because women are overrepresented in the sample, the researcher can weight the male responses more or weight the female scores less.

- Female scores are weighted 0.67 (thus 600 × 0.67 = ~400). Female scores are now in parity with the male scores.
- Male scores are weighted 1.5 (thus 400 × 1.5 = 600). Male scores are now in parity with female scores.
- Of course the change in the sample size will either increase error (smaller sample & lower cost) or increase cost (larger sample & lower error)

Re-Sample

Here researchers simply re-sample males to get 200 more men for the survey. This increase would put the total number of male respondents at 600, now in parity with the 600 female respondents. However this scenario means that the sample size is now 1,200, which reduces error (which is good) but increases collection costs and time from the project schedule (which is bad). This increase in collection cost and time would have to be approved by the research sponsor.

Reduce Sample

Because there are 200 more females than males, perhaps the researcher might simply and randomly remove 200 females from the survey leaving 400 females, now in parity with the 400 males. The impact of this approach is that it reverses the re-sample technique. In this case, because the combined sample size is now 800 (rather than the original target of 1,000) the error rate has been increased (which is bad) and the cost has been decreased (which is good). Either way, as in the re-sampling option, this approach would have to be approved by the research sponsor.

Multi-Adjust

Here the researcher can use a combination of the three approaches above. Perhaps the researcher will split the difference and re-sample 100 men and reduce the sample by 100 women; thus we now have 500 men and 500 women which is the original sample size target. Researchers can add a weight component as well if the results are still not 50/50. Researchers should be cautious before using too many approaches. Generally keeping the approach simple is best. In all cases, the approach must be approved by the research sponsor and be detailed in the *research methods* section of the research report.

Data Collection Methods and Increasing Response Rates

There are many ways researchers collect data. Remember that with focus groups or depth interviews the data collection is qualitative and in-person. These methods are somewhat labor intensive and require special attention to incentives. Without incentives, such as money, it's difficult to get people to take the time to be in a focus group or a depth interview—although usually there is no fee for a depth interview. Researchers often entice interviewees with pleas to their sensibilities to provide for the greater good of research. When researchers conduct surveys, the types of collection and incentive methods are quite varied, with each type bringing various advantages and disadvantages to the process. Researchers must consider the data collection methods, incentives/costs, and time issues when selecting a data collection method. The time impact is important given that some issues require quick data collection in order to ensure the results accurately capture the target audience's attitudes, beliefs, options, etc.

Suppose we are conducting a survey on religious beliefs. Conducting surveys over time might be acceptable since religious beliefs in general don't change that quickly. However, if the survey were about attitudes towards holiday shopping, taking several months to collect that data will likely produce dated results which will be of limited value to decision makers. Before a survey is launched, several major considerations, as shown in Figure 6.4, should be addressed.

Key Survey Considerations

Determining the data collection method is a key step in the survey process as it will have an effect on the time, cost, and response rate of the survey effort. In some cases researchers can combine data collection methods in order to maximize the number of survey participants. In this case, the researcher should ensure that surveys are identifiable by their collection method so that those surveys can be analyzed for

■ **FIGURE 6.4**

Key Survey
Considerations

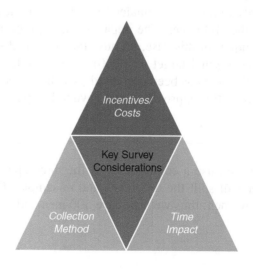

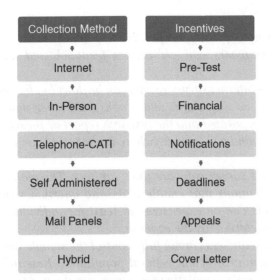

Collection Method	Incentives
Internet	Pre-Test
In-Person	Financial
Telephone-CATI	Notifications
Self Administered	Deadlines
Mail Panels	Appeals
Hybrid	Cover Letter

■ **FIGURE 6.5**
Data Collection Methods and Incentives

biases based on the collection method. Suppose we have 1,000 respondents to a survey on vacation destination preferences and that 600 were collected by telephone and 400 were collected through the Internet. Researchers will need to determine that there is not a statistically significant difference in how the 600 and the 400 responded to the survey. If there are statistically significant differences between the responses of each respective group, then the survey collection method ostensibly biased the results and thus the researcher really has two surveys—one of 600 and 400 respondents, respectively—instead of one survey of 1,000 respondents. There are several data collection methods and several incentives, as depicted in Figure 6.5 that can be used to increase response rates. Note that the incentives are applicable to all collection types and are not aligned specifically to one collection method.

Data Collection Methods

Internet

- Internet survey collection methods are primarily in the form of **online** or **e-mail surveys**. Online surveys are self-administered, whereby the respondent goes to a Web page and answers questions. E-mail surveys might prompt the respondent to go to a Web link or the questionnaire might be embedded in the e-mail.

■ **FIGURE 6.6**

Internet Data Collection has Grown Dramatically and has Reduced Collection Costs While Increasing Respondent Accessibility

Image © Iija Masik, 2011. Used under license from Shutterstock, Inc.

- **Advantages:**
  - **Cost**—*they are typically inexpensive to administer.*
  - **Speed**—*researchers can get instant feedback and tabulate the results continually.*
  - **Interfaces**—*Internet survey results can be downloaded quickly into statistical software and then charts and graphs (and other statistical outputs) can be easily incorporated into the research report or presentation.*
  - **Access**—*respondents from anywhere in the world can take the survey.*
- **Disadvantages:**
  - **Cost**—*not all survey software tools are free. The more sophisticated web survey applications that enable elaborate question sequencing and data analysis tools can be expensive—at least for individuals—but companies might be undeterred by the expense.*
  - **Sample**—*researchers cannot fully control the sample which can sometimes be unrepresentative of the general population. Researchers don't always know if the people completing the survey are the right sample.*
  - **Anonymity**—*depending on the issue, respondents might want anonymity. Researchers should be careful if promising anonymity when using online surveys as responses can often be traced to the computer IP address.*

- Some Internet survey sources:
  - www.vovici.com
  - www.surveymonkey.com
  - www.freeonlinesurveys.com
  - www.kwiksurveys.com
  - www.esurveyspro.com
  - www.zoomerang.com
  - www.keysurvey.com
  - www.cvent.com
  - www.surveygizmo.com
  - docs.google.com
  - www.qualtrics.com

In Person

In-person interviews, sometimes called "mall intercepts" in deference to its origins, are an effective way to collect information directly from respondents. This method involves stopping people in convenient, high-traffic locations, and asking them a set of questions. Some questions might be open-ended and others might be closed-ended questions such as a question asking someone to rate something on a scale of 1 to 10.

- **Advantages:**
  - **Sample**—*researchers can target who they want and can ensure they are speaking to the right person. If a researcher wants to survey someone who just shopped at the GAP—he can camp out in front of the store and approach the unsuspecting customer. Reaching certain market segments can be done through in-person interview.*
  - **Interactive**—*suppose a client wants to do a taste test or a hands-on product demonstration. This type of research cannot be done through a telephone or Internet survey. In-person interviews enable more flexibility and interaction with the respondent.*

- **Feedback**—*respondents have the opportunity to ask questions about the survey for clarification. In addition to ensuring the respondent understands the questions they are being asked, this give and take might yield additional and useful information about the research topic.*
- **Disadvantages:**
  - **Sample**—*although researchers can target who they want, the sample is not necessarily representative of the general population. Particularly important if projecting the sample to the general population is a goal of the researcher.*
  - **Cost**—*this collection method is labor intensive and involves hiring the right people with the skills and training to do the job. It's not sufficient to just hire a "body" to do the data collection. The interviewers must be trained in the art of interviewing and must have enough experience to answer respondent questions, in an unbiased manner, about the process and the questionnaire itself. Incentives to gain respondent participation also add cost to the project.*
  - **Time**—*it can take some time to get a large enough sample to be of use.*

Telephone—CATI

Computer Assisted Telephone Interviews (CATI) surveys are done through LAN lines or, more recently, to cell phones in some cases. Despite the growth of Internet data collection, telephone surveys are still widely used in some research circles and do offer certain advantages that other data collection methods do not.

- **Advantages:**
  - **Sample**—*researchers can determine they have the correct respondent through a series of respondent screening questions.*
  - **Speed**—*when the president gives the State of the Union address, major news organizations report the polling results, often within an hour or two, of how the public rated the speech. This research is done through telephone surveys. Obviously many callers are needed if researchers are to get several hundred (typically at least 500) respondents in an hour or two.*
- **Disadvantages:**
  - **Cost**—*costs vary widely depending on survey length, incidence (the percent of qualified respondents), complexity, and time needed to collect the data. If researchers need 1,000 respondents by tomorrow, that can be accomplished for a cost. Telephone surveys require people to speak to each respondent and thus can be expensive. Those making the calls, much like interviewers, must be trained on how to ask questions in an unbiased and effective way.*
  - **Complexity**—*for researchers needing to collect significant amounts of information, or long questionnaires involving big scales (1 to 10 for example), telephone surveys are not advised. Respondents answering questions on the phone do not have the time to spend on a lengthy survey. Typically a telephone call of more than 10 minutes will result in some respondents opting-out of the survey or cutting-off during the survey. This issue is exacerbated when conducting cell phone surveys. An additional hurdle to cell phone surveys is the issue of connectivity and some laws prohibiting cell phone surveys unless respondents opt-into that research.*
  - **Response Rates**—*telephone survey response rates are often low and thus require more incentives to raise participation. With caller ID and family screeners, it's difficult to reach respondents.*

- **Segmentation**—*segmentation is becoming more of a challenge since some target respondents might not have a LAN line phone. Getting respondents to opt-in cell phone surveys is more of a challenge than LAN line survey efforts. With LAN lines, at least the respondent is stationary.*
- **Focus**—*when people take telephone surveys, they are often doing other things—the so-called multi-tasking. This practice often results in respondents not fully engaged or focused on the questions. This lack of focus can result in respondents' not understanding the questions or failing to provide the best answers.*

Self-Administered

Self-administered surveys are taken by the respondent without the researcher being present. These surveys are often in the form of mail surveys sent through the postal service or an Internet survey. Sometimes these surveys involve respondents taking the survey at a set location on a computer, such as after a conference or event when the organizers want to gauge reactions immediately.

- **Advantages:**
  - **Length**—*respondents are taking the survey on their own time so the survey can be longer than it might be if it were a telephone survey.*
  - **Cost**—*this type of collection can be relatively inexpensive.*
  - **Market Segmentation**—*researchers can buy or rent mailing lists to target certain households.*
  - **Less Pressure**—*Respondents have the option of taking the survey over a period of time; thus, they are not required to complete the survey in one session. Respondents have time to compete the survey, assuming the issue being surveyed is not time sensitive.*
- **Disadvantages:**
  - **Response Rates**—*given that the respondent has the survey in hand and can take it, or not take it, at leisure, response rates are low. Respondents might simply forget to respond or lose the survey. In a telephone survey, the respondent is "captive" and must complete the survey on the spot. Mail surveys are not in the researcher's control and thus response rates are low.*
  - **Mailing List Quality**—*depending on the market, particularly in international research, the quality of the mailing list might be poor. Researchers might get a number of returned questionnaires or questionnaires that go to a home where the targeted respondent has moved.*

■ **FIGURE 6.7**

Questionnaires Provide a Quantitative Method for Collecting Data.

Image © Jirsak, 2011. Used under license from Shutterstock, Inc.

- **Lack of Control**—*even though the questionnaire might get to the right household, how do researchers know the correct person is completing the survey? If the survey is of men who like baseball, perhaps someone else in the house decides to complete the survey? Researchers can't easily confirm who actually completed the survey.*
- **One-Way Communication**—*A respondent who has a question about the survey, has no one to ask. Therefore, the questionnaire must be as clear and as straightforward as possible. Respondents who do not fully understand a question might answer it anyway and thus provide poor quality data.*
- **Time**—*if a researcher needs information about a fast-moving topic quickly, a mail survey is probably not the best option because it might take a few months to collect and validate the sample. Consider the possibility that after getting the 1,000 respondents, the Researcher has to redo the survey due to a lack of representativeness among the 1,000. Now it could take several more months to complete the survey project. If it takes three months to complete a survey, how do researchers know that the people who took the survey at the beginning of the three months have the same opinion by the time these slow respondents take the survey? Mail surveys fail to fully capture opinions as a snapshot in time.*

Mail or Online Panels

Panels are groups of people who agree to be in a long-term (longitudinal) survey or are shorter-term convenience samples on a variety of research topics. These respondents are surveyed periodically on various issues, but on the same issues, to gauge their opinions over time. Challenges related to mail or online panels include changes in the panelists that might affect the survey. Perhaps it's a mail or online panel of people who are married with three children and during the course of this several-year panel survey some people get divorced or are widowed. If

■ **FIGURE 6.8**

With a Quality List, Mail Surveys are an Effective way to Collect Survey Data

Image © TRINACRIA PHOTO, 2011. Used under license from Shutterstock, Inc.

these people do not recuse themselves from the survey, the researcher will continue to include them unless panelists are re-screened each time. Ensuring a good initial sample is a critical part of executing successful mail or online panels. If the initial sample is not representative of the target population, then the research result will be skewed from the start. This error will only be compounded with each iteration of the mail panel or online survey. These panels can be segmented by demographics, behavior patterns produced, service usage rates, etc.

- **Advantages:**
  - **Cost**—*the cost can be relatively low if the mail panel is not too specialized and that there is a large enough sample so that not everyone has to respond to everything. And if respondents are not contacted that often, perhaps yearly, the costs might not be to high. A special group of mail panel members, such as ophthalmologists, might require participation incentives.*
  - **Measuring Trends**—*because researchers are gathering information over time, they are able to determine who changes opinions, and then perhaps why their opinions changed, or did not change, as the case might be. This information is valuable in that it enables marketing researchers to detail more precisely what is happening in the marketplace. Market trend analysis is possible when this type of longitudinal research is done.*
  - **Expertise**—*a good mail panel will include opinion leaders. This access to expert, or at least well-informed respondents, will result in better quality data. Engaging thought leaders will add credibility to the research and might well result in the researcher's taking the research in different directions.*
- **Disadvantages:**
  - **Cost**—*keeping the same group of respondents in the panel over time is by definition time consuming for the respondents. Time is money so researchers will have to pay to keep folks in a mail panel as these respondents might have to commit to be in the panel for several years. Pharmaceutical panels might involve a twenty-year commitment in order for these companies to detail the long-term effects of various medical treatments.*
  - **Sample Integrity**—*maintaining a good sample becomes increasing difficult the longer the panel is engaged. Researchers should validate the sample with each iteration of the survey to ensure sample integrity.*
  - **Representativeness**—*panels are not necessarily representative of the target population.*
  - **Time**—*of course it takes more time to get information with this method than with other methods.*
  - **Professional Respondents**—*in some cases respondents might try to opt-in to more than one panel (perhaps many) and thus become professional respondents. A growing body of research is detailing "gamers," respondents who try to get into a number of panels.*

Hybrid

- Hybrid collection methods involve using multiple methods to collect the data. Suppose you need to survey 2,000 fans of your local football team. You make 3,000 phone calls but only get 1,500 to complete the survey. In order to get 500 more respondents, you decide to go to the next football game and stop passersby. Using this in-person intercept method, you collect the remaining 500.

- **Advantage:**
  - **Convenience**—*this method enables the researcher to maximize the opportunities to collect a sample.*
- **Disadvantage:**
  - **Representativeness**—*researchers need to validate the sample to ensure that the 1,500 telephone respondents are not statistically different from the 500 respondents who answered the survey at the football game. If there is a difference between those groups, then the data collection method itself has biased the integrity of the sample of 2,000.*

Choosing the Data Collection Method

Figure 6.9 highlights many issues to consider when deciding on which data collection method(s) to use.

- **Time:**
  - Time pressure can be driven by the need to get the information quickly for management, perhaps as required by the research sponsor, or because the issues are time sensitive and older information will be less relevant.
- **Budget:**
  - Research can be expensive and it's possible that the research sponsor prefers a mail or Internet survey because those methods are less expensive than in-person or telephone surveys. One method might be easier—thus typically less expense—to conduct.
- **Accuracy:**
  - Depending on the circumstances, some data collection methods result in a better representation of the population than other methods. For example, suppose you have an *average to poor* quality mailing or e-mail list, yet you have a very *sophisticated* random telephone calling system. If you want a more accurate sample, a telephone survey might be the best method in this case.

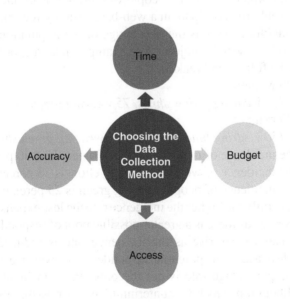

■ **FIGURE 6.9**

Issues in Choosing the Data Collection Method.

■ **FIGURE 6.10**

Four Characteristics of
Respondent Access

- **Access:**
  - Access is the extent to which researchers can reach the population through both their willingness to participate and the incidence of their occurrence in the population. Respondent characteristics are an important piece of the access issue. Marketing researchers must address four respondent characteristics as represented in Figure 6.10:
    1. **Willingness** to participate. Although researchers might have access to respondents, many potential respondents might not be willing to participate in the survey.
    2. **Suitability** to participate. Marketing researchers need to screen respondents as being knowledgeable enough to contribute substantively to the research. A lack of knowledge might result in a respondents' giving answers that the researcher incorrectly takes as credible. Respondents should be representative of the desired sample frame for the research project.
    3. **Ability** to participate. Someone might want or be willing to participate but perhaps they simply do not have the time or are not able to participate for whatever reason. People who do not have Internet access will not be able to participate in a web-based survey for example.
    4. The **incidence rate** is the percentage of the population who are qualified to be research subjects. For example, take a group of 500 people with the following breakdown :
       - 300 women:
         - *100 wearing yellow shirts, 75 wearing green, and 125 in red.*
       - 200 men:
         - *150 wearing blue shirts and 50 wearing green shirts.*
       - The incidence of men among the 500 people is 40 percent (200/500)
       - The incidence of women wearing yellow is 33 percent (100/300)
       - The incidence of people wearing green is 25 percent ((75+50)/500)
       - Generally the higher the incidence rate the less expensive it is to do the research as there is a greater possible pool of respondents. Marketing research costs rise as the incidence rate is reduced because there is less access to potential respondents. However a note of caution: The percentage rate is not the only driver in incidence rate costs. Although ostensibly counterintuitive, it's possible that an incidence

rate of 20 percent is more expensive than one of 10 percent. Suppose the 20 percent of potential respondents are doctors who are hard to reach and the 10 percent is of the general population who are women over 30 who have bought a car in the past month. Although a smaller percentage, this latter scenario is of a group that might well be easier to reach and more willing to participate.

Key Incentives to Raising Response Rates

Pre-Test

- Pre-testing the questionnaire involves administering the questionnaire among a small group, perhaps even a focus group, of appropriate respondents. Their feedback will be invaluable in revamping the questionnaire for clarity and for question relevance. With any luck, these test participants will make suggestions that will improve the questionnaire, resulting in more people interested in taking the survey. Pre-testing the questionnaire is of particular importance when dealing with sensitive or complicated issues as such issues are often a driver in non-response issues.
- **Advantages:**
  - **Clarify**—*creating a well-written survey will help increase response rates.*
  - **New Information**—*the pre-test group might identify other critical issues not included on the survey.*
- **Disadvantages:**
  - **Time**—*pre-testing takes time and can result in researchers' over analyzing the questionnaire. In some cases and at some point, researchers have to go with what they have and avoid making too many changes. It's unlikely the questionnaire will ever be perfect and too much time pre-testing might be better used executing the survey.*

Financial

- Financial incentives include money, prize giveaways, gift certificates, etc. Mail surveys might be accompanied by a dollar to entice participation, an online survey might offer a giveaway of a computer to every nth participant, and telephone interviews might tell potential respondents that they will get a chance to win a gift certificate to their favorite restaurant. Financial incentives should be enough to compensate respondents for their time and for *expressing* an opinion but not be so high that the respondent feels he is being *paid for a specific opinion.*
- **Advantages:**
  - **Effective**—*financial incentives usually increase response rates.*
  - **Variety**—*there are many types of financial incentives. Inventive marketing researchers can create almost anything as a way to entice survey participation.*
  - **Easy**—*offering incentives is relatively simple.*
- **Disadvantages:**
  - **Cost**—*depending on the incentive, this approach can be costly. A common mail survey incentive is a dollar. It might not sound like much, but the cost can add up quickly. However, it is often worth the cost if it results in getting enough respondents.*

- **Biases**—*incentives can bias the respondent as they might have some sense of obligation to respond a certain way, particularly if the incentive is too high.*

Notifications

- Informing potential respondents that they will be contacted to participate in a survey will increase response rates, particularly for mail (snail and e-mail) surveys. Many mail surveys look like standard junk mail destined for the trash. A pre-notification postcard informing potential respondents of the impending survey's arrival will result in more people looking-out for the survey. Some people who had thrown out the survey might well have taken it had they known it was coming. Pre-notifications are a courteous way to ease the researcher into the potential respondents' good graces.
- **Advantages:**
  - **Effective**—*notifying the respondents that they will be getting a survey will increase the likelihood that the targeted respondent will at least be more aware of the survey, and perhaps thus be more likely to respond to the survey.*
  - **List Verification**—*sending out a notice will help the researcher identify how good or bad the mailing list is. If notification letters are returned, the researcher can correct the addresses before sending out the questionnaire.*
- **Disadvantages:**
  - **Cost**—*sending out mailers adds to the survey costs. Sending e-mail notifications out is free—but might not be as effective as sending a notification through the mail.*
  - **Administrative Time**—*time spent on mailers detracts from the time the researcher could spend on executing the survey itself.*

Deadlines

- Deadlines convey a sense of urgency to the respondent to complete the survey in a timely manner. A ten-day deadline is a good guideline from which to start.
- **Advantages:**
  - **Effective**—*putting minimal pressure on respondents can help to increase response rates.*
  - **Free**—*putting a clearly marked deadline on the survey does not add to the research costs.*
- **Disadvantage:**
  - **Pressure Impact**—*putting too much pressure on respondents might cause a backlash of sorts. Respondents might not be predisposed to complete the survey if they feel overly pressured with a deadline that is too tight.*

Appeals

- Sometimes researchers make appeals to the respondent to complete the survey based on claims that the survey results will help a noble, or at least ostensibly important, cause. The U.S. Census Bureau uses this tactic and spends millions of dollars on advertising campaigns to convince citizens that completing the census will help to drive apportionment of funds that will help their communities.

- **Advantages:**
  - **Effective**—*depending on the level and reason for the appeal, it might add a sense of importance to a given survey and thus help to raise response rates.*
  - **Free**—*there is no cost for making a general appeal such as "this research will benefit first responders." However, getting an endorsement, which can help anchor the appeal, can be costly.*

- **Disadvantages:**
  - **Credibility**—*appeals have to be genuine and believable. Overblown appeals can reduce response rates if the respondent feels the researcher is being dishonest or disingenuous.*
  - **Source**—*not all appeals are appealing. Suppose the researcher is making an appeal to complete a survey that will aid in a community building project and that you are opposed to the building project because it will disrupt the neighborhood. This type of appeal will reduce the response rate for those people who do not support the appeal premise.*

Cover Letter

- In mail or web surveys researchers can include a cover letter or opening paragraph that will increase the survey response rate. Key components of the cover letter are: who you are, why you are doing the survey, how the respondent was selected, how long the survey will take, what will be done with the results and whether the survey is anonymous and confidential. Finally, always thank them for participating.
- **Advantages:**
  - **Effective**—*a well-written cover letter honestly addressing the survey process and conveying a genuine appreciation for their participation will increase the survey response rate.*
  - **Cost**—*there is minimal cost to writing a cover letter. However, mailing the cover letter before the survey adds to the postal costs. Including the cover letter with the survey will not increase the mailing costs as the survey was being mailed-out anyway. Of course e-mail letters are at essentially no cost.*
- **Disadvantage:**
  - **Credibility**—*poorly written cover letters can cause the respondent to lack faith in the quality of the survey.*

Research in Practice

Case:
- As the marketing manager for a large shoe store you have been asked to oversee a customer survey. The last survey was an Internet survey that yielded a very low response rate.

Assignment:
- Design a new data collection effort combining multiple data collection methods. What are the advantages and disadvantages of the types you selected? What incentives might you use to increase response rates?

Chapter Summary

Total survey research error is the combination of sampling and non-sampling error. Sampling error is a statistical reality bridging the gap between a sample and the total population. Sampling error is the error associated with the variance between the sample result and the projection of that result onto the population. Non-sampling error is error created by the design or execution (i.e., human error) of the survey. Non-sampling error is caused by either the respondent or researcher and can be intentionally or unintentionally caused. Some intentional errors include lying or data falsification. Some unintentional error includes misunderstanding of the questions, respondent fatigue, or researcher data entry errors. Pre-testing the questionnaire will help to reduce unintentional errors associated with poorly written questionnaires. Non-response error occurs when there is a statistically significant difference between those who responded and those who did not respond to the questionnaire. Three important factors that should be considered before conducting a survey are incentives and overall costs, the data collection method, and the time researchers have to conduct the survey. A number of common data collection methods include web, telephone, in-person, and mail surveys. Generally Internet surveys are inexpensive and can reach a wide audience. Telephone surveys enable quick data collection of targeted respondents, yet response rates are unpredictable. In-person, or "mall intercepts," as they had once been called, enable researchers to interact directly with respondents. Getting a representative sample and its potentially significant cost, are issues with this type of data collection. Generally mail surveys can be time consuming with unpredictable turnaround times and generally low response rates. Deciding on which data collection method to choose hinges on the research project's cost, time to execute, level of accuracy desired, and respondent access. Accessing respondents involves marketing researchers' determining respondents' willingness, ability, suitability (are they qualified to respond?), as well as the respondent incidence rate (the percent of respondents' meeting the survey screening criteria within the population). Marketing researchers can increase survey response rates through monetary (or related) incentives, pre-testing the questionnaire to ensure it's well written, sweepstakes or contest entries, appeals (touting the societal or related benefit), deadlines (applying minimal pressure to complete the survey), or a cover letter or survey pre-notification correspondence.

7 Causal Research and Experimental Design

Image © BenC, 2011. Used under license from Shutterstock, Inc.

Learning Objectives:

- Understand the role of causal research in marketing research
- Understand the three elements required to prove causation
- Learn the three types of variables in experimental design

- See how marketing researchers attempt to control extraneous variables
- Learn how to run an experiment and about experimental notation
- Understand the difference between true and pre-experiments

- Learn the difference between a lab and field experiment
- Understand how test marketing is used in marketing research

Chapter Seven

Exploratory, Descriptive, and Causal Research

Remember the three key marketing research approaches—exploratory, descriptive, and causal.

- **Exploratory** aims to gain basic information about an issue, topic, etc. and uses qualitative techniques such as focus groups, interviews, and secondary data.
- **Descriptive** research answers who, what, where, when, and how related questions. Its techniques are qualitative such as with certain observation studies, and quantitative such as statistically representative surveys.
- **Causal** research reveals the *why* behind the descriptive research results. Causal methods include surveys and various experimental designs, both simple and complex. Causal research documents the *cause-effect* relationship among the **independent, dependent,** and **extraneous variables** associated with your research topic.

Proving Causation

Proving causation requires rigorous testing. We might hypothesize that A caused B. However, has this ostensible connection actually been tested? Remember that three factors, as shown in Figure 7.2, must be present to prove causation:

- *Concomitant Variation—a statistically predictable pattern between responses/ variables.*
  - *If the team practices more, it will win more games.*
  - *When it rains, umbrella sales rise.*
- *Time Order of Occurrence—A must precede B if A is the **cause** of B.*
  - *Customers are happy **after** they receive good service.*
- *Systematic Elimination—all other possible causes have been eliminated.*
  - *We have tested and thus eliminated other possible causes to the change in variable B.*
- *It's rare to have one variable as the* only *cause of the change in another variable. Often variables A, B, and C, etc. affect variables D, E, and F, etc. Causal analysis can quickly become complicated. For example, the cause in the change of sales might be due to price, location, selection, and quality taken together.*

■ **FIGURE 7.1**

Proving Causation Requires Concomitant Variation, Appropriate Time Order of Occurrence, and Elimination of Other Possible Factors

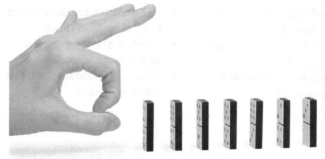

Image © Mazzur, 2011. Used under license from Shutterstock, Inc.

Experimental Variable Types

- **Independent:**
  - These are variables the researcher can control directly. Think of a restaurant. An independent variable might be product selection, hours of operation, store layout, lighting, number of staff, price, atmosphere, and service level. Because restaurant managers have direct control over implementing those variables they are independent in that they can be implemented regardless of the surrounding environment.
- **Dependent:**
  - Dependent variables depend on a change to the independent variable(s) for their effect. Think again of a restaurant example. Can restaurant managers change sales directly? No, they can change sales through manipulating (also called the **treatment effect**) the independent variable of, for example, price. In other words, if a restaurant manager wants to increase sales, she might lower price which results in increased sales. Thus in this case we have a cause-and-effect relationship between a change in price and the resulting increase in sales. Other examples of dependent variables include customer satisfaction, repeat customers, as well as consumer attitudes, opinions, perceptions, or beliefs. These variables are affected by manipulating or changing the associated independent variable(s).
- **Extraneous:**
  - Extraneous variables are variables that the researcher has no true control over but whose impact the researcher might be able to mitigate. For example, suppose a competitor to a given restaurant is opening soon. The restaurant manager might decide to preempt the impending competitor by offering a special that "steals their thunder" before the competition can open. Or perhaps an airline decides to have two hubs. They schedule flights during the winter through the Memphis hub and summer flights (hoping to avoid thunderstorms) through the Chicago hub. Although the airline can't control the weather, they can create a "workaround" to mitigate the negative impact of the weather. Other examples of extraneous variables include legal, regulatory, and political issues as well as competition, negative press, and road construction blocking easy access to your business. Good researchers do their homework to determine which extraneous variables are present and, to the extent possible, create strategies to handle or manage those variables.
  - Figure 7.3 shows the three main types of experimental variables.

Experimental Variables

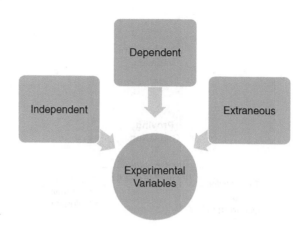

Marketing managers can identify many types of extraneous variables as well as a number of techniques to handle them, or at least mitigate their impact on the research. Remember that extraneous variables are often present and that the researcher can't necessarily "correct" for them, although the researcher is aware they might exist. The key extraneous variables are depicted in Figure 7.4.

Types of Extraneous Variables

- **Testing Effects:**
  - *This effect occurs when the effect of taking the tests affects the next time the test is taken.*
    - Consider a taste test experiment for a new energy drink. The first time you took the test you thought the drink was too bland. Various changes to the drink might or might not have taken place by the next time you take the test. After taking the taste test challenge a second time, your perception about the drink the second time was influenced by the first time you took the taste test. In other words the experience of having taken the test before might have an impact on how you answer the same questions the second time you take the test even though the product in this case has not changed.
- **History:**
  - *Events that occur which might have an impact on the test subjects.*
    - Let's suppose a township is testing residents' attitudes towards town services. During the course of the test, a snow storm cripples both the city and its snow removal operation for a couple of days. This winter event might well have an impact on the respondents' view of the city's services. Even residents who might have otherwise given the city high marks, might now temper their responses. How the snow event was handled might negatively skew their otherwise satisfied opinions of the city.
- **Regression to the Mean:**
  - *Occurs when test subjects gravitate towards the middle of a given scale.*
    - Imagine that you are an incoming freshman trying to register for college classes. You find the process frustrating, which results in your giving the school low ratings on a survey. Each semester the college surveys students to see how effective the students feel the administration is in running the college. As time progresses, you tend to soften your position for various reasons and thus begin giving increasingly less negative responses in subsequent surveys even though there has been no real

change in the college administration or its processes. Often, over time, respondents who gave very strong opinions tend to move more towards the center for no obvious reason.

- **Instrument:**
  - *Changes in the data collection instrument that affect the test subjects' responses.*
    - Consider a researcher testing community attitudes towards building a new bridge that will connect two parts of town. Because the project has been controversial, the city decides to do in-person interviews at the local mall. A few months go by, and the research company now decides to conduct surveys through the telephone or Internet rather than in person. The data collection method itself might cause a change in their responses. Suppose residents are more likely to give negative opinions on the Internet than to someone on the phone or, even more so, to someone in person. It might be that respondents feel more pressure to soften their responses to someone in person—even subconciously. The relative anonymity of a telephone survey, and the total anonymity of an Internet survey, provides sufficient cover to respondents to give more candid responses. Respondents might not knowingly tweak their views based on the data collection method, but it happens. In this case, the data collection instrument, or method, is causing a change in respondents' answers even though there has been no real change in the actual respondents, opinions.
- **Selection Bias:**
  - *This variable occurs when the test subjects are inappropriate for the research topic.*
    - Lowe's wants to determine what home improvement products are the most important to customers so the company decides to conduct a customer survey in its stores. At a given store a manager's research team stops customers and asks them ten pre-determined questions. As a key initial step, it is important to screen the respondents as appropriate to be in the survey. If this vetting is not done, the respondent pool might not be a good representative sample of the target audience. The store manager interviews 1,000 respondents in the store over one weekend.

This pool of 1,000 respondents is assumed to be a representative sample. However, suppose 10 percent of these respondents are customers just looking for appliances who are not interested in home improvement products, and 5 percent just dropped-in to get a light bulb or some other small item, and 3 percent came in for a coffee as, in this fictitious scenario, Starbucks is ensconced in the store. This example demonstrates that 18 percent of the sample should not be in the respondent pool. Additional sample selection bias can occur as a result of the time frame. If the store manager runs the survey for a weekend, he might not capture a true random cross-section of his customer base because not all people interested in home improvement products shop only on weekends. Weekday shoppers would be excluded from this survey.

- **Mortality:**
  - *These test subjects are lost during the experimentation.*
    - The longer the duration of an experiment, the greater chance the researcher will lose the test subjects through subject withdrawal, death, address change, etc. This issue becomes a problem if there is a disproportionate shift in the respondent demographic. For example, if it is critical to the research that there be equality, or a statistically insignificant inequality, between the number of men and women in the study, a disproportional drop in the number of men from the study might well skew the results towards the larger number of women in the experiment. Researchers must then determine how to handle this shift in the respondent demographic by perhaps either recruiting more men (although they will be "behind" in the study) or by releasing some women from the study in order to maintain relative equality in the number of men and women in the research.
- **Maturation:**
  - *This variable occurs when there are changes to the test subjects themselves.*
    - During the course of an experiment, the test subject might have situational changes to their lives that affect the integrity and independence of the experiment. Suppose a study is about researching how people feel about

■ FIGURE 7.5

A Taste Test Experiment Can Provide Researchers With Valuable Information as to the Likes and Dislikes Before a Product is Launched

Image © Serge Bikhenenko, 2011. Used under license from Shutterstock, Inc.

friendship and respondents are selected for a three-year period. Over the course of those years some of the respondents might have had a divorce and, in addition to the division of assets, there had been a splitting of friends. The marketing researcher might not be aware of the divorce and your resulting change in attitudes towards friends that is now driven by your new circumstances. Many things can happen to the respondents over the course of a research project that might affect the research, unbeknownst to the researcher, such as changes in respondents' health, financial status, living situation, or job. These changes might have a positive or negative impact on the research.

Now that we understand the major extraneous variables, we must determine how to handle them. It is difficult to eliminate these variables from the research entirely. In fact it is sometimes not clear to the researcher that they even exist. However, good researchers look for clues that some extraneous variables are in play and then design the research in such a way to either eliminate the extraneous variables from the study or lessen their impact on the research. The key methods for handling, or controlling for, extraneous variables are shown in Figure 7.6.

Controlling Extraneous Variables

- **Matching:**
  - *This method involves pairing like test subjects to alert the researcher of unexpected changes in one of the test subjects.*
    - If researchers are trying to determine why restaurant sales are declining, they might match store A with store B, first ensuring both stores A and B are similar. This way any untoward changes in the status of restaurant A that does not occur to store B will indicate the potential existence of an extraneous variable affecting store A.—presuming all other variables are constant.
- **Statistical Control:**
  - *This technique uses statistical adjustments to correct for imbalances in the test subjects.*
    - When the U.S. Census Bureau conducts its decennial census not everyone is counted. It's essentially impossible to literally count every American. How does the U.S. Census Bureau know they have or have not counted

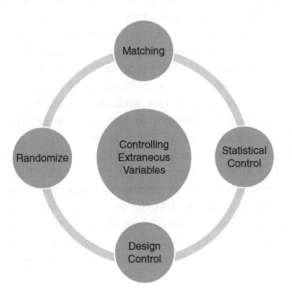

■ FIGURE 7.6

Controlling Extraneous Variables

everyone? The U.S. Census Bureau uses various statistical adjustments such as correlation analysis and Analysis of Variance (ANOVA) to determine where unexpected variances occur in the data. Then the Bureau adjusts the data to compensate, within a statistical error range, the presumed real mean parameters of the national population. Let's look at a practical example. Have you ever baked a cake? Take a look at the cooking directions on the back of a Betty Crocker cake mix box. You will notice that usually there is one set of cooking instructions. If you live in a high-altitude area, there are alternate directions. Suppose you don't have those high-altitude directions. Being an astute baker you know that higher-altitude cooking requires some adjustments. So instead of cooking the cake at 350 degrees for an hour, you statistically adjust the temperature to 375 degrees and cook the cake for 45 minutes. The baking result is the same. The extraneous variable of "altitude" needed to be handled through a statistical adjustment (the change in temperature and baking time). Now consider this: Do you always budget the same amount of time to get your coffee fix before class? Probably not. One assumes that you know that certain times will be busier, requiring you to statistically adjust the time you believe it will take to get your coffee and still be on time for class. Through experience, marketing researchers learn how much statistical adjustment needs to be done to remain confident that the extraneous variable's negative impact has been mitigated.

- **Design Control:**
  - *This approach involves designing the research in a manner that reduces the impact of the extraneous variable(s) in the first place.*
    - Researchers should use the most effective research design depending on the circumstances of the study. Perhaps focus groups are better than surveys, or Internet data collection is better than a mail survey, or a taste test in the local mall is better than a taste test at a research facility. The more a researcher knows about his subject matter, the better prepared he will be to preempt the extraneous variables before the research begins.
- **Randomization:**
  - *Randomly assigning test subjects to the study.*
    - The larger the respondent pool is, the better randomization works. If there is a flaw in some of the test subjects, randomizing their responses will reduce the overall impact. Think of selecting 3,000 people for a study. If researchers assign the 3,000 people to three separate experiment groups judgmentally, selection bias might cause one of the three groups to have a disproportional number of inappropriate test subjects, leading researchers to think that one of the groups is statistically different from the other two groups when in fact there is no difference. The difference is that the respondents in one group were handpicked and are not as statistically representative as the other two randomly assigned groups. If researchers randomly assign 1,000 people to each of the three groups, any error will be equally spread among all three groups.
    - If a random number generator in Microsoft Excel creates 1,000 numbers from 1 to 100, the average of those 1,000 randomly generated numbers will be about 50. Now if you attempt to "randomly" (thus manually) enter 1,000 numbers from 1 to 100, the average of those 1,000 numbers might well be much lower or higher than 50. This result indicates that the lack of true randomization had a negative impact on the integrity of the data because, all things being randomly generated, the average should be

around 50. Randomization helps to reduce error associated with extraneous variables.

Choosing the best method for handling extraneous variables depends on the level of knowledge researchers have about the impact and source of the extraneous variable(s) coupled with their marketing research expertise in selecting the most appropriate mitigation strategy.

Experimental Design Methods

Suppose a marketing research manager for a department store wants to determine why sales are declining. Documenting how much sales are declining, when, and with what products, is descriptive research. Descriptive research describes; causal research takes the research analysis to a more analytical level. Determining *why* sales are declining is more analytic than simply detailing that they *have* fallen. Analytic research builds on descriptive research and relies on marketing researcher expertise and insight to make sense of the data.

Experimental design is a form of causal research that tests the manipulation of independent variables to measure the corresponding change in the dependent variables.

Experimental design helps researchers to understand whether the variables of a given issue or problem are related and in fact connected. Not all relationships are causal. If every time it rains on Friday our basketball team loses on Saturday, are we really concerned whether it rains on Friday? Other than perhaps not liking rain, a Friday downpour is not the true cause of a Saturday loss. Rain and losing games appear to be "related" yet this pattern is simply statistically coincidental. Many variables can show a relationship but not be related in a cause-and-effect fashion. Consider taking a college exam. You might find that studying increases your exam score. In this case, the more you study, the higher your score. These variables (studying and exam score) appear to be both statistically *and* causally related. In other words, studying affects exams scores; the two variables are connected. The more you drive, the less gas there is in your tank. Again, both are statistically *and* causally related. Barring a leak or a siphoning thief, presumably the gas in your tank would not go down if you did not drive. Causal research formalizes the cause-and-effect relationship between and among variables. What is the difference between "between and among"? *Between* variables refers to two variables; *among* indicates three or more variables are in play. A sometimes overlooked distinction.

As with many aspects of marketing research, we engage in some form of experimental design in aspects of daily life. Have you ever made a peanut butter and jelly sandwich and can't get the jelly jar open? What do you do when you can't get a lid off a jar because it's too tight? Break the jar? Well, you experiment with various techniques to access this namesake component of your beloved sandwich. Perhaps you use a towel of some sort to increase your grip. Or maybe you decide to whack the sides of the lid to loosen it (that usually works). But as a last resort, because you know that lids are tight due to the vacuum pressure of its seal and not just how tightly it's screwed on, you decide to puncture the top of the lid to release pressure. In any case, you have tried three experiments to produce a cause-and-effect relationship. The lid opened as a direct result of some action you took. Even with this overly simplistic explanation, you can see that routinely we do "experiments" and process the resulting information for further action.

Marketing researchers use experimental design to solve complex business issues. During the first ten years of this century, the airline industry suffered billions of dollars of losses. How might airline CEOs have handled the business challenges related to the decline in revenues? What should they do? Simply wait for the market to return? Failure to take action would have resulted in lower revenue or perhaps the failure of a given airline. The airlines tried several experiments to see if they could increase revenue. Many changes took place, from increased charges for just about every service (I think peanuts are still free), to changes in airline schedules, cities served, aircraft used, minimizing fuel, getting more direct flight paths, and less time on the ground during connections. These variables are all independent variables because the airline has control of these variables and changes in those variables will, it is hoped, affect a change in the key dependent variable of sales. These changes represent experiments airlines employed to see if revenues would increase. Some cost-savings experiments were less traditional. Once planes are airborne, pilots often use the automatic pilot at cruising altitudes not unlike our using cruise control on the highway. However, when planes land, pilots take the controls manually even though most aircraft can land themselves. Some airlines instructed pilots, who objected, to allow the plane to land itself and take manual control only if necessary. This technique will save fuel, it was theorized because the automatic pilot is relatively efficient. Airlines know that pilots who manually land their planes often use more thrust that can increase control and lead to smoother landings. Use of more thrust burns more fuel and thus costs more. Finally, a Japanese airline thought it could save fuel costs by requesting that passengers use the bathroom before flying. The cost-saving result of this indelicate experiment is in question.

Laboratory vs. Field Experiment

Experiments can be done in a laboratory (lab) or the field. **Lab experiments** are conducted in a controlled setting. We often think of the burner or test tube lab experiments we did in junior high school. Lab experiments should not be thought of as only in a stereotypical lab setting. Laboratory experiments are really more correctly thought of as experiments where the researcher controls the setting and circumstances of the experiment. **Field experiments** are conducted in the marketplace, or a natural setting, and thus the environment is less controlled. The marketplace can be very broad or quite narrow. Suppose Holiday Inn decides it wants to change its hotel reservation system to see if it can improve the check-in process. Holiday Inn could launch the system nationwide or it could introduce it in a few hotels to see how well it works. A limited introduction, or experiment, enables Holiday Inn to test the system, and make any changes to it, before it's introduced nationally. Once launched nationally, system quirks will be magnified on a national scale; thus there are risks to releasing a system, or product, on a large scale before testing the marketplace waters first. However, an advantage to a national rollout is the jump marketers get on the competition. If Dunkin Donuts tests a new and innovative coffee flavor at a few local stores, it will show its hand to the competition, who might move quickly to launch their version of the drink nationally before Dunkin Donuts does. Being "first in" the marketplace might help this Dunkin Donuts competitor create a marketplace leadership perception despite not being the first with the product. Although field experiments can take a lot of time, be costly, and can tip-off the competition,

■ **FIGURE 7.7**

Field Experiments, Unlike Lab Experiments, are Done in an Environment not Under the Researcher's Control

Image © Goodluz, 2011. Used under license from Shutterstock, Inc.

they do offer marketers the opportunity to see how a product or service will actually perform when released in the marketplace. Additionally, problems associated with a product or a service that might escape the lab testing phase of research will surely be brought to light quickly when the marketplace, with its millions of "testers" uses the product. When a new technological gizmo hits the marketplace, how many of us check the web for blogs for guidance on how well the product is performing? You are conducting secondary research by the way. The marketplace greatly accelerates product testing. The key issues when considering a lab versus a field experiment are depicted in Figure 7.8.

Another type of field experiment is test marketing. **Test marketing** is when researchers bring a product or service to a limited market that is within the marketers' demographic target audience. For example, suppose you are selling raincoats. Rather than producing a vast number of raincoats and sending them to stores, you decide to pick a few stores, or cities, to test how well the product is received. Based on customer feedback, you make changes to style, price, color, etc. and then launch the newly updated raincoats in the larger marketplace. Test markets should be demographically and otherwise appropriate for your product or service. If we choose Las Vegas, which gets little rain, to test our raincoats, the data might not be very useful. Test market locations should be a microcosm of the targeted audience. Test marketing is less expensive than bringing a product to the national marketplace; however, there is a risk of alerting the competition. There are various forms of testing the market. Perhaps you have done a product or taste test in a local mall or you have received a box of laundry detergent or cereal in the mail. These techniques enable marketers to get a sense of how the product will sell. In a sense, marketers are conducting a lab experiment in the field to some extent because of the limited nature of some test marketing efforts. Most test marketing is field based since they are done beyond a mall environment or otherwise more controllable setting.

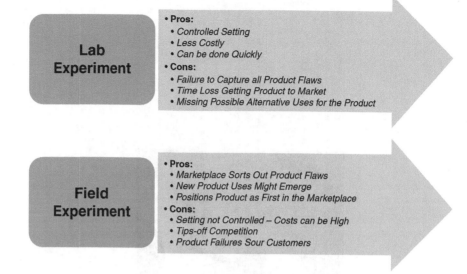

Research Validity

How do researchers know that they conducted the experiment correctly and that the results are right? **Validity,** the extent to which research results are correct or true, is a critical part of assessing the usefulness of the research.

Internal Validity

Internal validity refers to whether the researcher conducted the experiment using the correct cause-and-effect assumptions. Suppose you run an auto mechanic shop and sales have been flagging. In order to determine the cause, you decide to run an experiment that will test customer attitudes towards the service experience. You spend a lot of time and money testing various independent variables such as wait time, cost, and service quality. Your results are mixed but you think sales are declining due to customer attitudes that your price for repair is too high. You then lower the price, and you do not see a rise in customers. Later, a smart college student who is taking marketing research theorizes the real cause of the sales decline is road construction that has been making it difficult for customers to get to your shop. Because the wrong assumptions of cause and effect were presumed, internal validity was not realized here because your original premise as to the cause of the sales decline was wrong; thus, the experiment of lowering prices was doomed to fail.

External Validity

External validity is the extent to which the research results accurately reflect the results of the targeted population. Let's presume you conduct a taste test experiment to see how you should change the soup recipes at your soup shop. After running various taste tests, you confirm that the soups are too salty and heavy, thus, you decide to lighten the recipes before opening your soup shop to the public. However, your friends are overly health conscious and are not a true reflection of the general soup consuming population who apparently prefer salty and creamy soups. Your test subjects did not accurately reflect the true marketplace. In other words, your sample of soup samplers was not diverse enough to reflect the varied opinions of the larger population of soup consumers. Marketing researchers should test validity once the project is complete assess whether the research conclusions are valid.

Running an Experiment

Marketing researchers attempt to prove the cause-and-effect relationships between and among variables in order to inform managers as to the best course of action. As the owner of a car wash chain you want to determine what service mix will lead to the most business and, by extension, repeat business. You might simply decide to offer a certain service mix and see what happens. This approach might work. We say might because without some form of experimental design or customer survey whereby you test the impact of your independent variables, (i.e., service selection) you cannot be certain that the service options you offer have led directly to sales. You might assume that when customers are offered a free vacuuming with every car washed it will cause repeat business due to a customer perception or belief of value for the money. Testing the impact of varying service offerings on sales is the best way to truly determine how much of an impact changes in independent variables have on, in this case, the dependent variable of sales. Marketing researchers can run an experiment to test whether the survey findings are correct. Suppose a survey concludes that 80 percent of respondents say that they prefer the product color to be *blue,* but upon running an experiment testing product color preferences, respondents pick *green* more than any other color. Experimental design will identify customer's true preference.

True Experiment vs. Pre-Experiment Design

True experiments have both a control group and pre- and post-measurement of the dependent variables.

- A **control group** *is a set of variables whereby there is no manipulation of the independent variables to see the theorized change to the dependent variable.*

If you owned multiple car wash locations you might add the vacuuming service to five locations (the experimental group) and *not* add the vacuuming service to your five other locations (the control group). The control group enables the researcher to see if there is an impact on sales, in this case, despite changing or not changing any independent variables (the vacuuming service in this case). It's quite possible that sales at all ten locations might increase for reasons that are not the result of the added vacuuming service. Without a control group, the car wash operation might have assumed that adding the vacuuming service increases sales as sales did increase after the service was offered. However, it's possible that sales would have risen anyway, without the vacuuming service. Perhaps a competitor went out of business and thus sales at your car wash increased.

Consider a gym membership. If a gym manager has ten gyms with similar locations, sales, and demographics and she wants to determine how to increase customer satisfaction. The manager might change the independent variable of free gym classes at five locations and retain the fee for the classes at the other five locations. After some pre-testing period, customer satisfaction at all ten locations was established. The experiment of free classes lasted one month, at which time sales at all ten locations were re-measured. If sales between the test and control group were the same, the manager might conclude that the free classes did not change customer satisfaction. However if customer satisfaction improved at the free gym class locations only, the manager might determine that the free classes *caused* a change in customer satisfaction. Of course determining that no other independent or extraneous variables interceded during the experiment is a critical component of validating the impact of the independent variable manipulation's effect on the dependent variable change.

In addition to a control group, **a true experiment has a pre- and post-measurement** of the dependent variable. In our car wash example, researchers would measure the sales at the car wash, then add the vacuuming service, then re-measure sales to see if there was a change in sales. A change might indicate that the **experimental treatment,** which is the manipulation or change in the independent variable, caused a change in the dependent variable of car wash sales.

Experimental Notation

Experimental notation helps researchers to document the relationship between and among independent and dependent variables.

- **Experimental notation** *is a process that assigns designations to independent and dependent variables whereby* O = *the dependent and* X = *the independent variables, respectively.*

Once the researcher has identified which independent and which dependent variables are relevant to the experiment, he can notate the experiment. Take the car wash example a step further:

- *O* = Sales (dependent variable)
- *X* = Vacuuming service (independent variable)

A Sample of Experimental Designs

Pre-Experiments

Pre-experiments are often used as a precursor to the more rigorous requirements of a true experiment. Pre experiments might lack a control group or pre measurement and occurs without full randomization of variables. Unlike a true experiment, researchers don't have full control over the variables in pre experiments.

1. **One-Shot Test with Post-Measurement**
2. **One Group with Pre- and Post-Measurement without a Control**
   - **Notes:**
     - X = *independent variable*
     - O = *dependent variable*
     - O_1, O_2, *etc.* = *first, second, etc. measurement(s) of the change in the dependent variable resulting from manipulating or changing the independent variable.*

1. **One-Shot Test with Post-Measurement:**
   - A pre-experiment where there is a change to the independent variable and a measurement of the "change" in the dependent variable. This type of experiment lacks a control group (to truly determine the impact of changing the independent variable) and a pre-measurement of the dependent variable which

would enable the researcher to fully quantify the impact to the dependent variable change arguably attributable to the change in the independent variable.

- Although lacking the rigor of a true experiment, the one-shot test approach is useful in that such an experiment might help the researcher to understand what *might* be going on, as opposed to truly determining what actually is going on. Such an experiment can be a useful starting point.
- *Experimental Notation:* ***X O***

2. **One Group with Pre- and Post-Measurement without a Control:**
   - This pre-experiment technique involves taking a pre-measurement of the dependent variable, changing the independent variable, and then taking a post-measurement of the dependent variable. In this case, the researcher has some quantifiable data measuring the change in the dependent variable.
   - If a hotel is concerned about customer satisfaction (dependent variable), the hotel might remodel its rooms (independent variable) in an attempt to affect customer satisfaction. Using this experimental approach, the hotel might first measure customer satisfaction to get a satisfaction baseline, then remodel the rooms, then re-measure customer satisfaction to determine if remodeling the rooms affected (and by how much) customer satisfaction. Without a customer satisfaction pre-measurement, the hotel manager might be misled by only doing a customer satisfaction post-measurement. For example, suppose the hotel manager *did not* measure customer satisfaction before the remodeling and simply remodeled the rooms *and then* measured customer satisfaction. Let's suppose this customer satisfaction post-measurement yielded an 8 on a scale of 1 to 10. The hotel manager might think this result is good. It might well be good; however, an 8 is not very good if the customer satisfaction was a 9 before the rooms were remodeled. Without a pre-measurement, the hotel manager would not realize that customer satisfaction, although still high at an 8, actually slipped from a 9 before the remodeling. Perhaps customers liked the rooms better before.
   - *Experimental Notation:* O_1 ***X*** O_2

True Experiments

True experiments involve randomly assigning both the treatment and the test subjects to minimize biases and error. True experiments usually have both a control group and a pre- and post-measurement of the dependent variable. Some initial screening of experiential subjects is necessary, however. Researchers must make sure that the experimental and control groups are a good representative sample of test subjects. If there are ten coffee shops and nine of the ten are similar in size, product offering, clientele, etc. and the tenth is much larger and in a "nontraditional" location, this tenth store might not be the best one to use in an experiment as it's too different from the other locations to be used as a representative sample.

1. **After Only with a Control Group**
2. **One Set—Before and After Measurement with a Control Group**
3. **Multiple Sets—Before and After Measurement with Control Groups**

1. **After Only with a Control Group:**
   - In some texts this approach is labeled as pre-experiments as opposed to a true experiment. The discrepancy can arguably be settled assuming the test subjects are randomly assigned and there is a control group. Either way, this technique is not as thorough as the progressively rigorous methods outlined in 2 and 3 below.

- This approach involves at least two groups: a control group and an experimental group. The treatment, or change in the independent variable, is introduced to the experimental group but not to the control group.
- A post-measurement is done with both groups, but *not* a pre-measurement.
- This approach might be done when a manager needs to make a change immediately and does not have the time to do a baseline pre-measurement or perhaps he feels one is not needed.
- *Experimental Notation:* (A) $X O_1$
  (B) O_2

2. **One Set—Before and After Measurement with a Control Group:**
   - This approach involves two groups: a control group and an experimental group. The treatment, or change in the independent variable, is introduced to the experimental group but not to the control group.
   - A pre- and post-measurement is done with *both* groups.
   - Presume that group A and B are coffee shops.
   - First measure sales at both coffee shops; change an independent variable (price) at shop A but *not* B. Now re-measure sales at both shops A and B.
   - It is important that the pre-measurements at both shops are done at the *same* time and over some period of time to account for single-day anomalies. For example, perhaps researchers should measure the average sales for a month to get a solid baseline, then change the price at one coffee shop, then re-measure sales a month later at both shops. This time lapse will give the change in price a chance to work in the experimental group.
   - Also, remember that coffee shops A and B should be similar, thus making a comparison relevant.
   - *Experimental Notation:* (A) $O_1 X O_2$
     (B) $O_3 \quad O_4$

3. **Multiple Sets—Before and After Measurement with Control Groups:**
   - The difference between this approach and the one set technique above is a question of volume. This approach replicates, or multiplies, the effect of the one-set approach.
   - The advantage to the multiple-set approach is that the researcher can more clearly and definitively isolate the impact on the dependent variable from changing the independent variable since there are more sets to compare. Additionally, testing for the third component of proving causation, *systematic elimination,* is easier since there are more data sets to use as test subjects. In the case below, there are four coffee shops: two control and two experimental coffee shop locations. Now, there is no requirement to having four groups—the multiple-set approach could have 20 sets: 10 control and 10 experimental groups. Of course the time and cost of expanding the number of groups rises as the groups increase; however the prime advantage to more sets is the breadth of information the researcher will glean from running a large set of groups.
   - Remember that randomization is a key component of a true experiment. If the researcher spends too much time selecting test subjects, biases are bound to enter into the experiment. However, the researcher should ensure that the test subjects who are selected randomly are selected from a relevant, representative, and logical set of test subjects.
   - *Experimental Notation:* (A) $O_1 X_1 O_2$
     (B) $O_3 \quad O_4$
     (C) $O_5 X_2 O_6$
     (D) $O_7 \quad O_8$

Quasi-Experiments

- **Quasi-experiments** *are experiments done without full control over the treatment's influence.*

Sometimes researchers do not have full control over how the independent variable is disseminated. Let's says Sears is running an advertisement for a sale on dishwashers. Although there is a lot of marketing segmentation data around various media outlets such as TV, Internet, radio, and magazines, the researcher does not know when, or under what circumstances, the customers see the advertisement for the dishwasher sale. Sears controls the sale amount and the messaging campaign, but it does not fully control how the information is disseminated. Thus Sears might decide to do a rolling measurement of sales to try to "pin down" the effectiveness of its advertising.

When you hear radio or TV advertisements and hear the announcer say "tell them Jeff sent you" or "mention this ad and receive another 5 percent off", marketing researchers are trying to capture how effective the advertisements are in reaching the public. Sears running TV advertisements for a dishwasher sale does not mean the advertisement was effective even if dishwasher sales increased. Perhaps dishwasher sales would have increased with or without the advertisement for some other reason unknown to Sears.

1. **Interrupted Time Series**
2. **Multiple Time Series**

1. **Interrupted Time Series:**
   - In this case, the researcher has one experimental group whereby pre- and post-measurements of the dependent variable is ongoing in order to capture changes in the dependent variable as they happen.
   - A lack of a control group affects the reliability of the data.
   - Another shortcoming is the possibility that measuring the dependent variable multiple times might have an impact on future measurements of the dependent variables.
   - *Experimental Notation:* $O_1\,O_2\,O_3\,X\,O_4\,O_5\,O_6$
2. **Multiple Time Series:**
   - This method adds a control group to the process. Adding a control group results in a better ascription of the change in the independent variable.
   - *Experimental Notation:* $O_1\,O_2\,O_3\,X\,O_4\,O_5\,O_6$
     $O_1\,O_2\,O_3\quad\ O_4\,O_5\,O_6$

As a reminder, in all cases, controlling for (or attempting to control) extraneous variables is part of the process of conducting an experiment.

Pros and Cons of Conducting Experiments

There are many reasons why marketing researchers might decide to conduct or not to conduct an experiment. Weighing the pros and cons will provide the data business leaders need to make an informed decision as to whether running an experiment is a wise course of action.

- **Pros:**
  - *Enables researchers to determine the true cause and effect of relationships in the marketplace;*

- *Provides valuable data as to the possible results of marketing decisions;*
- *Gives business leaders a chance to incrementally launch products or services, make adjustments, and continue to roll-out the respective product or service.*
- **Cons:**
  - *Running an experiment takes time and money;*
  - *Results might be misleading or misapplied to the changing marketplace;*
  - *Correct implementation can be complex and thus potentially botched;*
  - *Business leaders might not act as they await the experiment's results, leaving an opening for the competition to act;*
  - *The experiment might alert the competition.*

Test Markets

Marketing research can also use test markets as a way to run an experiment, or simply to test a product in the marketplace to see how successful, or unsuccessful, it is in the marketplace. Consider McDonald's restaurants. You might have noticed the McCafe upgrade that McDonald's is introducing or perhaps you can only get a certain specialty drink at some Starbucks locations. In these cases, both McDonald's and Starbucks are testing the market in somewhat limited ways to see how these new products do in the marketplace. Some companies make various changes to their offering before launching a new product or service nationally. Recall the 4 Ps of marketing: price, product, promotion, and place. Companies like McDonald's and Starbucks use their respective place and distribution muscle to introduce new products or services in selected locations.

- **Test Marketing:** *The process of testing a product or service in a controlled marketplace before introducing the product or service on a larger, perhaps national, scale.*
- **Test Market:** *A suitable location to test your product or service.*

CBS NEWS Business Interactive listed what was billed as the top and bottom American cities to conduct test marketing from a list of the 150 most populated cities. This list is not necessarily a definitive compilation but it does serve as a good discussion point.

The top ten test market cities, which represent American consumers as a whole, are:

1. *Albany, NY*
2. *Rochester, NY*
3. *Greensboro, NC*
4. *Birmingham, AL*
5. *Syracuse, NY*
6. *Charlotte, NC*
7. *Nashville, TN*
8. *Eugene, OR*
9. *Wichita, KS*
10. *Richmond, VA*

The least favorable test markets, or cities that least represent American consumers, are:

141. *El Paso, TX*
142. *Columbia, MO*

143. *Tallahassee, FL*
144. *Brownsville, TX*
145. *Provo, UT*
146. *Ocala, FL*
147. *McAllen, TX*
148. *Honolulu, HI*
149. *San Francisco, CA*
150. *New York, NY*

Deciding to Conduct a Test Marketing Campaign

Many factors are important in deciding whether, when, and how to conduct test marketing. Marketing managers must decide whether they have the time and resources to introduce their product in a limited fashion to a subset of the market. Marketing managers might simply decide to launch a product nationally and fix any problems along the way. Perhaps IKEA, the Swedish furniture and house wares superstore (www.ikea.com), decides to introduce a new computer cabinet. IKEA's leadership might conclude that testing the cabinet, coupled with a successful sales history of comparable products, is sufficient to launch the product in all its stores. Many businesses introduce products or services having done more controlled, or lab-related, testing rather than a larger-scale field test that a test marketing campaign represents.

Test marketing can be time consuming, costly, and difficult to execute; it should not be done haphazardly. Marketing managers must commit to the lengthy process of conducting test marketing if it is to be done correctly. However, in some cases a small-scale effort might work. A local bakery might simply bake a few pies and other goodies as samples to be distributed at a widely attended community gathering. In this case, the bakery owner does not really need to do much research, or spend much effort in running this test marketing example. Again, usually full-scale test marketing of major products is time consuming and costly. In some cases, test marketing can be as simple as the baker's situation. Marketing managers must assess their current situation and what they hope to gain from executing a test marketing effort.

In addition to alerting the competition, a key drawback to conducting test marketing is cost. Many different costs are typical to executing a test marketing campaign. As one might expect, the larger the test marketing city is, generally the higher the cost is to run a test marketing effort.

Some typical test marketing costs:

- *Point of purchase materials—brochures, displays, etc.*
- *Product sample giveaways—Tide or Crest in your mailbox, for example.*
- *Local staffing requirements—hiring staff to hand-out samples at the state fair, for example*
- *Media advertisements (TV, radio, Internet, newspaper, etc.) time and exposure level and frequency*
- *Advertising firm to create the marketing materials and advertisements*
- *Event access and registration fees—having a booth at a community event, for example*
- *Staff time to conduct secondary research to identify the appropriate test market city*
- *Travel and setup costs once on-site*
- *Spending time on the test marketing campaign and not on selling existing products*

If businesses decide to test a product or service in a test market environment, they must do secondary data research into the demographics of the proposed city. The demographics of the selected city, or subsection of a city, should closely match the demographics of the desired customer lest the test pool be non-representative of the customer base. In other words, just a population of test subjects will not suffice. Researchers must ensure that the right test subjects are part of the test marketing campaign. Another consideration is the city's infrastructure or ability to execute the test marketing exercise efficiently. Researchers should know a lot about the proposed test market city before launching the experiment. Don't underestimate time and scheduling issues. As a marketing manager, you should have a clear timetable and schedule for executing all aspects of the test marketing campaign. Although the time commitment will vary depending on the complexity of study and the market size, generally six months is a good starting point for the time horizon for conducting a test market study. Additionally, periodic assessments and course corrections will be valuable in controlling extraneous variables while simultaneously making the research more precise.

Key Aspects of a Good Test Market City

It is true to say that the best test market cites have certain characteristics that position them as desirable test market cities. Figure 7.9 highlights a few of these key characteristics.

- **Diverse Media Outlets:**
  - *A variety of media outlets such as TV, radio, and newspaper enables researchers to segment and reach the target test population more effectively and efficiently. Measures of frequency, reach, and impact are most useful in determining how effective the test marketing has been.*
- **Demographically Suitable:**
  - *Again, the test market subjects should be demographically reflective of the targeted customers. It makes little sense to test winter coats in Honolulu.*
- **Compartmentalized Marketplace:**
  - *Marketplaces that are overly connected in tangible ways, such as large metropolitan areas whereby people move and work all over can cause marketplace assessments to get blurred. Remember that test marketing works when there is some control over the test subjects and related environment. If you are testing what Washington, DC people think of a product and you test the respondents during the day, the chances are that many people commuted from Virginia or Maryland thus you are really getting a skewed perspective despite thinking that the test subjects are from Washington. Of course it's impossible to find truly "isolated" cities (nor would researchers really want to), but the point is that researchers should strive to capture who they think*

■ **FIGURE 7.9**

Test Market City Characteristics

they are capturing. Too much overlapping or movement in the marketplace prevents the researcher from fully testing the targeted subjects.

- **Execution Method Flexibility:**
  - *Having the ability to test a product at a mall, then a community event, and then another venue will position the researcher to be able to react to changing circumstances. Multiple media outlets offer more flexibility in getting the message out to the targeted audience. Suppose one execution strategy does not work and there are limited options to change the test market execution. Then the researcher is faced with having to make due with the marketplace limitations.*

Research in Practice

Case:

- Suppose you are the manager of a popular Italian restaurant in the city and you notice a decline in dinner sales. Over the past year there have been changes to the food, parking, pricing, decor, management, and service level. You assume that one of these changes is the culprit in the sales decline but without data you are not sure where to begin.

Assignment:

- Design a true experiment to determine the cause of the sales decline. How would you run the experiment and how can the researcher tell what the possible causes are for the decline in sales?

Chapter Summary

A pillar of causal research is experimental design. Experimental design is the process of testing how independent variables affect, or do not affect, dependent variables. Three criteria are necessary to prove causation. Concomitant variation (a statistical pattern among variables), time order (independent variable change precedes dependent variable change), and systematic elimination (all other possible causal factors have been eliminated). The three main variables associated with causal, or experimental, research are independent, dependent, and extraneous variables. Independent variables are those controlled by the researcher (i.e., price); dependent variables (i.e., customer satisfaction) are those variables researchers hope to change by manipulation of various independent variables, and extraneous variables which, like the weather, are variables not under the control of researchers but should be considered during experimental design creation and execution. Dependent variables are notated by O and independent variables are notated by X. Other types of extraneous variables include regression to the mean, history, selection bias, instrumentation bias, and maturation. There are many ways of controlling for extraneous variables such as matching (pairing like test subjects to alert the researcher to unexpected changes in one of the test subjects), statistical control (adjustments to correct for imbalances in the test subjects), design control (designing the research in a manner that reduces the impact of the extraneous variable(s), and randomization (randomly assigning test subjects to the study). Lab experiments are done in a controlled setting and field experiments are done in an environment less, and in some cases not, under the control of researchers. Internal validity happens when the experiment was executed correctly and without undue internal variability. External validity is the extent to which the results correctly mirror the results of the general population. True experiments differ from pre-experiments in that true experiments have both a control group and a pre- and post-measurement of the dependent variables under experimentation.

A control group is an experimental group whereby there is no change to the independent variables associated with the experiment. There are several advantages to running an experiment, including the ability to determine the cause-and-effect relationship between variables, providing insight as to the effectiveness of marketing decisions, and giving business leadership the ability to incrementally launch new products, test their effectiveness, and make changes as needed. Cost, time, misapplied results, and alerting potential competitors are some disadvantages to running an experiment. Test markets are places where marketing researchers test products directly in the marketplace to determine how well a given product or service is received by customers. Good test marketing cities are microcosms of the target population. Running an experiment in a test market is an effective way for marketing researchers to try a product in a small setting before the financial risk of launching the product on a large scale. One disadvantage to running a test market campaign is that the exposure might alert your competition to your plans.

Measurement and Scaling

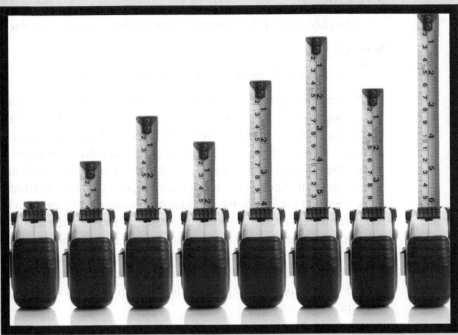

Image © Brian A. Jackson, 2011. Used under license from Shutterstock, Inc.

Learning Objectives:

- Understand how measurement is used in quantitative research
- Understand the four characteristics of data: *description, order, distance,* and *origin*
- Learn about the four data levels: *nominal, ordinal, interval,* and *ratio*

- Appreciate the uses of different data levels in decision making
- Understand the types and uses of comparative and non-comparative scales
- Learn the difference, and pros and cons, between forced and non-forced scales

- Learn about the uses of balanced and unbalanced scales
- Appreciate the impact of stability in the results during survey execution
- Understand the importance of reliability and validity in marketing research

As we have learned, secondary research leads to primary research. In order to be an effective interviewer or focus group moderator, the researcher has to have done extensive secondary, or background, related work. Once the researcher has conducted interviews and run some focus groups, developing a questionnaire is a logical next step in the marketing research process. Transitioning to questionnaire design requires an understanding of measurement and scaling.

Measurement and Scaling

Measurement:

- *Applying rules and assigning values to characteristics of objects or concepts.*

Scaling:

- *A continuum where measurement values are located.*

When a questionnaire is developed, a set of scales and related measurements are assigned to each question. Marketing researchers use these measurements during the statistical analysis research phase to transform data into information. Measures must be uniformly applied for each respective element. For example, if we are measuring a college track race and comparing how well students from one school performed compared to another school, we must measure using the same track event and time used. We would not compare a 100-yard dash to a 500-yard relay as equivalent events. We must compare the 100-yard dash from each respective university in order to generate meaningful and comparable results. The hackneyed expression of not "comparing apples and oranges" is applicable here. Scaling helps researchers to fully quantify the respective measurement. With scales, we assign numbers to values, enabling researchers to run a variety of statistical analyses on the data.

Types of Scales

Marketing has the four Ps (price, product, promotion, and place). Marketing research and statistics have, in ascending levels of sophistication, four levels of measurement: nominal, ordinal, interval, and ratio (NOIR). Any data example fits into one of these levels. Using a variety of these data types will maximize your data analysis options. A questionnaire limited to nominal or ordinal data only will not enable the researcher to conduct sophisticated data analysis. The more sophisticated

■ **FIGURE 8.1**

Measurement and Scaling
Enables Marketing
Researchers to Quantify
Data for Use in Analysis

the data are (ratio) the more information researchers have to make more informed decisions. All data are either nominal, ordinal, interval, or ratio. Futility reigns when trying to memorize which data are what level. In fact, it's not necessary. Researchers simply know the **four characteristics of data** and then apply whatever data confronts them against the four characteristics, and the answer will reveal itself. When assessing data, researchers first determine whether the data are descriptive (all data starts there), and then whether the data have order, then distance, and finally origin. Researchers work their way up the data characteristic chain to determine what level of data are present. Understanding these data levels is critical as the data level has an impact on the type of data analysis researchers can conduct. Nominal data are the least sophisticated type of data, then ordinal, then interval, and finally ratio. More sophisticated analysis is possible with higher-level data. A survey of only nominal or ordinal data limits the analysis options and sophistication available to the data analysis research team. The four data characteristics are shown in Figure 8.2.

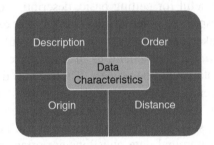

■ FIGURE 8.2

Four Characteristics of Data

The Four Characteristics of Data

Description:

- *The data are only descriptive. For example, when you think of car, computer, or doorknob, you have an instant image, or description, in your mind as to those objects. You know what they mean, but not how they are related to each other.*

Order:

- *Order refers to when there is a natural order to the data. For example, if you came in second in a three-person race, you know immediately that someone was in front of you and someone was behind you when completing the race. Order helps to frame data in a logical, sequential way.*

Distance:

- *Distance helps researchers determine the level of magnitude of the data order. For example, if you are given three colors—red, blue, green—and asked to put the colors in order of preference and you select green, blue, red—researchers know which you like best, but not by "how much." Suppose green and blue are essentially tied, but you really don't like red. Rating each color from 1 to 5 enables researchers to see how "far apart" each response is from the other choices.*

Origin:

- *Origin provides an anchor to the data. Suppose you read about someone having her 100th birthday party. You know in your mind how old that person might look—not just because she is 100 but because the 100 is anchored at 0. If someone is 50, you know they are half as old as this centenarian. The 0 provides a frame of reference.*

Now let's apply our understanding of the four data characteristics, shown in Figure 8.2, to the four levels of data: nominal, ordinal, interval, and ratio, in Figure 8.3.

Four Data Levels

Nominal Data

- *Mutually exclusive data that are categorical and descriptive only where there is no natural order to the data.*
- Nominal data are useful for getting basic, descriptive data. Only one code is assigned to each respective nominal data element. For example, if our nominal data are butcher, baker, and candlestick maker, we would assign a **code**, *a number representing each data element*, to each response. Researchers use these codes during the data tabulation process. These codes do not represent any related value of the nominal data element. For example, "butcher" could be code 1, 2, or 3. However, the code used for each data element must be consistent.
- When constructing surveys, it is often easier to ask nominal questions than other data types as nominal data questions are often less specific than other data types. Researchers should avoid this temptation as nominal only (or mostly only) surveys result in limited analysis options.
  - Nominal data examples: red, car, hotel, yes/no, gender, occupation, Paris, smartphone, pillow
  - Stand-alone nouns are nominal data.
  - Some types of analysis:
    - Cross tabulation, sums, frequency counts, and chi square.

Ordinal Data

- *Data with nominal characteristics plus demonstrating relative order to the data yet not the magnitude of that order.*
- Ordinal data are *ranking* questions, whereas interval data are *rating* scales. Ordinal rankings are very common in measuring customer satisfaction, agreement

■ **FIGURE 8.3**
Four Data Levels

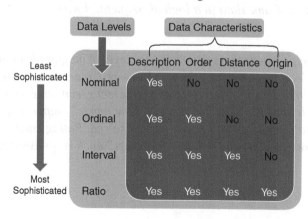

Data Levels	Description	Order	Distance	Origin
Nominal	Yes	No	No	No
Ordinal	Yes	Yes	No	No
Interval	Yes	Yes	Yes	No
Ratio	Yes	Yes	Yes	Yes

Least Sophisticated → Most Sophisticated

levels or importance type issues. These rankings establish relative data order which is very useful in describing how variables are related to each other.

- Ordinal data examples: first, second, third; small, medium, large; win, place, show
- Some types of analysis:
  - Cross tabulation, rankings, sums, and frequency counts
- Suppose you are asked to rank three ice-cream flavors—chocolate, vanilla, and strawberry—and you rank them as: 1) chocolate, 2) vanilla, and 3) strawberry. Perhaps you really love chocolate and vanilla, but really don't particularly like strawberry but, because it's last on the list, you rank strawberry third. Ordinal data does not enable researchers to understand how *far apart* the rankings are.

Interval Data

- *Data with nominal and ordinal characteristics plus demonstrating a measurable and equal distance between responses.*
- Interval data requires respondents to give more specific responses to questions. This data has various pros and cons. An advantage to specificity is that researchers will be able to conduct more precise statistical analyses on respondents' true feelings and opinions. The downside is that some respondents might not feel comfortable divulging such detailed information about their opinions. For example, consider providing feedback on your boss. If the questions were nominal and you were asked "would you rate him the best boss you have had," responding "no" is not necessarily negative as he might be a great boss but not the *"best."* An ordinal ranking of this issue requires more thought. "Of your past three bosses, rate your boss as the 1st, 2nd, or 3rd best boss." Again, even a three ranking might not be that negative if you have had many bosses. Consider an interval question. "Rate your boss from 1 to 10, 10 being the best." Now you are forced to reveal more clearly your true feelings about your boss. Interval data yields more quantifiable results than do nominal or ordinal data. However, the risks involve respondents either not answering the question or "fudging" their responses.
  - Interval data examples: on a scale of 1 to 10, temperature readings, and dates
  - Some types of analysis:
    - Correlation analysis, some cross tabulation, sums, frequency counts, some descriptive statistics (mean, median, mode, standard deviation), ANOVA, and correlation.

- *Let's revisit the ice-cream scenario. If you are asked to rate each ice-cream flavor from 1 (don't like) to 5 (like) and you rate chocolate a 5, vanilla a 4, and strawberry a 1, you have replicated the ordinal ranking but now you have added distance between the rankings revealing that, despite the potential misdirection of the ordinal data, you really don't like strawberry ice cream.*
- *Interval data adds a level of sophistication beyond ordinal data.*

Ratio Data

- *Numeric data with nominal, ordinal, and interval characteristics plus demonstrating a relation to zero.*
- Collecting ratio data can be a challenge. Remember that ratio data are numeric so there is an inherent level of specify to ratio data. Good ratio data tells the researcher much about the data in question because it's the most quantifiable data type. Consider this example. Suppose you are doing a research project measuring customer satisfaction at the business where you work. You gather 1,000 customer surveys asking various questions regarding their service experience. One question you ask is about age. You decide to ask age as a range: 20–30, 31–40, etc. This approach seems harmless enough. You now conduct the data analysis and submit the research report to your boss, who says he is most interested in how customers responded to the questions based on age. Because "age" was a question on the questionnaire you feel confident that you can answer the questions about age that your boss has posed. Now your boss begins asking you questions about the data. Firstly, he says he wants to know the average age of his customers, a basic starting question. How would you handle this question given that you asked the data on age based on interval, not ratio, data? You can tell him, for example, that 15 percent of the respondents were between the ages of 20 and 30, and that 43 percent were between 31 and 40 years old and so on. The trouble here is that those numbers are not averages; they are percentages ascribed to a range of age data. An average is one number. The way you asked data on the questionnaire (in interval ranges) now prevents you from providing the analysis your boss wants. He simply wants to know the average age of his customers. Not asking age as a ratio question has prevented you from reporting the results in an actionable way for your boss in this case. It is important to understand what you need or want to do with the data and the types of data analysis you want to run before creating the questionnaire. Selecting the right question for the data analysis required is critical.
- There are two primary pitfalls to asking ratio data:
  - Respondent's *inability* to recall accurately the information:
    - Because ratio data are numeric, asking someone how much TV they watched last month would be impossible to answer correctly without having kept a TV viewing log of some type. Respondents might be able to say that they had watched *more or less* than X amount, but would not be able to provide you with a *specific* number as required by ratio data. In other words, you are asking them to provide a certain level of specificity when only generalities will be remembered.
  - Respondent's *unwillingness* to answer:
    - Back to our age discussion. Asking age as a ratio data question can be perilous. Although getting precise numeric data is useful, some respondents do not want to provide that level of detail. Respondents might feel more comfortable answering age from an age range. So their unwillingness

■ **FIGURE 8.5**
Ratio Data are the Most Sophisticated Data and are Numeric With a Meaningful Zero

Image © Oria, 2011. Used under license from Shutterstock, Inc.

to answer might cause respondents to either skip the ratio question (the dreaded refusal) or *intentionally* provide an incorrect answer (i.e., saying they are 48 years old when they are really 52).

- Pre-testing the questionnaire in a focus group, or as a pre-test (conducting a small number of surveys before starting the full interviewing, just to test the questions), will help the researcher decide the most acceptable way to ask sensitive or complicated ratio data questions.
- Ratio data
  - Ratio data examples: age, weight, miles per gallon, number of people at a sporting event, or the time left on the "shot clock"
  - Some types of analysis:
    - Correlation analysis, descriptive statistics (mean, median, mode, standard deviation, kurtosis, skewness), rank and percentile, hypothesis testing, Analysis of Variance, conjoint analysis, and multiple regression.
  - Ratio data adds sophistication to the data. Suppose you are in a race and you finish third among 100 runners. One might assume that this placement is quite good based on this ordinal ranking. However, let's look at the ratio data. The first runner finishes in 5 minutes, runner two completes the race in 5 minutes 10 seconds, and you finish the race at 20 minutes with the remaining 97 runners right behind you at 20 minutes and 1 second. In this case, finishing third is essentially no better than the rest of the 97 laggards. Ratio data enables researchers to add precision and specificity to data.

Data and Decision Making

Generally, higher-level data enables more detailed and precise analysis options. This construct is the case even in seemingly simple decisions. Let's look at a practical example where you might use an ever-increasing level of data to make a decision. After you graduate from college you will begin a career. Let's assume that you are in such high demand that you receive several job offers and you subsequently weigh the pros and cons of each opportunity. You finally decide to pursue the engineering position with a prestigious architecture firm. There will be several points to negotiate such as work schedule, travel requirements, vacation time, and, of course, salary. How will you negotiate salary? Presumably, you will ask how much the position pays. Here is the possible conversation flow and the impact of data level on your decision making process:

Question 1:

- You: "What is the salary for this position?"
- Company: "Commensurate with experience" *(nominal data response)*
  - Will you accept the job? Did the company give you enough data to make a decision? Probably not, you would likely ask for more specificity.

Question 2:

- You: "How much is that?"
- Company: "Well, you will be in pay category B, where A is the highest salary category and C is the lowest category." *(ordinal data response)*
  - Will you accept the job? Again, probably not. Although they have given you more information about how the salary relates to other salaries, the salary data is still not specific enough.

Question 3:

- You: "OK, can you be a bit more specific?"
- Company: "Sure, you will be paid a 4 on a scale of 1 to 5 where 5 is the highest salary grade in the company. A 4 is between $80K–$90K." *(interval data response)*
  - Will you accept the job? At the interval level where you are given a scale with equal intervals (and the scale might in turn represent dollar value ranges), you might then decide whether to accept the job, particularly if the interval range is narrow. For example, suppose the salary offer had been between $80K–$85K. Given that the range is only $5K, that small amount might not be a "deal breaker." Perhaps you reject the job because even the top range is not high enough. Or perhaps you will accept the job because even at the lowest level you are thrilled to earn $80K. Interval data provide more information from which to make a decision, but not necessarily enough information for everyone.

Question 4:

- You: "Can you tell me the exact salary?"("exact" implies ratio data)
- Company: "The pay is $92,500." *(ratio data response)*
  - In this case, you have all the salary information. You will now be able to decide whether to take the job (assuming salary was the last issue to be resolved). Ratio data provide the most specific level of data.

You can see from this admittedly simple scenario that even if you are not aware of the data progression, you are continuing to request increasingly sophisticated data (from nominal to ratio) because you need higher-level and more precise data to make a decision. Although sometimes appropriate to the project, imagine trying to make complex marketing or business decisions with only nominal or ordinal-level data. Decisions such as how the product should be designed, promoted, priced, and distributed (the beloved 4 Ps again) are best made with the most precise data. The main take away here is that generally higher-level data provide the most precise information from which to make a decision. However, it's possible that lower-level data are sufficient.

It's important to know what the impact on or consequence to the research the level of data will have before the questionnaire is finalized.

In many cases, data are reported multiple ways. Take a look at the list of the world's busiest airports in Figure 8.6 as reported by the U.S. government. On the left, the airports are listed as ordinal data. On the right, we see the passenger data. The ordinal data are sorted based on the ratio data on the right.

Converting Data from Ratio to Nominal

One of the true advantages of ratio data is that ratio data can be converted to lower-level data, whereas the reverse is not the case. Take age as a ratio data point. If we have a list of ages as ratio data, we can convert them to interval ranges, ordinal rankings, or nominal descriptors. However, we cannot reverse this technique. Figure 8.7 depicts this concept.

■ FIGURE 8.7
Converting Data

Converting Data

Ratio	Interval	Ordinal	Nominal
20			
44			
67			
54	20–30		
23	31–40	Generation X	
45	41–50	Generation Y	Older than 40?
43	51–60	Baby Boomer	
45	61–70	Etc.	
67	71–80		
21	81–90		
23			
45	If ratio data are given, researchers can resort the		
67	data to create interval, ordinal, or nominal data.		
87			

Converting Data from Ratio to Nominal

Comparative vs. Non-Comparative Scales

Deciding whether to use comparative or non-comparative scales is a critical part of the questionnaire design process as that decision will drive how the questions are written. Figure 8.8 summarizes the differences between comparative and non-comparative scales.

Comparative Scales

- *Ordinal scales where data are ranked based on which data items are in the choice set.*
  - Example: Put these cities in order of most to least preferred as a vacation destination: Paris, London, or Rome. Your answer to this question will be based on which cities are on the list. Suppose London is first, then Paris, and then Rome. However, had Madrid been on the list, Madrid would have been first and London second.
  - Comparative scales give the researcher information on how items on the response set relate to each other but it does not account for items *not* on the list.
  - Comparative scales do not allow for ties as the respondent has to put the choices in order. Thus this process forces respondents to choose even if they really feel some of the choices are equal.

Non-Comparative Scales

- *Interval scales where data are rated independently of the other data items on the choice set.*
  - Example: Which cities would you like to visit?

	Not Like		□		Like
• Paris	1	2	**3**	4̲	5
• London	1	2	3̲	**4**	5
• Rome	1	2	**3**	4	5

- Non-Comparative scales reveal how respondents rate *each* item independent of other items on the response set.
- Non-comparative scales help to identify *ties* (that are not revealed in ordinal comparative scales).
- In the example above, Paris and Rome tied and London, although rated higher than Paris or Rome, still only rated a 4 on a 5-point scale. This rating should alert the researcher that there might be a city not on the list that should have been included because the top choice (London) did not score a 5.

■ FIGURE 8.8
Scale Types

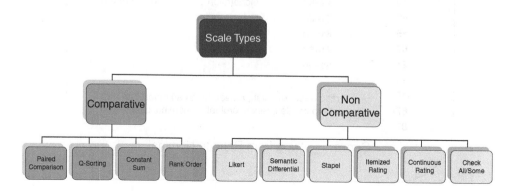

Types of Comparative and Non-Comparative Scales

Comparative Scales

- **Paired Comparison:**
  - These scales pit two items against each other and ask the respondent to put them in order of preference. Results might vary when pairing two items together rather than comparing three or more. Take a survey on soda preferences. Researchers might ask respondents to rate their preferences of Coke, Pepsi, and Sprite; all three together. However, when rephrasing the question by pairing items, results might vary as there is now a "head-to-head" contest. Figure 8.9 provides an example of this technique.
  - Let's look at another example. During the U.S. presidential election every four years there are typically a series of debates. When there are two candidates debating, the post-debate analysis focuses on "who won." With three or more candidates, the analysis centers on who did well and who did not. When there are three or more candidates, it's less likely that one person will have "won" as her performance, good or bad, will be somewhat diluted when there are three candidates.
  - Paired comparisons help to isolate and focus opinions as there are fewer options.
  - Sometimes called the *paired choice analysis*.

■ **FIGURE 8.9**
Head-to-head Contest

- **Q-Sorting:**
  - Q-sorting shown in Figure 8.10, developed by British psychologist and physicist William Stephenson in 1953 while teaching at the University of Chicago, is an effective way to reach a consensus. Suppose you run a computer repair company of 100 employees. It's time for your annual holiday party at a local restaurant. In an effort to select the restaurant that appeals to most people, you decide to do a Q-sort. Although the numbers below are for illustrative purposes only and each situation as well as the number of rounds will be different, here is how the process might unfold using our scenario above:
    - **Round 1:**
      - In an open-ended fashion, employees are asked to write down their top three (or X number of) restaurant choices, which produces potentially 300 different restaurants. However, because some employees named the same restaurant, in this case there are only 80 different restaurants named among the top three listed from each of the 100 employees.
    - **Round 2:**
      - Researchers take the 80 restaurant choices and winnow-down the list to say 10 restaurants. Why 10? Perhaps researchers decided to drop any restaurants not listed by at least "X" number of respondents. Now

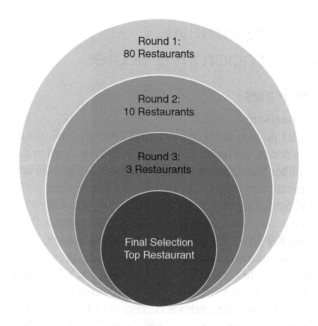

researchers take the list of 10 (a controlled list now) and resubmit the list to the employees and ask them to again rank their top three choices, but this time from the controlled list.

- **Round 3:**
  - Repeating the process of Round 2 yields the three (or X) most commonly selected restaurants.
- **Round 4**:
  - Now researchers ask the employees to select their *top* restaurant from the list now presented to them and a winner is selected.
- Q-sorting ultimately produces results that are the most acceptable to the largest number of respondents while simultaneously being the least objectionable to the most respondents.
- The name "Q" is the form of factor analysis that is used to analyze the data.
- The number of rounds and choices presented to respondents depends on the initial data collected. Researchers have to use their judgment in determining how many items make the progressively winnowed-down list.
- **Constant Sum:**
  - This type of scale is a comparative ratio scale whereby respondents ascribe a number (relative to zero) to items on a list based on total allowable points.
  - If respondents are asked to list all the features they want on their new car, they will list everything. A constant sum scale gives the respondent a "point budget" that they have to manage—in this case 100 points and five choices. Respondents must give points to items on the list based on what else is on the list. This method forces respondents to be more thoughtful about their choices.
  - Researchers who use constant sum scales should avoid having too many choices. If respondents are faced with 10 choices, distinguishing among the 10 becomes complicated, rendering it difficult for respondents to truly differentiate their likes and dislikes.
  - Also of note, avoid an awkward point total. A point total of 100, or 50, or 25 is relative easy for respondents to digest. If respondents are given several choices and a point total of 64, there will likely be a number of math errors, particularly if the survey is completed by hand and not controlled through a web-based survey that can be programmed to catch miscalculations.

- Finally, make sure the instructions are clear, otherwise respondents might *rate each* item from 1 to 100, rather than understanding that the total of *all* items should be 100.
- Figure 8.11 depicts a ratio comparative scale.

Most Desired Car Feature:
_____

Rear Seat TVs	_____
Navigation	_____
ABS Breaks	_____
Heated Seats	_____
All Wheel Drive	_____

Total Points: **100**

■ **FIGURE 8.11**
Most Desired Car Feature

- **Rank Order:**
  - These scales ask respondents to sort the items presented in a question in an order based on an established criteria. Unlike constant sum scales, there are no number assignments to each choice, just a simple order of items to be ranked based on preference.
  - Rank-order scales work well in determining respondents' preferences, as they relate to each respective item on the scale.
  - The number of items on these scales should generally not exceed six. If respondents are given a dozen choices to sort in order, the top few and bottom few will be relatively easy for respondents to select. However, the choices in the middle will be muddled.
  - If there are more than six items you want to rank, perhaps group the items into categories and submit two or more lists to respondents to rank.
  - Figure 8.12 depicts an ordinal comparative scale.

■ **FIGURE 8.12**
Favorite Car
Color

Non-Comparative Scales

- **Likert:**
  - Named after American psychologist and educator Rensis Likert.
  - Likert scales measure the level of *agreement or disagreement* to various questions.

- Often these scales are from 1 to 5 but have also been used on other scales such as 1 to 4, 1 to 6, or 1 to 10 scales. Generally, if the instructions are clear, there is little impact to having the "agree" (or whatever the positive descriptor is) as the 1 as opposed to having the "agree" as the 5 on the scale.
- Sometimes scales are labeled as "strongly agree" and "strongly disagree" as opposed to simply agree/disagree. A limitation of using the term *strongly* is that it is a very definitive rating for a small (five-point) scale. When using larger scales such as 1 to 10, respondents have more "room" on the scale to offer varied options. When using "strongly" on a five-point scale, other than the neutral 3 option, respondents have no option to "somewhat agree" because the 4 on the scale is "agree." There is no correct way per se, there are just implications to selecting the scale level and descriptors of the scale numbers.
- Likert scales are very common. Because respondents generally understand the Likert scales, researchers often use them.
- Figure 8.13 depicts a Likert Scale.

■ **FIGURE 8.13**
Sample Likert Scale

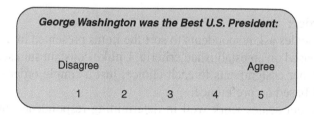

- **Semantic Differential:**
  - Like the name reveals, respondents are given a *paired set* of opposite words and are asked to rate the differences based on the meanings of the choices given.
  - These scales force respondents to make choices based on opposite meanings.
  - Oftentimes researchers include a list of questions related to one issue rated on a semantic differential scale in order to create a comprehensive picture of the issue at hand.
  - A challenge with semantic differential scales is quantifying the results, as often there is a line or blanks separating the choices, as opposed to numbers representing respondents' choices that can be used quantitatively.
  - These types of scales might well have numbers, a line, or radio buttons between descriptors. Be aware—if a line is used between the endpoints, quantifying the results will be difficult and not fully precise.
  - For example, in order to gauge customer opinions, your local dry cleaner decides to conduct a survey using semantic differential questions.
  - Figure 8.14 shows a semantic differential scale.

■ **FIGURE 8.14**
Sample of Semantic Differential Scale

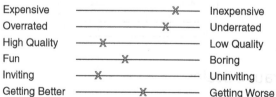

- **Stapel:**
  - Named after Jan Stapel, this usually 10-point scale places the research issue at the center and asks respondents to rate their opinion "around" the centered

item. These scales help respondents view the item more neutrally given that the rated item is at the center of the scale.

- These scales are typically depicted vertically.
- Current usage involves scale lengths other than 10.
- If a store manager wants to determine whether customers feel that the sales staff is helpful a Stapel scale might be used to capture this information.
- Figure 8.15 shows a Stapel Scale with the measured item centered around endpoints.

Please rate the staff:

+5
+4
+3
+2
+1
Helpful
-1
-2
-3
-4
-5

■ **FIGURE 8.15**
Stapel Scale

- **Itemized Rating:**
  - Giving the flexibility of scale length, these scales enable researchers to capture a wide variation of opinions.
  - Theses scales range from 1 to 4 through 10 and rate agreement (a Likert scale), importance, satisfaction, etc. Researchers can essentially rate anything on an itemized rating scale.
  - Typically these scales begin with 1 rather than 0—although some do begin with 0.
  - There is no correct or incorrect scale length. Picking the scale length is up to the researcher and those sponsoring the research. Selecting the scale length is a judgment call. Generally, the more diversity of opinions among your audience, the larger the scale should be to capture the nuances of those differences. If your focus groups revealed that respondent opinions are not that different, perhaps a small scale will capture all relevant opinions.
  - Much research has been done on the impact of scales. If there is no difference in which scale is used, one might expect that for two *equally randomly selected samples* if the average score on a 1 to 5 scale was 3, then the average score on a 1 to 7 scale should be 4. This result is not always the case. In some cases the scale itself can skew results. Researchers must take great care in selecting the right scale for their respective situation and sample base.
  - One of the key drivers in selecting the right scale is how much the researcher knows about the population. Greater opinion diversity might necessitate a larger scale.
- **Continuous Rating**—*sometimes called sliding scales:*
  - These scales are similar to itemized rating scales except the respondents are given a continuum—solid line—to mark their answer. This type of scale allows the respondent the freedom to mark any point on the scale, as opposed to forcing the respondent to select a particular number on the scale.
  - A drawback to these scales is in trying to quantify the results.
  - Sometimes these scales are used in a focus group to gauge general opinions and attitudes which are then examined in the focus group discussion.

- Figure 8.16 shows a continuous rating scale. Again, quantifying scales with lines between the endpoints is difficult.

■ **FIGURE 8.16**

Sample of Continuous Rating Scale

Was your recent car purchase a good or bad value?

Good Value ———————X——————————— Bad Value

- **Check All/Some:**
  - These scales ask respondents to check as many items that apply on the offered list. A variation of these scales is to limit the choices to perhaps picking two or three from a list. "Check all that apply" scales can be problematic. When faced with a "wish list" versus factual list, check all that apply can be unwieldy, leaving the researcher with little solid data. Let's look at an example.
  - Figure 8.17 shows a "check all that apply" type scale.
  - Under scenario A, respondents can select all that apply. Generally these types of questions have positive choices. Researchers would not include negative choices on the list such as a "bad boss" as no one would select that option. "Wish lists" are when respondents are asked what they "would like, or want" as opposed to gleaning facts such as what they actually have or have done. Respondents will simply check all choices because the options are positive and there is no limitation on how many items they can select. The researcher will be faced with respondents who want everything. Researchers will not be able to determine which items on the list are the most preferred. Under scenario B, respondents have to decide their top choices, which reveals more about the items that are most preferred. Using a factual list, such as "what features *do you have* on your car?" will yield more precise information than a wish list question such as "what features *would* you like on your new car?"
  - Remember that "check all that apply" works well when the questions are fact based. When asking respondents what they "would like" it might be better to limit the number of items they can choose.

■ **FIGURE 8.17**

Sample of Check All/ Some Scales

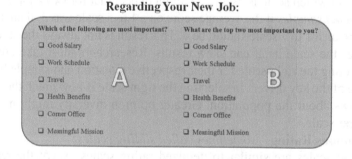

- **Balanced Scales:**
  - Balanced scales, as depicted in Figure 8.18, have an equal number of positive and negative choices in the response set.

Balanced vs. Unbalanced Scales

```
┌──────────────────────────────────────────────────────────────────────┐
│  Keep the coach: (balanced scale – choices not skewed)                 │
│                                                                        │
│                                                                        │
│  Disagree      Somewhat Disagree   Neither A/D   Somewhat Agree   Agree │
│     1                 2                 3              4            5    │
└──────────────────────────────────────────────────────────────────────┘
```

■ FIGURE 8.18
Balanced Scale

```
┌──────────────────────────────────────────────────────────────────────┐
│  Keep the coach: (unbalanced scale – choices skew positive)            │
│                                                                        │
│                                                                        │
│  Disagree      Somewhat Disagree     Agree     Somewhat Agree   Agree   │
│     1                 2                 3              4            5    │
└──────────────────────────────────────────────────────────────────────┘
```

■ FIGURE 8.19
Unbalanced Scale

- **Unbalanced Scales:**
  - Unbalanced scales, as shown in Figure 8.19, have more positive or more negative choices.
  - It is acceptable to use unbalanced scales provided they are done for a legitimate reason and that the nature of the scales is disclosed and explained as part of the *research methods* section of the research paper.
  - What constitutes a "legitimate reason" is debatable, but suppose your college basketball team made it to the NCAA Finals before losing to Carolina. The university then decides to conduct a student survey to gauge student support for the coach. Because the team had a good season, it stands to reason that the survey results would skew positive. In other words, many more students are likely to say keep the coach than fire the coach. In this example, an unbalanced scale would have more positive choices than negative choices to capture the gradations in the positive feelings about the coach.

Forced vs. Non-Forced Scales

- **Forced** scales have an even number of choices, thus forcing respondents to reveal an opinion because there is no "neutral" option. **Non-forced** scales have an odd number of responses, which allows for a "neutral" midpoint option. Figure 8.20 shows the difference between a forced and a non-forced scale.
- Deciding whether to use a forced or non-forced scale depends on what the researcher hopes to accomplish with the question. Researchers and research sponsors want the survey to reflect the respondents' true attitudes and beliefs as accurately as possible. For divisive or sensitive issues the researcher might want to force respondents "off the fence" as it's unlikely they don't have an opinion as reflected by a neutral response on an odd scale. However, for more general and less controversial topics respondents might truly have a neutral opinion and thus a non-forced scale might be better. The deciding factor is what you know about your audience and what you hope to accomplish with the survey. If during your focus group part of the research you determine that opinions are strong, why give the respondents a "safe out" by giving them a non-forced answer set? However, if your focus groups reveal that people are ambivalent towards the issue at hand, why force (by not having a neutral option offered on an odd scale) them to have an opinion through a forced scale?
- Neither forced nor non-forced scales is more correct. Researchers should just be aware of the impact of choosing one type over the other.

Forced Scale : (even number of choices)

Unimportant			Important
1	2	3	4

Non-forced Scale: (odd number of choices)

Unimportant				Important
1	2	3	4	5

- Finally, when using non-forced scales, be careful in *labeling* the middle value. Terms like *neutral, average*, or *no opinion* can be prejudicial. A better term for the 3 on a 1 to 5 "agree" to "disagree" scaled question might be "neither agree nor disagree."

Reliability and Validity

Reliability and validity are two critical issues in marketing research that must be addressed when assessing the quality of a marketing research study.

- **Reliability:**
  - *Reliability is the extent to which the survey responses are internally consistent and that researchers get the same result with repeat measurements.*
    - For example, on a survey if a respondent says that he does not have a car and later in the same survey he says that he owns a Ford Mustang, the respondent has given conflicting information within the same survey. Only one response can be true.
- **Validity:**
  - *Validity measures the extent to which the survey conclusions are a correct reflection of the opinions of the targeted general population.*
    - For example, if 65 percent of our survey respondents said they will vote for candidate Jones, then we would expect that 65 percent of *all voters* would vote for candidate Jones when the election occurs. If in fact only 50 percent voted for candidate Jones on Election Day, then the *survey conclusions* about the *general population* were proven invalid by the *actual* election results.
    - Researchers only know validly for certain if the whole population under study weighs-in on the survey results. When we see survey responses before elections, we only know whether the survey results are valid once the election occurs and the whole population has voted. The population vote is compared to the survey results. This delta will reveal how valid the survey results were and how good a predictor the survey results were of the general population.
    - Figure 8.21 shows a comparative view between reliability and validity.

Assessing reliability and validity inform the researcher of the level of **measurement error.** Measuring reliability can be done more quantitatively than measuring validity can be. Many measures of validity often require some researcher judgment component.

- *Measurement error, as seen in Figure 8.22, is the total difference between what the researcher tries to measure and what is actually measured.*

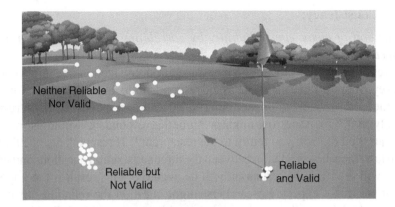

■ **FIGURE 8.21**
Reliability and Validity

© Matthew Cole, 2012. Used under license from Shutterstock, Inc.

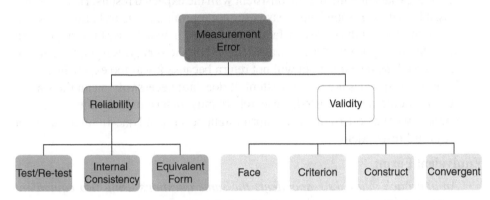

■ **FIGURE 8.22**
Measurement Error

Dealing with Measurement Error

Reliability

Test/Retest:

- *This method involves testing respondents more than once, asking them the same questions to gauge whether they give the same response.*
- One issue associated with this technique is the time between measurements. If respondents give different answers to the same questions over time, researchers might conclude that the respondents are giving inconsistent answers and thus their results are unreliable. If respondents are asked questions about where they were born; inconsistent answers would show that their responses are unreliable since their answers should not change over time. But suppose the questions are related to the type of job they have, or their favorite movie, or any illness they have. It's quite possible that over time respondents' situations might have in fact changed and thus different answers to the same questions might in fact be correct.
- An offshoot of this approach is asking about the same information but in a slightly different way. Myers-Briggs (www.myersbriggs.org) personality tests take this approach. Respondents are asked questions about their personality preferences and re-asked the same type questions in a different way to see if they give consistent answers.
- The next time you watch a courtroom drama, pay attention to the cross-examination scenes. What are the lawyers trying to do during cross-examination? They are attempting to discredit witnesses by showing that the witnesses are giving inconsistent answers to various questions that in some cases they have already been asked through a written, pre trial, questionnaire. If witnesses give inconsistent answers the second time, their reliability, or trustworthiness, is challenged. Lawyers are testing and retesting witnesses based on various facts.

Internal Consistency:

- *A method of measuring reliability by correlating responses to confirm presumed relationships.*
- If a restaurant manager wants to measure patron satisfaction, she might conduct a survey. Suppose three questions asked respondents to rate their satisfaction regarding the food, service, and location on a 1-to-10 scale. If respondents rate the restaurant highly on all three issues, one might presume that respondents would also rate highly the question of "will you return to the restaurant?" If respondents rate that question low, then the correlation between the three satisfaction questions and whether they will return to the restaurant will be negative. This result is the opposite of what we might expect. Researchers might question the reliability of these responses by labeling them as inconsistent with the expected results. However, it's possible that the respondents' reason for not returning to the restaurant was tied to "price" and not the three satisfaction questions. In which case the real problem with this survey is that "price" was not asked on the survey. Respondents might have loved the restaurant but will not return because it was too expensive.
- If survey responses are not consistent, it does not necessarily mean the survey results should not be trusted. Researchers must determine why the survey responses were inconsistent. The culprit might be a flawed questionnaire and not wayward respondents.

Equivalent Form:

- *An approach that asks respondents the same questions using two equivalent methods to measure question response consistency.*
- If 100 students are taking an exam and 50 get test version A and 50 get test version B whereby the questions are the same but the question sequence is different, researchers can correlate answers to determine reliability.
- The results are then correlated to determine if the scales measured the same thing.
- Three drawbacks with this method are cost, time, and data collection method bias.
  - **Cost:** *Given that this method involves interviewing respondents more than once, there are costs associated with maintaining the same sample and with executing a second or third survey over time.*
  - **Time:** *Depending on the questions, respondents' opinions can legitimately change over time. Different answers to the same question over time might be acceptable if the respondents' circumstances have changed.*
  - **Data Collection Method Bias:** *Respondents' answers might vary over time due to the data collection method. Suppose the data collection method was an Internet survey the first time and then an interview the second time. Respondents might not respond in the same way based on how the data are collected. Perhaps respondents felt more comfortable being candid on an Internet survey and less so when face to face with an interviewer.*

Validity

Face:

- *A method that relies on a judgment as to whether the research results are expected.*
- A question researchers might ask is whether the results "make sense" or "pass the smell test." Suppose the local power company doubles its rates and customers are surveyed to see if they approve of the rate increase. Not surprisingly, 85 percent of those surveyed oppose the increase. Researchers would conclude that "on the face of it" those results make sense and thus the survey results should be a valid reflection of the total population of power company customers.
- This method requires good researcher judgment.

Criterion:

- *This method measures whether respondents' answers are consistent with a series of criterion related to the issue at hand.*
- When research leader Gallup (www.gallup.org) surveys the public about various political candidates, they establish the difference between "registered" and "likely" voters. This determination is made by asking a series of criterion-related questions to determine if respondents who say they will vote (registered voters) will vote (likely voters). A series of criterion-based questions help researchers to establish who will and who will not vote. Researchers will ask respondents whether they will vote. Those who say "yes" might also be asked additional questions, that help establish that they meet the desired criteria, such as about the last time they voted, whether their spouse voted, whether they know who the candidates are, and where their polling location is, etc. If these registered voters respond negatively to these types of questions, they are not likely to vote even though they *said* they would vote.
- Imagine asking high school students about career choices and 50 percent say they want to be doctors. However, once a series of criterion questions are added, researchers might question the validity of those results. When researchers ask high school students about whether they are willing to commit to ten years of medical school and residency, whether they like hospitals, and about their tolerance for sick people, researchers realize that, although 50 percent of high school students say they want to be doctors, when researchers apply a criterion list to the mix, the number of high school students who are likely to pursue medicine as a career plummets.

Construct:

- *This approach involves assessing whether the respondent fully understands the construct, or concept, being measured.*
- Many researchers assume that if respondents answer survey questions, they understand the questions. This assumption might not be correct. Respondents might not understand the underlying concept or construct associated with the questions—or might think that they understand. This issue is of particular note when doing international or cross-cultural research when words and concepts are translated. For example, in the United States there are generally two verdicts in criminal cases: guilty or not guilty. In some countries there are three possible verdicts: guilty, not guilty, or not proven. For many Americans the concept of "not proven" is difficult to understand correctly. If Americans were taking a survey that addressed these three verdicts, they might guess at what this third verdict means. Guessing on surveys leaves researchers with little confidence that the survey results are valid.

Convergent:

- *A form of construct validity, this method measures whether survey scales positively correlate and whether multiple research methods result in the same conclusion.*
- When measuring aspects of the *same construct* in a survey, researchers look for questions to correlate. When high correlations are found between issues related to the *same construct* convergent validly can be established.
- Researchers might also argue for survey validity based on the convergence of multiple methods finding the same or materially similar results. If a survey reports that 60 percent of its respondents eat out at least once a week, the researcher might argue for convergent validity due to other surveys, secondary

data, or information from the restaurant association that came to the same conclusion. Essentially the researcher is saying that the *convergence* of other research corroborates her findings.

Stability in Survey Execution

Before acting on the survey results, those receiving the survey results should determine over what time period the research was conducted. If the survey was about past aspects of respondents' lives, a survey taken over a number of days or months might be just as stable as a survey that had been done over a few days.

Survey Execution Stability:

- *The extent to which the length of time in executing the survey affects the survey results. This issue is important when the survey respondents at the end of a survey period have been affected by events during the survey execution. These respondents thus have materially different opinions from those who were surveyed at the beginning of the survey period.*
- Take the scenario below asking the public if they support the president's foreign policy. Although most (although mail surveys might) surveys are not taken over 20 days, this example demonstrates the concept. Here are the scenario particulars:
  - **Survey 1**—taken over just four days shows that on average the survey respondents give the president high marks. The responses are relatively stable at 70 percent.
  - **Survey 2**—taken over 20 days shows that support for the president dropped. Perhaps something happened that had a negative impact on people's perceptions. After the 20 days the average support was about 60 percent.
  - Spreading a sample over a long period of time must be revealed and justified in the *research methods* section of the research report.
  - In essence, a sample spread over a long period of time might not be considered one sample representing a snapshot in time, as will be presumed unless explained by the researcher.
  - In fact, many of the people in Survey 2 who supported the president might well have responded differently if they had been surveyed after the 20 days as events during the survey execution period might have affected or "polluted" the survey results.
  - Figure 8.23 compares stability between surveys.

■ **FIGURE 8.23**

Stability Issues in Surveys 1 and 2

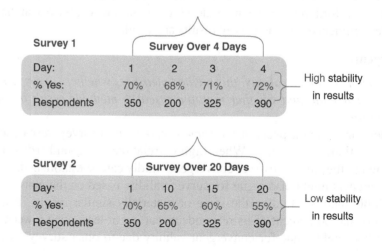

Research in Practice

Case:
- After reporting the survey findings to department store company shareholders, you are challenged on the results because they seem conflicting. Some respondents indicated that they had never shopped at the department store yet they also said that they had returned items to that store.

Assignment:
- Defend the research by demonstrating that you tested your survey for reliability and validity. What combination of reliability and validity tests would you use and why?

Chapter Summary

Quantitative research, in the form of questionnaires, requires an understanding of the data levels and of measurement in general. Measurement is the quantitative way in which marketing researchers add definition and impact to qualitative statements. All data falls into four levels listed in order from least sophisticated be most sophisticated: Nominal ordinal internal, and ratio. The four characteristics that define data levels are description, order, distance, and origin (a relation to zero). Nominal data, such as hotel, green, doctor, and desk, are categorical data that can stand alone in relation to other data. Ordinal data have nominal characteristics but with a natural order to the data such as first, second, and third or small, medium, and large. Interval data have ordinal characteristics with a definable distance between the data elements such as on a scale of 1 to 10. Ratio data (the most sophisticated data level) share all the data characteristics with the added component of a relation to zero. Ratio data are numeric such as age (25), or number of children (3), or hours worked in a given day (8). Comparative scales offer two or more items from which comparisons are made. For example, asking respondents to *rank* colors by placing three colors in order of preference depends on what colors are on the list. Green is listed as the number one color because blue was not on the list. Non-comparative scales enable respondents to *rate* each item, in this case color, individually and thus independently of other items on the list. Types of comparative scales include paired comparison, Q-sorting, constant sum, and rank order. Types of non-comparative scales include Likert, semantic differentiation, Stapel, itemized rating, continuous rating, and check all that apply. Balanced scales are scales with an equal number of positive and negative descriptors. Unbalanced scales have more positive or more negative descriptors on the scale. Forced scales (with no neutral choice) are even scales such as a scale from 1 to 4 and non-forced scales are odd scales (with a neutral choice) such as a scale from 1 to 5. Reliability and validity are critical elements to ensuring the integrity and usefulness of the research. Reliability is the extent to which the survey responses are internally consistent. Respondents who said that they do not have a car and later in the survey state that they own a Ford, indicates unreliability. Validity is the extent to which the survey results are an accurate reflection of what the researcher thinks is being measured and that the results are transferable to the population of interest. There are several ways to check for reliability such as test/retest, internal consistency, and equivalent form. Validity tests include face, criterion, content, and convergent validities.

ISSUE IN THE
SPOTLIGHT Managing a Focus Group Facility—*The View from the Top*

Jay White, CEO
Baltimore Research
www.baltimoreresearch.com

As the CEO of a large focus group facility, I often have a "bird's eye" view of a wide assortment of projects. What makes the view even broader is the large number of industries served. While Qualitative Research may have its roots in Consumer Packaged Goods, focus groups have now become a corporate favorite for those in Politics, Pharmaceuticals, IT, Business to Business, Financial and Automotive Industries. Even the legal profession is weighing-in, as mock trials and jury analysis projects are on the rise.

I attribute the popularity of focus groups to the cross fertilization of career marketers. Executive recruiters encourage their clients to look beyond their respective industry when conducting a search for marketing executives. It is very common for large firms to "cherry pick" marketing talent from a firm in a completely unrelated industry. Naturally, these marketers, many from consumer products, take their research tool box with them. This practice has led to a proliferation of qualitative research across a variety of vertical industries.

I like to tell clients that they cannot make a million dollar decision based solely on the opinions of 12 members of a focus group. Most firms blend results with a variety of qualitative and quantitative methodologies. Rigorous statistical analysis should always be merged with the sensitivities captured in a well-conducted focus group study.

Having been on the client (end user) side of the business only enriches and expands my abilities in the running of a Qualitative House. Naturally, I get to see the proverbial good and not-so-good ways clients view the findings. While not overly common, some clients hear what they want to hear from the targeted audience, and there are times when the decision makers simply proceed with a product or service in spite of what their research (qualitative and quantitative) tells them.

I guess the bottom line is a focus group can either dash a person's dream completely or provide insights that allow marketers to make positive adjustments thus saving time, money and maybe a career or two.

Questionnaire Design

Image © Paperboat, 2011. Used under license from Shutterstock, Inc.

Learning Objectives:

- Understand the questionnaire design steps
- Understand what multidimensional questions are and their importance to research

- Learn about skip patterns, question branching, and coding
- Learn about types of scales and the role of open-ended questions
- Appreciate several key dos and don'ts in writing a questionnaire

- Appreciate the impact of the Internet in survey execution
- Learn about question flow, format, and layout

Chapter Nine

Marketing researchers learn about people through primary research such as focus groups, interviews, observations, experimental design, and questionnaires. Many marketing research projects culminate with a questionnaire that aims to inform researchers as to what the general target population thinks about an issue. The qualitative forms of primary data collection such as interviews, focus groups, observation, and experimental design—tell researchers quite a bit about what the target population *might* be thinking. The sample size for these research methods is often too small to statistically represent the population. Questionnaires, due to the larger sample sizes that typify their collection, are designed to statistically represent the population. Unlike the aforementioned qualitative primary research methods, questionnaires are static because researchers generally do not have the opportunity to change the questions during the questionnaire administration, particularly for Internet or mail-based surveys as these are self-administered. Although the questionnaire design process should be tailored to the specific research situation, the questionnaire design process detailed below is useful for most situations. Although there is general linear progression in the design process, many steps in the questionnaire design process overlap and in fact can be done simultaneously. Figure 9.1 shows the main steps in the questionnaire design process.

Questionnaire Design Process

Survey Objectives

- The survey objectives are derived from what the research sponsor hopes to accomplish and learn from the survey. The objectives might be to simply learn more about the audience on a variety of issues or the objectives might center on a specific business or marketing problem. If the survey objectives are not clear, then the questionnaire might fail to satisfy the research sponsor. Asking a set of random questions will result in a "hodgepodge" of data of marginal use. Once the survey is distributed, it is too late to introduce survey objectives. Researchers who develop surveys without clear input from the survey sponsor risk failing to deliver a useful and actionable research report. The questions should be directly related to the research objectives.

Data Collection Method

- Deciding on the data collection method will have an impact on the types of questions on the questionnaire. Suppose you decide to do a telephone survey. The questionnaire should not be lengthy nor should it be composed of complex scales because respondents have more difficulty visualizing questions that they

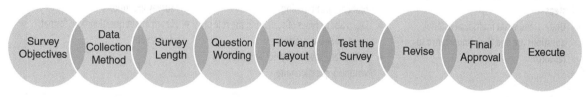

■ **FIGURE 9.1**

Questionnaire Design Process

■ **FIGURE 9.2**
Sometimes
Questionnaires are
Collected Through
One-on-One
Interviews

Image © sellingpix, 2011. Used
under license from Shutterstock, Inc.

hear as opposed to seeing the questions in print. If researchers are collecting the survey through mall intercepts, they can ask more complex questions, provided the interviewers are well trained. Generally, the four most common survey data collection types are telephone, Internet, mail, and in-person.

Determine Survey Length

- Survey length is an important decision to make and is based on time, budget, and burden. If a researcher does not know how long the questionnaire should be, she might well create a questionnaire that is too long or too short.
  - *Time: A survey that is too long might result in high degrees of non-response or cutoffs. A questionnaire with too few questions will limit what is asked while possibly omitting questions critical to the survey sponsor.*
  - *Budget: Longer questionnaires, particularly those with complex questions, take more time to administer and analyze; thus, the survey cost generally rise with its length. Also of note is the cost of pre-testing the questionnaire with focus groups. Longer questionnaires will be more costly to pre-test. Researchers should have a firm understanding of the research project budget.*
  - *Burden: Burden refers to the effort the survey requires of the respondents as well as how invasive the survey is to respondents. The higher the level of respondent involvement, the greater the risk the respondent will not participate in the survey. Surveys that ask respondents invasive or otherwise personal questions can lead to respondents' being less than forthright or refusing to answer outright.*

Question Wording

- Selecting the right words and phrases results from careful attention to respondents' understanding of what the words or phrases mean. In this phase, researchers must be very careful to select the questions that will elicit the types of answers they want. As we saw with reliability and validity, it's possible that researchers will get reliable and valid answers, but perhaps not useful responses because the right questions were not asked. Questions that are **multidimensional** as opposed to **one-dimensional** greatly improve the utility of the survey responses. Identifying concepts and constructs to be measured and writing the right questions is a key part of this process.

• **Multidimensional** *questions examine several characteristics about an issue or topic. This approach helps researchers build a profile of the issue or topic.*

• **One-dimensional** *questions reveal only one major aspect of an issue or topic.*

Suppose you are in the market for a new lawnmower and you want one that is reliable. You toddle into your local Sears to conduct a little research on their substantial lawnmower selection. You tell the salesperson that you want a durable lawnmower. What does "durable" mean? On the face of it, "durable" is one-dimensional because the salesperson did not ask you about the components of durability. The salesperson simply presented you with a lawnmower that he said was durable. An astute shopper will ask multiple questions related to durability in order to make his own determination as to whether the proposed lawnmower is durable. A series of follow-up questions establishing the components of durability transform a one-dimensional question into a multidimensional assessment that, in this case, provides the customer with more precise information about the lawnmower in question.

A one-dimensional assessment of durability focuses on one aspect of durability; repair record, for example, or perhaps the word *durability* itself is considered evidence of the same. Figure 9.3 depicts a possible multidimensional examination of the concept of "durability":

Developing good questions takes time. Part of the questionnaire design process includes testing the questionnaire with a sample of respondents. Researchers might test specific, perhaps sensitive questions before the entire questionnaire is executed in order to gain insight from respondents as to the quality of the questions. **Data equivalence,** addressed more fully in Chapter 14, should be established before a questionnaire is executed.

Other applications of multidimensional research include how researchers might track two very common issues often included on questionnaires:

■ FIGURE 9.3

Multidimensional Components of "Durability"

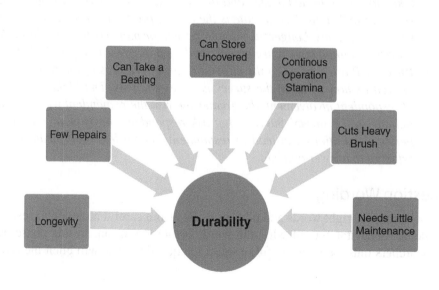

"importance-" and "satisfaction-" related questions. Customer satisfaction is a staple focus of many survey efforts because organizations often want to know how satisfied their customers are about certain aspects of their business. Often the assumption here is that satisfaction is a surrogate variable for the likelihood of repeat business. This assumption might well be true in many cases, but not necessarily in all situations. A limitation of measuring just satisfaction is that it does not totally captured intent, although it is often assumed to.

● Consider this scenario: You own a dry cleaning business and you want to gauge customer satisfaction because business has been flat. You interview some customers and then perhaps run a focus group or two to identify the key issues of concern. After this initial qualitative primary research, you decide to do a survey to measure the six customer satisfaction issues raised during the initial phase of your research effort. You now decide to administer a five-point satisfaction rating survey to measure customer satisfaction on these six issues related to customer satisfaction of your dry cleaning business:

- Quality of Cleaning
- Hours of Operation
- Parking Convenience
- Staff Friendliness
- Speed to Complete Cleaning
- Undamaged Return of Clothes

Based on the results below, the dry cleaner manager might decide to fix *parking* first and then *hours of operation* because respondents were the most *unsatisfied* with these issues. However, without an importance rating compared to the *satisfaction* rating, researchers will not know how to advise organizational leadership on which issues should be addressed *first*. Tables 9.1 and 9.2 show satisfaction and importance interval scales respectively.

	Unsatisfied				Satisfied
Hours of Operation	**1**	2	3	4	5
Parking Convenience	**1**	2	3	4	5
Staff Friendliness	1	2	**3**	4	5
Speed to Complete Cleaning	1	2	3	**4**	5
Undamaged Return of Clothes	1	2	**3**	4	5

■ TABLE 9–1
Unsatisfied/Satisfied Scale

	Unimportant				Important
Hours of Operation	**1**	2	3	4	5
Parking Convenience	**1**	2	3	4	5
Staff Friendliness	1	2	3	**4**	5
Speed to Complete Cleaning	1	2	**3**	4	5
Undamaged Return of Clothes	1	2	3	4	**5**

■ TABLE 9–2
Unimportant/Important Scale

Now consider comparing *satisfaction* with *importance*. When researchers ask respondents the importance they place on the same questions, a profile emerges that provides leadership with a more multidimensional view of customers' beliefs.

When we consider the relative importance of each factor, a more precise picture emerges. Researchers might recommend to the dry cleaner manager that he focus on fixing *undamaged return of clothes* first and then *staff friendliness* because those two issues have the lowest satisfaction and highest importance ratios.

Data Equivalence:

- *Measures the extent to which respondents understand the questions and the questions are interpreted the same way by respondents.*

- Marketing researchers must ensure that the survey questions are interpreted the same way by all respondents and that the data collection method is understood by all respondents. Marketing researchers test questionnaires to ensure that the data are interpreted the same way by respondents. Researchers might administer the questionnaire to a sample group and then conduct a focus group of those same people to determine whether they interpreted the questions the same way. Questions that are not interpreted the same way by all respondents should be rephrased or dropped from the questionnaire. Additionally, scales are tested to ensure that respondents understand the scale and that respondents interpret that scale in the same manner. Again, more on data equivalence in Chapter 14.

Open- vs. Closed-Ended Questions

- **Open-ended questions** ask the respondent to provide a response in his own words. Generally, a large-scale quantitative survey should have a limited number of open-ended questions since they are difficult to tabulate. Too many open-ended questions will become unwieldy to manage. If researchers want to ask many open-ended questions because they feel that they don't have enough information about the topic and thus need respondents to provide input, they should have probably done more focus groups and interviews where open-ended questioning is the norm.

  - **Unprobed** open-ended questions are broadly based questions that do not lead the respondent towards addressing specific aspects of the question at

■ **FIGURE 9.4**

Questionnaires with Interval Rating Scales are Common and Allow for a Number of Useful Analysis Options

Image © Chad McDermott, 2011. Used under license from Shutterstock, Inc.

hand. For example, the question: "What did you think of the restaurant?" is an open-ended unprobed question as it gives the respondent freedom to talk about any aspect of the restaurant experience.

- **Probed** open-ended questions give the respondent a little more direction as to what aspect of the question the researcher is interested in examining. For example, "What did you think about the food quality at the restaurant?" In this case, the researcher is probing, or directing, the respondent to provide an open-ended response about a specific (food quality) aspect of the restaurant experience. When doing large surveys, probed open-ended questions allow respondents freedom in responding to questions while engineering some *commonality* in what aspect of the question will be examined.
  - **Advantages:**
    - Allows for respondents to be free and open in their responses.
    - Respondents might identify critical aspects of an issue heretofore unbeknownst to the researcher.
    - Easier for researchers to write than controlled response scaled questions.
  - **Disadvantages:**
    - Responses might be so broad that there are no discernable patterns, thus inhibiting researchers from making sound judgments about the whole population based on a sample.
    - Analysis is subjective and can be cumbersome.
- **Closed-ended questions** are questions that force the respondent to answer questions according to some type of scale such as:
  - **Dichotomous:** Choice between two choices such as "yes/no" questions.
  - **Multiple Choice:** Choose among three or more choices such as "check all that apply" questions.
  - **Scaled Response:** provide a scale such as from 1 to 5 whereby respondents *rate* each response without regard to the other items on the list.
  - **Ranking:** Asking respondents to put items in order of preference.
  - **Advantages:**
    - The collection and analysis process is more structured.
    - The questionnaire execution process is repeatable.
    - All respondents are asked the same questions using the same scales.
    - Requires less work or involvement by the respondent because they do not have free-form responses.
  - **Disadvantages:**
    - Limits respondents to the scale provided, which might reduce the amount of information collected.
    - The scale might not completely capture hidden feelings, attitudes, beliefs, or perceptions because respondents will only answer on a scale as opposed to writing answers.

Flow and Layout

- Selecting the right flow and layout will result in increased response rates. Questionnaires that are too cluttered, wordy, or sloppy in appearance dissuade respondents from completing the survey. Figure 9.5 shows a typical questionnaire flow.
- **Skip Patterns:**
  - The sequence of questions based on how respondents answered previous questions. Respondents might be instructed to skip certain questions based

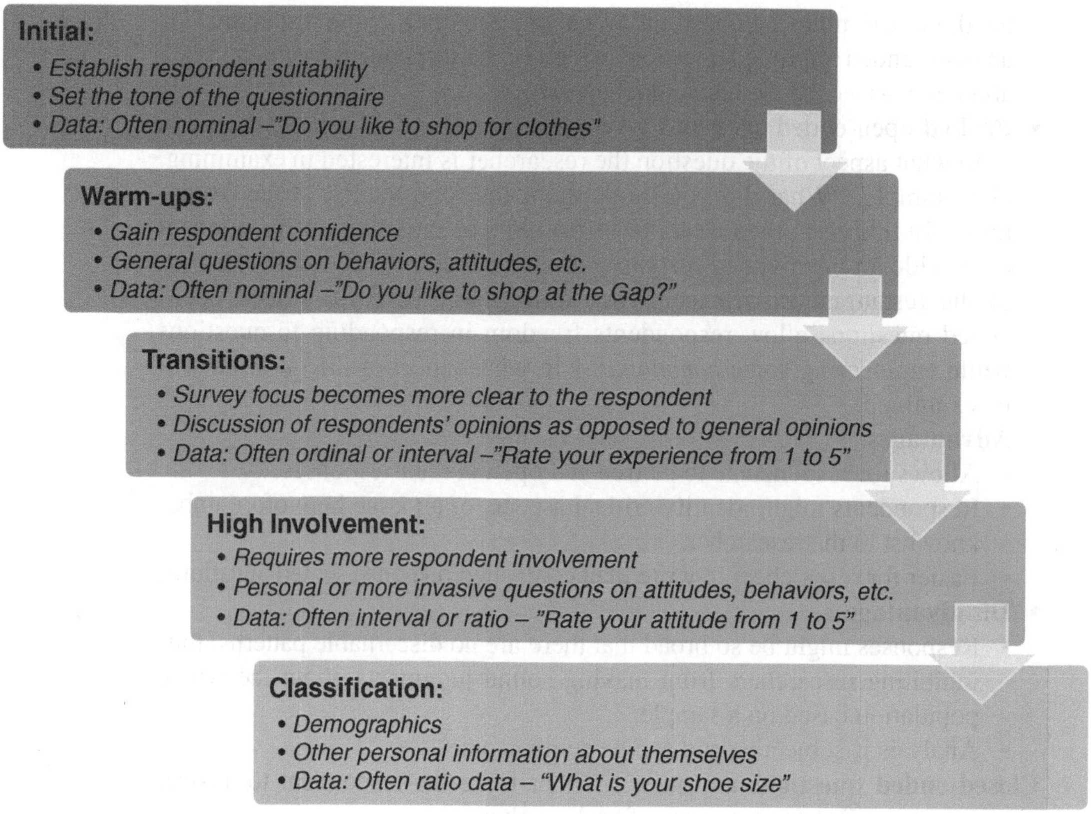

Initial:
- *Establish respondent suitability*
- *Set the tone of the questionnaire*
- *Data: Often nominal –"Do you like to shop for clothes"*

Warm-ups:
- *Gain respondent confidence*
- *General questions on behaviors, attitudes, etc.*
- *Data: Often nominal –"Do you like to shop at the Gap?"*

Transitions:
- *Survey focus becomes more clear to the respondent*
- *Discussion of respondents' opinions as opposed to general opinions*
- *Data: Often ordinal or interval –"Rate your experience from 1 to 5"*

High Involvement:
- *Requires more respondent involvement*
- *Personal or more invasive questions on attitudes, behaviors, etc.*
- *Data: Often interval or ratio – "Rate your attitude from 1 to 5"*

Classification:
- *Demographics*
- *Other personal information about themselves*
- *Data: Often ratio data – "What is your shoe size"*

■ **FIGURE 9.5**
Typical Questionnaire Flow

on how they answered various other questions on the questionnaire. Skip patterns allow for longer questionnaires that can capture more information. For example, suppose an airline wants to understand its customers' attitudes about its services. The questionnaire might have 100 questions (which is too long for a such an endeavor) but the average respondent might only answer 25 questions based on "skipping" past certain questions that might not be applicable to that particular respondent. Researchers should be careful to ensure that skip patterns are minimized and that the respondent is not continuously being directed to different parts of the survey. However, with Internet questionnaires respondents are unaware of their being "skipped"; thus, researchers can create more skip patterns for web-based surveys.

- **Codes:**
  - Codes are numbers assigned to survey responses which are used in the data tabulation process. Ratio data are self-coded because they are numeric data (unless the researcher wants to group ratio data into interval ranges which would then be coded). Codes can be created for interval, ordinal, and nominal data as needed. Some interval data are self-coded as well. For example, "rate the movie on a scale of 1 to 5"; 1, 2, 3, 4, and 5 are the codes for the respective question. The same approach might be used for ordinal data: "put these movies in order from best to worst." If there are four movies, the ranking (1, 2, 3, and 4) become the codes for that question. Because nominal data are categorical such as "red, blue, green," these colors need an associated number or code such as 1 = red, 2 = blue, and 3 = green. Researchers can then use these codes during the analysis phase of the research as needed.

- **Flow:**
  - The questions should flow from simpler to more difficult (personal) or high involvement questions towards the end. Respondents should buy into the questionnaire by being led from more general to more specific questions.
- **Sequence Bias:**
  - Sequence bias, sometimes called *order effects*, occurs when the order of the questions has a deleterious impact on the results. Marketing researchers can randomize the questions to reduce, and perhaps eliminate, this type of bias.
- **Position Bias or Halo Effect:**
  - Similar to sequence bias, position bias occurs when respondents give disproportionate weight, positive or negative, to a question based on where the question is located in the survey. If a question is located near positive issues raised in a questionnaire, a *halo effect* might occur if a given respondent sees the question in a more positive light due to its proximity to positive issues addressed in the questionnaire.

Potential Questionnaire Flow

- When developing the questions, there should be a natural connection between and among the various questions. If a questionnaire is simply a group of unrelated questions without any recurring themes, researchers will be limited in the questionnaire analysis that can be done. For example, if you are asking questions about the respondent's opinion on the quality of the food at a restaurant, there should be natural follow-up questions that emerge. Perhaps respondents should be asked the reasons they liked or did not like the restaurant and detail the key factors associated with that opinion, or gauge their intent to return or willingness to recommend the restaurant. Interrelationships among the questions enables researchers to connect the dots of information to create a respondent profile. Researchers will find few correlations among questions if the questions are "stand-alone" questions and there is no logical connection between the questions. Regarding flow, there are two main views on whether related questions should be close to or separated from each other on the questionnaire. Take the example of the dry cleaning business questions on "satisfaction" and "importance" discussed earlier. In that example, we are asking the respondent about the same issues in two different questions. One question focused on "satisfaction" and the other question on "importance." One might argue that it makes sense to have these two questions in sequence, as opposed to separating them in the questionnaire because separating them will disrupt the survey flow. Another approach is that by separating those two questions the respondent might be more likely to not let how he answered one question affect how he answers the next question(s). Separation can help to isolate similar questions in a manner that aids the respondent in clearing her mind before each question. Neither way is right or wrong. However, researchers, and those sponsoring the research, should be aware of the respective impact of each approach.
- **Layout:**
  - State instructions clearly and be consistent with fonts, bolding, and italicizing. It's often useful to bold key components of the instructions, particularly if there might be some confusion as to what the questionnaire is asking of the respondent.

- In order to increase response rates, researchers generally send some type of pre-notification of an impending survey or at least an opening paragraph/narrative on the survey itself to tell the respondents:
  - *Who you are and why you are doing the survey*
  - *How they were selected*
  - *Whether the results are anonymous and confidential*
  - *How the survey results will be used and to whom they will be given*
  - *How long the survey will take*
  - *The deadline*
  - *An appeal to complete the survey*
  - *Thank them for participating*

The questionnaire layout is not important for telephone surveys because respondents don't see the survey. However, researchers should be careful not to use large interval scales (above 1 to 5) on telephone surveys because it is difficult for respondents to *visualize* a scale that they *hear.* If a respondent is faced with a 1-to-10 scale on a telephone survey, the tendency will be to gravitate towards the scale's endpoints with the middle part of the scale getting lost. It's very difficult for telephone respondents to keep the middle of a large scale straight in their mind.

Primacy and recency issues are important considerations when writing a questionnaire.

- **Primacy:**
  - *The tendency for respondents to give more weight to what they heard or saw* ***first*** *or at the* ***beginning*** *of the process.*
- **Recency:**
  - *The tendency for respondents to give more weight to what they heard or saw* ***last*** *or at the* ***end*** *of the process.*

The questionnaire should appear neat, clean, and professional. Cleanly align the questions and scales to give the questionnaire a streamlined appearance. When descriptors above the endpoints of interval scales, ensure that the descriptors are centered over their respective number and that they do not overlap other points on the scale. Figure 9.6 reveals well and misaligned descriptors.

FIGURE 9.6
Sample of Well-Aligned/Misaligned Scales

Well Aligned	Poor					Excellent
Speed	1	2	3	4	5	6
Taste	1	2	3	4	5	6
Color	1	2	3	4	5	6
Ambiance	1	2	3	4	5	6
Price	1	2	3	4	5	6

Misaligned	Poor				Excellent	
Speed	1	2	3	4	5	6
Taste	1	2	3	4	5	6
Color	1	2	3	4	5	6
Ambiance	1	2	3	4	5	6
Price	1	2	3	4	5	6

Mail *(self-administered)* or in-person questionnaires should have plenty of "white space" between the questions lest the respondent feel overwhelmed with cluttered copy. Take a look at: www.samplequestionnaire.com for some guidance.

Should the questions be numbered?

- **Mail** or otherwise paper questionnaires: Yes, numbering the questions gives the survey a professional appearance and provides order to the questionnaire.
- **Telephone** questionnaires: Numbering the questions might be useful for the interviewer but does not add much value to the respondent as they do not *see* the questionnaire. However, interviewers should tell the respondents how long the survey will take as opposed to telling the respondent that the survey is "X" number of questions. On the telephone, respondents can better visualize the time component than the number of questions.
- **Internet** questionnaires: Generally numbering the questions is not necessary on Internet surveys if researchers' provide a progress bar at the bottom of the screen. It's useful to have one question per Internet page as opposed to the *entire* questionnaire on one page. Also, numbering the questions might be confusing to respondents if there are skip patterns on the questionnaire. If respondents answer "no" to question 5 and are then skipped to question "11", they might wonder what happened to questions 6 through 10, prompting them to try to go back in the survey.

Test the Survey

- Once the draft questionnaire is ready, researchers should test the survey with a sample group of the *target population*. Testing the questionnaire can be in the form of a focus group where the researcher asks participants to take the questionnaire as though they were really taking the survey. Researchers are looking for several issues related to the questionnaire construction such as:
  - *Typos—are there misspellings or sentence structure problems?*
  - *Do the questions make sense—are they clear?*
  - *Are there questions that were not asked that should have been asked— what's missing?*
  - *Is the question wording acceptable, particularly for sensitive related questions?*
  - *Is the look and feel of the questionnaire professional?*
  - *Are the skip patterns clear?*
  - *Are there any questions that should not be asked or are not value added?*
  - *Are some questions too objectionable to ask?*
  - *How should sensitive questions be asked?*
  - *Are the instructions clear?*
  - *How long does it take to complete the survey and is that amount of time reasonable?*
- There are different types of pre-tests using peers, subject matter experts, and the target population of interest. Also, pilot studies can be done to test the questionnaire before it is launched to the target population.

Revise

- After a couple of rounds of testing the questionnaire, it is now time to revise the survey based on respondent feedback. After the revisions are made, researchers might want to retest the updated survey with another set of respondents. This second round of pre-testing might be with only one group of test respondents.
- Researchers should make the distinction between correcting the questionnaire and making material changes to the survey. A group of test respondents might

suggest changes to the questionnaire that would significantly alter the focus of the survey. These types of changes are probably not wise as they will result in a questionnaire that might not meet the research objectives.

- The revised questionnaire should now be taken to the survey sponsors (perhaps organizational leadership) for review and approval.

Final Approval

- The completed survey is now ready for approval from its sponsor—a given company president let's say, who will have her team review the questionnaire. It's quite possible, and often likely, that the president and her team will request various revisions be made to the questionnaire in accordance with the agreed to research objectives.
- A question that often arises is how much "push back" the researcher should give to the research sponsor when the sponsor requests changes. Researchers should be upfront about the impact to the research project that the changes will have. In some cases, the changes might result in lower response rates if, for example, the sponsor wants more invasive questions asked or if the survey length is increased.
- Finally, there should be some process that formalizes the questionnaire approval by both the research sponsor and the researcher. Researchers should not administer a questionnaire without *written approval* of the *exact* questionnaire and the *precise* data collection method and timetable.

Execute

- At this stage the researcher executes the survey as called for in the research plan through the Internet, telephone, mail, in person, or otherwise agreed to method.

- Researchers are now in the collection and monitoring phases. Researchers should monitor whether they are getting enough responses in a timely manner. Researchers should send out reminders to respondents if the response rate is low.
- The research sponsor will inevitably ask the researcher for a status report that details the response rate demographics. Establishing that the *non-response* rate is not statistically different from the *response rate* is critical to maintaining the statistically representative integrity of the survey. If there is a significant difference in those who responded versus those who did not respond, the researcher should have a correction strategy in place to account for this variance.
- Providing managers frequent updates and running tabulations of the data during the survey execution process will help to set the stage for the research report.

Dos and Don'ts in Questionnaire Design

- There are many guidelines in developing questionnaires that generally fall into the *questionnaire wording* phase of questionnaire design. Careful attention to avoid these pitfalls will greatly enhance the precision of your questionnaire. Remember that the purpose of a questionnaire is not simply to ask questions but to ask the *best questions in the right way.* Figure 9.8 provides an accounting of mistakes to avoid when writing a questionnaire.

Questionnaires Should:
- *Be grammatically simple;*
- *Use the respondent's vocabulary and word usage;*
- *Be as brief as is appropriate for the target audience;*
- *Generally have numbered questions;*
- *Use consistent scales;*
- *Have clear instructions;*
- *Use plenty of white space between the questions.*

Things to Avoid in Question Construction

Types of Question Constructions to Avoid

- **Doubled Barreled:**
  - *Double-barreled questions ask two questions in one question.*
    - In the quest to shorten questionnaires, avoid the temptation to ask two questions in one question.
      - Question: "Did you receive fast and friendly service at the restaurant?"
      - Respondent: "Well, they were fast but not friendly so how do I answer this question?"
    - Researchers should measure these two issues separately.
    - In some cases, a tandem pair might be considered one issue and thus might be included together. For example, suppose you wanted to know if your respondents liked "cold and windy" weather as a pair. Thus if they liked cold but not windy weather they would answerer "no" to the pair. Determining whether they like both cold and windy together can be captured by grouping the pair in one question. In most cases however, researchers often want to know how respondents would answer each question separately.

■ **FIGURE 9.8**

Issues to Avoid in
Question Construction

- **Leading:**
  - *Leading questions offer a clue to the respondent with regard to the type of response the researcher is looking for which can cause the respondent to answer in a way he might not have otherwise done.*
    - Legitimate research organizations do not want to lead the respondent to a specific answer. However, researchers might inadvertently lead the respondent towards an answer based on how the question is worded.
    - Pre-testing the questions by asking respondents to rephrase the question in their own words or by asking the respondents what they think is the crux of the question might reveal a bias in the question.
    - Special-interest groups seeking favorable results might embed leading questions to sway results.
      - Question: "Do you really believe that the parking policy is fair?"
      - Respondent: the term *really* leads the respondent to say "no."
- **Guessing:**
  - *Guessing questions ask respondents to state what they would or will do in hypothetical situations.*
    - These types of questions are too conditional to provide solid data as to actual, predictable behavior.
      - Question: "Will you read the chapter before class?
      - Respondent: "Yes, of course!"
      - Question: "Would you support the policy if it saved lives?"
      - Respondent: "Of course, because it saves lives!"
        - This second example is also leading.
    - It might be better to ask the student a more direct question such as "Did you read the chapter for this week's class?" In this case, the researcher is asking for actual behavior (with the inclusion of the word *did*) as opposed to asking respondents what they *might* do. Often respondents will answer what they *think* they should do or what the researcher *expects* that they should do as opposed to what the respondent *actually* will do.

- Similar to establishing validity, researchers can ask a series of screening questions to determine if the students are likely to read the chapter before class. Such screening questions might include whether they read last week's chapters or whether they know what chapters are due.

- **Beyond Ability:**
  - *Questions in this category are asking respondents questions that they are not qualified to answer or otherwise do not have the knowledge or frame of reference to answer accurately.*
    - This issue is demonstrated in national surveys that ask questions of respondents who simply have no way of knowing the answer.
      - Question: "Do you think this legislation will pass?"
      - Respondent: This question might gauge their perception about its passage but not the actual chance of passage because respondents do not have the inside information needed to answer this question.
    - Answering these types of questions are akin to guessing.
    - Sometimes researchers ask respondents for a specific answer when only generalities will be remembered. For example, if asked how much was spent on food last week, a respondent will not be able to tell to the penny how much was spent unless it had been documented. Instead, researchers should ask a more general question such as "Did you spend more or less than $100 on food last week?" Even though the first question asks for specific ratio data and the second question asks general nominal data, it is better to ask less specific information that the respondent can answer accurately than asking for details that will be incorrect.
    - Other types of questions in this category ask respondents such questions as what someone else is thinking, what might happen in situations where they have no control, or behaviors of people not directly in their view.
    - As a caveat to this issue, if researchers ask these types of questions they should couch the analysis in terms of respondent *perceptions* about the question at hand as opposed to portraying their responses as hard data or a factual representation of knowledge.

- **Specifics for General Case:**
  - *These questions ask respondents to provide a general answer when using a specific case as an example.*
    - Suppose you turn on the evening news and hear about someone who went into an art gallery and spray painted two works of art. As a result of this incident, we are being surveyed about the situation and asked: "In light of what happen at the art gallery, should all works of art be behind glass?" Here respondents are asked about a proposed new general rule applied to all art museums based on the specific happenings at *one* gallery involving *one* person.
    - These types of questions can also be leading in that the underlying assumption is that placing art behind glass will thwart vandals when this might not be the case.

- **Assumptions:**
  - *Questions that assume that respondents have a certain knowledge base.*
    - Question: "Do you think Mr. Watson is doing a good job?"
    - Respondent "Who is Mr. Watson?"
      - Here the researcher is assuming that the respondent knows who Mr. Watson is and also that the respondent is qualified to offer an informed opinion about Mr. Watson.

- Question: "Do you think NASA's budget is too small?
- Respondent: "Who/What is NASA?"

Or

- Question: "Is the new return policy at the clothing store fair?"
- Respondent: "What is the new return policy?"

- Using names, acronyms, or information without knowing if the respondent is aware of those meanings will lead to confused respondents. In the case of an interview, the respondent can ask for clarification since the interviewer is standing before the respondent asking the questions. The interviewer should be well trained and versed on the objectives, content, and purpose of the questionnaire that he is administering. However on mail or Internet self-administered questionnaires, respondents do not have anyone they can ask for clarification. Be aware that respondents' not fully understanding the questions does not mean that they will not answer the questions anyway.
- Another aspect of this concept is the notion of asking respondents questions to which the answers seem pre-determined but that the impact of the answer is not fully examined. For example:
  - Question: "Are you in favor of lower taxes?"
  - Respondent "Yes."

  Revised question

  - Question: "Are you in favor of lower taxes if it means a reduction in city services?"
  - Respondent: "No."
  - In these cases, researchers get opposite answers for the same basic question.
  - This question is not loading assuming a reduction as city services will happen and is factual.
- Secondary research along with interviews and focus groups will help the researcher establish what the respondent knows and does not know about the issue being researched. It is unwise for researchers to assume that respondents are as well versed on the issues raised in the questionnaire as are those developing the questionnaire. Remember that the researcher developing the questionnaire has been involved in the project presumably for some time giving him an inherent knowledge advantage over respondents who see the questionnaire for the first time.
- **Confusing Meaning:**
  - *These questions are interpreted differently among respondents or are otherwise written in a confusing manner.*
    - Open-ended question: "Where did you read about the sale?"
    - Respondent 1: "In the newspaper."
    - Respondent 2: "In my kitchen drinking my coffee."
  - Pre-testing the questionnaire will help to ensure the questions are clearly understood by all respondents.
  - Sentence construction that uses double negatives can also cause confusion among respondents.
- **Overstating the Condition:**
  - *Questions that overstate an issue, exaggerate the impact of the issue, overplay the proposed solution to the issue, or obfuscate relevant facts surrounding the issue.*
    - Question: "The university's policy on student meal plans will cause meal prices to rise 50 percent. Should this policy be implemented?"
    - Respondent: "Wow, a 50 percent increase, that's huge—no, I do not support the policy."

- In addition to leading the respondent, this question seems to be a dramatic assessment of the policy shift. Perhaps meal costs will rise, but stating that they will rise 50 percent might well be exaggerating the impact. Perhaps the real increase is only 10 percent.
- Including too much commentary as part of the question should be a *red flag* for researchers and respondents alike. The questions should be as simple and as straightforward as possible with limited adjectives characterizing aspects of the questions.

Other Issues in Administering a Questionnaire

Branching Questions

- *Questionnaires that use skip patterns to examine multiple aspects of various issues in one questionnaire.*
- Branching is very useful when researchers are interested in exploring several different, yet related issues. Suppose Ford Motor Company (www.ford.com) wants to know what its customers think of its vehicles. If Ford wants to sample Ford Explorer owners, the survey will focus on the features associated with that brand. Instead of focusing on one brand, Ford decides it wants to conduct a broader survey asking questions about all its cars in one survey by filtering respondents based on the type of car they own. The survey might have 100 questions yet the branches, and skip patterns, result in no one responding to more than perhaps 25 questions. Figure 9.9 shows vacation preferences using this technique.

Managing the Process

- There are several major considerations to weigh before a questionnaire is launched as represented in Figure 9.10.
- Successful survey projects involve extensive planning and a keen understanding of the marketing environment in which the project will be executed. Neither the researcher nor the research sponsor gets everything she wants when conducting a research project. Of course, the research provider would like a substantial budget and plenty of time to conduct the research. However, the research sponsor might have a somewhat limited, or perhaps a very limited budget, and wants the results quickly. The research provider might well feel time and budget pressures particularly if they plan to conduct both qualitative and

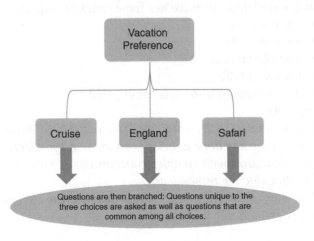

■ **FIGURE 9.9**
Vacation Preference

■ FIGURE 9.10

Managing the
Questionnaire Process

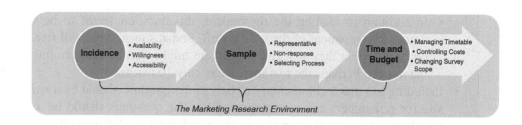

quantitative research. The incidence rate, the percentage of qualified respondents in the population, has a significant impact on the research project's timeline and budget. Projects with low incidence rates require more time and money to reach qualified respondents. Once the researcher makes contact with the respondent, the respondent must be available and willing to participate in the survey. A clear understanding of the profile of potential respondents will give both the researcher and the research sponsor a sense of the level of difficulty in getting a "complete"—a survey respondent who completes the survey.

● The issue of representativeness must be addressed if the survey is to be an accurate representation of the general population. If a sample is randomly selected, the probability that the sample will be an accurate reflection of the general population is greater than if the sample had been selected in a non-random manner. Researchers must determine how representative they want the survey respondents to be of the general population.

  ● **Representativeness:**
    ● *The extent to which the sample is a statistically representative subset of the target population.*

The Internet Impact

● Of course the Internet has had a significant impact on many aspects of marketing research, not least of all on questionnaire design and execution. Before the Internet, data collection was much more labor intensive and time consuming. The Internet has greatly facilitated executing the questionnaire component of marketing research. Figure 9.11 offers an overview of the advantages and disadvantages of the Internet impact on questionnaire design.

  ● **Advantages:**
    ● Speed:
      ● *Questionnaires can be developed, edited, and distributed much more quickly than can be done with manual questionnaire development.*
    ● Analysis:
      ● *The various Internet software applications have made quick and sophisticated analysis possible. Some common sources:*
        ● *www.sas.com*
        ● *www.spss.com*
        ● *www.systat.com*
        ● *www.minitab.com*
        ● *www.microsoftStore.com/Excel_2010*
    ● Complexity:
      ● *Questionnaires with complicated skip patterns or branching are easily done online and done unbeknownst to the respondents.*
      ● *Questionnaires with complex concepts can contain various web links to help guide the respondent.*
      ● *The Internet also allows for visual demonstrations to aid respondents in understanding various concepts.*

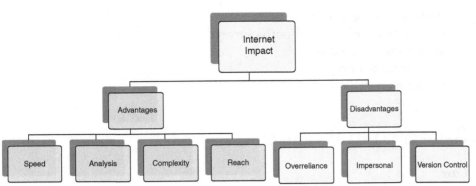

- Reach:
  - *Online questionnaires can reach anyone in the world with an Internet connection—which is particularly important when reaching people in remote areas or people who are otherwise hard to reach; certain professional people are not easily accessible.*
- **Disadvantages:**
  - Overreliance:
    - *Online questionnaires do not "write themselves." Software can create, post, and distribute the questionnaire, but the researcher still must develop a questionnaire in a methodical way.*
  - Impersonal:
    - *Surveys that are created online might appear to have been created by a machine as opposed to having been created with a sense of look and feel that are best developed with personal attention.*
  - Version Control:
    - *Too many changes to the questionnaire might result in different versions getting accidentally posted or distributed.*

Marketing researchers can use a variety of online survey writing tools to help create and collect data. Some tools are free, whereas others are offered for a fee. Generally the free services have various limitations on how elaborate the survey can be; whether skips and branching are permitted, on how many questions are permitted, and on how many respondents are allowed. Other possible limitations include time limits on how long the survey can be posted and a lack of access to download the raw data. Many free sites offer rudimentary analysis tools but require a fee for more elaborate data analysis. Depending on the researcher's goals, many free services might well be adequate. However, if doing a long-term complex survey with a large sample and sophisticated analysis requirements, a paid service is probably best. Here are some questionnaire services that might be helpful.

Sampling of Questionnaire Development Sites

- www.vovici.com
- www.surveymonkey.com
- www.zoomerang.com
- http://freeonlinesurveys.com
- http://docs.google.com
- http://www.keysurvey.com
- www.surveygizmo.com

- www.NoviSystems.com
- www.VisionCritical.com/Firefly-Surveys
- www.kwiksurveys.com
- www.limesurvey.org
- www.surveymethods.com

Research in Practice

Case:
- After having done extensive secondary research, employee interviews, and three employee focus groups, you have enough data to begin building a questionnaire to determine why employee satisfaction at the company has been declining. However, your boss feels that the time and cost of a questionnaire is unwarranted given the other secondary and primary research that has already been done. The company of 10,000 employees is based in Seattle and produces aircraft parts as a subcontractor to Boeing.

Assignment:
- Make the case to your boss that a questionnaire is the next logical step in quantifying employee opinions and include a discussion of the pros and cons of conducting a survey. Design a 20-question questionnaire to determine why employee satisfaction has been declining and discuss the steps and methods necessary to execute the survey.

Chapter Summary

Built on secondary data and many types of qualitative primary research, questionnaire design has several important steps. The steps are establishing the survey objectives (driven by the survey sponsor), deciding on the data collection method (i.e., telephone, Internet, mail, or in person), determining the survey length, developing the questions, constructing the survey flow and layout, testing the survey (with a focus group of typical respondents), revising the survey based on test subject feedback, gaining final written approval to execute the survey (from the survey sponsor), and distributing the survey. Multidimensional questions involve asking about multiple aspects of a given issue or topic to gain a more complete view of the totality of that issue or topic under study. Data equivalency, the extent to which respondents understand and interpret the data elements, or survey questions, equally, is a critical part of the questionnaire design process. The key components to data equivalence, that will be discussed in chapter 14, are item (understanding the actual words used on a questionnaire), content (understanding the idea raised in the questions), and

construct (having the cultural and educational frame of reference needed to fully comprehend the questions and their meaning). Open-ended questions on questionnaires should be used sparingly and can be either probed or unprobed. Unprobed open-ended questions that are truly open-ended are questions such as: "Please comment on the restaurant," whereas probed open-ended questions direct the respondent to respond some aspect of the experience such as "Please comment on the *service* at the restaurant." Probed open-ended questions result in respondents providing open-ended answers that are more precise than unprobed open-ended questions. Other types of questions involve scales such as from 1 to 5 or 1 to 10. These types of questions reveal the relative strengths of answers. Skip patterns enable marketing researchers to direct respondents to different parts of a questionnaire based on how they respond to various questions. Branching questions lead respondents to different parts of the survey. Codes are numeric representations of responses on a questionnaire such as 1 = yes and 2 = no. These codes help researchers quickly tally responses and can be used with different types of data analysis techniques. It is important to establish an efficient question flow. A good question flow is typified by initial screening questions, warm-up questions, transition, high involvement, and finally classification (more invasive) type questions. The questionnaire layout should be clean and professional looking with adequate white space and with properly aligned scales and numbered questions. Internet surveys are often best when presented with one question per page. Generally Internet survey questions should not be numbered if using skip patterns as respondents can get confused when they are redirected to questions seemingly not in sequence. Instead, use a progress bar to indicate how far along the respondent is in the survey. Questionnaire questions should be grammatically simple, use the respondent's core vocabulary, be as brief as is appropriate for the audience, use consistent scales, and have clear instructions. In writing questions, avoid questions that are doubled barreled (asking two questions at once), making assumptions about what respondents might already know, using confusing wording, asking leading questions, asking questions that require respondents to guess, and asking questions that ask for general opinions based on a specific incidence. Generally, the Internet impact on survey execution has been positive. Advantages include time, cost, access to respondents, access to secondary data, ability to use visual stimuli or an interactive component to the questionnaire, and speed and flexibility in the data collection and analysis phases. Disadvantages include overreliance on its capabilities, an impersonal feel, and version control.

ISSUE IN THE SPOTLIGHT   Keys to Questionnaire Success

Timothy Triplett, Senior Survey Methodologist
Statistical Methods Group
Urban Institute—www.urban.org

CHECKLIST OF THINGS TO AVOID WHEN WRITING SURVEY QUESTIONS:

- *Is your question asking about more than one thing (double barreled)?*
- *Are you using any terms that some respondents may not understand?*
- *Are your response options exhaustive and mutually exclusive?*
- *Are the response options good enough to disseminate respondents' views?*
- *Do your scale questions have balanced alternatives?*
- *Can you get the information from another source (reduce burden)?*
- *Will all respondents have the same interpretation of the question?*
- *Is the time frame clearly stated and reasonable for recall questions?*
- *Does the question contain double negatives?*
- *Is there any unnecessary neutral, don't know, or no opinion option?*
- *Are you using reasonable intervals for numeric response options?*
- *Does the wording seem to advocate a particular answer (leading)?*
- *Are you using an acronym that has not yet been defined?*
- *Are you asking respondents to rank a series of items or some other task that appears burdensome?*

RESPONSE OPTIONS OFTEN DISSEMINATE RESPONDENTS' VIEWS BECAUSE:

- *There are often cultural differences in responding to scale questions*
- *Asian respondents tend to avoid endpoints or extreme options*
- *Male respondents are more likely to choose endpoints or extreme options*

THINGS KEEP IN MIND WHEN ASKING PEOPLE TO RECALL EVENTS:

Make sure the recall period is explicit:
- *Poor Question: On average how many hours of TV do you watch?*
- *Better: About how many hours of TV do you watch on a typical weekday?*

Saliency is the key to recall:
- *For instance, people can probably still remember where they were and what they were doing on September 11, 2001, but cannot remember anything*

about where they were or what they were doing six months ago.

Motivation is the other key:

- *For instance, if you are doing a survey about global warming, people who feel this is an important issue will more likely think harder when asked to recall prior events or activities.*

Social desirability leads to telescoping:

- *For instance, when asking people about volunteering during the past 12 months, people often include an event that occurred over 12 months ago (which is called* telescoping*) because volunteering is something that people like to report doing.*

Other considerations:

- *Consider seasonal effects*
- *Easier to get income estimate in April*
- *Easier to get information about schools towards the end of the school year*
- *Easier to get information about outdoor activities in the summer*
- *If possible, avoid changing the recall period*
- *If you have to, make sure to emphasize when a change occurs*
- *Cognitive testing is important to knowing whether the recall period is reasonable*
- *Focus groups can also help you learn what people are able to recall*

10 Sampling Methods

Image © olly, 2011. Used under license from Shutterstock, Inc.

Learning Objectives:

- Appreciate the role of sampling in marketing research
- Understand the key considerations in selecting a sample
- Understand the broad approaches to sampling

- Learn the different techniques in selecting a sample
- Understand the various methods for determining the sample size
- Understand the difference between probability and non-probability sampling

- Learn the four methods of probability and four methods of non-probability sampling
- Understand the statistical foundations of determining a sample size

Chapter Ten

Sampling is one of the most critical areas in marketing research for it enables researchers to make statistical projections about a population based on a small sample of that population. Like many aspects of marketing research, we engage in a version of sampling ourselves. Let's look at a practical, albeit oversimplified, example to start our examination of sampling. Monday night arrives and you decide to take a study break and go to Pundio's, a new local eatery, for dinner. Because this trip to Pundio's was your first visit to the restaurant you did not know what to expect. Sadly, you were underwhelmed by the meal and concluded that the restaurant was average. However, believing in second chances, you return to the same restaurant on a Wednesday night some weeks later. Upon your second visit, the restaurant succeeded in meeting your expectation that the restaurant would again be average, which solidified your opinion. You now resolve that you will not return to Pundio's. However, one Saturday night your friends ask you to join them for dinner, and alas they are going to Pundio's. Were you just going with a couple of friends, you might suggest a different place. However, recognizing an inability to overcome the critical mass of friends' pressure, you relent and sacrifice a good meal for great conversation and join the group. Your reluctance to return to Pundio's a third time is based on an assumption: that the two previous times were a large enough sample of the restaurant to determine that the restaurant would be bad on *all* nights. Although this sample size is clearly too small, you are still making a judgment on the population of *all* nights at the restaurant based on just *two* visits. Similar to national political polls that do not need to ask everyone in order to gauge public opinion (they take a sample) you would not need to go to the restaurant seven nights a week for a year to determine that it is not a good restaurant because a good sample (more than two) would prove enough statistical information to make a judgment. By the way, the third time was the charm as Pundio's, now under new management, was fabulous.

Marketing researchers use sampling to make statistical judgments about a population so they don't have to ask the entire population.

Sample vs. Census

Both a sample and a census are based on populations.

- **Population:**
  - *The total universe of elements sharing the same characteristics.*

- **Sample:**
  - *A subset of the population.*

- **Census:**
  - *An exact enumeration of all elements of a population.*

What is better a sample or a census? Typically a good sample is better than a bad census. With a small population, perhaps an organization with 2,000 members, a census is doable. Conversely, if you need the opinions of the people of Houston, Texas, a sample is the best way to collect data because a census of a city the size of Houston is daunting and generally not doable (unless it is a well-funded project). Given that a good sample will accurately reflect the population within a margin of error, a census in generally overkill.

Every ten years the U.S. Census Bureau (www.census.gov) conducts a census, ostensibly counting everyone in the U.S. The first U.S. Census was conducted in 1790 and managed under the direction of then Secretary of State Thomas Jefferson.

Key Sampling Considerations

Management sponsoring the research should keep close track on the research study methods and its progress towards meeting the research goals. Good leaders, although perhaps not always connected to the details of a specific project's methods, should have a clear view of the overall process and should know enough about the research project to ask the right questions. Before launching a survey the marketing researcher must settle on a sample plan. Several key considerations, as shown in Figure 10.1, should be weighted before finalizing the sampling plan.

- **Adequacy:**
  - Adequacy refers to the extent to which the sample size is large enough to represent the target population of interest. The sample size should be large enough to reveal patterns that are then extrapolated to represent the entire target population.
- **Incentives:**
  - Incentives have an impact on the number of people who will respond to the survey. The better the incentive is the higher the response rate will be. Marketing researchers must oversample to compensate for people who refuse to be in the survey. For example, if 50 percent of the people contacted agree to be in the survey, the researcher will have to approach 2,000 people to get 1,000 respondents to agree to be in the study. The willingness to participate rate will increase as the incentives get better. The incentives should be high enough to make it "worth their while" for respondents to give their opinion, but not so high as to bias their responses.
- **Desired Accuracy:**
  - There are several statistical methods for determining the sample size. These methods include a margin of error. For argument sake, let's presume a 3 percent margin of error and say that 40 percent of people in our survey stated that they liked broccoli. Remember that the 40 percent who liked broccoli are 40 percent of the sample, not the whole population because we did not in fact ask the whole population. We presume that the 40 percent sample would represent the entire population (plus or minus 3 percent) had we conducted a census. In other words, if we had conducted a census, between 37 percent and 43 percent (the average being 40 percent if we assume a normal distribution) would say that they like broccoli.

■ **FIGURE 10.1**

Sample Size Considerations

- Researchers, along with the research sponsor, must determine how accurately they want the sample to reflect the population. Is it acceptable to have a 5 percent margin of error? Several considerations come into play, such as time and budget, which will have an impact on the desired accuracy decision. Suppose you are managing the political campaign of upstart lawyer and Senate aspirant Drew Hunter. If the election were a year away it might be acceptable to have a survey with a large margin of error given the length of time before the election. Perhaps your candidate simply wants to get a feel for the electorate and more specifics are not yet warranted. However, as the election approaches, your candidate will likely want more reliable data enabling him to manage his campaign more precisely with regard to the realities of the electorate. Generally the more critical the business decision is, the more accurate (lower margin of error and larger sample size) the research should be.

- **Collection Method:**
  - The collection method might have an impact on the sample size. Suppose you are a research provider and your client wants you to do a survey of women over 50. Your client wants you to collect the data in person at the local mall and wants the data collected over the weekend. Given the research budget, you tell your client that you can accomplish the data collection but that you will only be able to collect 500 interviews due to the time it takes to conduct the interview. In this case the sample size is driven by the data collection method.

- **Time and Budget:**
  - Time and budget play a key role in the sample plan. If a researcher has $5,000 to conduct a survey and it costs $100 per respondent, the sample size will be 50 people. Similarly, if the researcher only has a day to collect the data, the sample size will be affected.

- **Possible Biases:**
  - Certain biases can play a role in determining the sample size. If the researcher is conducting a *random* probability sample, fewer biases are present and thus perhaps a smaller sample size will work. More biases are present when the researcher selects respondents through non-probability (or non-random)

■ **FIGURE 10.2**

A Well-Chosen Sample Can Inform Organizations about what the Population Thinks. Researchers do not Need to Ask Everyone to Learn their Opinions

Image © Rafael Ramirez Lee, 2011. Used under license from Shutterstock, Inc.

methods. Suppose a researcher is hand-selecting 100 passersby to be in a survey and that the researcher has a tendency to select people who appear more approachable. Marketing researchers might need to increase the sample size through probability means to balance-out the potential inequities resulting from the non-probability sample.

Strategic Sampling Issues

It is important to understand the overall sample issues from a strategic level. The sampling design process details the steps marketing researchers take in developing the sample of respondents for a marketing research survey. Before delving into the details of the sampling plan, a broad understanding of the major sampling decision points provides students of marketing research a quick reference to the critical aspects of sampling that serve as a foundation to remembering the role of sampling in research. These three issues are *identifying who to include in the survey, how to select respondents/how to get the respondents,* and *how many respondents to select.* These three concepts (who / how / how many) are detailed in the research design process but are offered here as a summary of the key issues related to sampling. Figure 10.3 shows the three main issues that should be addressed when formalizing the sampling plan.

Who Are the Respondents?

- This decision involves marketing researchers determining who to include in the survey as directed by the research study sponsor. In other words, who are the targets, or subjects, of the marketing research study?

How to Select and Get Respondents?

- This step involves determining how researchers will select the sample that will be in the survey and deciding whether the selection process will be random or non-random?
- Researchers also need to determine how they will collect the data such as through the Internet, telephone, mail, in person, and so forth. The data collection method will have an impact on the number of respondents and the way the researcher reaches them.

■ **FIGURE 10.3**

Major Sampling Decision Points

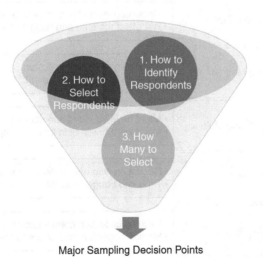

Major Sampling Decision Points

How Many Respondents to Select

- Researchers must decide how many people they need to respond to the survey and not just ask to be in the survey since there will be some people who will decline to participate.

Sampling Design Process

The process of executing a sampling plan, shown in Figure 10.4, involves a number of steps that require marketing researchers to make decisions that can affect the integrity of the process. Samples that are not selected appropriately, or that are not large enough, will not accurately reflect the population of interest, thus casting the quality of entire research project in question. Transitioning from the qualitative data collection methods we have examined such as focus groups, interviews, and observation to quantitative measures must be done with precision or the quality of the research will suffer.

Define the Target Population

- In this step marketing researchers must determine the population of interest for the study. Broadly put, who are you trying to reach? Marketing researchers will get this information from the research sponsor as detailed in the objectives of the study's research design. Suppose the city of Santa Fe, New Mexico, decides it wants to gauge the business climate in the city. The city might determine that it needs to survey business owners to capture their insights as to the business growth, and potential growth, of Santa Fe. In this case, the target population is business owners.

■ **FIGURE 10.4**
Sampling Design Process

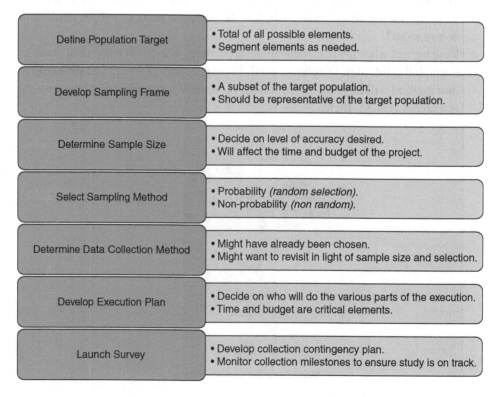

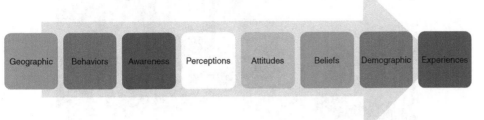

Figure 10.5 lists many different bases for segmenting populations. Perhaps the research study requires that the target population be based on a geographic characteristic such as the midwestern United States or the south of France. Ultimately researchers will survey people; however, the initial geographic target example in this case is based on location. The target might also be behaviorally based. Perhaps marketing researchers need to survey people who eat steak at least once a week or who get their hair cut every month, or who watch certain TV programs. Knowledge or awareness levels are also potential bases of segmentation. The target population can be based on many aspects beyond simply a demographic such as age, income, ethnicity, or gender. Oftentimes we think of a target population or market segments as just demographic characteristics when in fact there are many ways to segment the population into targeted respondents.

Develop Sampling Frame

Sample Frame:
- *A manageable subset of the target population.*

The sample frame enables researchers to get a more manageable segment of the population to then target. Suppose Wal-Mart wants to gauge customer satisfaction about its latest product offerings. Wal-Mart has thousands of stores worldwide. Targeting all these customers would be unwieldy. The target population is Wal-Mart customers; the sample frame is a subset of Wal-Mart customers. Suppose Wal-Mart decides to survey 200 people at ten of its stores. These 2,000 respondents are a subset of the hundreds of thousands of customers worldwide. This subset must be a statistically representative sample of the total universe of Wal-Mart customers in order for these 2,000 customers to adequately represent the customers *not* surveyed.

It is unlikely that the sample frame will precisely match the proportions in the target population. However, it is important that the sample be a statistically representative subset of the target population lest the sample not reflect the responses of the entire population. Perhaps the university dean wants to survey business school students to determine course registration satisfaction levels. Once researchers collect the sample, they realize that only students who live on campus were captured in the sample frame. The researcher could change the objective of the research study to look at only students on campus. By narrowing the objective, researchers can refine the sample frame to match a newly defined target population—such a change must be approved by the research sponsor.

Determine the Sample Size

Before a U.S. election, numerous polls are taken. How is it possible for 1,000 randomly selected Americans to accurately represent the over 200M registered voters?

■ **FIGURE 10.6**

Mall Intercepts are a Common Form of Non-Probability Convenience (high-traffic location) Sampling

Image © Dmitrijs Dmitrijevs, 2011. Used under license from Shutterstock, Inc.

It's not witchcraft that enables researchers to use samples to represent populations, but simple statistics. Before a survey is launched, marketing researchers, along with the research sponsor, must determine the desired sample size. Figure 10.7 provides an overview of the main sample size methods.

Sample Size:
- *The number of respondents needed to complete the survey—not only the number of people the researcher approaches.*
- *Although the population size has a role in determining the sample size (particularly for small populations), the key driver in the sample size is the **variance** within the target population.*
- **Movie night decision:**
  - Suppose you were deciding whether to see a particular movie that you had heard was good. Because the movie is in the genre of movies you typically like, you decide to do a little research before deciding whether to go. You conduct some secondary research by reading about the movie's plot and characters, and its reviews, both professional and lay reviews through various websites. To augment your secondary findings you conduct some primary research in the form of interviewing three friends (a sample of the population of friends) whose opinions you view as *equally reliable.*
  - **Scenario 1 Interview Results:** One friend loved the movie, one hated it, and the last friend thought the movie was so-so. Are these mixed results

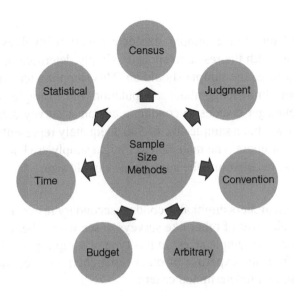

definitive enough to make the decision about seeing the movie? Probably not. You would likely determine that you should ask more friends until a critical mass of opinion developed.

- **Scenario 2 Interview Results:** All three friends loved the movie. Now are these three same opinions reliable enough to make a decision? In this case you will probably not feel the need to ask more friends as even with three friends a clear pattern has emerged.

- Take-away: The key to a good sample size is not the population size but the variance, or differences, within the population. The more varied, or different, the population is the larger the sample should be to adequately represent the total population. Remember that in neither scenario was the population (total number) of friends the issue, but the variance within the friends' opinions was the key. As a caveat to this rule, the population size can play a role in the sample size if the population size is quite small.

Sample Size Methods

Census:

- Although a census is not a sample, it's an important issue to address in the discussion of sampling. A census is an exact enumeration. If there are 30 students in a classroom, asking all 30 about their views on the course would be a census of students' opinions. In small populations it might be relatively easy to conduct a census. However, when the population is large (so defined and determined by the researcher or research sponsor) a representative sample of the population is warranted. A key issue surrounding taking a census is ensuring that the researcher has in fact captured everyone. A representative sample is better than an incomplete census. Every ten years the U.S. government takes a census of the population. The government tries to survey everyone, yet there are some segments of the population thought to be undercounted. In these cases, the Census Bureau makes statistical adjustments, based on sophisticated modeling, to correct for presumed inequalities and inaccuracies in the census data.

Judgment:

- This type of qualitative sample size determination involves the researcher, perhaps along with the research sponsor, simply determining, based on some criteria, how large the sample should be. This sampling technique is typically based on prior knowledge about a population. For example, suppose a shopping mall manager decides to conduct a customer survey and, based on past surveys, knows that a sample size of 500 adequately represents the population of all mall customers. The mall manager might simply use knowledge about her customer base to determine the appropriate sample size.

Convention:

- Marketing researchers might also conduct secondary research to determine the relative sample sizes of other like surveys to see what other experts have used as their respective sample sizes. In this type of sampling, marketing researchers benefit from the expertise of other researchers in selecting a sample size that meets some predetermined criteria.

Arbitrary:

- In arbitrary sampling the sample size determination is less clear. Using this approach, marketing researchers might select a sample size that is some percentage of the target population. For example, in an organization of 10,000 employees the marketing researcher might randomly select 10 percent of these employees to be invited into the sample. In this case, the researcher is using ostensibly reasonable and presumably defendable criteria. Other arbitrary methods might include when a researcher quite simply arbitrarily picks a sample size because it seems reasonable.

Budget:

- In an era of limited budgets, many organizations give the research provider a budget from which to develop and execute the marketing research project. Suppose a research firm is given $8,000 dollars to obtain the sample and it costs $50 per respondent to conduct a telephone survey. In this case, the sample size is a function of the budget, thus 8,000/50 = 160 respondents. What if this sample size is unacceptably low to the research sponsor? What options does the researcher have to raise the sample size? Marketing researchers can change various aspects of the research project to reduce non-sample costs and then redirect those funds to increase the sample size. Figure 10.8 highlights some cost reducing strategies, in addition to increasing the budget, marketing researchers often use.

■ **FIGURE 10.8**

Cost Reducing Strategies: Increase Budget/Reduce Project Scope/Change Collection Method

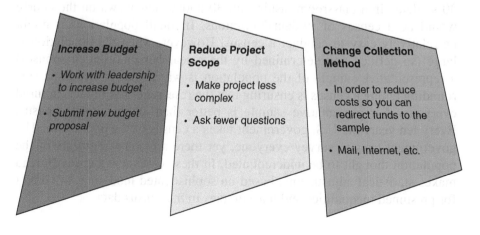

Increase Budget

- Work with leadership to increase budget
- Submit new budget proposal

Reduce Project Scope

- Make project less complex
- Ask fewer questions

Change Collection Method

- In order to reduce costs so you can redirect funds to the sample
- Mail, Internet, etc.

Time:

- In some cases time might have an impact on the sample size. When conducting surveys for the U.S. government, the inaptly named Paperwork Reduction Act mandates that the amount of time respondents can spend on a survey—so-called "burden hours" is limited to X. In other words, for a given survey the researcher might only be allowed 50 total hours of burden time which, if a survey takes 10 minutes to complete, produces a sample size of 300. A larger sample would require that the survey length be shortened to reduce the time to complete the survey and thus the sample size would rise. The thinking behind this law is that the U.S. government aims to reduce the imposition on the public that these surveys are perceived to create.
- In a business setting, the research sponsor might only give the researcher X amount of time to complete the survey. If a researcher must collect all surveys within 24 hours, as opposed to two weeks, she will likely have a small sample size due to the tight deadline.

Statistical:

- Statistical methods are used by most researchers who want a statistically valid and defendable sample size. Several concepts are important to understand in the discussion of the statistical approach to sampling.

The Central Limit Theorem:

- This theorem states that as the number of observations grows the distribution of those observations will increasingly approximate a normal distribution.
- This theorem was developed and quantified by French mathematician Abraham de Moivre and introduced in a 1733 article demonstrating the theorem through the predictable probabilities revealed by consecutively flipping coins.
- If you flip a fair coin the probability of heads or tails is 0.5 or a 50 percent chance that the coin will be either heads or tails. However if you flip a coin twice, how confident are you that it will be heads once and tails once? If you flip the coin ten times, presumably your confidence of some combination of heads and tails increases. In other words you might well get two heads in two flips but you are very unlikely to get ten heads in ten flips. The more flips there are, the closer the results will be to the theorized 50 percent heads and 50 percent tails. Table 10–1 depicts the probability outcomes based on an increasing number of coin tosses. We see from Table 10–1 that if we flip a coin 100 times, the biggest statistical spread we might expect is 56 heads and 44 tails.
- Let's look at a practical example to highlight the principle concept behind the central limit theorem. If you are driving down the road and the traffic light at the upcoming intersection is turning red, you will stop. Another time the light turns yellow just before you get to the intersection so you are able to make the light. On a given day, do you think you make or do not make the traffic lights on your route? You might make all five lights on your route one day and miss

Number of Flips	Number of Heads	Probability of Heads
4	1	0.25
100	56	0.56
1,000	510	0.51
10,000	4,988	0.498

■ TABLE 10–1
Coin Toss Probabilities

all five traffic lights another day. However, taken over a long period of time, say a month, you probably make the lights as often as you miss them (assuming your trips are at random times). In other words, over time and given a large set of data (if this case represented by traffic lights) the chances of making or missing the light are likely going to be equal and will in fact become more equal as the number of observations (or traffic lights) increases.

The Normal Distribution:

- A bell curve statistical distribution whereby the data distribution is symmetrical around the mean and that the mean, median, and mode are equal.

The Standard Normal Distribution:

- A normal distribution with a mean of zero and a standard deviation of one.
- This distribution and related formula enable researchers to determine the Z-Score for any value X drawn from normally distributed data.
- The formula is:

$$z = \frac{X - \mu}{\sigma}$$

- Where:
  - z = the number of standard deviations a given value is from the mean
  - X = the value of a given variable
  - μ = the mean of a given variable
  - σ = the standard deviation of a given variable

Some Key Characteristics of a Normal Distribution

Given that the normal distribution is statistically derived, there are aspects of this distribution that are constant for all perfectly normally distributed data—although it's rare to find perfectly normally distributed data in the routine course of conducting marketing research. However, the larger a population is, generally the increasingly normally distributed the data become. Figures 10.9, 10.10, and 10.11 cover many key concepts that typify normally distributed data.

- A bell curve, symmetrically distributed around the mean, is a probabilistic distribution whereby 68 percent of the data observations fall evenly (i.e., plus or minus) around *one* standard deviation from the mean, 95.4 percent of the data fall evenly around two standard deviations from the mean, and 99+ percent

■ **FIGURE 10.9**

Key Characteristics of a Normal Distribution

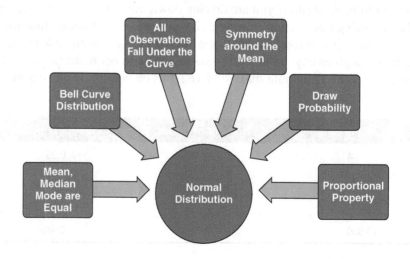

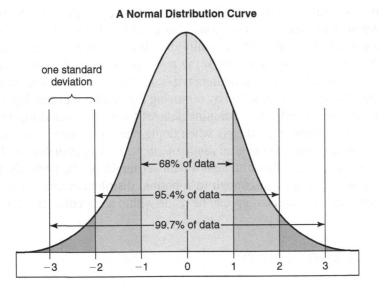

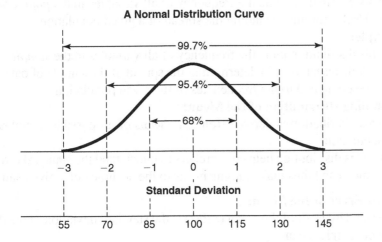

of the data fall within three standard deviations from the mean. Observations falling more than plus or minus three standard deviations from the mean are considered statistical outliers. The **Empirical Rule** is the principle that defines this distribution around the mean.

- **Draw Probability** refers to the probability of where the data lie if a randomly selected data item were selected. In other words, suppose Figure 10.11 represents basketball scores for the top NBA team over the past ten years. On average, the team scores 100 points per game. If we were to draw a score from a hat containing all basketball scores for this team over the past ten years, there is a 68 percent probability that the score we drew would be between 85 and 115; there is a 34 percent chance (half of 68 percent) that the score would be between 85 and 100 or 100 and 115, respectively.

- **Proportional Property** states that the *number* of observations between the mean and a given standard deviation(s) is the *same* for all normally distributed data. In other words, the percentage of respective observations one, two, and three standard deviations from the mean are the same for all normally distributed data sets. This property enables researchers to apply the statistical concepts and constants of normally distributed data to all normally distributed sets of data.

- In a perfectly normally distributed data set, all data fall under the bell curve within three standard deviations plus or minus from the mean. Most data are not, in fact, perfectly normally distributed. Again, data that fall outside three standard deviations from the mean are *statistical outliers*. Data with an inordinate number of outliers will not produce a bell curve. In this case, the data should be *stratified* by removing the outliers and creating a separate set of data whereby the remaining data set forms a normal distribution. This process is used by marketers when doing market segmentation. Oftentimes researchers will see the term *approximates a normal distribution*. This term refers to the fact that although a data set might not be perfectly normally distributed it is close enough to a normal distribution that valid statistical inferences and predictions can be made within acceptable error levels.

Other Distributions

- **Population:**
  - This distribution plots the frequency of all variables in the *population*.
    - Useful for understanding the spread of a given population.
- **Sample:**
  - This distribution plots the frequency of all variables in the *sample*.
    - Aids researchers in determining the spread of the sample of data that can be compared to the frequencies of the given population.
- **Sampling Distribution of the Mean:**
  - This distribution is derived from the means of all possible samples from a population.
    - This distribution helps researchers to understand the standard error of the mean and thus make judgments as to the accuracy of a given sample.

Standard Error of the Mean:
- The standard error of the mean (SEM) is the standard deviation of the distribution of sample means.
  - Assuming equal variability, as the sample size increases the error decreases. Thus as the sample size increases it approaches a census in which case there should be no error, assuming no human error.

$$SE_{\bar{x}} = \frac{s}{\sqrt{n}}$$

Standard Deviation:
- Standard deviation measures the relative dispersion that a sample statistic is around the mean of the population of that statistic. The standard deviation helps researchers to determine the relative variability of a data set. Understanding the standard deviation and its applications are quite useful during the data analysis phase of marketing research. There is a difference between calculating the standard deviation of a population versus a sample.
  - For example, suppose we want to calculate the standard deviation of the number of course credits 1,000 college students are taking. The first question to ask is "Do we know the total number (i.e., population) of student course credits?" If we do, then we use the standard deviation formula that presumes we know the total population of students' course credits; if not we use the standard deviation formula for a sample.

- **Scenario 1:** We *know* that all 1,000 students are taking a combined 12,000 course credits because our survey asked all 1,000 students.

$$\sigma = \sqrt{\frac{\sum (x_1 - \mu)^2}{N}}$$

where:
σ = *the standard deviation*
x_1 = *each value in the population*
μ = *the mean of the values*
N = *the number of values in the population*

- **Scenario 2:** If we *do not* know the total population of students' course credits, we use the standard deviation formula for a *sample*. For example, suppose we had only asked 50 of the 1,000 students about the number of course credits they were taking and thus we had to estimate the remaining 950 students' course load.

$$S = \sqrt{\frac{\sum\limits_{n}^{n} (x_1 - \bar{x})^2}{n-1}}$$

where:
S = *the standard deviation*
x_1 = *each value in the sample*
$\bar{x}$ = *the mean of the values*
n = *the number of values in the sample*

Results for Scenario 2:

- The data of the 50 students' course load is represented in Table 10–2 and Figure 10.12 respectively:
- The average course credit load is 12 and the standard deviation is 2.15 (let's use 2 for simplicity) course credits. In other words, assuming that the data are normally distributed, Figure 10.12 shows the course credit distribution we would expect were we to have surveyed all 1,000 students. The distribution of all 1,000 students' test scores is below. This data reveal that 68 percent of students take between 10 and 14 credit hours, 95 percent take between 8 and 16 credit hours, and 99 percent of students take between 6 and 18 credit hours. Students' taking fewer than six credit hours or more than 18 credit hours fall beyond the normal distribution and are thus statistical outliers.
- *Note: The use of 48 percent for two standard deviations is rounded for simplicity. The actual percentage is closer to 47.7 percent or plus or minus two standard deviations from the mean.*

Student Total Credit Hours per Semester									
11	9	14	10	12	15	15	15	11	15
10	12	8	12	10	15	10	10	11	13
14	15	12	10	15	12	10	11	9	8
12	15	10	14	13	11	10	14	14	10
15	10	11	15	12	10	10	12	14	14

■ TABLE 10–2

Total Student Course Credit Hours

■ FIGURE 10.12

Student Course Credit
Hours

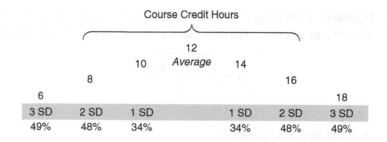

Point Estimate:

- A point estimate is the data point or percentage that is the result of the sample surveyed. For example, if a survey concludes that 65 percent of students like the new meal plan, then "65 percent" is the point estimation of what the population of students think. It is called a point estimate because it represents only one data point (in this case 65 percent) and not a range of data.

Interval Estimate:

- Interval estimates result from the point estimate and its margin of error. Remember that point estimates are actual data collected directly from respondents. Interval estimates are the projection from the point estimate to the population, which consequently includes the margin of error. The "jump" from the sample results (known data) to the population estimation (not fully known data) results in some level of error because researchers are essentially guessing (using statistical and usually quite accurate guesses) about the population in general. In our example above let's presume a 3 percent margin of error. Therefore were we to have interviewed all students we would expect that between 62 percent and 68 percent (65 percent ± 3 percent) of the total student body population would like the new meal plan. The range between the 62 percent and 68 percent is the "interval" component of the equation.

Confidence Interval:

- A confidence interval is a statistical value that quantifies how accurate the results of an estimate are and whose interval includes the true population mean. It is usually between the margin of error ranges. For example, presume a survey of 1,200 randomly selected grocery store shoppers concludes that 55 percent are unhappy with the quality of the produce department. With an error rate of 3 percent and using a 95 percent confidence interval, statistically speaking if this survey were conducted 100 times, 95 out of a 100 times the results would fall within the 52 percent and 58 percent interval range. The results will likely fall in this range 100 percent of the time due to the random error associated with chance variations that occur when going from a sample to the population.

Margin of Error:

- The margin of error is the delta between the observed sample results and the actual results compared to a census of the whole population. For example, if 45 percent of the public reported having run a red light in the past week, plus or minus 3 percent, then we would expect that if the entire population were asked if they had run a red light, between 42 percent and 48 percent of the entire population would report having run a red light in the past week. The amount of error is largely a function of the sample size. Generally, with the variance and confidence interval being the *same*, the larger the sample size the

Standard Deviation	Age
−3 SD	35
−2 SD	40
−1 SD	45
Mean Age	50
1 SD	55
2 SD	60
3 SD	65

■ **TABLE 10–3**
Z-Score Chart

lower the error is. In other words, the more people asked in a survey, the more accurately that sample will represent the entire population.

Sampling Distribution of the Mean:
- A normal distribution occurs when the frequency distribution of the means of all possible samples are calculated. In other words, as the number of samples grows, collectively they increasingly resemble a normal distribution.

Standard Error of the Mean:
- This type of error occurs when the standard deviation of the distribution of the sample means is calculated.

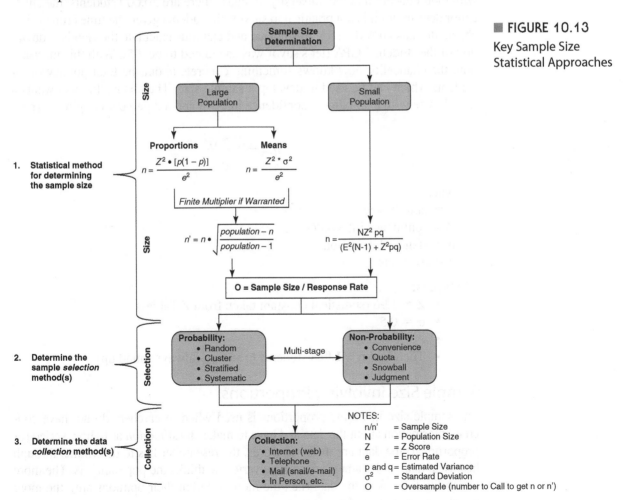

■ **FIGURE 10.13**

Key Sample Size
Statistical Approaches

Z-Score:

- A Z-Score indicates how many standard deviations from the mean a particular data element is. For example, let's suppose we have normally distributed population age data and the average age is 50, with a standard deviation of five years. Using the empirical rule, we calculate the age distribution as represented in Table 10–3:

    Using a 95.4 percent confidence interval, the Z-Score is 2 (2 standard deviations from the mean); thus a 95 percent confidence interval, which is quite common, has a Z-Score of 1.96, slightly less than 2 because 95 percent is slightly less than 96 percent. Several key sample size statistical approaches are identified in Figure 10.13.

Sample Size Involving Means

This method presumes that the researcher can calculate the standard deviation from existing data or that the standard deviation is otherwise known. Using the sample size as a function of the mean is useful if the researcher knows the standard deviation of the data from which a sample will be drawn. Perhaps there had been previous surveys done and the researcher was able to calculate the relative standard deviations among the responses.

Scenario 1:

The university chancellor wants to survey students to determine if they are satisfied with their education at the university. Because there are 30,000 students, the chancellor determines it is not practical to survey all students given the time crunch. The chancellor has GPA data for all students and can thus calculate the standard deviation of the students' GPA (let's say it was calculated to be .05). With this information, the chancellor now knows something concrete about the total population of students which can be used to develop a sample size. The chancellor also wants a sample size with a 95 percent confidence interval and a 3 percent margin of error.

$$n = \frac{Z^2 * \sigma^2}{e^2}$$

where:

n = sample size
Z = confidence interval (Z-Score)
σ = standard deviation
e = error rate

Inputs:

- $Z = 1.96$ (statistical constant taken from Z Tables)
- $\sigma = 0.5$
- $e = 3$ percent
- Therefore **n = 1,068** students to survey (always round up)

Sample Size Involving Proportions

The sample size involving proportions is used when researchers do not have concrete information about the data and have to make an *estimation* as to how varied (or proportional) the data are. In other words, the researcher has to determine, through historical data, or by a best guess, how varied he thinks the population is. The more variability there is in the data (i.e., the more different their opinions are), the more people are needed for the survey.

Scenario 2:

The mayor of Santa Fe wants to survey business owners about whether they approve or disapprove of a new zoning plan. The mayor cannot ask all 10,000 business owner, so she decides to take a sample. Not knowing much about the opinions of the business owners, the mayor presumes the proportion in the Santa Fe population (the number of people who approve versus disapprove of the plan) is equally divided; 50 percent for and 50 percent against the new zoning plan. Again, without any knowledge or history of the people's opinions, assuming equal variability gives the researcher the highest probability of being the least wrong about the actual variability in the population. The mayor decides to use a 3 percent error rate with a 95 percent confidence interval (meaning that if we conducted the survey 100 times, 95 out of a hundred times the survey results would fall within the prescribed margin of error).

$$n = \frac{Z^2 * [p(1-p)]}{e^2}$$

where:

n = sample size
Z = confidence interval (Z-Score)
p = estimated variance
e = error rate

Inputs:

- $Z = 1.96$ (a 95 percent confidence interval)
- $p = 0.5$
- $e = 3$ percent
- Therefore **n = 1,068** business owners to survey

Let's now assume that the mayor has done surveys in the past and has determined that the opinions of the Santa Fe business owners are not as varied as 50/50. In past surveys the public had similar opinions on average 60 percent of the time, which now becomes our new estimation of the variability in the population of business owners. Let's recalculate the sample size.

New Inputs:

- $Z = 1.96$ (a 95 percent confidence interval)
- $p = 0.6$
- $e = 3$ percent
- Therefore **n = 1,025** business owners to survey
- The sample size is lower because with less variance, fewer people are required to represent the population of business owners.

Finally, let's say the mayor decides the town budget will not cover surveying more than 1,000 people. Consequently the mayor decides to raise the error rate to 3.5 percent to reduce the sample size.

New Inputs:

- $Z = 1.96$ (a 95 percent confidence interval)
- $p = 0.6$
- $e = 3.5$ percent
- Therefore **n = 753** business owners to survey
- The sample size is lower because with a higher error rate, fewer people are required to represent the population of business owners.

The Finite Multiplier

This technique is used to reduce a sample size while maintaining the *same level* of accuracy. The revised sample size (n') resulting from the **finite multiplier** enables researchers to reduce the number of required respondents *without* sacrificing accuracy.

For example, presume a sample size of 1,000 based on proportions with a margin of error of 3 percent. What will happen to our survey accuracy if we only get 999 respondents? Is that one respondent missing from the 1,000 enough to change the results? If 58 percent of the 999 respondents said "yes" to a given question would asking one more person (to get to the 1,000) be enough to "move the needle" from 58 percent to either 57 percent or 59 percent? With 1,000 respondents, each person represents only 1/10 of 1 percent. Thus we would have to have 10 people to represent 1 percent of 1,000 respondents. It is highly unlikely that one person would be enough the change and entire overall percentage. Would asking 998, 997, or 996 respondents be statistically significantly different from asking 1,000? Still, probably not. However, what about asking 950 respondents? There is a point at which the margin of error becomes affected by the reduced sample size. The finite multiplier helps researchers to revise-down the sample size within the same margin of error.

Let's continue the survey the Santa Fe mayor wants to conduct using 753 business owners. Using the formula below (remember the Santa Fe population of business owners is 10,000), the 753 becomes 724.13 (round up to 725).

In other words, asking 725 people is as statistically accurate (within the 3 percent error margin) as asking 753 people. The researcher just reduced the sample pool by 28 people, which will save time and money, again without sacrificing accuracy.

$$n' = n \times \sqrt{\frac{population - n}{population - 1}}$$

$$725 = 753 \times \sqrt{\frac{10,000 - n}{10,000 - 1}}$$

This formula is best used for relatively small populations, perhaps 25,000 or fewer people. The larger the population, the greater the impact of each respondent because each respondent represents more people. For example, a sample of 800 people representing a population of 10,000 is different from 800 people representing 1,000,000 people because each of the 800 people represents proportionally more people as the population rises.

Sample Size for Very Small Populations

Not all surveys involve large populations. Although there is no official definition of a small population, 5,000 is a good benchmark. Another consideration is if the calculated sample size (using the regular sample size formulas) is more than 20 percent of the population size; using a sample size calculator for small populations is advised. Suppose a company with 500 employees wants to survey its employees to gauge their opinions on the new office cafeteria. Using the regular statistical formula involving proportions, we arrive at a sample size of 1,068 using a 95 percent confidence interval, maximum variance (0.5/0.5), and an error rate of 3 percent. This sample size makes little sense because it's twice as large as the population of employees, which is 500 people. To address this situation, marketing researchers can employ a sample size calculator for small populations.

$$n = \frac{N Z^2 \, pq}{(E^2(N-1) + Z^2 pq)}$$

Let's follow our example above using the sample size calculator for *small populations* to calculate a sample size for the employee survey gauging staff satisfaction of the new office cafeteria.

where:
n = sample size
N = population size
Z = confidence interval (Z-Score)
p = estimated variance
e = error rate
q = (1–p)

Inputs:
- $N = 500$
- $Z = 1.96$ (at 95 percent confidence interval)
- $p = 0.5 / q = 0.5$
- $e = 3$ percent
- Therefore **n = 341** employees to survey
  - FYI: *If we used the formula for large populations using the formula for proportions and arrived at 341, the error would be very high, the variance less pronounced, and perhaps the confidence interval would have to be reduced. Thus the sample size formula for small populations is the better approach.*

Oversampling

Unless the researcher has exceptional incentives, there will likely be a number of potential respondents who decline to be in the survey. Based on data from past surveys, coupled with expert judgment from the researcher, an estimated response rate is determined. For the sake of our example, let's assume that the researcher has determined that there will be a 40 percent response rate; thus 60 percent of those contacted decline to be in the survey. The oversampling formula, whose result will inform the researcher as to how many people to contact, is below. The researcher would need to contact 1,813 people to get the 725 respondents because only 40 percent of those approached will complete the survey or 853 people (using n = 341).

$$O = \frac{n'}{response\ rate}$$

$$1{,}813 = \frac{725}{.40} \quad \Big/ \quad 853 = \frac{341}{.40}$$

Selecting the Sampling Method

There are two overall approaches in determining how to obtain the sample. The two approaches are **probability** and **non-probability** sampling and each approach has four methods. The essential difference between these methods is whether the respondent *can or cannot calculate* their chance of being selected into the sample,

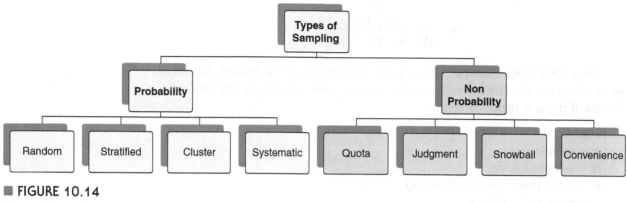

■ FIGURE 10.14
Types of Sampling

or whether it's knowable at all. Figure 10.14 shows the different types of sampling approaches marketing researchers employ.

Probability Sampling

- *The chance (or probability) of selection into the sample can be calculated.*

Non-Probability Sampling

- *The chance of selection into the sample is not random and not fully known or easily calculated.*

Probability Sampling Methods

Random:

- *Simple random sampling (SRS) results when an element of the population has a known and equal chance of selection into the sample.*
- Examples of simple random sampling include the lottery where each ticket has a 1 in X (X being the total number of tickets sold) chance of winning. If you have two tickets, you have twice as good a chance of winning as someone with one ticket. The probability of winning is known and equal (per ticket).
- The term *random* is often misused. For example, suppose the professor needs a student to take the course evaluations to the departmental office and that a student in the class will be chosen at random to perform this duty. If the professor simply chooses a student, this method is most decidedly not random because the professor made a choice based on unknown criteria. If the professor assigns a number to each student and a random number generator picks a number, the student with the corresponding number can be said to have been selected randomly.
- Many telephone surveys are done through **Random Digit Dialing (RDD)** whereby telephone numbers are called randomly through a computerized scrambler method to ensure that everyone who has a telephone has an equal and known probability, or chance, of being selected into the telephone sample.
- Sample RDD providers:
  - www.hosteddialer.com
  - www.insidesales.com/Dialer
  - www.call-em-all.com
- Statistical software such as SPSS, SAS, and Microsoft Excel can generate random samples.
- SRS does not guarantee a representative sample. Marketing researchers might have to take additional samples from the source data, or discard part of the SRS, if the SRS is not representative.

Stratified:

- *Stratified sampling is a two-step process used when the source data are not normally distributed necessitating that the data be stratified, or broken-down, into normally distributed subgroups from which a random sample is then taken.*
- Suppose researchers are trying to determine the average net worth of people living in a particular ZIP code. Suppose there are 10,000 people in that ZIP code and 8,000 have a net worth of X and the remaining 2,000 are all relatives of the Sultan of Brunei (we should be so lucky) and have a net worth of 50X. The average net worth is thus the combined net worth of about 11X. If researchers were to randomly select 100 people from these 10,000 we would expect the average net worth to be around 11X if the data were normally distributed. But as just demonstrated, neither groups' net worth is near the 11X. In this case, the data should be stratified into two groups: one of the 50X and one of the X net worth groups, respectively. Then two random samples are drawn from these groups, revealing two market segments (the 50X and X groups, respectively).

Cluster:

- *Cluster sampling is a process whereby like elements of the target population are separated into clusters from which random samples (or a census if the cluster is small enough) are drawn.*
- Cluster samples are useful when conducting market testing. If a cereal company wants to test a new product, it might locate a cluster of potential customers from a city, or locale, that demographically matches their desired customer base.
- Suppose the university dean wants to know what students think about the new student center on campus. Rather than conduct a university-wide survey, she decides to conduct a cluster sample. The dean researched the demographics of various classes and realized that three general business courses of 50 students each demographically mirror the student population. The dean recommends that the researcher go to each of those three classes and conduct a census by asking all 150 students from the three classes. Because these classes are a representative demographic snapshot of the whole student body, these classes are a suitable subset, or microcosm, of the overall student population.
- If the cluster is large, such as a city representing the nation, a census is not realistic and thus a random sample is drawn from the cluster.

Systematic:

- *Systematic sampling is done by skipping every nth element in a randomly scrambled target population. The skip interval is calculated by dividing the sample size into the population size*
- Suppose we are conducting a survey of grocery store frequent shoppers. There is a population of 10,000 shoppers and the proposed sample size is 1,000. Researchers would divide 10,000/1,000 to calculate a skip interval of 10. Thus researchers would start at some point in the randomized list of 10,000 shoppers and select every tenth shopper, which would result in 1,000 shoppers selected.
- Systematic sampling works well with relatively small populations. If we had a population of 100 million and needed a sample size of 1,000 the skip interval would be 100,000. In larger populations, simple random sampling is generally a better alternative to systematic sampling.

- This type of sampling is common when doing in-person interviews such as mall intercepts. Marketing researches might stop every fifteenth person leaving a store or every tenth person on the street. Demographics can play a role in systematic sampling. For example, marketing researchers might need to stop every fifth woman, or every tenth Asian male, or every fifteenth person wearing a hat.

- It is important that the target population list from which the nth person is selected be randomly presented. Suppose a researcher takes an alphabetized list and selects every tenth name from the list. Someone with the last name of Ashley will never be selected if someone else on the list has a last name of Aaron (supposing Ashley is second on the list). Failure to start the sample selection process from a random list results in both an inability to calculate the chance of being selected into the sample and in a lack of equality of selection probability, both hallmarks of probability sampling.

Non-Probability Sampling Methods

Quota:

- *Quota sampling involves researcher judgment in selecting respondents based on a quota that needs to be achieved.*

- Suppose we are surveying university students about their spring break preferences and that we have an equal number of freshman, sophomores, juniors, and seniors. When we select our sample, we realize that freshman and sophomores are overrepresented. Perhaps more students of those classes live on campus thus the researcher stopped more underclassman. A quota sampling technique might be used whereby the researcher is instructed to revisit the student pool and collect more juniors and seniors in order to create year-in-school parity among the sample.

- Quota sampling can be done to correct for sample imbalances among the respondent base. It can also be done to meet some other pre-determined quota, such as when researchers and research sponsors decide they need more students who have never lived on campus or who have always lived on campus. This type of quota sampling might be done for reasons other than to ensure that the sample is representative of the population.

- Because this type of sampling is inherently judgmental, researcher-created sample selection biases can cause increased research error.

Judgment:

- *As a form of convenience sampling, this non-probability sampling procedure involves researchers, and the research sponsor, using their collective expertise and judgment to select the sample. In many cases researchers might follow some conventional approach by selecting a sample based on some common industry practice or based on "what has worked before."*

- Because the selection is judgmental, marketing researchers must be careful to avoid obtaining a biased sample.

- As the manager of a large appliance store, let's assume that you have conducted many customer surveys over the past several years. It has been your experience that handpicking the sample has worked well in the past and that those samples have seemed to reflect accurately the total population of customers. Your experience, and ostensible expertise, enable you to select a non-probability sample with relative accuracy. In this case, a judgment sample might well work. However, researchers and research sponsors are ill-advised to improvise when using judgment samples. If the researcher and/or research sponsor has little substantive knowledge about the potential respondent base, a probability sampling technique, perhaps simple random sampling, will likely yield more representative results.

Snowball:

- *Snowball sampling is a non-probability pyramidal sampling technique that involves selected respondents referring other respondents into the sample. This technique is built from an initial probability or non-probability-based sample.*

- Snowball sampling can be executed by any number of referral rounds. For example, suppose you randomly selected 100 people to be in a dishwashing liquid usage survey. Once the researcher has the 100 respondents, she can then ask those 100 to each refer X number of people into the survey. Those new respondents are then asked to refer another X number of respondents into the survey and so on. Depending on the number of referral iterations, this method can result in a large sample over a potentially short period of time.

- Researchers should be cautioned that with each referral iteration the survey purpose can get increasingly lost, or at least muddled. The more complex the survey purpose, the less reliance the researcher should place on the increasingly distant referred respondents. In our dishwashing example, it's likely that because this purpose seems simple, the referred respondents could accurately explain the survey's purpose to each round of referred respondents. However, if the survey were about cultural or buyer behaviors, motivations, and related issues, the referred respondents lack the expertise to explain the survey purpose well. And remember, by the time more than one referral iteration has occurred, the respondents are increasingly removed from the marketing researcher who is conducting the study. Thus snowball samples might result in less than qualified respondents as the referral process expands. Marketing researchers might decide it's best to have only one or two rounds of referrals to maintain some control over the sample. Also, each respondent should be coded so researchers know when in the snowball sample they were selected.

Convenience:

- *Convenience sampling is aptly named. These non-probability samples are collected in high-traffic or otherwise "convenient" locations. The interviewer makes the selection usually based on some pre-determined criteria.*

- You have seen the mall survey taker with a clipboard ready to pounce on unsuspecting passersby. What reaction do you have when you see them? Avoid them, feign an illness, pretend to be on your cell phone, or simply prepare to shrug them off? Why do we have that reaction? The central reason for this reaction is that convenience sampling is non-probabilistic. In other words, you do not know the *chance* of being selected into the sample. Let's revisit this scenario with probability sampling. Suppose you notice that the clipboard-wielding marketing research is stopping every tenth person: systematic sampling. Because you know that you are the third person passing by you are confident that you will not be selected because with probability sampling you know the chance, or probability, of selection into the sample.

- Convenience samples are an effective method for collecting quick information.

- Marketing researchers can target specific demographics based on where the data are collected.

- Marketing researchers should be careful before assuming that a convenience sample is a representative sample of the target market. In many cases it will not be a representative sample yet it might well yield valuable information about your target population segment.

- These types of samples are good for product testing or otherwise high respondent involvement research as the respondent is present.

Multistage Sampling

- *Multistage sampling involves combining any number of sampling techniques.*
- This type of sampling can be used when one sampling technique fails to yield a suitable sample in both size and/or composition.
- Researchers should code respondents based on the way in which they were recruited into the sample in order to determine if sample selection biases are present. For example, suppose you need 1,000 people in your survey about types of TV news programs people watch. Your research staff goes to local malls to collect the data. After a hectic weekend of data collection, your research team reports 700 respondents. The research sponsor wants 1,000 respondents in order to maintain the 3 percent error rate; thus, your research team must collect 300 more respondents over the next 24 hours. Having exhausted your mall data collection patience, you decide to collect the remaining 300 though random digit dialing, a telephone probability technique. You now have the required 1,000 respondents. When reporting the results, this multistage technique must be explained in the *research methods* section of the research report. The researcher must also code which respondents came from the mall (non-probability sampling) and which respondents were reached by a random digit dial telephone method (probability sampling). Failure to code the questionnaire and thus keep track of the telephone versus mall respondents will prevent the researcher from comparing the 700 respondents against the 300 respondents to ensure that their answers on the same questions correlate in order to make the case that the researcher has one set of 1,000 respondents rather than two sets of 700 and 300 respondents, respectively. The researcher needs to prove that the data collection method itself did not affect the results. In other words, if 65 percent of the mall intercept respondents reported that they watch *CBS News* then we would assume that 65 percent of the telephone respondents should also watch *CBS News*. If only 30 percent of the telephone respondents watch *CBS News* then there is a statistically significant difference between how the telephone respondents and the mall intercept respondents answered that question. Thus the researcher really has two separate data sets: one of 700 and one of 300 respondents.
- Figure 10.15 summarizes the sampling types that can be combined to create multistage sampling.

Online Sampling

- One of the major challenges in Internet marketing research is in obtaining a representative sample. When a news station asks the public to go online and respond to a survey on an issue, it is collecting a self-selected sample. The Internet survey might collect 100,000 respondents in a matter of hours (or less), yet this sample size, although very large, is neither randomly generated nor judgmentally selected. It's quite possible that despite the lack of randomness of the sample, excellent and insightful information might well

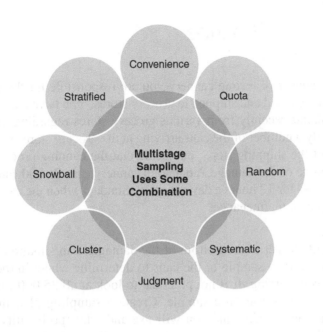

be collected. However, researchers must be aware of the limitations of self-selected samples because the researcher is removed from the sample selection process. Another issue is that the researcher cannot truly determine who is responding to a given survey. How does the researcher know who actually responded to a given Internet survey? As a partial remedy, marketing researchers can select the sample through a random process and invite those respondents into a *password-protected* survey.

- A sampling of online sampling resources:
  - www.startsampling.com
  - www.surveysampling.com
  - www.thesamplenetwork.com
  - www.synovate.com

■ **FIGURE 10.16**

Politicians Use Many Types of Sampling Methods When Conducting Polls to Gauge Public Opinion

Image © Kalim, 2011. Used under license from Shutterstock, Inc.

Research in Practice

Case:

- As the manager of a soup cannery you are responsible for the quality of the soup being canned and shipped to grocery stores. You have received a number of complaints recently from various grocery stores regarding damaged cans. Apparently a number of the cans arriving at the grocery store are dented. After ruling out the shipping step, you decide that the canning process itself is the likely source of the damage. Your soup cannery cans 25,000 cans of soup per day and runs for 12 hours a day except on Sundays when the cannery is closed for equipment maintenance.

Assignment:

- You decide to get to the bottom of the damaged can situation and you will do so by taking a sample of the cans to determine where in the process the damage is occurring. It is not practical to look at all 25,000 cans in a given day; thus, you settle on a sample. Create a sampling plan that addresses which sampling technique you will use and why (probability versus non-probability) and how many soup cans you will sample. You want to conduct the study assuming a 95 percent confidence interval and a margin of error of 3.5 percent. You conducted a quality control soup can survey two years ago and found that 60 percent of the cans had some defect in the label affixation. Also, you decide to revise-down the sample size while maintaining the same level of accuracy. Finally, you expect that the response rate (in this case the number of soup cans that should be included into the sample) is 80 percent.

Sample Size Exercises:

1. **Scenario A:**
   - The university has 18,000 students. The chancellor wants to survey the students to determine their support of policy changes. Due to time and budget constraints, there is not time to ask all 18,000 students so you will do a survey. The chancellor wants to be 95% confident that the results from the sample are within 3.5% of the results were you to ask all students. In past student surveys, students had similar opinions on average 65% of the time. In order to save some money, you decide to reduce the sample size while maintaining the same level of accuracy of 3.5%. Once you have this revised sample size determined, you realize that seniors are underrepresented in your sample as they represent 25% of the student body but are only 20% of the revised sample—thus you must adjust your revised sample size accordingly without increasing the total revised sample size number. Finally you are using an Internet survey and expect about a 40% response rate.

Questions

- Using the statistical method of determining a sample size, how many students would you need to complete the survey and how many students would you have to ask to get the desired number of respondents?
- How many seniors should be added to the survey?

2. **Scenario B:**
   - You work for a small furniture company with 1,500 employees and the boss wants to survey employees regarding their satisfaction with working for the company. The boss wants to be 95% confident that the results from the sample are within 4% of the results if you were to ask all employees. Since this survey will be the first one done, there is no clear understanding of the employees' opinions. Finally, you are using an Internet survey and you expect about a 75% response rate since incentives were offered.

Question

   - Using the statistical method of determining a sample size, how many employees would you need to complete the survey and how many employees would you have to ask to get the desired number of respondents?

Chapter Summary

A staple of marketing research is using samples to represent populations. Ensuring a representative sample using online sampling has been challenging for marketing researchers. A normal distribution is a data distribution whereby the mean, median, and mode are the same. The Central Limit Theorem states that as the size of a population grows, its distribution will increasingly approximate a normal distribution. A census is an exact enumeration of the target population of interest and a sample is a subset of the population. The three major issues in sampling include who to sample, how many people to sample, and how to select the sample. There are many considerations that marketing researchers should weigh before executing a sampling plan such as the time, budget, level of accuracy desired, and access to respondents. Several steps are involved in designing a sampling plan. These steps are defining the target population, developing a sample frame (a subset of the target population), determining the sample size, selecting the sampling method (the way by which the researcher will select the sample), determining the data collection method (telephone, Internet, in person, or mail), developing an execution plan, and launching the survey. An important distinction in sampling is the difference between determining the sample size and the method by which researchers select respondents into the sample. The sample size is a function of the variability within a population. There are several methods for determining the sample size including budget

(what is affordable), time (how much time is available), arbitrary (some rule of thumb), judgment (using the researcher's experience), and conventional (learning from others). Two main statistical sample size methods include determining the sample size through understanding the population's mean or by estimating the population proportions. There is a separate statistical formula for small populations (a population notionally under 5,000). Marketing researchers should code the respondents by their respective selection method to ensure that there are no biases resulting from the sample selection method itself. Target populations can be segmented a number of different ways such as by geography, behavior, awareness, perception, attitude, belief, demographic, or experience. Point and interval estimates are important to understanding the impact of a sample representing a population. Point estimates are single data points such as 80 percent sampled liked the product. The interval estimate takes the point estimate and incorporates the margin of error as is required when going from a controlled known sample to the sample representing the population at large. Standard deviation is a measure of dispersion that quantifies the distance a particular observation is from the mean of the data. Good samples can accurately reflect the population of interest. There are two overall approaches to selecting the sample: probability and non-probability sampling. Probability sampling is a sampling technique whereby each respondent has a known chance of being selected into the sample. Probability methods include cluster, systematic, stratified, and simple random. Non-probability sampling is sampling whereby the respondent does not know the chance of being selected into the survey. Non-probability methods include judgment, convenience, snowball, and quota. Multistage sampling occurs when researchers combine sampling techniques.

ISSUE IN THE SPOTLIGHT   A Solid Sample

Jackie Lorch, Vice President,
Global Knowledge Management
Survey Sampling International
www.surveysampling.com

A solid sample is the essential foundation for any research project. Offline sample (aka landline telephone, mobile/wireless, mail) is still used for many government, syndicated, and public release projects. Online, however, is the dominant sample methodology today (ESOMAR Global Market Research 2010). This trend toward online has been driven by lower costs, speed of results and the flexibility of the online mode, where researchers can show product packaging, ads, or other visuals. There is also some evidence that respondents answer more candidly online when questioned about topics such as smoking, diet, health or other personal issues.

Whatever the mode, the basic elements of a good sample remain the same. It must accurately reflect the population under study, it must incorporate random selection, and controls must be in place to minimize potential biases such as non-response and non-coverage. An example of non-coverage bias would be using a sports website as the sample source for a study to understand TV watching among the general public. Non-response bias would occur if a telephone study targeting sports fans was conducted during a major sporting event.

Most online research today is conducted via large panels of people who have agreed to take surveys. However, the pool of people willing to join a research panel is limited compared to the total online population, so sample companies are now blending samples from additional sources, such as social media and web destinations, to create a more diverse, representative online sample. Blending must be managed carefully to ensure that the sample composition is consistent and as representative as possible of the total online population. Sample providers use various techniques to achieve this, including profiling of respondents and matching with known data points and benchmarks.

Similar challenges exist for other sample methodologies. According to the National Health Interview Survey, January–June 2010, 98 percent of U.S. households can be accessed by telephone; however, 27 percent only have a cell phone, and an additional 16 percent consider themselves cell phone dominant. To be representative, a telephone sample must include both landline and cell phone households.

During the early years of online research, some researchers expressed concern about the quality of online samples, because it is more difficult to verify identities online. In response to these concerns, sample companies developed controls, including digital fingerprinting, quality checks and verification procedures to minimize duplication and other quality concerns.

One of the biggest challenges of online research today is giving research respondents a good enough experience so they will continue to take part in market research in the future. Many online surveys are too long, or are tedious, confusing or poorly designed. Without a live interviewer, there is a danger that such a survey will cause a respondent to answer carelessly, or quit before finishing. The researcher of the future must respect the participant's time and provide an enjoyable, engaging survey-taking experience.

The sample of the future is likely to be independent of mode. Individuals will be identified and offered the opportunity to take a survey via whatever mode they prefer, whether telephone, handheld device, PC, or other device.

11

Data Preparation and Cross Tabulations

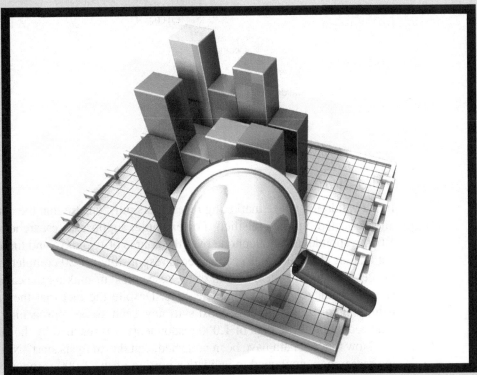

Image © Norebbo, 2011. Used under license from Shutterstock, Inc.

Learning Objectives:

- Understand the steps researcher's take before analyzing data
- Learn methods of validating data
- Understand the different coding rubrics for the different data levels

- Learn the difference between editing and coding
- See typical ways that survey datasets are formatted in software
- Learn about bivariate and multivariate cross tabulations

- Understand the difference among the cross-tabulation data views
- Learn about marginals and their use in marketing research

Chapter Eleven

Once the data are collected, the process to ensure that the data are ready to be analyzed begins. Remember that when conducting a survey the sample represents the target population. Any error in the sample is amplified when then used to represent the population. Marketing researchers must ensure the integrity of the data before the analysis process begins. Figure 11.1 is a starting point.

■ FIGURE 11.1
Validating Data

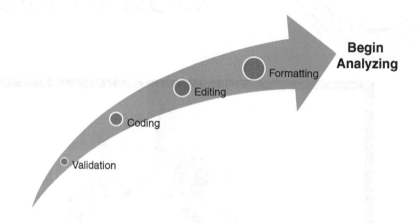

Validation

In the validation phase marketing researchers must ensure that the data were actually collected and not falsified. For example, suppose a researcher is collecting 1,000 respondents by telephone over the course of two days and there are 50 people making the calls, thus each caller is responsible for 20 completed surveys. As the deadline approaches, several of the research staff making the calls are running short of their goal of 20 complete calls. Despite the fact that they appear to be behind in collecting the data, most staff now seem to be approaching the job with renewed vigor as the goal of 1,000 respondents was reached by the deadline.

Now that the data have been collected, can the analysis start? Not yet, marketing researchers now need to validate a portion of the 1,000 respondents to ensure the integrity of the data. This process is done through **Call Backs**.

Call Backs:
- *The process of calling back, or otherwise contacting, survey respondents to verify their participation in the survey.*
- Call backs might be done for Internet or mail surveys if the survey is not anonymous.
- For Internet and mail surveys, respondents can indicate that they are receptive to a call back to verify their survey responses. In this sense, call back refers to re-contacting the respondent to verify his questionnaire responses.
- The call backs might be initiated on a random bases and then progress to more targeted call backs based on the data found. For example, if of our 50 agents making the calls, we find that a few agents in particular seem to have collected faulty or fabricated data, researchers would refocus the call back process on those agents.

When doing call backs, marketing researchers are primarily looking to ensure that the survey responses were completed and correct as well as verifying refusals/cutoffs and checking for biases. There is overlap among these four concepts during the call back process. Figure 11.2 covers the key issues in data validation.

Validating the Data – Key Call Back Issues			
Complete	**Correct**	**Refusal/Cutoff**	**Biases**
• Were all questions answered • Any missing data	• Filled-out correctly • Answers correct • Verifying skip patterns	• Why & on which questions • Understand the difference	• Interviewer • Pressure • Wording

- **Complete:**
  - During call backs marketing researchers want to be confident that the 1,000 respondents in our example answered the entire questionnaire. Part of the call back process might include asking the respondent a few of the questions from the questionnaire to ensure that they were in fact asked those questions. Generally, asking a few questions *(likely not the whole questionnaire)* will inform researchers as to whether the respondent was asked all of the questions. Typically respondents will be asked a few questions from the beginning, middle and end of the survey to increase the odds that the researcher will catch whether they were asked all the questions on the questionnaire.
  - It's possible that on a 25 question survey, all respondents for researcher X were only asked the first 20 questions. Why might the researcher have failed to ask the remaining five questions per respondent? Perhaps those questions took too long to complete and the researcher decided to leave them blank—or complete those five questions himself (unethical researcher behavior) to expedite getting all 20 respondents he needs to complete his work on the project.
  - However, we should not assume that a 20 question questionnaire requires that respondents complete all 20 questions. If a questionnaire has skip patterns, it's quite possible that a respondent would only complete 15 of the 20 questions. In determining how *complete* the survey is the marketing researcher needs to be aware of the skip patterns and ensure that respondents were not asked questions that should have been skipped based on their previous answers. Respondents might well answer a question that should have been skipped if they had been asked the question (perhaps incorrectly) by the researcher. Researchers should verify that the skip patterns were followed.
- **Correct:**
  - During the call back process, marketing researchers need to determine whether the responses received by the respondents were correct—i.e. were the answers the respondent gave the right answer for a respective question. Let's say respondent #45 was *asked* all questions on our questionnaire and in fact *responded* to all of them. Marketing researchers will want to verify the response itself—not just whether the respondent was asked and answered the question. The correctness of the answer must be verified as well. If respondent #45 was asked her favorite color and her response was recorded as "red" marketing researchers will verify that, during the call back process, "red" was the answer recorded during the initial call. If the respondent says that she told the researcher that her favorite color was purple not red, the marketing researcher should question the entire questionnaire by verifying more questions on that questionnaire. If more

than one question is incorrectly recorded, the marketing researcher should check the other respondents who were called by that researcher to verify those respondents' answers.

- If a survey has an incorrect answer, that answer should obviously not be used—although it is not necessarily a given that the entire questionnaire should be discarded. Marketing researchers must use their judgment in determining whether a questionnaire should be discarded due to the unreliability of the answers.
- A researcher making the calls might have intentionally or unintentionally recorded the respondents' answers incorrectly.
  - *Unintentionally recording incorrectly:* Perhaps the researcher simply misunderstood the respondent's answers or accidentally recorded the response incorrectly *(perhaps entered "yes" instead of "no")*. Fatigue or poor interviewer training might be in play here.
  - *Intentionally recoding incorrectly:* Perhaps the researcher wants to skew the data in a particular way and incorrectly records a respondent's answers.
- **Refusal/Cutoff:**
  - If the marketing researcher verifies that all questions were asked, yet not all were answered, researchers can investigate the cause and benefit from determining why some questions were skipped. Suppose we have 20 questions in a questionnaire and there is a pattern of respondents not answering question 8 *(presumed refusal)* or a pattern of no questions being answered after question 15 *(presumed cutoff)* the researcher needs to know why. Perhaps the question is in some way offensive to the respondent. The question would thus need to be rephrased or removed from subsequent surveys. Maybe respondents simply did not understand a given question and consequently refused to give an answer. This cause might be the result of a poorly worded question or stem from a lack of interviewer training on how to address respondents' questions about the survey. Perhaps the question is complex or technical and the interviewer is not trained to elaborate on the question's meaning.
  - Based on the numbers of cutoffs and refusals, marketing researchers can revisit the questionnaire and address those problem areas for subsequent questionnaires.
- **Biases:**
  - There are many types of biases that can have an impact on the integrity of the data. During the call back process, researchers should determine how the initial interview was perceived by the respondents. Key questions to ask:
    - Did the respondent feel pressured to have a certain opinion?
    - If the respondent was indecisive, did the interviewer sway them one way or another?
    - Did the respondent feel intimidated or ill at ease by the interviewer?
    - What was the interviewer's tone and manner?
    - Did the respondent feel rushed?
    - Was the respondent multitasking to a fault during the interview?
    - Were all the questions clear?
  - Identifying biases can be tricky because their impact is less quantifiable than some of the other methods used to assess the validity of the questionnaire.
  - Researchers need to use expert judgment in determining if biases exist, and if so, what to do about them.

Coding

Coding is the process of ascribing a numeric code to non-numeric variables. These codes are useful in the analysis phase of the research project. Additionally, the survey

67	12,40	830,80	4,47	67	12,40	830,80	15,63	8
169	13,70	2315,30	11,27	169	13,70	2315,30	35,00	287(
110	13,70	1507,00	7,37	110	13,70	1507,00	35,00	43
190	54,17	10292,30	12,6	190	54,17	10292,30	35,00	70(
75	54,17	4062,75	5	75	54,17	4062,75	35,00	105(
112	54,17	6067,04	7,5	112	54,17	6067,04	35,00	192
30	207,50	6225,00	0,2	30	207,50	6225,00	9,36	15
165	14,25	2351,25	1,1	165	14,25	2351,25	5	83
418	15,90	6646,20	2,8	418	15,90	6646,20	244	15
269	15,90	4277,10	1,8	269	15,90	4277,10	75	18
)025	8,32	0,50	0,245	0	8,32	0,00	0	
5	1666,67	8333,35	0,337	5	1666,67	8333,35	180	14
244	6,50	1586,00	1,63	244	6,50	1586,00	100	27
75	25,00	1875,00	0,5	75	25,00	1875,00	150	37
4	33,33	1,33	0,2	0	33,33	0,00	10	41
)	8,32	1497,60	1,21	180	8,32	1497,60	10	10
)	27,50	2750,00	0,667	100	27,50	2750,00	6	17
)	25,00	3750,00	1,01	150	25,00	3750,00	2	7
240	4,91	1178,40	12	240	4,91	1178,40	363,99	7
76	20,34	1545,84	3,8	76	20,34	1545,84	1281,80	256
67	12,40	830,80	4,47	67	12,40	830,80	15,63	84
169	13,70	2315,30	11,27	169	13,70	2315,30	35,00	287(
110	13,70	1507,00	7,37	110	13,70	1507,00	35,00	437
190	54,17	10292,30	12,6	190	54,17	10292,30	35,00	70(
75	54,17	4062,75	5	75	54,17	4062,75	35,00	105(
112	54,17	6067,04	7,5	112	54,17	6067,04	35,00	192
30	207,50	6225,00	0,2	30	207,50	6225,00	9,36	154
165	14,25	2351,25	1,1	165	14,25	2351,25	5	833
418	15,90	6646,20	2,8	418	15,90	6646,20	244	158
269	15,90	4277,10	1,8	269	15,90	4277,10	75	187
)025	8,32	0,50	0,245	0	8,32	0,00	0	
5	1666,67	8333,35	0,337	5	1666,67	8333,35	180	149
244	6,50	1586,00	1,63	244	6,50	1586,00	100	275
75	25,00	1875,00	0,5	75	25,00	1875,00	150	375
4	33,33	1,33	0,2	0	33,33	0,00	10	41
)	8,32	1497,60	1,21	180	8,32	1497,60	10	109
)	27,50	2750,00	0,667	100	27,50	2750,00	6	174
)	25,00	3750,00	1,01	150	25,00	3750,00	2	72
240	4,91	1178,40	12	240	4,91	1178,40	363,99	72
76	20,34	1545,84	3,8	76	20,34	1545,84	1281,80	256
67	12,40	830,80	4,47	67	12,40	830,80	15,63	84
169	13,70	2315,30	11,27	169	13,70	2315,30	35,00	2870
110	13,70	1507,00	7,37	110	13,70	1507,00	35,00	437

FIGURE 11.3

Survey Data Formatted in Columns and Rows will Facilitate the Data Analysis Process

itself should be coded to reflect when and how it was collected. For example, suppose researchers collected 500 surveys by telephone and 300 through the Internet. Researchers need to be able to determine which surveys came from the telephone and which ones came from the Internet so they can determine if the survey responses are materially different based on the data collection method itself. The same is true with mail surveys. Researchers should code the responses as they arrive in order to measure the impact of time. Researchers need to know if mail responses that arrive after a week are statistically different from those that arrived a month after the survey was launched. If different, this information enables researchers to segment the responses. Researchers should then explore the possibility that some extraneous variable(s) intervened during the collection period that untowardly affected the survey results.

Surveys should have either the question codes written directly on the questionnaire or have a coding sheet the researcher uses when entering or downloading the data into a spreadsheet.

As a review, the four data levels are nominal, ordinal, interval, and ratio. All of these data levels can be coded—although ratio data, and some interval data, are essentially self coded as ratio data are numeric. However, coding comes into play even with ratio data.

Researchers can use whatever codes they like; however consistency should prevail. For example, if the code for "yes" is 1 and the code for "no" is 2, those codes should be used for all yes/no questions on the questionnaire. Also, researchers can reuse codes. For example, the question about your sex can be recorded as "male" 1 and "female" 2. Reusing codes is acceptable, and in fact common because, in our example, the question number itself will differentiate what the code "1" means. Think about the impact of using unique codes on a 100 question questionnaire. Such a coding scheme would be unwieldy.

Coding Nominal Data

- Nominal data examples with potential codes:
  - *Do you like to travel?*   *Yes (1) / No (2)*
  - *What is your profession?*   *Doctor (1), Dentist (2), Lawyer (3)*
- Open-ended questions pose more of a challenge. Take a survey of 1,200 vacationers. If asked to reveal what they liked best about their respective vacations we will get multiple answers for each respondent. The key with coding open-ended questions is grouping like answers and coding those. For example, on our vacation survey suppose 500 people responded with variations on the weather such as: *great weather, sunny, hot and wonderful, a great break from the winter, etc.* These answers are all unique in their word choice but common in their meaning. Marketing researchers could simply create a nominal category of "weather" and code it as "1". Marketing researchers would then go through all the open-ended questions looking for patterns of responses that could be, like our weather example, grouped into a single category. In many cases marketing researchers might include the full breadth of the open-ended comments in an appendix to the research report and might also discuss how the groupings were done in the *research methods* section of the research report.
- *"Check all that apply"* questions might have quite a number of choices. Let's suppose we have a survey with 10 car features listed *(leather seats, sun roof, etc.)* and we ask respondents to check all of the features their car has. In this case we would have 10 codes, one for each feature. Not everyone would check all 10 items, but we still have the codes.

Coding Ordinal Data

- Ordinal data examples with potential codes:
  - *What is your color preference?*   *Red (1), Blue (2), Green (3)*
  - *Put these items in order of preference.*   *Apple (1), Fig (2), Plum (3)*
    - It is important not to confuse the item's code with its relative rank. In other words, apple is coded as a 1 but it might be the 3rd snack choice. Thus we have a coded notation of 1(3) meaning apple was ranked 3rd by a particular respondent.
- The data can then be displayed using the relative codes as depicted in Figure 11.4.

■ FIGURE 11.4

Snack Rank Data

Survey Data	Apple	Fig	Plum
1	1	3	2
2	2	1	3
3	1	2	3
4	3	2	1
5	1	3	2
6	1	2	3
7	2	3	1
8	3	2	1
9	2	1	3
10	3	1	2

Snack Rank

Respondent

Relative ranking from 1 to 3 for each item by respondent.

- When cleaning this type of data, marketing researchers should check if there are any duplicate recordings. In an ordinal ranking scale, there should be no ties. In other words, suppose respondent 3 listed in Figure 11.4 ranked Apple as 1, Fig as 2, and Plum as 1. Now there is a discrepancy in the rankings because ties are not permitted in this type of ordinal ranking. If found, researchers should remove those responses from the analysis.
- Remember the difference between a ranking *(ordinal data)* and a rating *(interval data)* when cleaning the dataset.

Coding Interval Data

- Interval data examples with potential codes:
  - *Rate the movie:*   *Poor 1 2 3 4 5 6 Excellent*
  - *Rate the snack:*
    - *Apple*   *Don't Like 1 2 3 4 5 6 Like*
    - *Fig*   *Don't Like 1 2 3 4 5 6 Like*
    - *Plum*   *Don't Like 1 2 3 4 5 6 Like*
- In these cases, the data are essentially self-coded from 1 to 6.
- When coding this type of data, there can be ties because respondents are *rating* each item on its own merits as opposed to *ranking* them in relation to other items on the list.
- Figure 11.5 shows interval rating codes.

Coding Ratio Data

Ratio data are already coded. For example, the age expressed as a number (25) is itself coded as 25 becomes the code. However, in some cases, the researcher might want to code ratio data when the data are being revised to a lower level of data. Let's look at age again. Here is the list of ages from our survey and the steps to convert to codes.

- Step 1: *Place ages in the order received from respondents*
- Step 2: *Sort ages in ascending order*
- Step 3: *Group according to some desired rubric (in our case 10 year ranges)*
- Step 4: *Assign a code to each grouped age range*

This process enables researchers to group ratio data while providing codes to those groupings for use in the analysis phase of the research. Researchers can now say how many people are in, for example, group 3, the 40–50 year old range, we have two observations, 43 and 47 years old respectively. Figure 11.6 details this approach.

Survey Data	Snack Rating		
	Apple	Fig	Plum
1	1	6	1
2	3	3	2
3	2	2	2
4	4	6	1
5	3	5	6
6	5	5	3
7	4	6	4
8	6	4	2
9	4	4	2
10	3	3	2

Respondent

Each item is rated from 1 to 6 by respondent.

■ FIGURE 11.5

Snack Rating Data

■ FIGURE 11.6

Age Chart

Age	Ascending	Grouped with Code
25	21	
34	23	1
21	25	
65	31	
43	32	
32	32	2
56	34	
78	36	
62	43	
31	47	3
47	53	4
32	56	
36	65	
76	68	5
68	62	
53	76	6
23	78	

Editing

Editing primarily involves ensuring that the open-ended comments are edited as appropriate. In some cases respondents might include inappropriate open-ended comments—or at least comments that the researcher might not want to include in the report. Of course, as directed by a given contract, the verbatim open-ended comments and responses are submitted to the research sponsor for review; however, comments included in the research report should be edited for clarity. Additionally, perhaps a respondent revealed some proprietary information that should be redacted. Asking open-ended questions can yield valuable information. However, it can also produce data that might not be of much use. Marketing researchers often edit open-ended comments and include only the most salient, insightful, and useful information in the general research report while perhaps submitting the verbatim responses in a separate attachment.

Formatting

Once the data are collected, it's time to format the survey responses in a useful data sheet. If the data are collected through the Internet, the software will create a raw dataset that can be exported into SPSS, Microsoft Excel, or some other data analysis tool. It is also possible to conduct data analysis directly from the software tool. This practice is quite useful for a number of analysis techniques. However, if the researcher wants to manipulate the data himself, or if the research sponsor wants the raw data, it will be necessary to download the data. When collecting the data in person, on the telephone, or through the mail, data sheet formatting is more labor intensive—except perhaps with telephone collection depending on the data collection software tool.

■ **FIGURE 11.7**

Cleaning the Data
by Looking for
Errors, Omissions, or
Inconsistencies will
Enable Researchers to
Produce More Accurate
Results

Image © Tischenko Irina,
2011. Used under license from
Shutterstock, Inc.

Generally, survey responses are best formatted in rows and columns with the rows representing the respondent and the columns representing the questions. Each data element should be in a unique cell and should neither be merged with other data cells nor have more than one data element per cell. The more discretely the data are entered into the spreadsheet the more analysis options the researcher will have.

The survey data below records the responses of 30 people regarding how they rated various restaurant experiences. The questions, depicted in Figure 11.8, reveal both the code and the corresponding text for that code. In some cases, having both the code and the text will be useful in the analysis. Also, all four data levels are represented.

- *Note the respondent count on the left most column*
- Q1: The nominal data question asked respondents about the restaurant they most recently visited.
- Q2: The ordinal data question asked respondents to rank three items (*food, service, and price*) from 1 to 3 based on their satisfaction with the respective restaurant.
- Q3: The interval data question asked respondents to rate their overall satisfaction of the respective restaurant from 1 to 10 (*whereby 1 = very unsatisfied and 10 = very satisfied*).
- Q4: The ratio data question indicates the number of employees at the given restaurant.
- Figures 11.3 and 11.8 show a typical formatting and coding rubric.

Of course most surveys are more complicated than this four question 30 respondent example. However, this pattern for formatting is useful for large scale surveys. Notice that in the dataset each response item has its own cell. This technique enables researchers to *"mix and match"* any data elements though multivariate cross tabulations and other analysis tools.

■ **FIGURE 11.8**
Data Formatting Chart

Respondent	Q1	Restaurant Type	Q2a - Food Rank	Q2b - Service Rank	Q2c - Price Rank	Q3 - Overall Satisfaction	Q4 - Number of Employees
1	1	Mexican	1	2	3	1	30
2	2	French	1	2	3	3	200
3	5	Chinese	2	1	3	5	100
4	1	Mexican	2	1	3	6	150
5	1	Mexican	2	1	3	7	105
6	5	Chinese	1	2	3	5	225
7	2	French	1	2	3	5	210
8	5	Chinese	1	2	3	5	150
9	6	Mediterranean	3	2	1	4	88
10	2	French	3	2	1	2	165
11	3	American	3	2	1	2	150
12	2	French	3	2	1	3	270
13	1	Mexican	3	2	1	5	105
14	6	Mediterranean	1	2	3	6	700
15	5	Chinese	1	2	3	9	285
16	2	French	1	2	3	10	330
17	1	Mexican	1	2	3	10	150
18	5	Chinese	2	1	3	10	90
19	5	Chinese	2	1	3	1	30
20	6	Mediterranean	2	1	3	1	120
21	5	Chinese	1	2	3	1	90
22	2	French	1	2	3	4	135
23	2	French	1	2	3	4	60
24	5	Chinese	1	2	3	5	75
25	2	French	2	1	3	2	200
26	6	Mediterranean	2	1	3	3	225
27	3	American	2	1	3	5	180
28	5	Chinese	1	2	3	8	180
29	1	Mexican	1	2	3	6	75
30	2	French	1	2	3	6	435

Cross Tabulations

Once the data are entered into a spreadsheet, the data analysis, including cleaning or checking the data for errors, can begin. Let's look at a truncated sample survey as represented in Figure 11.10, of 30 questions asking respondents about issues related to local restaurants. The survey format would be more formally presented but are offered here in abbreviated form for expedience.

As detailed in Ed Sugar's piece in Chapter Five and though Peter Van Brunt's perspective at the end of this chapter, marginals and cross tabulations are critical analytic techniques.

- **Marginals** are uni-tabulations of the totals for each question.
  - *Uni-variate—the summary of one variable.*
- **Cross tabulations** are cross referenced calculations pairing one question with another *(or multiple)* questions.
  - *Bivariate—comparing two variables.*
  - *Multivariate—comparing three or more variables.*

In our survey example, a top line marginal report would result in at least 30 outputs—a summary of each question. For example the survey results for question 1 might be:

Question 1 Marginal:

- *25 percent American*
- *15 percent Italian*
- *23 percent Chinese*
- *Etc.*

Question 6 Marginal:

- *There might be two types of output for this question:*
  - *Total number of employees*
  - *Average number of employees*

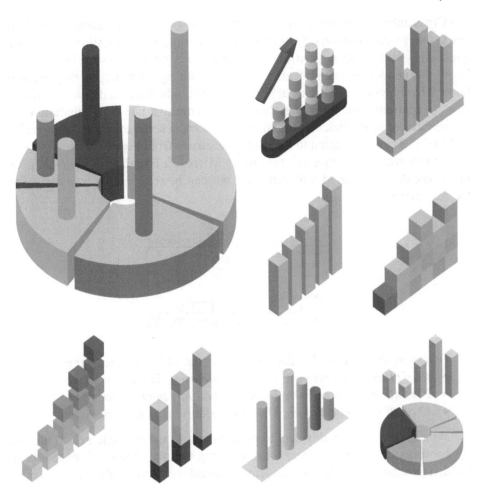

■ **FIGURE 11.9**

Cross Tabulations Can be Charted for Additional Clarity and Impact

Image © Sabri deniz kizil, 2011. Used under license from Shutterstock, Inc.

■ **FIGURE 11.10**

Restaurant Survey

Restaurant Survey		
1. Restaurant type	11. You liked the restaurant	21. Service satisfaction
2. Restaurant location	12. Overall satisfaction	22. Price satisfaction
3. Year opened	13. Gender	23. Location satisfaction
4. Years of staff experience	14. Race	24. Prestige satisfaction
5. Sales	15. Average entrée price	25. Atmosphere importance
6. Number of employees	16. Customer age	26. Food importance
7. Do they deliver?	17. Number of seats at the restaurant	27. Service importance
8. Opened on weekends?	18. Food, service, and price rank	28. Price importance
9. The food is good?	19. Atmosphere satisfaction	29. Location importance
10. The chance you will return	20. Food satisfaction	30. Prestige importance

Cross tabulations, often simply called *"cross tabs"* are another staple of marketing research reports. Cross tabulations compare one question, or multiple questions, with another question(s). For example, perhaps researchers want to know the gender of respondents combined with age. Or maybe they want to know what types of restaurants are open on weekends that also deliver. Bi-variate cross tabulations look at two variables whereas multivariate cross tabulations examine three or more variables together. Let's look at some examples of bi-variate and multivariate cross tabulations using the survey from Figure 11.10. It's worth noting that when creating cross tabs using Microsoft Excel, *(called Pivot Tables in Excel),* data are sorted alphabetically but can be resorted anyway that suites the researcher.

Restaurant Type	City	Rural	Urban	Total
American	8	27	16	51
Chinese	36	28	19	83
French	57	15	25	97
Italian	23	20	15	58
Mediterranean	7	4	4	15
Mexican	42	40	29	111
Total	173	134	108	415

- Bi-variate cross tabulation data analysis of the 415 respondents reveals:
  - *36 of all respondents were Chinese restaurants in the city.*
  - *25 of all respondents were French restaurants in urban locations.*
  - *40 of all respondents were Mexican restaurants in rural areas.*

We can now convert this data to percentages. In the example below, the data are converted to a *percentage of total,* meaning that the individual responses are divided into the total of 415 respondents to reveal the *percent of total.*

Restaurant Type	City	Rural	Urban	Total
American	2%	7%	4%	12%
Chinese	9%	7%	5%	20%
French	14%	4%	6%	23%
Italian	6%	5%	4%	14%
Mediterranean	2%	1%	1%	4%
Mexican	10%	10%	7%	27%
Total	42%	32%	26%	100%

- Bi-variate cross tabulation data analysis of the 415 respondents reveals:
  - *9 percent of all respondents were Chinese restaurants in the city.*
  - *6 percent of all respondents were French restaurants in urban locations.*
  - *10 percent of all respondents were Mexican restaurants in rural areas.*

Other ways to cross tabulate the same data are as a *percentage of row* and *percentage of column.*

Restaurant Type	City	Rural	Urban	Total
American	16%	53%	31%	100%
Chinese	43%	34%	23%	100%
French	59%	15%	26%	100%
Italian	40%	34%	26%	100%
Mediterranean	47%	27%	27%	100%
Mexican	38%	36%	26%	100%
Total	42%	32%	26%	100%

- Bivariate cross tabulation data analysis of the 415 respondents reveals:
  - *43 percent of **Chinese** restaurants were in the city.*
  - *26 percent of **French** restaurants were in urban locations.*
  - *36 percent of **Mexican** restaurants were in rural areas.*
  - *In this case, the percentage totals are in the rows creating six sub sets of data segmented by restaurant type.*

Restaurant Type ▾	City	Rural	Urban	Total
American	5%	20%	15%	12%
Chinese	21%	21%	18%	20%
French	33%	11%	23%	23%
Italian	13%	15%	14%	14%
Mediterranean	4%	3%	4%	4%
Mexican	24%	30%	27%	27%
Total	100%	100%	100%	100%

- Bivariate cross tabulation data analysis of the 415 respondents reveals:
  - *21 percent of **City** restaurants were Chinese.*
  - *30 percent of **Rural** restaurants were Mexican.*
  - *23 percent of **Urban** restaurants were French.*
  - *In this case, the percentage totals are in the columns creating three sub sets of data segmented by restaurant location.*

As noted, multivariate cross tabulations involve more than one variable—usually three or more because using two variables is captured with the term bi-variate cross tabulations, as just demonstrated. Multivariate cross tabs are useful particularly when researchers need to delve more deeply into the data in search of sub groups within a given population. With multivariate cross tabs, researchers are essentially peeling more layers of the onion in search of data that might not be readily apparent. When researchers are presented with a large dataset of perhaps 50 questions and 5,000 respondents, there are many combinations of data analysis options. Marginals are useful in determining initial results from which the researcher can explore other aspects of the data. For example, suppose the marginals reveal that 90 percent of the women in a survey indicated that they had no interest in going on a cruise for a vacation. This finding might be somewhat surprising to the researcher, prompting him to explore that aspect of the data first. Conversely, data showing large differences in responses are another possible target for further analysis. Colloquially expressed but nevertheless true, researchers have to "pick their fights"—it's not practical or necessarily insightful to analyze *every* question *every way*. Researchers must decide, based on the project's research objectives and on direction from the research sponsor, what questions to focus on more intently. Software can run data analysis ad nauseum, but it's the researcher's expertise that will reveal the most important survey findings.

Cross Tabulations Using Nominal Data

Let's look at our restaurant example using multivariate cross tabulations examining three variables—restaurant *type, location,* and *whether they are open on weekends.* Heretofore we have looked at bi-variate cross tabs which are very useful. Now let's show how multivariate cross tabs can add an additional layer of sophistication and insight into understanding data. The multivariate cross tab data below are the numeric counts of the data which can be converted to a percentage of total, row, and column respectively as done for the bi-variate cross tabulations in the examples above.

Opened on Weekends Y/N & Location									
	No			No Total	Yes			Yes Total	Grand Total
Restaurant Type	City	Rural	Urban		City	Rural	Urban		
American	3	22	7	32	5	5	9	19	51
Chinese	21	13	9	43	15	15	10	40	83
French	30	8	15	53	27	7	10	44	97
Italian	6	9	6	21	17	11	9	37	58
Mediterranean	4	4	1	9	3		3	6	15
Mexican	14	20	15	49	28	20	14	62	111
Grand Total	78	76	53	207	95	58	55	208	415

- Using three variables, the multivariate cross tabulation data analysis of the 415 respondents reveals:
  - *21 of the 415 restaurants were Chinese restaurants that are located in the city that are not open on weekends.*
  - *53 were urban located restaurants that are not open on weekends (all restaurant types).*
  - *9 were Mediterranean restaurants that are not open on weekends (all restaurant locations).*
  - *27 were French restaurants in the city that are open on weekends.*
  - *20 were Mexican restaurants in rural locations that are open on weekends.*
  - *19 were American restaurants that are open on weekends (all locations).*
  - *15 were Mediterranean restaurants. The far right column essentially negates the interior of the table where the cross tabulations takes place.*

A word of caution when using cross tabulations when analyzing survey data is warranted. As detailed in the sampling chapter, sample sizes have associated margins of error. Let's assume that the margin of error for this restaurant survey of 415 respondents is 5 percent. As we cross tabulate the data, the "N", or number of respondents for a given question, falls. For example, the data above show that only 15 of the 415 restaurants were Mediterranean eateries. Of the 15 Mediterranean restaurants nine were not open on weekends. If we then concluded that 60 percent of Mediterranean restaurants (9/15) in general were not open on weekends we would be making a generalization about the population of Mediterranean restaurants based on only 15 restaurants. As data are cross tabulated examine the subsets of the total data, the number of respondents falls and thus the sample size is affected. Consequently it's incorrect to assume the results of a subset of the population (*the 15 Mediterranean restaurants*) represent the whole population of Mediterranean restaurants. However, researchers can say that 4 percent (15/415) of the general population of restaurants are Mediterranean restaurants with a 5 percent margin of error. As long as we use the original sample size as the anchor, we can use its associated error rate.

Thus far we have looked at various forms of cross tabulations using nominal data. As you recall, there are four data levels—nominal, ordinal, interval, and ratio. Cross tabulations can be used with all data levels, but the ways in which the tabulations are created differ.

Cross Tabulations Using Ordinal Data

Cross tabulations using ordinal data and nominal data are similarly constructed. Let's look at a cross tabulation using ordinal data. In the data below, respondents were given three items to rank in order of importance: food, service, and price. As we can see from the data below, 44 respondents rated the food quality at Chinese restaurants as the most important factor. The importance of food quality came in second for Mexican restaurants as rated by 27 respondents, and third for 20 French restaurant respondents. One might think that food quality should be rated first.

However this assumption might not always be a correct one to make. Perhaps speed of service or location is more important to some customers than food quality. Presuming some acceptable level of food quality is likely a given, however.

Restaurant	Food Rank		
	First	Second	Third
American	22	14	15
Chinese	44	19	20
French	54	23	20
Italian	34	11	13
Mediterranean	8	2	5
Mexican	57	27	27

There are other ways to look at ordinal data beyond cross tabs that we will examine in the next chapter on data analysis techniques. However, marketing researchers often use cross tabulations for ordinal data to gain a level of insight as to the relation of the ordinal rankings. It's worth noting that multivariate cross tabs are also useful in examining ordinal data.

Women	Food Rank		
Restaurant	First	Second	Third
American	13	5	8
Chinese	18	11	8
French	14	10	12
Italian	17	6	4
Mediterranean	5	1	3
Mexican	28	15	12

In the case above, we have segmented the data by gender (women). We now have three variables—gender, restaurant type, and food rank. This multivariate cross tabulation offers a more precise level of insight as we are now dissecting the data by segmenting the data by gender. As we can see, 18 female Chinese restaurant respondents ranked food quality first in importance, 15 female Mexican restaurant respondents ranked food quality second in importance, and 12 female French restaurant respondents ranked food quality as third in importance—perhaps ambiance and service were more important (*thus pushing food quality to third*) to the female French restaurant respondents.

Cross Tabulations Using Interval Data

Cross tabulations are useful in highlighting interval data. Let's look at the question asking respondents from our restaurant survey to rate (*not rank*) their level of satisfaction on the food quality at the respective restaurant—(*from 1 = very unsatisfied to 10 = very satisfied*). A cross tabulation using interval data enables researchers to see the spread of this type of continuous data.

Food Satisfaction	Restaurant Type					
	American	Chinese	French	Italian	Mediterranean	Mexican	Grand Total
1 Very Unsatisfied	8	7	3	7		12	37
2	8	14	12	6		17	57
3	7	10	9	2	1	13	42
4	4	10	22	8	5	15	64
5	17	11	13	16	6	21	84
6	4	3	6	7	2	12	34
7		7	13	2		2	24
8	1	7	8	8		14	38
9	2	11	4		1	1	19
10 Very Satisfied		3	7	2		4	16
Grand Total	51	83	97	58	15	111	415

■ **FIGURE 11.19**

Restaurant Bar Graph

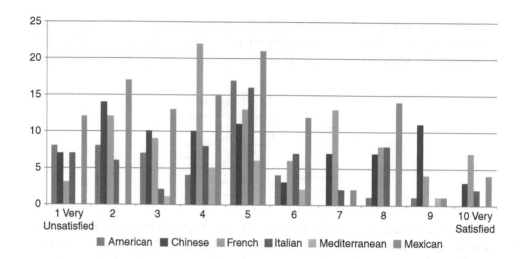

The data output in Figure 11.19 is analyzed based on the ten-point satisfaction rating scale. Ten respondents rated the food quality at Chinese restaurants as a "4", 97 respondents rated French restaurants *(varying ratings from 1 to 10),* and 19 people rated various restaurants a "9". We can also look at the data graphically as shown in Figure 11.19 producing more insight as to the data distribution and its relation to the other data elements.

Cross Tabulations Using Ratio Data

Remember that ratio data are numeric such as, in our restaurant survey, the number of seats in a given restaurant. These data in the survey are numeric—34, 56, 109, seats in a given restaurant and so on. If we cross tabulate with ratio data using that data in column or row fields *(where the restaurant type and location are depicted in the above examples),* there will have too many data elements. Ratio data are best used in the center of the pivot table thus we are cross tabulating by that data. For example:

Restaurant Type		City	Rural	Urban	Average Number of Employees
American		214	193	475	285
Chinese		178	246	214	209
French		254	165	289	249
Italian		168	198	180	181
Mediterranean		261	168	144	205
Mexican		286	219	204	240
Average Number of Employees		233	209	260	232

In the case above, we use the ratio data in the center to cross tabulate the restaurant type by location by average number of employees. We see that on average French restaurants in the city employed 254 people, Mediterranean restaurants employed 205 people *(all locations combined),* and rural restaurants employed on average 209 people *(all restaurant types combined).* Using ratio data as the anchor around which the other data are tabulated provide an additional level of analytic insight.

In addition to looking at the data using averages, researchers can look at the same data multiple ways. Below are the total number of employees, the standard deviation of the number of employees, and the maximum and minimum number of employees. Cross tabulations enable researchers to see the data at a high level from which decisions can be made to delve more deeply into subsets of the data.

Restaurant Type ⌄	City	Rural	Urban	Total Number of Employees
American	1,710	5,220	7,595	14,525
Chinese	6,399	6,901	4,065	17,365
French	14,459	2,478	7,220	24,157
Italian	3,865	3,950	2,705	10,520
Mediterranean	1,828	672	575	3,075
Mexican	12,015	8,764	5,903	26,682
Total Number of Employees	**40,276**	**27,985**	**28,063**	**96,324**

The data above reveal the total number of employees by restaurant location and type.

- There are 14,459 employees at French restaurants in the city.
- There are 27,985 employees *(all restaurant types)* located in rural areas.
- There are 3,075 employees who work in Mediterranean restaurants *(all locations)*.

Restaurant Type ⌄	City	Rural	Urban	SD Number of Employees
American	206	120	428	292
Chinese	156	247	116	185
French	176	64	273	197
Italian	86	104	157	113
Mediterranean	134	167	39	131
Mexican	248	174	169	205
SD Number of Employees	**187**	**165**	**255**	**201**

The data above show the standard deviation *(a measure of how dispersed or spread the data are around the mean)* of employees by restaurant location and type.

- The SD is 176 for employees at French restaurants in the city.
- The SD is 165 for employees *(all restaurant types)* located in rural areas.
- The SD is 131 for employees who work in Mediterranean restaurants *(all locations)*.

Restaurant Type ⌄	City	Rural	Urban	Maximum Number of Employees
American	700	375	1,170	1,170
Chinese	660	700	500	700
French	825	225	825	825
Italian	375	495	600	600
Mediterranean	400	400	180	400
Mexican	975	975	750	975
Maximum Number of Employees	**975**	**975**	**1,170**	**1,170**

Restaurant Type ⌄	City	Rural	Urban	Minimum Number of Employees
American	75	60	75	60
Chinese	18	22	30	18
French	18	30	60	18
Italian	75	75	60	60
Mediterranean	88	22	110	22
Mexican	75	60	30	30
Minimum Number of Employees	**18**	**22**	**30**	**18**

Finally, the two cross tabs above show the relative maximum and minimum *(or most and least)* number of employees by restaurant type and location.

- The French restaurant in the city with the most employees had 825 staff and the one with the fewest number of employees had 18 people working at the restaurant.
- Of *all* rural restaurants of all restaurant *types*, the restaurant with the most employees had 975 people working there and the rural located restaurant with the fewest employees had 22 people working at that restaurant.
- Of *all* Mediterranean restaurants in *all* locations, the one with the most employees had 400 staff and the restaurant with the fewest number of employees also had 22 people working at the restaurant.

Research in Practice

Case:
- The manager of a local bicycle shop is lamenting the decline in his customer base. He is speculating that the decline is due to several factors: competition, price, substitute methods of exercise, and a reduction in the types of bikes he offers. He also wonders if there are differences in the decline related to gender.

Assignment:
- How might marketing researchers use multivariate cross tabulations to address the potential reasons for the decline in the bicycle shop's customer base? Create a set of questions that could be used to determine the decline in sales and demonstrate how these questions could be cross tabulated to provide the bicycle manger insight as to the potential causes of the sales decline.

Chapter Summary

Before survey data is be analyzed, marketing researchers must ensure that the data that was collected is quality data by first preparing the data. One of the first tasks is to validate the data. Validating the data is the process of verifying that the data were actually collected. For example, if a researcher says 100 people responded to a survey, validation verifies that those people *(by calling back some of them)* were contacted and that they gave the answers as recorded. Coding, editing, and formatting the data are the next key steps in the data preparation process. Coding is the process of assigning numbers to the survey responses to facilitate the data analysis process. Editing involves ensuring the data are entered correctly and are free of inconsistencies. For example, if a respondent says that they do not own a car and later in the survey they report owning a

Ford, they have given inconsistent answers and the data cleaning process should identify those inconsistencies. Formatting the data sheet involves putting the dataset in a usable structure that facilitates analysis. Many statistical software packages can be used to host the data. Typically, the questions are entered as columns and the respondents' answers are entered in the rows of the data spreadsheet. Two of the most common initial data analysis techniques are marginals and cross tabulations. Marginals involve summarizing each question respectively in the questionnaire by the number and percentage of responses. This technique informs the analysis process by highlighting large variations in respondents' answers that can be further explored using other data analysis techniques. Cross tabulations *(sometimes simply called cross-tabs)* are the next logical step in the data analysis process. Cross tabulation involves taking two *(bivariate)* or three or more *(multivariate)* questions in a questionnaire and comparing them. For example, researchers might say that 50 percent of the sample are women *(a marginal)*, or that 25 percent of the sample are women who were born in New Mexico *(a bivariate cross tabulation)*, or that 12 percent of the sample are women, born in New Mexico, and have traveled overseas *(multivariate cross tabulation)*. Cross tabulations reveal the predominate relationships, in number/percentage but not causation, amongst the data which can then be analyzed using increasingly more sophisticated data analysis techniques.

ISSUE IN THE SPOTLIGHT   Cross tabulations - *a Research Staple*

Peter Van Brunt, President
ReData Inc.
www.redatainc.com

Tabulations both uni-variate and multivariate are one of the basic tools which researchers make use of to evaluate and understand results from quantitative research studies. They are also one of the most underutilized and over utilized tools available to the researcher. This would seem to be contradictory, let me explain.

HOW TABULATIONS ARE OVER USED:

All too frequently researchers see Cross-tabulations as a magic tool which will explain all the results from their study. They take an approach of cross tabulating every variable with every other variable with the hope that some result will bubble to the surface. What frequently happens is that they are then faced with a thousand pages of numbers to look at, and are overwhelmed trying to find something significant to report.

It makes much more sense to approach each question remembering why it was asked. With that in mind, the important results are the ones reported, and the unimportant ones are ignored. A perfect example of where this frequently occurs is on a grid of scale questions. All too often full distributions (every value) are tabulated, but only the summary (top 2 or top 3 box) tables are actually ever looked at or utilized. This doesn't make sense.

Another error that is frequently made is the tendency to focus on the percentage giving a particular response, and ignoring the frequency count associated with the percentage as well as the base on which the percentage was calculated. This can lead to erroneous conclusions as base sizes in cross-tabulations often get quite small particularly when skip logic is taken into account.

HOW TABULATIONS ARE UNDERUSED:

Many quantitative researchers fail to take full advantage of the full analytical capabilities of tabulation software. Researchers often only look at uni-variate and bivariate tabulations. Tabulation software is capable of combining multiple variables into complex combinations which can delve deep into understanding the research findings. In addition, the software is capable of weighting results, sorting the responses, building multiple nets, and highlighting significant differences. Utilizing some or all of these capabilities can make it easier to build tables which illuminate the finding in a more efficient manner. Researchers need to give more thought and planning to what data they want to tabulate and think beyond just presenting the answers from a single question or variable in each table.

CONCLUSION:

Tabulations are the most basic tool that the researcher has for understanding the results from a quantitative study. Like any tool it is best when applied properly. Understand their limitations, maximize their full capability, and you will find cross tabulations to be a true asset. But be careful to understand statistical tests and their limitations, and be sure to understand which statistics make sense in a given situation, otherwise you can be mislead as to what the data are actually indicating.

Data Analysis

Image © Elena Elisseeva, 2011. Used under license from Shutterstock, Inc.

Learning Objectives:

- Understand the difference between descriptive and inferential statistics
- Learn how to handle qualitative data analysis
- Learn about statistical notation between sample and population data
- Understand the difference between categorical and continuous data
- Learn about center, shape, and spread in descriptive statistics

- Understand the concept and measures of central tendency
- Learn the difference between a between group and within group analysis
- Learn about measures of dispersion and how they are used in marketing research
- Understand the concept of degrees of freedom
- See how histograms, rank and percentile, and correlation analysis are used research

- Learn about the applicability of Chi Square, ANOVA, and regression
- Learn about box plots and stem and leaf plots as useful methods for displaying data
- Become aware of some pitfalls to avoid in the data analysis section of a research report

Chapter Twelve

The data analysis phase of a research project is where the true value and utility of marketing research takes shape. Without solid data analysis, a marketing research project has little impact on aiding the business decision process. Once the data have been collected, entered into a data analysis tool and prepared, the quantitative data analysis can begin. There are pros and cons to using the different types of software. SPSS (www.spss.com) and SAS (www.sas.com) are high level statistical software packages that are commonly used in sophisticated and complex data analysis projects. When doing elaborate subgroup analysis, SPSS and SAS are well suited to building those types of relationships. Microsoft Excel requires more data manipulation however Microsoft Excel data analysis is easily integrated across other Microsoft applications such as Word and PowerPoint. There are many options when selecting the data analysis software tool.

Generally there are two main data analysis approaches that can be taken—**descriptive** or **inferential** statistical data analysis as depicted in Figure 12.1.

- **Descriptive Statistics:**
  - *Data analysis that describes data typified by the mean, median, mode, skewness, kurtosis, rank and percentile, percentages, counts, relative frequency histograms, and standard deviation.*

- **Inferential Statistics:**
  - *Data analysis that aims to explain patterns in data used to make inferences about that data under study. Some data analysis tools used in inferential statistics include correlation analysis, regression, exponential smoothing, conjoint analysis, chi square, Analysis of Variance (ANOVA), and hypothesis testing.*

Population vs. Sample Statistical Notation

The study of statistics and data analysis involves a number of formulas with various statistical notations. There are different statistical notations based on the population and sample statistics respectively. These notations are frequently used when presenting the various statistical formulas common in data analysis.

■ **FIGURE 12.1**

Descriptive and Inferential Statistics

Descriptive Statistics	Inferential Statistics
• Mean	• Pearson Correlation
• Median	• Regression
• Mode	• Exponential Smoothing
• Kurtosis	• Conjoint Analysis
• Skewness	• Hypothesis Testing
• Standard Deviation	• Analysis of Variance
• Rank & Percentile	• Chi-Square Test
• Percentages	
• Counts & Sums	
• Histograms	

- **Population Statistics Notations:**
  - N = Size (of the population)
  - μ = Mean
  - σ = Standard Deviation

- **Sample Statistics Notations:**
  - n = Size (number of observations in the sample)
  - $\bar{X}$ = Mean
  - S = Standard Deviation

Categorical vs. Continuous Data

When approaching data analysis, there are two types of data that require different data analysis approaches as represented in Figure 12.2. Categorical data are qualitative data whereby the distance between the data elements is not fully known *(ordinal data)* or nonexistent *(nominal data)*. Continuous data are data where the distance between the data is known and in progressive order *(interval and ratio data)*.

There are different data analysis techniques for each type of data. Lower level data such as nominal and ordinal data lend themselves to less sophisticated, albeit useful and common, types of data analysis such as percentages, Chi-square statistical significance tests, sums, and counts. Higher level data such as interval and ratio data enable researchers to conduct more sophisticated data analysis such as standard deviation, rank and percentile, correlations, hypothesis testing, Analysis of Variance, as well as more insightful mean and median calculations and interpretations.

One of the first tasks before beginning the analysis is to determine what type of data is to be analyzed, categorical or continuous, and the relative tools for those types. Outlining the data analysis strategy before beginning the analysis will streamline the data analysis process.

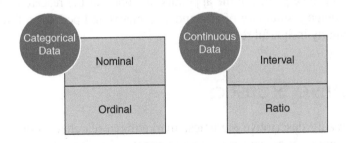

■ **FIGURE 12.2**

Categorical vs. Continuous Data

Analyzing Qualitative Data

One advantage to asking open-ended questions during interviews, focus groups, and surveys is that respondents can elaborate on key issues. These comments often provide additional insight to researchers. In addition, perhaps respondents address a heretofore unknown issue. Open-ended questions are useful but a challenge to analyze because they lack the numeric aspects of quantitative data. Marketing researchers must do content analysis to determine patterns of answers that might be

useful. Grouping answers into like concepts and then conducting frequency counts of those groups will help to quantify the data. Suppose respondents were asked to rate the ambiance at a new upscale restaurant. Answers such as *"great", "loved it", "wonderful"*—should be grouped into one category with a frequency count of three. This process takes expertise and judgment to ensure the respondents' answers are being characterized and categorized appropriately. Although a summary of all responses can be placed in the appendix, the body of the research report should generally include a summary of respondent patterns and perhaps a few comments from particularly insightful respondents.

Descriptive Statistics

When analyzing descriptive statistics, marketing researchers look for data that reveal the center, shape, and spread components of a given dataset. A number of measurements associated with center, shape and spread, as seen in Figure 12.4, used together enable researchers to understand a given dataset more clearly.

There are several key descriptive statistics measures that are common to marketing research. The challenge for researchers is to decide which combination of descriptive and inferential statistics to use. The type and level of data will drive the appropriate types of data analysis that should be performed. Generally, interval and ratio data are the most useful data levels for analysis using descriptive statistics. Let's look at a summary of descriptive statistics in Figure 12.5 based on a survey asking business owners about how many employees they have.

Descriptive statistics describe the data leaving the interpretation, or analytic observations, to the researcher's expertise. There are several key descriptive statistics

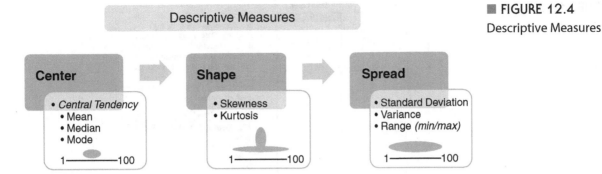

Number of Employees		Summary Definition
Mean	232	The average - sum all observations, divided by the number of observations
Standard Error	10	The estimated standard deviation of a given statistic
Median	180	The middle value of an ordered set of data
Mode	75	The most commonly occurring response / answer
Standard Deviation	201	The relative dispersion of the data around the mean
Sample Variance	40,552	Squared SD - another measure of variability
Kurtosis	6	The steepness to which the data are peaked around the mean
Skewness	2	The extent to which the data are disproportional in a given direction
Range	1,152	The difference between the minimum and the maximum observations
Minimum	18	Smallest / lowest response value
Maximum	1,170	Largest / highest response value
Sum	96,324	Total value of all responses given
Count	415	The number of respondents for a given question

that can be analyzed to provide researchers with a broad overview of the data being analyzed. Let's look at the descriptive statistics for the data in Figure 12.6 which captures the number of vacation days each of the 30 hotel employees has used in the past year. We will analyze the data in subsequent sections.

- **Measures of Central Tendency**:
  - Measures of central tendency help researchers to understand where the middle of the data lies. The key measures of central tendency are mean, median, and mode. Figure 12.7, 12.8, and 12.9 provide some useful data to analyze.

  - **Mean:**
    - What is typically called an average, the mean is calculated by summing all observations and then dividing the result by the number of observations. The mean is an effective measure of central tendency. In normally distributed data, the mean can be taken to represent the central tendency of the data. In data not normally distributed, or are skewed, the mean can be misleading.
    - In Figure 12.6, the mean number of vacation days is 27 meaning that on average the hotel staff take 27 days of vacation.
    - Useful for interval and ratio data.

  - **Trimmed Mean:**
    - *A mean calculated after a certain percentage (as per the researcher's discretion) of the highest and lowest observations are omitted.*
    - Helps to minimize the impact of disproportionately high and low data observations.

■ FIGURE 12.6
Data Output

Data Input

Number of Vacation Days
49
24
16
26
3
51
36
17
49
13
59
23
26
10
57
25
42
21
12
6
32
47
2
47
5
14
18
40
29
11

Microsoft Excel can run descriptive statistics through the *Data and Data Analysis Tabs* then the *Descriptive Statistics* dropdown box. You might have to add the Data Tab through the *Microsoft Icon (top left color icon), Excel Options, Add-ins, Analysis Tookpak* path.

Data Output

Number of Vacation Days	
Mean	27
Standard Error	3
Median	25
Mode	49
Standard Deviation	17
Sample Variance	290
Kurtosis	-1
Skewness	0
Range	57
Minimum	2
Maximum	59
Sum	810
Count	30

- The researcher must justify what percentage of the high and low observations are being omitted.
- The rank and percentile tool is useful here. Researchers might take the Interquartile range—or some such range—as the new data range. However, researchers need to clarify why a certain top and bottom percentage will be trimmed and what will be done with that trimmed data. Do the trimmed data sets become market segments in their own right or are those data considered statistical outliers that have a disproportionate impact on the inner range of the data?
- It is beneficial to conduct some additional analysis on the data omissions to support their omission from the remaining dataset.
- Generally, the percentage of high and low observations being omitted should be the same unless there is a valid reason otherwise.

- **Grand Mean:**
  - *The grand mean is the average of the averages.*
  - Grand means can help to smooth-out data to provide insight as to how groups of data are averaged.
  - Figure 12.7 shows the students' average score for five classes and then the grand mean *(the average of the averages)* to see how students are doing with their overall course load.

■ FIGURE 12.7
Student Course Grades

Student Course Grades				
Marketing	Accounting	Finance	History	Philosophy
79	61	98	96	90
77	84	87	76	84
95	87	92	82	81
61	93	95	88	98
95	94	92	99	97
70	60	82	76	91
87	90	95	72	100
77	80	84	86	80
98	87	87	79	76
91	86	100	66	87
64	68	89	78	84
77	73	94	93	66
93	69	82	98	99
82	79	91	84	87
Respective Course Averages				
Grand Mean				85
(82+79+91+84+87)/5				

Favorability Rating	Day	Three Day Moving Avearge
45%	1	#N/A
46%	2	#N/A
43%	3	45%
50%	4	46%
46%	5	46%
48%	6	48%
48%	7	47%
49%	8	48%
50%	9	49%
54%	10	51%
52%	11	52%
49%	12	52%
55%	13	52%
56%	14	53%
53%	15	55%
56%	16	55%

55% { 56%, 53%, 56% }

Day 16 Polling	
Average	Three Day Moving Avearge
50%	55%
averages all 16 days	*averages three rolling days*

- **Moving Average:**
  - *A moving average is a mean using a certain number (as determined by the researcher or research sponsor) of previous observations as the baseline for the new average calculation.*
  - Moving averages help researchers smooth-out data by giving the most recent observations more weight in the mean calculation.
  - Oftentimes political polling organizations use moving averages to capture the currency of events. Suppose there are fast moving issues and a political candidate wants to know where she stands with the public. A moving average which averages each of the three (or some other number of) previous days will help her stabilize the polling data that might take an anomalistic jump or decline on one of those days. A moving average partially compensates for any daily spikes by using previous days averaged as a balance. Political pollsters use moving averages when doing **tracking polls** to gauge the state of a given political race day by day. Let's look at an example of a moving average for a political campaign.
  - In Figure 12.8 we see that the moving average is likely a better representation of the data than averaging all 16 days because opinions have likely changed during those 16 days and generally more recent opinions are more accurate. Why not just take the average on day 16 as the best indicator? Of course many researchers will take the last observation. However, smoothing the average by including the two previous days can reduce the impact of statistical error in any one day. In other words, if there is 2 percent error in the survey taken on day 16 but no error in the survey taken on day 15, the more accurately done results of day 15 will help to mitigate the negative impact of the error that occurred on day 16. However, if there is error on both days, the inaccuracies get compounded. Neither approach is necessarily the right way. Marketing researchers should just be aware of the consequences of the types of averages they use when analyzing survey data.

- **Median:**
  - *The median is the middle value in an ordered set of data.*
  - In Figure 12.6 the median number of vacation days is 25 meaning that half of the staff take fewer than 25 vacations days per year and that half take more than 25 vacations days per year.
  - Useful for interval and ratio data levels.

■ FIGURE 12.9
Median, Mean, and Mode
Data

Survey I
Number of Sugar Packs

	1
	2
Mean	3	**Median**
	4
	5

There is no mode since each observation was reported only once.

Survey II
Number of Sugar Packs

	1
	2 (mean 2.8)
	3	**Median**
Mode	4
	4

- **Mode:**
  - *The most frequently occurring observation.*
  - In Figure 12.6 the most common number of vacation days taken was 49. The mode is often not that useful when analyzing ratio data. In fact, there might be more than one mode. The mode is more useful when analyzing nominal, ordinal, and interval data levels.
- Let's look at some other examples directly comparing the mean, median, and mode relationships. Suppose we surveyed two groups of five people about how many sugar packs they use in their coffee. As revealed in Figure 12.9, the mean and median are the same in Survey I but the spread between the mean and median begins to grow with Survey II. The larger the data set the more potential the spread is between the mean, median, and mode
- Great disparities between, in particular, the mean and median, should alert researchers to the likelihood that the data are not normally distributed. Non-normally distributed data are good candidates for data stratification by separating the data into normally distributed sub groups from which data extrapolations and generalizations about the population from the sample can be made.
- In the vacation example, suppose the mean number of vacation days was 75 and the median number was 20. This data should cause the researcher to presume that there are a few lucky people who get to take very long vacations which is disproportionately skewing the data to the right of a plotted curve. It might be wise to identify the data outliers and re-run descriptive statistics without them. In other words, although the mean is 75 vacation days, that result is not indicative of the central tendency of the data because a few data observations are pushing the average higher.
- Suppose for the past 30 trips to work you spend exactly 10 minutes a day getting there. Thus the average trip time is 10 minutes. On the 31st trip, the bridge en route to your work is closed and thus you have

to take an alternate route. Your commute to work on the 31st day was 240 minutes. We now calculate the average commute time over the past 31 days to be 17.4 minutes. Although this new average of 17.4 minutes is the correct arithmetic mean, it does not represent what we might say is the *true* average because the 31st day disproportionately skewed the results. Researchers must be alert to the impact that a few data points can have on the totality of the data.

- When analyzing nominal data, such as the respondents' favorite color, the mode (considering the mean, median, and mode) is the only useful descriptive statistics because the mean and median are only useful for continuous data. The mode can provide insightful information for categorical data. The researcher could defendably say that *blue* is the favorite color because it was the mode of the data.

- **Measures of Dispersion**:
  - Measures of dispersion enable researchers to identify the relative spread of data and how the data relate to the mean of the dataset. Measures of dispersion provide a level of insight that measures of central tendency can't quite achieve. There are several measures of dispersion that help reveal the relative spread of the data. The key here is not only what the spread is but what it says about the data. Marketing researchers look for significant spread levels that lead researchers to ask various questions—chiefly where is the large spread and what might be causing it.

- **Standard Deviation:**
  - *The principle measure of dispersion and variability in data, the standard deviation shows the data's average distance from the mean.*
  - We reviewed the components of standard deviation during the sampling chapter, but here again is the formula:

$$S = \sqrt{\frac{\sum_{k=1}^{n}(x_k - \overline{x})^2}{n-1}}$$

  - The notion of variability in data anchors the foundational understanding of standard deviation. The standard deviation formula calculates the square root of the squared sums of each data observation minus the mean of the data divided by the **degrees of freedom** (*the number of observations minus 1).*

- The **Degrees of Freedom (DF)**:
  - *Represents the amount of variability a set of data has by demonstrating the extent to which variables are free to vary within a dataset.*
  - Degrees of Freedom, depicted in Figure 12.10, are very common in many statistical formulas due to the necessity of preventing overestimating variability in a given data set. Degrees of Freedom are particularly important in sample size formulas. Lower variability will decrease the sample size whereas data that have high levels of variability result in larger sample sizes.
- When marketing researchers run descriptive statistics on data resulting in, among other statistics, the mean median, mode, and standard deviation, special note should be taken when comparing these statistical

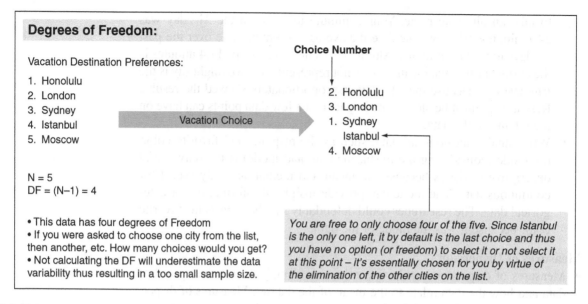

FIGURE 12.10

Degrees of Freedom

Age - Preshoolers	
Mean	5
Standard Error	2
Median	3
Mode	3
Standard Deviation	14
Minimum	2
Maximum	100
Sum	246
Count	50

FIGURE 12.11

Preschooler Age Data

outputs. Similar to the issue regarding the spread between the mean and the median and what it reveals about the central tendency of the data, the standard deviation also alerts researchers to data that might be skewed in one direction or another. Consider the data in Figure 12.11 on the age of preschoolers and the statistical relationships addressed below.

- What observations might a researcher make?
  - The median age is 3 *(half of the pupils are above 3 and half are below 3)*
  - The mode is 3 years old *(more kids are 3 than any other age)*
  - The mean age is 5 *(indicating some older kids are raising the average)*
  - The oldest child *(maximum)* is 100 *(quickly revealing an error in the data)*
  - The standard deviation is 14 *(applying the 1, 2, and 3 SD rule with related percentages (Empirical Rule) reveals skewed data, the 100 aged child error is the culprit)*
  - Marketing researchers should examine the *closeness* of the *mean* and *median* as well as how the *standard deviation* compares to the *mean* by using the **Empirical Rule** to determine if the appropriate number of observations fall within 1, 2, or 3 standard deviations from the mean of the data of interest.

- **Range:**
  - *The range defines the spread of the data and is represented by the difference between the minimum and maximum variables.*
  - Let's suppose a university chancellor wants to learn how many credit hours students are taking per semester. The campus-wide survey reveals that students are taking an average number of 16 credit hours for a given semester with the fewest number of credit hours being 4 and the most being taken is 20 credit hours per semester. Thus the range of credit hours is 16 (20−4).
  - This data provides researchers with insight as to the scope of the data by showing the relative spread of the data.

- **Interquartile Range (IRQ):**
  - *The IQR is the range of data whereby 25 percent of the data are above the IQR and 25 percent of the data are below the IQR. Thus the IQR*

Exam Scores
58
60
64
66
70
72
76
77
79
80
82
84
85
87
87
88
89
90
90
92
92
93
94
98

Lower Quartile – bottom 25%

IQR = 50% of Observations

Upper Quartile – top 50%

■ FIGURE 12.12
Quartile Ranges

*represents the middle 50 percentile of the data. Also known as the **Fourth Spread** because the data are in four ranges of 25% each.*

- The IQR is a useful tool in helping to frame the scope of the middle 50 percent of the data by eliminating potential data outliers that might reside in the top or bottom 25 percent of the data respectively.
- The IQR is particularly relevant when using box plots.
- Sometimes marketing researchers use techniques like the IQR to get a sense of where the true average of the data might be expected to fall.
- The IQR is best used when the data sample is large enough *(whereby the IQR sample size is recalculated and the error margin and confidence interval are acceptable)* and when researchers theorize that data disproportionality might affect the credibility of the data analysis conclusions.
- Figure 12.12 shows this relationship.

- **Median Absolute Deviation (MAD):**
  - *The MAD is a median measure of dispersion that accounts for outliers thereby greatly reducing their ability to skew the data results.*
  - Suppose a local eatery hired a research company to conduct a focus group of seven residents to determine how many times per week they eat out. Here is the data on how many times these seven people eat out per week.
  - Figure 12.13 provides data for the MAD analysis.
  - The data 1,1,2,4,5,6,15 has a median if **4.** The absolute deviations around 4 are 3,3,2,0,1,2,11 *(i.e. the median of 4 is 3 deviations from 1, and again 4 is 3 deviations from 1, 4 is 2 deviations from 2 etc.)* which when put in sequential order—**0,1,2,2,3,3,11** produce a MAD of **2.**

- **Histograms:**
  - *Histograms are graphical depictions of data that are displayed cumulatively or are sorted from the highest to lowest (or vice versa).*
  - Histograms, shown in Figure 12.14, provide researchers with a quick visual display of the data distribution from which other analyses stem.

Times Eating out Weeky
1
1
2
4
5
6
15

Median
4

MAD
2

■ FIGURE 12.13
Median Absolute Deviation

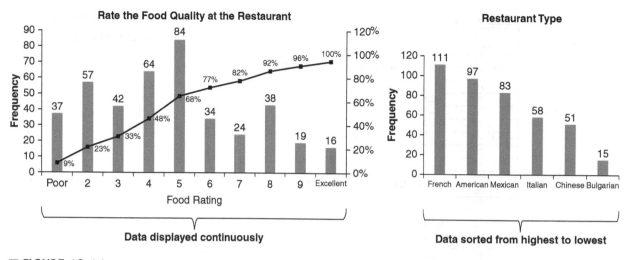

FIGURE 12.14

Histogram Data

Once the histogram distribution is displayed, researchers might be alerted to anomalies in the data warranting further investigation. At a glance, researchers can see from the data in Figure 12.14 that more than half of the people rated the restaurant food quality below average. Researchers might now conduct sub group analysis to determine if there are demographic trends on the lower end of this rating scale. Perhaps men over 50 are the primary driver of the lower rating or maybe women are less pleased with the restaurant than are the men. In any event, histograms help researchers gauge the scope of the data distribution.

- Histograms are useful for all data levels—nominal, ordinal, interval, and ratio.

- **Kurtosis:**
  - *Kurtosis is the measure of how peaked the data are around the mean. It is a measure of the shape of the data.*
  - A kurtosis of zero represents the kurtosis of normally distributed data called **mesokurtic kurtosis**. Data with high kurtosis, called **leptokurtic kurtosis**, is highly peaked with longer, wider tails. Data with low kurtosis, called **platykurtic kurtosis**, have a more rounded peak and the tails are shorter and thinner. Let's look again at the data from the number of vacation days survey.
  - Figure 12.15 displays Kurtosis output.
  - A kurtosis of 12 indicates the data are highly peak around the mean of 26 days giving researchers insight as to the data distribution. Marketing researchers might take data with high or low kurtosis and dissect that data to determine the key drivers of the high or low kurtosis. Perhaps a particular demographic is skewing the data which would prompt further analysis of that demographic.

- **Rank and Percentile:**
  - *Rank and percentile sorts data in order from highest to lowest with the corresponding percentile each data element is of the total observations.*
  - Useful for understanding the relative position one data element has in relation to other data elements and with the data overall. Rank and percentile calculations are best used with ratio data.

Number of Vacation Days	
Mean	35
Standard Error	7
Median	26
Mode	49
Standard Deviation	38
Sample Variance	1430
Kurtosis	12
Skewness	3
Range	198
Minimum	2
Maximum	200
Sum	1064
Count	30

FIGURE 12.15

Kurtosis Result

- Students often want to know the class average exam score—presumably to compare their score to the class average. However, a *rank and percentile* of exam scores will tell students much more about how well they performed relative to the other students in the class. Let's assume that a student scored a 91 percent on the last exam and wants to know how his score compared to the rest of the class. As revealed by the data in Figure 12.16, the average exam score of 82 percent does not tell the whole story. The student performed well given that he was *above* the average. However, he ranked 7th out of 20 students and he was in the 68 percentile meaning that he did better than 68 percent of his peers. Remember that the average score of 82 percent was brought down by *students with much lower scores (perhaps disproportionately lower scores)*. If one student received a 10 on the exam, the average would be significantly reduced. Be aware that sometimes one score can have a disproportionate impact.
- Figure 12.16 displays rank and percentile data.

Exam Scores	Rank	Percent
99	1	100%
96	2	95%
94	3	79%
94	3	79%
94	3	79%
93	6	74%
91	7	68%
86	8	63%
84	9	53%
84	9	53%
82	11	47%
79	12	42%
77	13	37%
76	14	32%
72	15	26%
70	16	16%
70	16	16%
66	18	11%
64	19	0%
64	19	0%

	Exam Score 91	
Average	Rank	Percentile
82%	7	68%

FIGURE 12.16
Rank and Percentile

Within and Between Group Differences

One of the major data analysis research areas is the notion of sub groups. Marketing researchers identify data sub groups which form the basis for target marketing or market segmentation. Market segmentation is everywhere in the marketplace. Music, clothes, vacation packages, sports marketing, cars, food, electronics, airline seats—and the list goes on—are all highly segmented and targeted markets based on an understanding of their relative sub group within a given population. Understanding the difference **between a group** and **within a group** is an important distinction.

Using the data from Figure 12.17, let's suppose we surveyed three groups of five students per group *(men, women, and freshman (m/w))* who were asked to rate *(from 1=unsatisfied to 5=satisfied)* their opinion of the class registration process at their university. What might researchers report about the results below?

It appears that the difference *between* men, women, and freshmen *(each representing a "group")* is zero because all of their averages were "3". Remember, we are comparing the aggregate of each group as opposed to the individual responses within a group. However, the analysis of the difference *within* each group reveals a much different story. There is great variance amongst the men because none of the men gave the same satisfaction rating. The women had the significant variability between satisfaction rating highs and lows because 40 percent gave the top rating and 40 percent gave the lowest rating. The freshman showed no variability because everyone rated his/her satisfaction the same at a "3". Although

Class Registration Satisfaction Rating		
Men	Women	Freshman
1	1	3
2	1	3
3	3	3
4	5	3
5	5	3
Averages 3	3	3

FIGURE 12.17
Comparing Between and Within Group Differences

a researcher might be correct in saying that there is no difference between how men and women answered this question, that finding would misdirect the reader to think that men and women share the same opinion when in fact the differences between their respective genders is high even though the average satisfaction rating between men and women was the same. Marketing researchers must be careful not to report, through omission, data in misleading ways.

Inferential Statistics

- **Pearson Correlation:**
  - *As a **measure of association**, the Pearson Correlation is a linear measurement as to the extent to which two or more data elements move or do not move in a predictable pattern in relation to each other.*
  - It is designated as: *r*
  - The correlation range is from −1 *(perfect inverse correlation)* to 1 *(perfect positive correlation)*. The closer the correlation is to "0" the less association there is between variables.
  - The Pearson Correction formula and corresponding data is shown in Figure 12.18. Assume 10 people were interviewed to gauge their liking of warm weather and whether they would like to go to Hawaii. The correlation of .74 indicates a moderate positive correlation. In other words, people who like warm weather tended to indicate that they would like to go to Hawaii. A question researchers might ask is *"why was the correlation not stronger"*— because one might think that the data should have correlated more strongly? Perhaps some people who like warm weather said that they would not want to go to Hawaii because perhaps it's too far, or they have been there recently, or they have another destination in mind. There could be a host of reasons why the correlation is not higher than might be expected.
  - Correlation shows the relative association between variables—but not necessarily causation.
  - The Pearson Correlation is used on interval to interval or ratio to ratio data comparisons whereas a **Spearmen Rank Order Correlation** is used to determine the correlation among ordinal data.

Correlation Range																				
-1	-0.9	-0.8	-0.7	-0.6	-0.5	-0.4	-0.3	-0.2	-0.1	0	0.1	0.2	0.3	0.4	0.5	0.6	0.7	0.8	0.9	1
Strong Inverse		Moderate					Weak			None	Weak				Moderate				Strong Positive	

■ FIGURE 12.18
Correlation Data and Formula

Data (X=weather / Y=Hawaii)	
Like Warm Weather	**Like Hawaii**
1	1
2	3
3	2
2	2
3	2
4	3
5	4
5	3
5	4
4	5

Correlation = .74

Numerator				Denominator				
Sum XY	Sum X	Sum Y	N	Sum X$_2$	(Sum X)$_2$	Sum Y$_2$	(Sum Y)$_2$	N
110	34	29	10	134	1156	97	841	10

$$r = \frac{\sum XY - \dfrac{\sum X \sum Y}{N}}{\sqrt{(\sum X^2 - \dfrac{(\sum X)^2}{N})(\sum Y^2 - \dfrac{(\sum Y)^2}{N})}}$$

Numerator	11.4
Denominator	15.4
Correlation	0.74

- Marketing researchers use correlation analysis to see if two or more variables are associated or related in some manner. Correlation analysis should not be taken to mean that the relationship between data is *causal.* Many variables can show a strong correlation but are not related. Suppose the correlation between the Washington National's baseball scores and temperature in Sydney, Australia are highly correlated. We can presume that the baseball team's performance has no impact on the temperature in Sydney. These types of correlations are simply statistical coincidences. However, in general data that are highly correlated should lead the researcher to explore the possibility of a causal relationship among the variables. Now suppose that students' test scores highly correlate to the amount of time the respective student spends studying for an exam. In this case it's quite possible, in fact likely, that this correlation also indicates causality in that the more students study the better their test scores are and the less they study the worse they perform on exams.
- Marketing researchers should not dismiss low correlations simply because they are low. The descriptive results might indicate an insignificant correlation but the analytic observation might be critical to understanding the issue under study. Suppose a local dry cleaning business correlates customer satisfaction ratings to the speed of service. Presumably these variables should correlate because (let's assume) the researcher's earlier data identified service speed as the key driver in customer satisfaction. A low correlation in this case should prompt the researcher to ask *why the correlation was low* given that the researcher *expected* the correlation to be high and it was not.
- By using a **Scatter Plot,** as seen in Figure 12.20, marketing researchers can quickly tell if two variables appear to have a linear relationship and can determine the positive or negative aspect of a given relationship. Data showing an apparent relationship can be further examined by running a correlation analysis.

- **Scatter Plot:**
  - *A graphical representation of two data elements revealing the extent to which the data elements have or do not have a linear relationship.*

- **Analysis of the three scenarios in Figure 12.20:**
  - **A:** With a strong positive correlation of **.80**, it appears that the people who said that they liked the food at the restaurant are generally likely to return. And those who did not like the restaurant are not particularly likely to return.
  - **B:** As expected there is a very weak *(essentially none)* correlation of **.10** indicating that there is no clear pattern between student exam scores and the temperature in Sydney.
  - **C:** There is a very strong inverse, or negative, correlation of **−.95** indicating that the farther someone drives, the less gas there is in his tank. This finding makes sense and is in fact presumably causal.

- **Setting Markers:**
  - *Markers identify the points on a scatter plot.*
  - Markers enable researchers to see trends or patterns of data based on respondent demographics or based on how respondents answered a particular question.
  - The results of these markers might warrant additional analysis if apparent data patterns emerge.

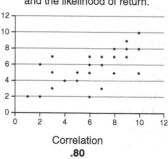

A. Liked the food at the restaurant and the likelihood of return.

Correlation
.80

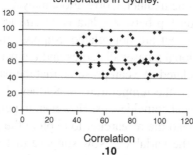

B. Student exam scores and temperature in Sydney.

Correlation
.10

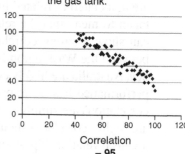

C. Miles driven and gas left in the gas tank.

Correlation
−.95

■ **FIGURE 12.20**

Scatter Plot Output

■ **FIGURE 12.21**

Scatter Plot Data Markers

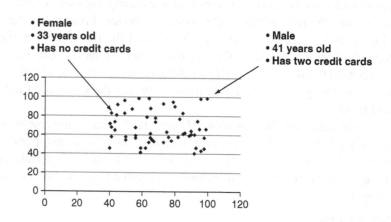

• **Female**
• **33 years old**
• **Has no credit cards**

• **Male**
• **41 years old**
• **Has two credit cards**

• **The Coefficient of Determination:**
  • *The coefficient of determination, often interpreted as a percent, reveals the relative impact of one variable over another variable under study.*
• It is designated as: r^2
• The coefficient of determination provides a useful statistic for it enables researchers to ascribe a certain percentage impact of one variable on another. In our example above where the correlation between respondents *liking the food at the restaurant* and *whether they will return to the restaurant* was .80—thus the r^2 is .64 *(.8*.8)*. We can say statistically that 64 percent of the reason for returning to the restaurant is due to the fact that they liked the food at the restaurant. This result now invites the question—what are the other reason(s) why people will return to the restaurant? Perhaps a combination of service, location, price, parking, or atmosphere are the remaining factors affecting the customer's decision to return to the restaurant.
• When marketing researchers need to focus the research on the *"why"* type questions—why people behave the way that they do—the coefficient of determination sheds some light on the reasons behind behavior people engage in or opinions they have.

- **Conjoint Analysis and Regression:**
  - *Considered to be regression, conjoint analysis is a statistical method that considers jointly the relative impact that a combinational set of independent variables has on the dependent variable(s) under study. Regression analysis examines a predicted linear relationship between variables accounting for the relative impact on the dependent variable based on changes from the independent variable(s).*
  - This method presumes that a *combination* of variables has a greater impact on the dependent variable than independent variables taken in *isolation*.
  - Most decisions involve making trade-offs. Conjoint analysis produces data that informs researchers as to the most and least desirable combination of variables associated with a preference or decision of some kind. For example, when students decide on where to go for spring break, they weight a series of factors, or criteria—presumably ascribing some notional weight to these criteria—before making a decision. Conjoint analysis reveals the relative impact independent variables have on the dependent variable(s).
  - Let's expand on the spring break example by looking at the criteria set in Figure 12.22. The dependent variable ultimately is the decision to choose one vacation choice over another. The spring break location is the variable that is dependent on the various criteria *(or independent variables)* that constitute the basis for the decision. The order of the independent variables does not matter because the regression analysis will account for all possible independent variable combinations. The independent variables associated with the spring break decision are shown in Figure 12.22.
  - **Combinations:** The total possible combination of attributes is 27 *(3 types × 3 distances × 3 lengths)*. As the number of attributes and choices increases, the total possible combinations increase exponentially. If there were another variable in addition to these three, the total number of combinations would be 81 (27 × 3). Conjoint analysis can get complicated quite quickly. With only a handful of variables one might think the relationships and relative impact of the independent variables could be estimated by simple observance. However, when more variables are included, the exponential number of possible combinations quickly outpaces one's ability to make judgments based on simply looking at the data.
  - **Coding:** Respondents now rate each of the 27 combinations on a preference scale—let's use a 1 to 10 preference rating for each possible combination provided by the respondents whereby 1=least preferable and 10=most preferable choice combination. Statistical Software needs numbers, not text, to calculate the regression thus the variables (data must be coded whereby 1=yes and 0=no *which is considered a **dummy variable** because it represents a null response*). Also, each attribute is coded as a 1, 2, 3, etc. *(depending on how many variables there are)*. In this case, there are three variables whereby 1=sight seeing, regional, and 3 days; 2=beach, national, and 1 week; and 3=cruise, international, and 10 days.

Spring Break Critera Set		
Type	Distance	Length
Sight Seeing	Regional	3 days
Beach	National	1 week
Cruise	International	10 days

■ FIGURE 12.22
Criteria Set

■ FIGURE 12.23
Coded Data

Spring Break Critera Set				
Choice	Type	Distance	Length	Preference
1	Sight Seeing	Regional	3 days	1
2	Sight Seeing	Regional	1 week	2
3	Sight Seeing	Regional	10 days	8
4	Sight Seeing	National	3 days	7
5	Sight Seeing	National	1 week	6
6	Sight Seeing	National	10 days	10
7	Sight Seeing	International	3 days	10
8	Sight Seeing	International	1 week	3
9	Sight Seeing	International	10 days	4
10	Beach	Regional	3 days	6
11	Beach	Regional	1 week	7
12	Beach	Regional	10 days	7
13	Beach	National	3 days	8
14	Beach	National	1 week	6
15	Beach	National	10 days	2
16	Beach	International	3 days	9
17	Beach	International	1 week	8
18	Beach	International	10 days	10
19	Cruise	Regional	3 days	2
20	Cruise	Regional	1 week	1
21	Cruise	Regional	10 days	5
22	Cruise	National	3 days	5
23	Cruise	National	1 week	4
24	Cruise	National	10 days	8
25	Cruise	International	3 days	2
26	Cruise	International	1 week	8
27	Cruise	International	10 days	3

Codes →

Spring Break Critera Set				
Choice	Type	Distance	Length	Preference
1	1	1	1	1
2	1	1	2	2
3	1	1	3	8
4	1	2	1	7
5	1	2	2	6
6	1	2	3	10
7	1	3	1	10
8	1	3	2	3
9	1	3	3	4
10	2	1	1	6
11	2	1	2	7
12	2	1	3	7
13	2	2	1	8
14	2	2	2	6
15	2	2	3	2
16	2	3	1	9
17	2	3	2	8
18	2	3	3	10
19	3	1	1	2
20	3	1	2	1
21	3	1	3	5
22	3	2	1	5
23	3	2	2	4
24	3	2	3	8
25	3	3	1	2
26	3	3	2	8
27	3	3	3	3

- Figure 12.23 shows the total possible number of combinations with the preference ratings for each possible combination and then the coded version of the same:
- Finally, before the final coding sheet can be created, researchers must correct for **linear dependence.**
  - **Linear Dependence:**
    - *The predictability of one independent variable based on the disposition of other independent variables.*
    - In other words, suppose there are five known factors affecting the decision to select a particular restaurant. Once four of the five possible variables identified as the *most to least* important are identified, researchers can *predict* by virtue of elimination that the unselected fifth factor is the *least* important factor. Multiple regression analysis requires that *predictable* combinations of options be eliminated from the data.
- **Final combination coding sheet:** Creating the final coded sheet requires accounting for linear dependence by eliminating one column of data for each variable, which despite its omission, is essentially accounted for by the remainder of the possible variable combinations. Thus it really does not matter which column of data is omitted as we see in Figure 12.24.
- The regression statistics function, in Figure 12.25, can be found in Excel under the Tools, Data Analysis tab once the Analysis ToolPak has been installed.
- The results of running the regression tool on the data are in Figure 12.26.
- For this respondent, the key driver in the decision making process was an international beach location for 10 days. The correlation was relatively low at .30 perhaps indicative of the random nature of the preference ratings given that this data is not actual data from respondents but created for illustrative purposes.
- Regression analysis enables researchers to determine the most effective combination of variables involved in the decision making process. Business leaders use regression analysis to help make decisions on the appropriate *marketing mix of price, product, promotion, and place* that best meets the customers' needs, wants, and expectations.

Choice	Sight Seeing	Beach	Cruise	Regional	National	International	3 days	1 week	10 days	Preference
1	1	0	0	1	0	0	1	0	0	1
2	1	0	0	1	0	0	0	1	0	2
3	1	0	0	1	0	0	0	0	1	8
4	1	0	0	0	1	0	1	0	0	7
5	1	0	0	0	1	0	0	1	0	6
6	1	0	0	0	1	0	0	0	1	10
7	1	0	0	0	0	1	1	0	0	10
8	1	0	0	0	0	1	0	1	0	3
9	1	0	0	0	0	1	0	0	1	4
10	0	1	0	1	0	0	1	0	0	6
11	0	1	0	1	0	0	0	1	0	7
12	0	1	0	1	0	0	0	0	1	7
13	0	1	0	0	1	0	1	0	0	8
14	0	1	0	0	1	0	0	1	0	6
15	0	1	0	0	1	0	0	0	1	2
16	0	1	0	0	0	1	1	0	0	9
17	0	1	0	0	0	1	0	1	0	8
18	0	1	0	0	0	1	0	0	1	10
19	0	0	1	1	0	0	1	0	0	2
20	0	0	1	1	0	0	0	1	0	1
21	0	0	1	1	0	0	0	0	1	5
22	0	0	1	0	1	0	1	0	0	5
23	0	0	1	0	1	0	0	1	0	4
24	0	0	1	0	1	0	0	0	1	8
25	0	0	1	0	0	1	1	0	0	2
26	0	0	1	0	0	1	0	1	0	8
27	0	0	1	0	0	1	0	0	1	3

Spring Break Criteria Set
Remove shaded *(adjust for linear dependence)* columns to run regression

■ **FIGURE 12.24**
Criteria Set

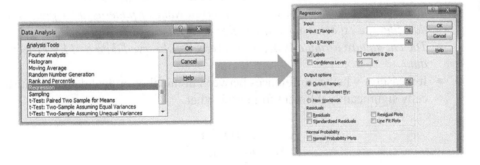

■ **FIGURE 12.25**
Regression

Criteria	Coefficients
Intercept	4.30
Beach	1.33
Cruise	-1.44
National	1.89
International	2.00
1 week	-0.56
10 days	0.78

Regression Statistics	
Multiple R	0.55
R Square	0.30
Standard Error	2.76
Observations	27

■ **FIGURE 12.26**
Regression Output

Chi Square Analysis

Chi Square analysis is a relatively common statistical tool that reveals whether observed data falls in an expected range of data. In other words, are the data results what we expect them to be? We discussed cross tabulations earlier as a means of gaining good descriptive data. However, cross tabulations do not tell researchers if there are statistically predictable patterns or differences in the data. Cross tabulations simply display the numbers and percentages of various combinations of data. Chi square tests take the data analysis a step further by ascribing an expected pattern or relationship between variables and by determining if the difference between nominal or ordinal data pairs are statistically significantly different from each other.

■ **FIGURE 12.27**

Survey Results are Just
a Jumble of Numbers
Until Transformed into
Information Through
Data Analysis

Image © Kudryashka, 2011. Used
under license from Shutterstock, Inc.

- **Chi Square—Notation X²:**
  - *A statistical test between two or more nominal or ordinal (categorical) data elements that determines how well the observed value or patterns fit the patterns of data they are expected to fit. Also called a "goodness of fit" determination.*
  - *The chi-square formula is below whereby 0=observed data and E=expected data.*
  - It measures whether differences between nominal or ordinal data are statistically significantly different from each other.

$$\chi_c^2 = \sum \frac{(O_i - E_i)^2}{E_i}$$

Type I and Type II Errors

When conducting hypothesis testing there is, by its very nature, the chance that the researcher will arrive at incorrect conclusions about a given hypothesis. When creating a hypothesis *(or argument),* such as *"the sales decline is due to poor customer service"* marketing researchers have essentially two conclusions from which to decide the merits of the hypothesis—the **null hypothesis** and the **alternative hypothesis.** There are two major types of error: **Type I** and **Type II** as depicted in Figure 12.28.

- **P-Value:**
  - The p-value statistic is a test of statistical significance whereby a p-value of less than .05 indicates that the null hypothesis should be rejected in favor of the alternative hypothesis that there is a statistically significant difference

Hypothesis Testing - Types of Error

between variables. The .05 result indicates that there is a 5 percent chance of rejecting the null hypothesis when in fact it is true—or a Type I error. Rejecting the null hypothesis essentially means that there is statistical significance in the difference between the variables under study.

Hypothesis Testing:
* *A statistical test to examine the theorized impact of changes made by independent variables on dependent variables while accounting for variations attributed to chance variation.*

Null Hypothesis—denoted by H_0:
* *A conclusion stating that the independent variable under study **has no** statistically significant impact on the dependent variable.*
  * *"The sales decline is **not due** to poor customer service"*

Alternative Hypothesis—denoted by H_1:
* *A conclusion stating that the independent variable under study **has a** statistically significant impact on the dependent variable.*
  * *"The sales decline **is due** to poor customer service"*

Type I Error:
* *A false positive error whereby the researcher rejects the null hypothesis when in fact the null hypothesis is true.*
  * *The sales decline was **"not"** due to poor customer service—but it really **was**.*
  * *Perhaps a test shows that someone **has** chicken pox, but he really **does not**.*

Type II Error:
* *A false negative whereby the researcher fails to reject the null hypothesis (thus accepting the alternative hypothesis) when in fact the null hypothesis should have been rejected in favor of the alternative hypothesis.*
  * *The sales decline **was due** to poor customer service—but it really **was not**.*
  * *Perhaps a test shows that someone **does not have** chicken pox, but he really **does** have chicken pox.*

Let's look at the restaurant survey again and examine two key questions on that survey—their sex and favorite type of restaurant. Researchers might want to determine if there is a *statistically significant* difference between how men and women answered this question. We know there is some difference between the data by virtue of the fact that their answers are not identical. The more important issue is to understand the *nature* of the difference. Is the difference due to chance variation *(random variation)* or is the difference statistically significant meaning there is some *reason* for the difference? The questions and survey results are below.

1. *"What is your sex?"*
2. *"What is your favorite type of restaurant?"*

■ FIGURE 12.29
Survey Questions

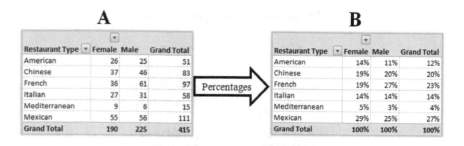

■ FIGURE 12.30
Chi Square Table

Chi Square Distribution Table

DF	P				
	0.995	0.975	0.20	0.10	0.05
1	0.0000393	0.000982	1.642	2.706	3.841
2	0.0100	0.0506	3.219	4.605	5.991
3	0.0717	0.216	4.642	6.251	7.815
4	0.207	0.484	5.989	7.779	9.488
5	0.412	0.831	7.289	9.236	11.070
6	0.676	1.237	8.558	10.645	12.592
7	0.989	1.690	9.803	12.017	14.067
8	1.344	2.180	11.030	13.362	15.507
9	1.735	2.700	12.242	14.684	16.919
10	2.156	3.247	13.442	15.987	18.307

Performing a Chi Square Test:

Step 1 - State Hypothesis

- **The null hypothesis:**
  - *There is **no** statistically significance difference between men and women's restaurant preference.*
- **The alternative hypothesis:**
  - *There **is a** statistically significant difference between men and women's restaurant preferences.*

Step 2 - Select and Find the Critical Value

- This step involves comparing the actual, or observed value, with an expected value.
- The degrees of freedom for **Table A** is (2-1) *for the columns* and (6-1) *for the rows*—thus the DF = 1*5 = 5.
- The critical value for a chi-square with 5 degrees of freedom at the 95 percent confidence level is rounded to **11.1** from the standard Chi Square Distribution Table in Figure 12.30.

Step 3 - Calculate the Test Statistic

- Calculating the chi-square test statistic involves comparing the actual *(or observed)* data to its expected data. Expected data are the results researchers would expect if the null hypothesis were true.

- Using Table A data from above we calculate the **expected** frequencies:

Female	E = 51/415*190	E = 83/415*190	E = 97/415*190	E = 58/415*190	E = 15/415*190	E = 111/415*190
	23.3	38.0	44.4	26.6	6.9	50.8
Male	E = 51/415*225	E = 83/415*225	E = 97/415*225	E = 58/415*225	E = 15/415*225	E = 111/415*225
	27.7	45.0	52.6	31.4	8.1	60.2

- Once we have the **expected** calculated values, they can be compared to the **observed** values *(from Table A data above)* to calculate the chi-square statistic using the Chi Square Formula:

$$\chi^2_c = \sum \frac{(O_i - E_i)^2}{E_i}$$

- Comparing the observed data to the expected data using the chi square formula:
  - (26−23.3)(26−23.3)/23.3+(37−38)(37−38)/38+(36−44.4)(36−44.4)/44.4+(27−26.6)(27−26.6)/26.6+(9−6.9)(9−6.9)/6.9+(55−50.8)(55−50.8)/50.8+(25−27.7)(25−27.7)/27.7+(46−45)(46−45)/45+(61−52.6)(61−52.6)/52.6+(31−31.4)(31−31.4)/31.4+(6−8.1)(6−8.1)/8.1+(56−60.2)(56−60.2)/60.2 = **5.39**
  - Chi Square = 5.39

Step 4 - Analyze the Results

- Because at the 95 percent confidence interval the chi square test statistic is **11.1** *(as taken from the chi square table)* and the actual chi square calculation yielded **5.39**, the null hypothesis is not rejected. In other words, the null hypothesis that there was *no statistically significant difference* in how men and women answered the question regarding their favorite restaurant type is likely true.
- Do not reject the null hypothesis when the chi test statistic is greater than the calculated chi square statistic based on the data. Reject the null hypothesis in favor of the alternative hypothesis when the chi square statistic is greater than the chi square test statistic from the chi square table.

When using **Microsoft Excel,** there are three main steps to conducting a chi square analysis that provide a shortcut to the more detailed version just explained. Let's use these steps to look at a survey of color preferences by sex and determine whether men and women like different colors.

1. **Create a pivot table** *(of the nominal or ordinal data)* **to create the "observed" values. Let's presume the following data were actual data results from a survey:**

Observed	Men	Women	Totals
Red	25	30	55
Blue	17	15	32
Green	7	26	33
Totals	49	71	120

2. **Create the "expected" values:**

- This value is what we would "expect" to see if there was no statistically significant difference in color preference between men and women. For example, if we had two color choices (purple and yellow) and 100 respondents (half men and half women), we would "expect," assuming randomness and no "reason" for there being a preference difference, this distribution to be as follows:

- 25 men like purple
- 25 men like yellow
- 25 women like purple
- 25 women like yellow

Observed	Men	Women	Totals		Expected	Men	Women	Totals
Purple	25	25	50	AND	Purple	25	25	50
Yellow	25	25	50		Yellow	25	25	50
Totals	50	50	100		Totals	50	50	100

- Return to the example from step 1 above, and copy and paste the pivot table using "paste special—values."
- Delete the interior of the data (the shaded area from the previous step).
- Create the expected ranges (the new shaded area) using this formula:
  - Column total × row total / grand total

    1. $49 \times 55 / 120 = 22.5$ (Men column and red row)
    2. $49 \times 32 / 120 = 13.1$ (Men column and blue row)
    3. $49 \times 33 / 120 = 13.5$ (Men column and blue row)
    4. Repeat the process for the Women column.
    5. Note that the red/blue/green distribution is not evenly distributed, unlike the distribution in the previous purple/yellow example, because there is **not** an even number of men and women.

Expected	Men	Women	Totals
Red	22.5	32.5	55
Blue	13.1	18.9	32
Green	13.5	19.5	33
Totals	49	71	120

3. **Run the Chi Square test and interpret its P-value. Excel automatically converts the Chi Statistic to its P-value** (accounting for the appropriate degrees of freedom):

- The formula in Excel: =chitest(actual_range, expected_range).
- Note that the actual range = observed range.
- The actual and expected ranges are the interior (shaded) regions of the data from the previous step and do not include the data totals.
- P-value = .021.
- Since P< .05 (at the 95% confidence level), there is a statistically significant difference in color preference by sex when we consider all three colors. Apparently, men and women like different colors. However, remember that parsing data into subgroups might affect the statistical significance.

Analysis of Variance (ANOVA)

- ANOVA:
  - *A statistical test with interval and ratio data to determine if the group means and variances among (at least three) normally distributed datasets are statistically different from each other.*

Three types of ANOVA are commonly used:

1. Single factor
2. Two factor without replication
3. Two factor with replication

1. Single factor:

- This type of ANOVA presumes each data element (*each cell*) represents an individual respondent; thus, each cell represents *a different* person doing *one* thing.

- Example:
  - Student test scores—*each* student is taking only *one* section of marketing research. Therefore, there are 36 students in the table, each doing *one* thing (taking one exam).

Marketing Research Class Sections		
Monday Professor Parekh	Wednesday Professor Setlur	Friday Professor Smith
60	78	57
87	15	69
88	33	96
51	73	77
92	92	66
66	44	100
64	87	77
22	20	100
54	44	77
97	91	69
20	92	57
56	84	95

ANOVA - One P-Value	
Source of Variation	*P-value*
Between Groups	0.21326

- Analysis:
  - There was *not* a statistically significant difference (P = .213, thus > .05) in how students performed compared to each other by class *section*. In other words, students generally did equally good or bad on the test regardless of class section. It appears that none of these professors is "easier" or "harder" than another.

2. Two factor without replication:

- In this ANOVA approach, *each row* represents an individual respondent; thus, *each* respondent is doing *two or more* things.

- Example:
  - Student test scores—*each* student is talking *four* classes (arts, language, sports, and history). Therefore, there are 12 students in the table, each doing *multiple* things (taking four exams each).

- Analysis:
  - Case A:
    - There is *not* a statistically significant difference (P = .82, thus > .05) in how students (rows) performed, *compared to each other*, across the four courses

Student	Arts	Language	Sports	History	Average
1	88	100	99	78	91
2	90	95	79	65	82
3	87	78	88	69	81
4	78	88	85	79	83
5	100	85	87	81	88
6	81	91	78	94	86
7	65	94	94	77	83
8	87	87	93	73	85
9	81	83	89	82	84
10	84	82	95	88	87
11	91	77	97	84	87
12	94	91	93	72	88
Average	86	88	90	79	85

By Student

By Course

Case A

Courses	
Arts / Language / Sports / History	

P-Values	
Between Students	0.82
Between Subjects	0.01

Case B

Courses	
Arts / Language / Sports	

P-Values	
Between Students	0.70
Between Subjects	0.44

they took. Note that the student averages (far right column) do not appear to be very different from each other, which is one indicator that the variance in the scores might also not be very pronounced (confirmed by a P-value of .82).

- However, there is a statistically significant difference (P = .01, thus < .05) in students' performance by class subject when considering all four classes. Apparently, some classes were easier or harder for students.

- Case B:
  - In this case, we remove the history class from the analysis and run the ANOVA on the arts, language, and sports columns. Note that the average test scores by class subject reveal that perhaps the history class was the main source of the class performance variation (P = .01 from Case A). because its average of 79 (see the bottom row) is quite a bit lower than the averages for the other class subjects—86, 88, and 90, respectively. In other words, perhaps the history class was so hard that it "pulled down" all the other classes to make it appear that there was a difference in class performance among the four classes—in fact, if we remove the history class from the analysis, there was not a statistically significance difference (P = .44, thus >.05, from Case B) among the other classes (arts, language, and sports).
  - Note that the slight difference in row P-values (.82 in Case A and .70 in Case B) in the samples above is due to removing the history class from the analysis, which leaves fewer data points.
  - It is important to do this type of subgroup analysis in order to determine the source of variation in data, or at least what the source might be.

3. **Two factor with replication:**
- In this type of ANOVA, each respondent is doing *two or more* things *and* the data are broken into two or more *subgroups.*

- Example:
  - Student test scores—*each* student is taking *four* classes—divided by *subgroup*—per school year. Therefore, there are 12 students in the table,

Year	Student	Arts	Lauguage	Sports	History	Average
Freshman	1	88	100	99	78	91
	2	90	95	79	65	82
	3	87	78	88	69	81
Sophmore	4	78	88	85	79	83
	5	100	85	87	81	88
	6	81	91	78	94	86
Junior	7	65	94	94	77	83
	8	87	87	93	73	85
	9	81	83	89	82	84
Senior	10	84	82	95	88	87
	11	91	77	97	84	87
	12	94	91	93	72	88
Average		86	88	90	79	85

By Student

By Course

P-Values	
Between Students	**0.80**
Between Subjects	**0.001**
Group Interaction	**0.09**

with four from each year in school (subgroup), and all are doing multiple things (taking four exams each).

- Analysis:
  - In this case, there is *not* a statistically significant difference (P = .80, thus > .05) in how students performed by class rank (sample), nor is there a statistically significant difference (P = .09), thus P > .05) in the interactions between the students by class rank. In other words, no group of students (by class rank) positively or negatively affected other class ranks. The argument that freshmen will not perform well if they take the exam with seniors in the room (i.e., that somehow seniors being in the room will have an impact on the freshmen's performance) is not a valid argument. However, further subgroup analysis might yield significant differences given that the P-value, at .09, is close to .05. At .001, there is a statistically significant difference in how well students performed by subject matter. Perhaps some subjects are easier or harder than others.

Finally, if the P-value is close to .05 but not below, consider breaking the data into subgroups. Statistically significant differences may be revealed when the data are parsed into smaller groups.

Let's look at test scores for three sections of a marketing research class that one professor teaches to determine if the variances among the three class scores are statistically significantly different from each other. If there is a statistically significant difference among the scores, the question raised is *"why is there a difference?"* Perhaps there is some difference in the students themselves or in how the professor approached each class. ANOVA will identify if there is a difference beyond what we might expect from mere chance variation by comparing the variances between sets of interval or ratio data. The *within and between group* variances are important here. ANOVA is comparing the *within and between group differences* and determining whether the within group variance is high. If so, it's presumed that the within group variance, or difference, is essentially masking the between group difference unless the difference between the groups is large enough to compensate for the large within group variance.

There are several data requirements to note. The dependent variable must be continuous data—either interval or ratio *(in this case we are using ratio data—test scores)* and the independent variable must be categorical—nominal or ordinal *(in this case we are using nominal data—class 1, 2, or 3)*. Below is the data with the ANOVA single factor output using the data analysis ToolPak in Microsoft Excel.

Student Exam Scores

Class 1	Class 2	Class 3
77	86	79
73	67	93
68	64	86
77	67	75
96	77	83
88	61	98
63	96	91
86	89	98
80	97	98
96	89	80
72	67	88
74	85	90
62	81	88
93	77	85
87	87	98
61	80	75
80	82	81
73	78	95
70	98	78
68	78	73
98	78	88
65	88	97
70	69	84
78	80	78
99	72	98
78	81	88
80	79	86
77	76	91
61	96	92
60	93	80
84	86	95
97	63	90
85	88	99
84	70	75
76	66	95
78	**80**	**88**

Averages

Three Classes

SUMMARY

Groups	Count	Sum	Average	Variance
Class 1	35	2,736	78	131
Class 2	35	2,791	80	108
Class 3	35	3,073	88	60

ANOVA

Source of Variation	Sum of Squares	Degrees of Freedom	Variance	F	P-value	F crit
Between Groups	1,868	2	934	9.4	0.0	3.1
Within Groups	10,153	102	100			
Total	12,021	104				

Two Classes

SUMMARY

Groups	Count	Sum	Average	Variance
Class 1	35	2,736	78	131
Class 2	35	2,791	80	108

ANOVA

Source of Variation	Sum of Squares	Degrees of Freedom	Variance	F	P-value	F crit
Between Groups	43	1	43	0.36	0.55	3.98
Within Groups	8,116	68	119			
Total	8,159	69				

$$F = \frac{\text{Between Group Variance}}{\text{Within Group Variance}}$$

- **Class Analysis:**
  - Three Classes F Value: 934/100 = 9.4
  - Two Classes F Value: 43/119 = .36

At the 95% confidence interval when F is greater than F critical, P becomes less than .05 and there is a *statistically significant difference* between the samples. Thus we *reject* the null hypothesis that there is no statistically significant difference in favor of the alternative hypothesis that there *is* a significant difference between the datasets. It appears that there is **not** a statistically significant difference between class 1 and 2 but there is a statistically significant difference when class 3 is included. In the two class analysis—for class 1 and 2, F is less than F critical and thus P is greater than .05. Therefore, there is no statistical difference in variation between classes 1 and 2. However, in the three class scenario, the F value is much greater than the critical value, which means at least one of the groups *(class 1, 2, or 3)* is statistically different from the others. In this case class 3 is the variance culprit because we know that there is no difference between class 1 and 2.

Marketing researchers use ANOVA to determine if the difference between variables is due to some reason *other* than chance. If so, the challenge is to find the reason(s) for the variance.

T-tests

t-tests tell researchers whether the difference between the **averages** of two interval or ratio datasets (of at least 30 observations) is statistically significant. Remember that ANOVA reveals whether the **variances** in datasets are statistically significantly different.

Suppose we have 40 scores each from a sports exercise and a history exercise, and we want to determine whether the respective averages (sports = 18.9 and history = 16.1) are far enough apart to justify a researcher stating that these scores are statistically significantly different from each other. If so, the difference is *not* due to chance and is not random, and thus there is some *reason* they are different.

The following data reveal, in addition to some descriptive statistics and correlation output, that the P-values for **both** a one-tail test (essentially meaning that one score is higher than the other: P = .02) and a two tail test (essentially meaning that one score is either higher or lower than the other: P = .04) are below .05; thus, we can say that there is a statistically significant difference between the averages of the sports and history scores.

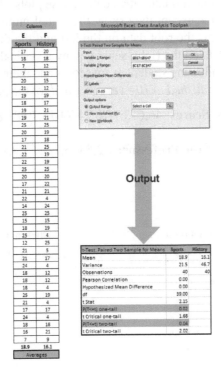

Box Plots

Box plots, which can be created in SPSS, SAS, and in Microsoft Excel, visually ratio data. Box plots provide an easy way to understand visual representations of the distribution of data. The more centered the box is between the whiskers, the more normally distributed the data are likely to be. Not all box plots have outliers—data above the upper or lower 25 percentile. The more narrow, or compressed, the middle 50 percentile box is, the higher peaked (kurtosis) the data are. The distance between the whiskers is the data range—outliers notwithstanding. A sample box plot is presented in Figure 12.32

■ **FIGURE 12.32**
Box Plot

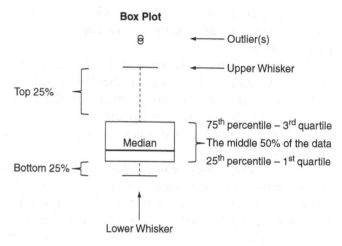

Stem and Leaf Plot

Stem and leaf plots, also called stemplots, are visual displays of data that highlight the shape and distribution of quantitative data. These plots, shown in Figure 12.33, are similar to histograms except they show the actual numeric value of the data. Stem and leaf plots show the root data on the left and the digit data extension for each respective root data on the right, separated by a vertical line.

Let's assume the following student exam scores and their respective satisfaction rating *(from 1=very unsatisfied to 10=very satisfied)* of the professor for that class.

- **Ratio Data Exam Scores**: 46,67,67,70,74,74,76,79,81,84,88,88,88,89,92,92, 94,96, and 99
- **Interval Ratings of the Professor:** 1,2,5,6,6,7,7,7,7,8,8,8,8,8,9,9,9,10,10

■ **FIGURE 12.33**
Stem and Leaf Plot

Ratio Data	
Stem	Leaf
4	6
5	
6	7 7
7	0 4 4 6 9
8	1 4 8 8 8 9
9	2 2 4 6 9
10	

Interval Data	
Stem	Leaf
1	1
2	1
3	
4	
5	1
6	1 1
7	1 1 1 1
8	1 1 1 1 1
9	1 1 1
10	1 1

- With a large set of ratio or interval data, the stemplot will become increasingly complex while simultaneously yielding insightful information about the data distribution. When using a stemplot for interval data, the leaf calculation is simply the number of observations, or ratings, per item on the scale.
- Stem and leaf plots are another way to visually display and represent the distribution of data while including the data value (for ratio data).

Data Analysis Pitfalls to Avoid

Marketing research reports contain varying levels of data analysis. When conducting data analysis, researchers must decide which analysis tools to use and why. There are simply too many statistical tools to use thus selecting the correct and appropriate tools are critical given the objectives of each respective research report. Here are a few pitfalls to avoid when deciding which type of data analysis technique and approach a researcher might use in a report.

- **The Wrong, or Incorrectly Applied, Statistical Tool:**
  - **Example:** Doing a correlation on nominal data. Using the wrong statistical tool guarantees that the reader will lose confidence in the quality of the report.
- **Overanalyzing—Analysis Paralysis:**
  - **Example:** Making data extrapolations and conclusions not fully supported by the data or drawing analysis conclusions from limited descriptive data. Suppose 80 percent of respondents do not like the product color in blue and the researcher determines that the color of choice is green despite the lack of soliciting such information from respondents. In this case, the researcher apparently assumed that because blue was not desired, green was the most likely alternative for whatever reason. Avoid crowding the report with "one of each" data analysis tools, instead focus on a few tools most relevant to your research objectives.
- **Under Analyzing:**
  - **Example:** Failing to run a marginal report or failing to include "obvious" multivariate cross tabs, or perhaps not conducting correlation analysis despite having an interval based questionnaire. Relying too much on qualitative observations as opposed to quantitative analysis limits the utility and impact of the research report results, conclusions, and recommendations. A value added component of a marketing research report is conducting sub group analysis. Sub group analysis delves more deeply into the data and uncovers data patterns that are not readily apparent. Suppose when correlating "age" and "number of hours exercised" the correlation is .40. Researchers might conclude that age and hours of exercise are not significantly related. However, when looking at a sub group—women over 30—the correlation is .80 indicating that as women over 30 age, they exercise more than women under 30 and more than all respondents when considered as a group. Sub group analysis is a leading tool in market segmentation research.
- **Ignoring the Research Objectives:**
  - **Example:** Remember that many marketing research reports have a sponsor. Perhaps your boss wants to conduct a marketing research study on ways to better serve customers or maybe a company hires a marketing research firm to conduct a customer satisfaction study. In the latter case, the marketing research firm has a paid client with expectations. A period of time, perhaps

a significant period of time, will have elapsed by the time the researcher gets to the data analysis phase of the project. This time lag might result in a disconnect between the original research objectives and the data analysis that should examine those objectives. Marketing researchers should ensure that the data analysis supports the original research objectives and that the data analysis is not simply a "data dump" of information.

- **Equating Correlation with Causation:**
  - **Example:** Correlation is a measure of association or a measure of how statistically related data are. Correlation uncovers patterns, or lack of patterns, among data. However, do not assume that highly correlated data mean that one data element caused the other. There are innumerable examples of statistical coincidences that are not cause and effect related.
- **Incomplete or Unclear Graphics:**
  - **Example:** Bar and pie charts are very common and generally quickly understandable. However, when using histograms, radar graphs, box plots, stacked bar charts, area graphs, or other statistical tools be vigilant in ensuring that the graphs depict the data correctly and convey the information clearly. It might be wise to test the data clarity with a small sample to validate whether the data displays are effective.

Research in Practice

Assignment:

- Using the Microsoft Excel data set provided with this book through the publisher or directly from the text's author—David Ashley at dashley@gwu.edu—write a five page research report using the tools discussed in chapters 11 and 12.

■ FIGURE 12.34

Even Martian Business Leaders Analyze Data Before Making a Business Decision

Image © Konstantinos Kokkinis, 2011. Used under license from Shutterstock, Inc.

Chapter Summary

The data analysis and report writing phase is the culmination of the marketing research process. The final report is driven by both the qualitative and quantitative research findings. Analyzing qualitative data largely involves creating frequency counts from like responses. Descriptive statistics describes data though measures of central tendency, shape, spread, and frequency. The chief forms of central tendency involve the mean *(the sum of the observations divided by the number of observations)*, median *(the middle value in an ordered dataset)*, and mode *(the most commonly occurring observation)*. Measures of data shape include kurtosis *(how peaked the data are around the mean)* and skewness *(the level of spread in one direction or another)*. Measures of dispersion or spread include range *(the difference between the highest and lowest observation)*, variance *(the standard deviation squared)*, and standard deviation *(a measure of variability around the mean)*. Inferential statistics involve data whereby inference or conclusions about relationships among data items can be made or extrapolated. Histograms can be used with nominal, ordinal, interval, and ratio data. Histograms are cumulative frequency bar charts and are good tools for displaying the impact of data such as understanding how many respondents rated *(cumulatively)* a certain item 1, 2, and 3 on a scale of 1 to 10. Rank and percentile, used with ratio data, sorts the data in descending order and labels each observation by its relative rank and percentile relative to the entire dataset. Categorical data are qualitative data that are descriptive and mutually exclusive such as nominal data. Analyzing categorical data typically involves frequency counts, percentages, and cross tabulations. Continuous data are more ratio in nature (can be interval) whereby the data have a natural progression such as age when expressed numerically. Many statistical tools such as descriptive statistics, regression, correlation, and Analysis

of Variance (ANOVA) can be used on continious data. Regression analysis uses interval or ratio data to determine the varying and weighted impact of independent variables on dependent variables. Pearson correlation analysis uses interval or ratio data to establish statistical patterns, or lack of patterns, among data elements. Correlation is a measure of association and should not be extended to presume causation. Chi square is used to determine if two or more categorical data elements are statistically different from each other. Analysis of Variance is used to determine if ratio or interval data variances are statistically significantly different. There is a difference between within groups and between groups analysis. Within groups measures the variance within one group such as the variance of ages of people in Seattle. Between groups variance measures the difference between groups such as comparing the age averages of people from Seattle to people from Albuquerque. Box plots and stem and leaf plots are used to show data dispersion. Box plots show ratio data as anchored around the median with the relative quartile ranges. Stem and leaf plots use the root of ratio or interval data as the stem and the extension of each root as the leaf which results in a histogram like display— except the relative value of each data element is apparent. Finally, a number of data analysis pitfalls should be avoided when writing the research report. Over and under-analyzing the data, using the wrong data analysis tool or using a tool incorrectly, failing to tie the data analysis to the original research objectives of the research sponsor, presuming that correlation means causation, and using unclear or inconsistent graphics. The data analysis phase is where marketing researchers tie together the secondary and primary qualitative and quantitative research findings in a written report that answers the original research question and meets the purpose of doing the research.

ISSUE IN THE SPOTLIGHT   NPR Understanding its Audience

Lori Kaplan, Director
Department of Audience Insight & Research
National Public Radio
www.npr.org

CASE STUDY—NPR PROJECT ARGO

PROBLEM STATEMENT:

Over the last 40 years NPR has grown from an organization offering one news program on a couple of dozen stations to a major presence in the news and information space, reaching more than 27 million listeners weekly on the radio and 17 million digitally on a monthly basis. At the same time local stations have been growing their footprint and are universally interested in growing their local news capacity, particularly in light of the void left by newspapers shuttering their doors. In an effort to address this public radio system need, NPR and its VP of Digital Media, Kinsey Wilson, conceived of a concept to drive traffic to station sites. It was dubbed Project Argo, referencing the Greek mythological quest for the Golden Fleece.

PROPOSED SOLUTION:

While many have touted the mantra of hyper-local content as a solution for what ails local newspapers and content providers, Wilson argued for a different approach. Project Argo proposes that stations develop a specific area of content expertise, for example, health, education or the military. This content would be collected on a station site in three ways: original content provided by an expert blogger, smart aggregation, and a vibrant online community. Wilson suggests that this approach would likely generate a longer-term win. Station leadership could propel local content into the national spotlight as stations develop their expertise. Wilson based this hypothesis on his experience at USA Today developing two popular travel-themed blogs.

QUESTIONS RAISED BY THIS PROPOSAL:

Would this translate from a national outlet to local outlets?

Is this project scalable to small markets?

What should the sites look like?

Would we see demand for the content through increased site traffic?

RESEARCH PLAN:

NPR first needed to make a decision as to whether to seek and invest resources for a pilot project to test the viability of the Project Argo strategy. In order to proceed, NPR needed to assess whether the idea had legs from a listener perspective—would listeners actually visit such a site and would they trust the content from the local station? For this we decided to speak with existing listeners in one-on-one interviews. Using this method allowed us to spend substantial time (up to 50 minutes per person) to understand each person's relationship to media, to search out information and to assess the barriers to adoption. We also needed to understand the competitive landscape. Are others ready to jump into this space? Are there models we should be examining? Are those who are exposed to consumers beyond our own aware of limits to this concept? For this set of questions we turned to expert one-on-one interviews.

EXPERT INTERVIEWS:

Expert interviews consist of individuals who are responsible for development, execution or authority over strategies, policies or insights. These people may also have access to privileged information about target subject matter or persons. The value in conversations with them lies in their aggregated knowledge and exposure to many different organizations or scenarios do to their vantage point. They know what has and has not worked and are in a position to share that information with us. In this case, we structured the interviews, but were flexible during the conversation to allow for each expert to share whatever relevant information they deemed appropriate. We included those we had a contractual relationship with—those who had expressed previous interest in helping NPR. During those conversations we asked if there are others that we should be speaking with. Best practices indicate that each expert would receive a copy of the final summary document. We scheduled interviews with media thought leaders and strategists to get both their reaction to the Argo concept and gauge any concerns. We spoke with individuals at USC's Annenberg Center for the Digital Future, Knight Foundation Journalism Program, Edison Research, Forrester Research and Free Press.

The people we spoke with are optimistic about the future of public radio and were very receptive to the concept of Project Argo and bullish on its potential. Critical to its success will be three key elements: moving to fill the shrinking supply of local news and information, doing so in a fashion that makes use of pre-existing conversational momentum around specific topic areas and ensuring that that coverage is relevant both locally and globally. Some expressed concerns about the ability of public media to accommodate the culture shift required to thrive in this new space. Despite this, the people we interviewed generally found the concept to be sound. All the shifts they are observing in news consumption point to a need for less centralized approaches to local news coverage, where success is defined less by massive reach and scale of audience than by the facilitation of coverage and conversations around specific topics.

LISTENER INTERVIEWS:

Armed with expert information, we slated one-on-one interviews among regular and fringe listeners to NPR stations. While one would imagine that visitors to Project Argo sites would expand beyond existing listeners, the initial exposure and evangelists will be from this group. We spoke with 25 individuals in Ann Arbor, MI; Southfield, MI; and Washington, DC. Interviews were conducted by Paul and Fred Jacobs of Jacobs Media. During the conversations, we sensed that public radio listeners are generally open to the idea of special interest sites produced by local public stations, but their enthusiasm is tempered by their need to see how these sites might actually look and work. It will be important for each participating station/site to state the rationale behind the effort on various promotion platforms. In considering the Argo concept, several respondents felt that if public radio developed sites devoted to areas that reflect its "sweet spots"—specifically politics or news oriented interest areas—it could be successful.

USABILITY TESTING:

With validation of experts and listeners, NPR proceeded and secured a grant from the Corporation for Public Broadcasting. The project advanced under the leadership of Joel Sucherman, formerly of USA Today. The team developed wireframes for the local sites. Before launch, we tested the design among NPR listeners recruited from an existing NPR online advisory panel. We invited individuals to review pages. This critical phase revealed important design modifications regarding user expectations, navigation, aggregation tools, share tools and the support banner.

We found that the station name and NPR branding are important to the identity of the site. Additionally subtitles below the blog title are important for newcomers and should clearly message the mission of the site. Along these lines, the blogger identity was not clear to visitors. Potential site visitors indicated that the credibility of the blogger is essential to establishing the value of the site. As a result the head shot and mini bio were moved to a more prominent location. The "email this" functionality—critical to building traffic and site exposure— was added to all pages.

OUTCOME AND IMPACT:

Project Argo sites launched in August 2010 with 12 stations. All 12 sites saw an increase in page views and unique visitors because going live. The two stand outs, WBUR (CommonHealth) in Boston and KQED (Mind/Shift) in San Francisco, experience 50,000 or more page views each month. CommonHealth's coverage of the September 2010 Similac recall was so powerful that Abbot Lab's Similac Team responded to questions on the lively community forum.

During this initial period, stations have invested significant time training newspaper reporters to blog actively on the sites. The next phase for the site is promotion—on station's air and rotation on NPR.org for posts with national resonance. NPR is also in the process of developing open source platform technology so that the template for sites can be replicated without additional expense for new station sites.

13

Presenting the Results

Image © Konstantions Kokkinis, 2011. Used under license from Shutterstock, Inc.

Learning Objectives:

- Appreciate the importance of effectively presenting the research results
- Learn the key components of a marketing research report
- Understand the concept of Return on Investment and its applicability to research

- Appreciate the difference between the research methods and research findings sections
- Learn how to demonstrate the value of marketing research to clients
- See why addressing reliability and validity in a research report is important

- Learn some methods of effectively presenting the research results
- Appreciate the benefit of separating the secondary and primary data findings.

Chapter Thirteen

The Research Report Purpose

The major function of the research report is to summarize the research study purpose, research methods, and findings for the benefit of the research sponsor. After the lengthy process of data collection and analysis are completed, it is time to produce a written report. Typically, in the initial phase of a research project, the research sponsor and the research provider will have coordinated the deliverable and managed expectations. In the absence of clear guidance from the research sponsor, the research provider should produce a draft outline of the deliverables early in the research project life cycle to ensure there are no major surprises at the end of the research project.

Establishing credibility in the research report involves clearly conveying the research methods, primary and secondary sources, and the analysis used in the research report. The reader of the report must feel that the researcher has the credentials and expertise to produce a quality report. Marketing researchers will benefit from having plausible and actionable recommendations based on the data and they should be honest brokers in analyzing the data in an unbiased manner.

Careful marketing researchers work closely with the research sponsor during the research execution phase of the project to ensure that they are on in agreement and that the research sponsor's expectations are being met. Oftentimes, but not always, the research sponsor will want to receive all major facets of the research study and will expect regular project updates. It is incumbent on the researcher to manage the research study in accordance with a given contract while deftly managing the client's exceptions. The research report is the culmination of the research study and generally marks the end of the engagement between the marketing researcher and the research sponsor.

When marketing researchers compile the research report, considering the needs and wants of the report recipient is critical. Many marketing research reports are statistics-heavy documents that might be difficult for the research sponsor to absorb fully. Creating an elaborate statistical document is not overly difficult given the breadth of available software. However, writing and presenting a research report in a meaningful way that provides actionable recommendations and insight with understandable statistics and analysis, will create value in the research report.

Is the Research Worth the Cost? *The Return on Investment Debate*

Failure to communicate the results of the marketing research study to clients effectively will represent a missed opportunity to the research supplier to demonstrate the value of conducting the research. In many cases the marketing researcher will present the results to a variety of interested parties who might not be fully versed on the research purpose and thus need to be *"sold"* that the research was worth the cost. For example, suppose researchers are conducting a market segmentation study for the Gap which wants to expand to new markets. The marketing manager for the Gap hires a marketing research firm to conduct the study. After the study has been completed, the researcher presents the results to the marketing manager who, satisfied with the results, arranges a meeting with the Gap senior leadership and various stockholders to review the report. The presentation of the research report becomes contentious when several key stockholders question the value of the research. These stockholders point out that the research project cost $100,000 and the results and recommendations generated by the report fail to show how the costs will be recouped though the recommended market segmentation strategy. Whereas some clients conduct research for research sake (such as basic as opposed to applied research) hoping that the basic research might yield some valuable and actionable data, most business clients expect the marketing research results will provide an appropriate *Return on Investment* (ROI) lest the marketing research project not be worth the cost. If the marketing researcher does not adequately explain and demonstrate the value of the research, it is likely that someone in the client leadership chain will challenge the value of having done the research. Marketing researchers should be cautious and realize that the research sponsor who hired the marketing researcher to conduct the study has more direct involvement with the research project than many senior organization leaders might have and thus will see the research value more easily than other people in the reporting chain who do not have adequate prior knowledge or appreciation of the research project.

Return on Investment:

- *The calculation, and thereafter assessment, of the cost of an investment compared to the tangible and/or intangible benefit(s) from the investment.*

- ROI References:
  - *www.investopedia.com/video/play/return-on-investment-basics*
  - *www.solutionmatrix.com/return-on-investment.html*
  - *http://en.wikipedia.org/wiki/Rate_of_return*
  - *www.roiformula.net*

- ROI Calculators:
  - www.ehow.com/how_4927969_calculate-return-investment-excel.html
  - *www.money-zine.com/Calculators/Investment-Calculators/Return-on-Investment-Calculator*

- ROI Formula:

$$ROI = \frac{Gain/Benefit - Cost}{Cost}$$

Let's refine the example above to demonstrate how a marketing researcher might show the value of the marketing research investment. In most cases calculating the actual ROI will be more complicated than our example above assuming that the gain/benefit components will be more complex. It's worth noting that the marketing research cost will be generally clear — a client will know how much they spent on the contract with the marketing research company. However, it is possible that the benefits might be questioned particularly if the benefits are either intangible *(increased goodwill, higher customer satisfaction, or "visibility" in the marketplace)* or are long-term benefits whose true value is difficult to fully realize. There are essentially two major categories of tangible benefits of interest to business clients:

- Two tangible benefits resulting from marketing research:
  - Revenue increase:
    - Suppose the marketing research recommendations resulted in the Gap increasing its market share by 10 percent yielding a 15 percent increase in overall sales.

- Costs savings:
  - Now suppose the research was geared towards cost savings and that the research study recommendations increased the efficiency of the Gap's operation and thus saved the company money.

Let's complete the Gap example by assuming the revenue increase resulting from the marketing research study recommendations is $500,000. We know that the cost of the research was $100,000. The ROI is calculated:

$$ROI = \frac{\$500,000 - \$100,000}{\$100,000}$$

$$ROI = 4$$

Thus the benefit of the investment was four times greater than the investment itself and therefore apparently worth the cost of the marketing research investment.

Finally, it is important that the marketing researcher has a solid and defendable list of assumptions for both the intangible and tangible benefits. These assumptions should be reasonable and should be accompanied by supporting documentation. Generally, it is very helpful to offer a detailed write-up explaining the ROI calculation. When claiming intangible benefits, marketing researchers need to make the case for the value of the research using more qualitative language and "selling"

Careful Proofreading of the Research Report will Prevent Costly and Embarrassing Errors

the client on the value of the research based on the intangible benefits arising from the study. Well armed with data, marketing researchers can show that the marketing research study was worth the cost.

The Research Report Components

Usually the final product includes a written report perhaps coupled with a Microsoft PowerPoint presentation and the raw data file, as well as the focus group and interview transcripts and related recordings. There is no officially correct format or content for a research report, although there are many components of a research report that are common. Ultimately the researcher conducting the study should be guided by what the client wants. The major components are depicted in (Figure 13.1).

Title Page

The focal point of the title page should be a title that encapsulates the most critical aspects of the research study. This title is often centered and in bold type and will typically have the research sponsor prominently positioned below the title. White space is critical on the cover page because a cluttered title page loses impact and is less likely to stand out. A professional look, perhaps with a splash color, is a good approach.

Letter of Transmittal

Essentially a **Letter of Transmittal** is *the acknowledgment from the marketing researcher to the research sponsor that the research report is being delivered and is thus the de facto property of the research sponsor for his use.*

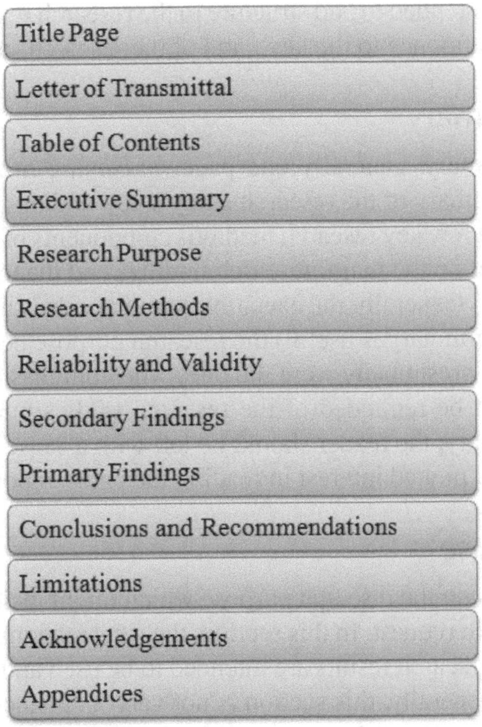

Title Page

Letter of Transmittal

Table of Contents

Executive Summary

Research Purpose

Research Methods

Reliability and Validity

Secondary Findings

Primary Findings

Conclusions and Recommendations

Limitations

Acknowledgements

Appendices

■ FIGURE 13.1

Major Components of a Marketing Research Report

■ **FIGURE 13.2**

Sample Letter of
Transmittal

The letter of transmittal notifies the research sponsor that the research project has been completed. This *"hand off"* between the marketing researcher and the research sponsor indicates the formal conclusion of the research study.

Letters of transmittal are not just for marketing research studies. When a work product such as study or report, etc. is submitted to the sponsor in accordance with the completion of a contract or otherwise stated agreement, it constitutes a letter of transmittal of some type. A sample letter of transmittal is shown in Figure 13.2.

Table of Contents

The table of contents should neither be too general nor too detailed. The table of contents should guide the reader through the research report at a high level. The table of contents is intended to add structure to the research report while simultaneously serving as a reference to the key parts of the research study.

Executive Summary

The executive summary, generally one page *(maximum two)*, should provide a leadership level summary of the research study's key findings. The executive summary should cover a few key research methods components of the study but should primarily be focused on the major research findings and the top few recommendations from the study. Generally the executive summary does not need to discuss at length (although a summary is useful) the research purpose because the executives reviewing the study presumably were the ones who commissioned the project and thus likely need not be reminded of the research study's purpose. After reading the executive summary, the reader should be left with a sense of the totality of the research study and a piqued interest in reading the entire report.

Research Purpose

This section focuses on the research purpose which might include some history, or origin, of the research request. In this section, the researcher might add some information on how the research results are intended to be used and to whom the results will be delivered. Generally, this section is not very long since it primarily serves as a quick reference to the reader to prevent his having to search through the report for its purpose. Discussing the top three or four major questions that the research is designed to answer is a useful strategy to solidify the importance, relevance, and impact of the research study.

The Research Methods

The research methods section is very important to establishing the credibility of the research report. If the reader feels the report lacks rigor, the findings will have limited impact. Marketing researchers should not assume that the research report reader will not know much about methodology issues or standards. In many cases there will be quite informed readers while other times the research method details might be of limited interest to the reader. However, marketing researchers should err on the side of providing more not less on the research methods section of the report. In this section the researcher *does not include the results* of the methods used, he addresses the step by step approach of *how* the research was conducted. The next section of the research report discusses the research results.

Separating the secondary data findings from the primary data findings is important. Marketing researchers should convey a sense of progression in the research report to demonstrate the research process was structured. Combining the secondary and the primary research findings results reduces the impact of the sequence of research steps and consequently the value that each step brings to the process (Figure 13.3). Showing how the secondary data was used in the primary data phase is useful as well tying together both methods when it enhances the understanding of the research results.

Secondary:
- Secondary research serves as a foundation piece of the marketing research report. If the reader suspects the secondary data research and analysis lacks rigor, he is likely to look at the entire research report with a critical eye. In

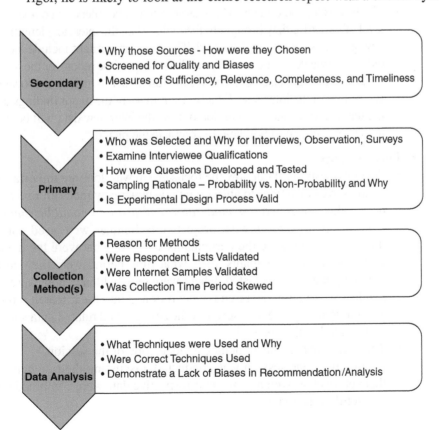

■ FIGURE 13.3
Research Methods Steps

Secondary
- Why those Sources - How were they Chosen
- Screened for Quality and Biases
- Measures of Sufficiency, Relevance, Completeness, and Timeliness

Primary
- Who was Selected and Why for Interviews, Observation, Surveys
- Examine Interviewee Qualifications
- How were Questions Developed and Tested
- Sampling Rationale – Probability vs. Non-Probability and Why
- Is Experimental Design Process Valid

Collection Method(s)
- Reason for Methods
- Were Respondent Lists Validated
- Were Internet Samples Validated
- Was Collection Time Period Skewed

Data Analysis
- What Techniques were Used and Why
- Were Correct Techniques Used
- Demonstrate a Lack of Biases in Recommendation/Analysis

fact, the reader might discount the entire report if the secondary data and analysis thereafter is not of quality. Refer to Chapter 3 for details on some key methods for assessing the quality of the secondary data. However, the researcher should pay close attention to not only the sources of secondary data, but also *how* it was used in the research report.

- Remember that the secondary data should be screened for relevance, completeness, timeliness, accuracy, and sufficiency. There should be a section in the research report that speaks to how the marketing researcher checked the secondary data for quality.
- Also included in this quality check is an accounting of how the secondary data were collected, why those sources were chosen, and how they were used in the marketing research report.
- Marketing research clients want to see that the marketing researcher used a variety of sources and that the breadth and depth of those sources was thoroughly researched.
- Finally, if content analysis of the secondary data was done, the researcher should include the key findings of that analysis and a discussion on the content analysis method — in other words, how it was done.

Primary:

- There are a number of different primary data sources that can be used in a research report. As is the case for secondary data, for primary data each method requires the researcher to support how these data were collected, why these types were used, and how they were incorporated into the research report. Below are some typical primary data collection methods and related questions that should be addressed in the marketing research report to provide the reader of the report with confidence that the data are quality data.

  - **Interviews:**
    - The research should detail who was selected to be interviewed and what level of expertise they brought to the table. Also, the interview length and key questions should be discussed. The researcher might include a copy of the interviewer guide in the appendix section of the report for the reader to review. It might also be useful for the researcher to include the location and setting of the interview. Finally, a summary of the major findings during the interview and a discussion of how the interview data will be used in the research report will help to complete the picture.

  - **Focus Groups:**
    - Several questions about how the focus group was done are important to address. Key questions to answer include how many focus groups were done, who moderated *(the moderator qualifications could be summarized in the appendix)*, what projective techniques were used during the session, how were the participants selected, what were the demographics of the participants, over what time period were they done, how long the sessions lasted, where were they held, and how were the results (information data trends) incorporated into the research report.
    - The moderator guide, transcript of the session, and related data should be included in the appendix.
    - The researcher will also include a video copy of the session.
    - If more than one session was conducted, discussing the rationale for that approach as well as how their respective data were combined will be useful to the reader.

- **Observation Research:**
  - If observation research was used, the reader will be very interested in the types of observation that were done and why those methods were chosen.
  - Because many observation research techniques are qualitative, marketing researchers must show the reader that the observation selectees and analysis of their respective behaviors lacked biases.
  - Discussing the objectives of the observation and including an observation guide *(for structured observation)* in the appendix is useful.
  - One of the pitfalls of observation research that needs to be addressed is that the subjects might not always be a representative group. For example, if the researcher goes to the local shopping mall to see what types of clothes people typically wear, only people at the mall on that day will be captured. Extrapolating data from observation studies and attempting to transpose those findings to predict behavior of the general population should not be done without other quantifiable supporting data. However, if the researcher is studying people at that mall, he might be more likely to be able to make a supportable link between the sample and the general population. The takeaway here — establish a rationale, justification, and applicability of the subjects being observed.
  - If mystery shopping was used, include a copy of the script and a justification for the ones being *"mystery shopped"* in the appendix.

Collection Method(s):

Given the variety of collection methods this section is critical. If the reader deems the collection methods faulty, the research report quickly loses credibility.

Assumption: *Suppose a customer satisfaction survey of 1,500 Caribbean cruise customers was done to determine the best ways for the cruise company to improve its offering.*

Below are the major issues to be addressed in the collection method assessment of the report regarding this cruise ship customer survey.

- **The Sample:**
  - Questions related to the *sample* that must be addressed include:
    - How was it determined that 1,500 was an appropriate sample size? In the case above, were all respondents cruise passengers? What if 300 never took a cruise but somehow got included into the sample? The sample should be verified as the right group.
    - How were the 1,500 respondents selected *(probability vs. non probability)?*
    - If non-probability — elaborate on how this selection was done and how selection biases were avoided.
    - Over what time period was the sample selected?
    - How was the sample validated to ensure it adequately represented the target population?
    - If used, what was the method for selecting the Internet sample?

- **Collection:**
  - Questions related to the data *collection* that must be addressed include:
    - What collection type was used and why — telephone, Internet, mail, in person, other?
    - Was only one collection type used? If more than one type was used, how were the different collection methods validated to ensure that there were no biases in the collection method? In other words, was there a difference

in the results from the 500 collected through the Internet and the 1,000 collected though the mail? If there is a difference, how was this difference handled to ensure the integrity of the sample?

- If different collection methods were used, were the responses coded to enable researchers to determine which respondents responded through which collection method?
- How long did the data collection take? Was there an impact on the responses based on a time lag to collect the data?
- Was the data collection method appropriate for the type of questionnaire? In other words, were long, complicated questionnaires with large scales *(from 1 to 10)* used for telephone surveys *(which they should not be)?*

Data Analysis:

Although some recipients of a research report will not have a statistical background, marketing researchers should never assume the recipient of the research report is not well versed on data analysis techniques or statistics in general. An easy way for a research report to squander credibility is through weak, or even incorrect, data analysis.

A weak analysis might include failure to analyze key questions in the most relevant way. Suppose a marketing researcher did not do marginals — or running tabs or summaries of each question and thus did not identify which questions to analyze further. This oversight might prevent the researcher from conducting the most relevant analysis. The benefit of running marginals is that these high level summaries can often help identify areas requiring additional analytic work. Or perhaps using a rank and percentile is the most appropriate tool to measure students' test score standings but the researcher fails to employ this technique. To be sure, not every question can be analyzed every way, but the researcher should use the best tools and techniques her judgment and experience dictate.

An incorrect analysis involves using the wrong statistical tool for the type of data analyzed. For example, suppose the researcher wanted to determine the correlation between the *sex* of the respondents and related ranked favorite *color* and used a Pearson Correction analysis tool. Because *sex* and *color rank* are *nominal* and *ordinal* data respectively, a Pearson Correlation, for which only interval and ratio data should be used, is the incorrect analytic tool to use for this type of analysis. Marketing researchers are increasingly challenged in this area as the data sophistication rises.

Reliability and Validity

After the discussion on the research methods, it's important to support the research methods by accounting for the reliability and validity of the data. If the reader does not have confidence in the credibility of the report, the report will have little impact. As discussed earlier, reliability is the extent to which the questionnaire is internally consistent. In other words, if a respondent said they had never been to Hawaii and later in the survey indicated they loved their trip to Honolulu, one might question the consistency, or reliability, of that respondent's answers. Marketing researchers should address how they tested the questionnaires for internal consistency and thus by extension making the case that the questionnaire responses should be trusted as being consistent.

The researcher also needs to address the validity issue, or the extent to which the research results measure what the researcher thinks is being measured. If a restaurant customer satisfaction survey concluded that 80 percent of restaurant patrons did not consider the restaurant food quality as *"important"*, one might conclude the research results are not valid since they don't seem to *"make sense."* Addressing ways in which the validity, or the extent to which the reader should trust and value the survey results as a true reflection of the population's opinions, will add credibility to the research findings.

A failure to discuss the credibility of the report through addressing both reliability and validity puts the research in a vulnerable position during the inevitable report scrutiny period.

Secondary Findings

The secondary findings section of the research report is where the marketing researcher summarizes the secondary data findings while dovetailing the analysis to the research objectives. This section should be more than just a *"data dump"* of the sources and summaries thereof, which the researcher found. The secondary data findings provide the foundation for the rest of the research report. Failure to produce credible and insightful secondary findings will have a deleterious, perhaps unrecoverable, impact on the entirety of the research report.

Including secondary sources not used can also provide some value to the reader. Suppose the reader wonders why the researcher did not include a well known article on what cruise ship customers want. Perhaps there had been such a study published by a travel company. It might well be the case that the researcher indeed looked at that article but deemed it inappropriate for use for this study for some reason. Including an accounting of key secondary sources that were *not* used and *why* they were not used can serve to preempt questions the reader might have as to why certain sources were not used.

A full accounting, or listing, of the secondary research sources should be included in the appendix of the research report.

Primary Findings

The primary research findings section includes both the descriptive and analytic results of the primary methods such as the observation research, experimental design, focus groups, and surveys. Descriptive analysis answers the who, what where, when, and how related questions. Descriptive analysis sets the stage for the analytic, or interpretative, phase of the analysis. Analytic work involves explaining what the descriptive results might mean, or reading between the lines, by extrapolating perceptive conclusions from the descriptive results.

When compiling the survey results, researchers should demonstrate how the research was built from the secondary and primary data sources while simultaneously linking the research findings with the stated research objectives. When multiple primary research methods are used, link the analysis from one research type to the next type as opposed to simply explaining each primary research type in a vacuum without a connection to the other primary research methods used. In other words, discuss how the results of one primary research method were used as a building block to the next phase of the research. The research progression should be clear.

Whereas qualitative data are typically confined to written, descriptive analyses, there are quite a number of visual ways to display the quantitative data in a marketing research report. Edward Tufte (www.edwardtufte.com) has written a number of books on creative ways to display quantitative data that are quite interesting.

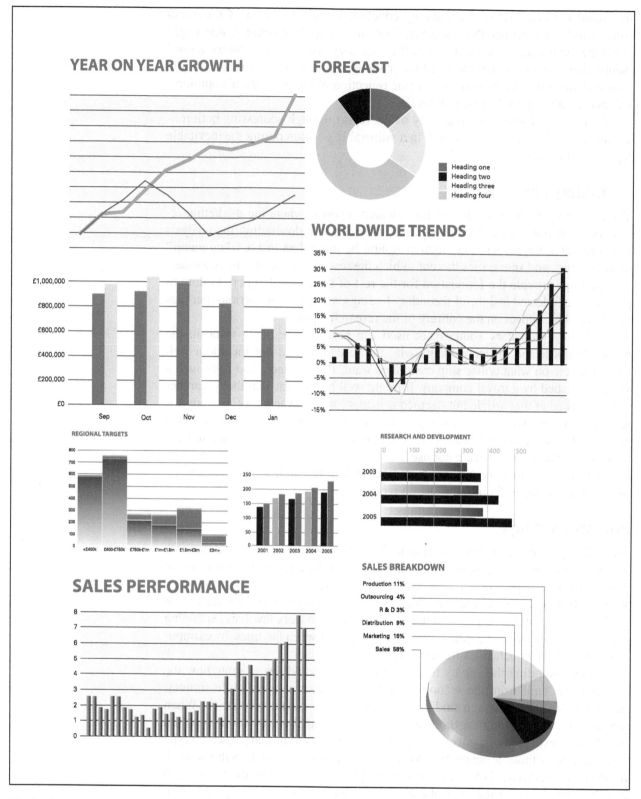

Displaying Data a Variety of Ways Adds Interest and Impact to the Research Report

However, in the absence of the software tools, techniques, and expertise to produce these creative data displays, marketing researchers can use many standard, and effective, means of conveying quantitative data visually. Although we saw a few data display methods in the discussion of cross-tabulations in Chapter 11, there are a number of other ways to display data. Below are data, restaurant type and restaurant location, displayed in different ways.

Side by Side Column Chart

- These charts are useful for showing the relative relationship between and among research variables (Figure 13.4).
- In order to keep the data bars in proportion, the data should be somewhat comparable in range. For example, annual sales figures from five grocery stores could be compared side by side in this type of bar chart. However, if the *total sales* for *all five grocery stores* were included as the right most bar on the chart, that figure would appear disproportionately high as compared to the bars for each of the five grocery stores. This disproportionality will reduce the bar height of each of the five stores thus producing a potential misdirection by leading the reader to think the sales were low for each store because the bars are low. Marketing researchers can embed a "total" number *(with no associated bar)* near the legend of the chart to both provide the data while maintaining clarity in the chart.

Stacked Column Chart

- These charts help many readers see how a group of data relates as a proportion of the whole of that given data.
- In Figure 13.5 all three restaurant location choices are stacked in one bar and separated by restaurant type. This depiction enables the reader to see how each of the three restaurant location types relates to the other two location types under the umbrella of the *totality* of all three restaurant location types.

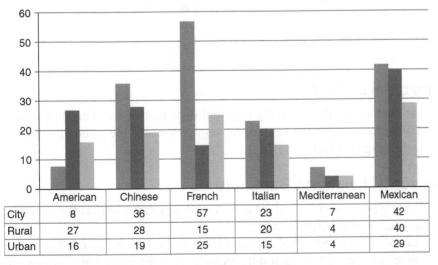

■ FIGURE 13.4
Side by Side Column Chart

	American	Chinese	French	Italian	Mediterranean	Mexican
City	8	36	57	23	7	42
Rural	27	28	15	20	4	40
Urban	16	19	25	15	4	29

■ City ■ Rural ■ Urban

■ **FIGURE 13.5**
Stacked Column Chart

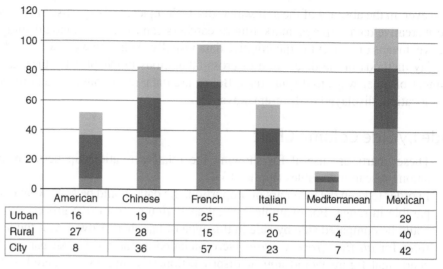

	American	Chinese	French	Italian	Mediterranean	Mexican
Urban	16	19	25	15	4	29
Rural	27	28	15	20	4	40
City	8	36	57	23	7	42

■ City   ■ Rural   ■ Urban

■ **FIGURE 13.6**
Horizontal Bar Chart

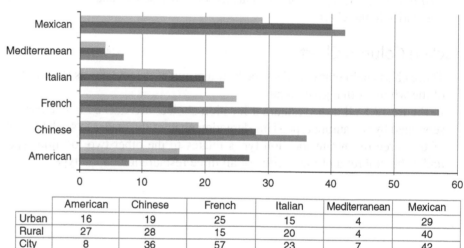

	American	Chinese	French	Italian	Mediterranean	Mexican
Urban	16	19	25	15	4	29
Rural	27	28	15	20	4	40
City	8	36	57	23	7	42

■ City   ■ Rural   ■ Urban

Horizontal Bar Chart

- Bar charts provide a visually different depiction of the data. Horizontal bar charts create a sense of flow or movement towards the right which might be useful (Figure 13.6).

Horizontal Relational Bar Chart

- These types of charts produce a relational way of looking at the data by connecting the data being researched.
- The use of percentages along the horizontal axis helps researchers to gauge the relative impact of each data element as a percentage of all observations (Figure 13.7).

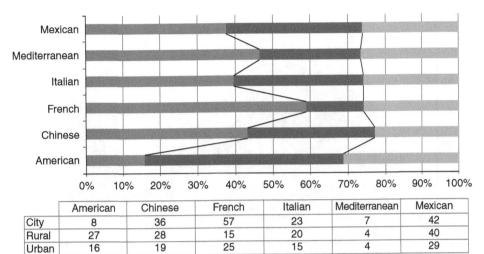

■ FIGURE 13.7
Horizontal Relational Bar
Chart

	American	Chinese	French	Italian	Mediterranean	Mexican
City	8	36	57	23	7	42
Rural	27	28	15	20	4	40
Urban	16	19	25	15	4	29

■ City   ■ Rural   ▦ Urban

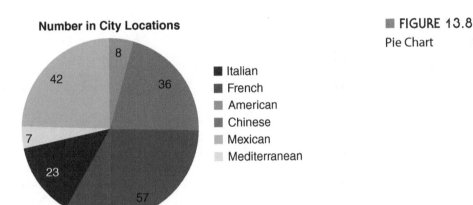

■ FIGURE 13.8
Pie Chart

Pie Chart

- Pie charts are a very common and easily understood data display tool that graphically depict how one data element compares to a list of other data elements. In Figure 13.8 displayed is the restaurant type by city location. If a client wanted to see a pie chart of multiple location types against the restaurant type — the better tool is a column or bar chart because the pie charts are not designed to capture data in that way.

Area Chart

- Area charts are not very common as their interpretation is not intuitive. However, area charts can help researchers gain a sense of the impact of each data elements as they relate to the other data elements in the area chart (Figure 13.9).

Line Chart

- Line charts are quite common and useful to establish trends and to see the relative distance between categories.

■ FIGURE 13.9
Area Chart

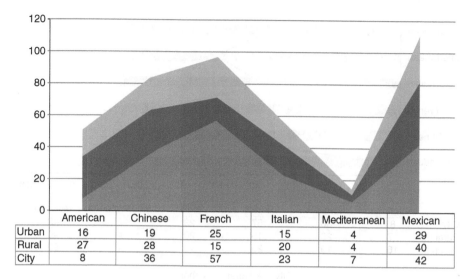

	American	Chinese	French	Italian	Mediterranean	Mexican
Urban	16	19	25	15	4	29
Rural	27	28	15	20	4	40
City	8	36	57	23	7	42

■ City   ■ Rural   ■ Urban

■ FIGURE 13.10
Line Chart

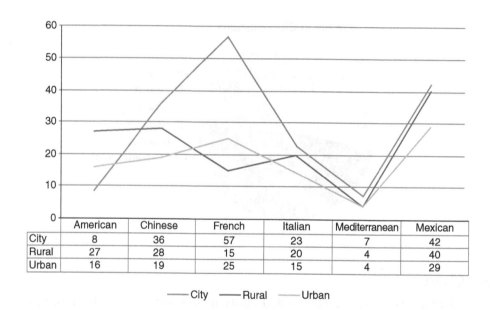

	American	Chinese	French	Italian	Mediterranean	Mexican
City	8	36	57	23	7	42
Rural	27	28	15	20	4	40
Urban	16	19	25	15	4	29

—— City   —— Rural   —— Urban

- Also, the peaks and valleys among the data can help researchers, and managers, identify possible issues, positive or negative, that need to be addressed (Figure 13.10).

Cumulative Frequency Histogram

- When using interval or ratio level data, cumulative frequency histograms yields useful results. This distribution quickly reveals the highs and lows of the data in question from which additional analysis will be borne.
- The cumulative distribution line shows the progressive combination of data as it reaches 100 percent of observations. Marketing researchers can say that 73 percent of the respondents rated the food quality as a "5" or lower on a scale of 1 to 10 (Figure 13.11).

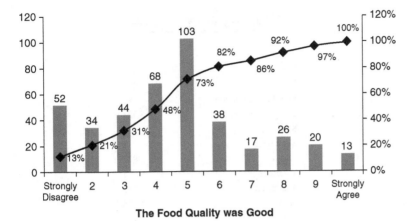

■ **FIGURE 13.11**
Cumulative Frequency
Histogram

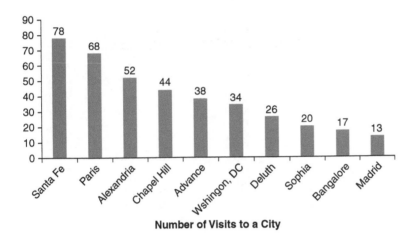

■ **FIGURE 13.12**
Pareto Frequency
Histogram

Pareto Frequency Histogram

- Pareto frequency distribution sorts the data from the most to the least observation. This type of distribution is useful for nominal data to dramatize which data elements have the greatest and least impact on the research question.
- Marketing researchers can prioritize the depth of the subsequent analysis based on the data with the greatest impact to the marketing research study (Figure 13.12).

Descriptive Statistics

- Descriptive statistics provide the researcher with an overview of the data distribution that can be used for more in-depth analyses.
- In addition to displaying the summary data of the entire sample, descriptive statistics analysis can also be used to analyze sub groups or segments within the sample (Figure 13.13).

Rank and Percentile

- Rank and percentile data are useful when data are skewed and the researcher wants to see what data might be causing the skewness. If a rank and percentile analysis reveals 5 percent of the sample is disproportionately higher than the rest of the

■ **FIGURE 13.13**
Descriptive Statistics

Number of Seats in the Restaurant	
Mean	147
Standard Error	5
Median	120
Mode	150
Standard Deviation	93
Sample Variance	8,728
Kurtosis	3
Skewness	1
Range	487
Minimum	25
Maximum	512
Sum	61,086
Count	415

■ **FIGURE 13.14**
Rank and Percentile

Number of Seats in the Restaurant	Rank	Percent
512	1	100%
500	3	99%
500	3	99%
450	7	98%
450	7	98%
400	12	97%
400	12	97%
350	14	97%
320	15	95%
320	15	95%
320	15	95%
320	15	95%
300	23	91%
300	23	91%
Etc...		
55	369	11%
55	369	11%
50	371	4%
50	371	4%
50	371	4%
45	399	3%
45	399	3%
45	399	3%
25	405	0%
25	405	0%
25	405	0%

sample, the researcher might conclude the top 5 percent of observations should be removed and analyzed separately as statistical outliers (Figure 13.14).

Conclusions/Recommendations

The secondary and primary research phases should provide a thorough accounting of the research results. The conclusion and recommendations sections tie together the entire research report in a comprehensive fashion. The conclusion section is perhaps a page and summarizes the key points of the research by highlighting the totality of the research findings. The analysis foundation of the conclusion is typically descriptive followed by analytic observations. The recommendation section differs from the conclusion section in that the researcher proposes a course of action resulting from the research report findings. Usually the researcher will clarify why the proposed action should be taken and offer a prediction of the result of taking the action. It might be that the researcher recommends no action be taken. For example, suppose a grocery store conducted a research study to determine if the store should expand its space and increase its product offering. The store hires a marketing research company to study this question. Suppose the research results concluded that expanding the store will not be worth the cost thus the recommendation to the grocery store from the marketing research company is not to expand the store size or product offering. Not taking action is a perfectly acceptable recommendation since, in this case, taking action might in fact be more costly.

A caveat to this section is the instruction the marketing research provider gets from the research sponsor. If a company hires a marketing research company to conduct a customer satisfaction survey, the company might instruct the research suppler to conduct descriptive research and not offer recommendations. In this case, perhaps the hiring company simply wants the research results and does not want recommendations from the researcher to encumber its ability to offer its own analysis and recommendations as to what actions to take or not take.

Limitations

To be sure, the researcher should not belabor the hurdles and problems associated with the report, but he should address any issues that presented challenges to completing the study. In addition, a discussion of the solutions to those problems — or "workarounds" — will help to instill confidence in the reader that the marketing researcher is an honest broker in being forthright about challenges to the research study. Types of hurdles faced might include difficulty in reaching the sample, loss of data, survey execution delays, focus group no-shows, and a lack of good secondary data. The researcher should identify relevant challenging issues and then demonstrate how these challenges were handled and discuss, if true, how these challenges ultimately had no negative impact on the quality of the research report. The researcher might also want to include a summary of "best practices" that detail how subsequent research might be conducted in a way to avoid any problems that arose during this study.

Acknowledgements

It is unlikely that marketing researchers will complete a research report without some assistance from various people or groups. The acknowledgements section lists the people or groups who helped the researcher in the research project process. Suppose a marketing research project involves surveying students about their career plans and the marketing researcher needs access to students. The university chancellor approves access to the student body by allowing the marketing researcher to distribute surveys during class time. The marketing researcher might list the chancellor as someone who helped facilitate the survey execution. Or perhaps the researcher had a mentor who provided guidance and insight into the research process or benefitted from student work on the project. The acknowledgements section is a professional way to share in the success of the marketing research project and can be done at no cost.

Appendices

The appendices include whatever the researcher feels is needed to add credibility, utility, or clarity to the marketing research report. Although there is no rule for what has to be in, or should not be in, the appendices, the following items are common in the appendix section of marketing research reports — but do not comprise an exhaustive list of all items that can be in the appendix.

- A copy of the questionnaire
- Statistical formulas
- Numeric tables
- Focus group or interview transcripts
- A comprehensive listing of the secondary sources
- The raw survey data provided in electronic format
- Case studies relevant to the research study
- Four group moderator guide

The Report's Look and Feel

Branding is a critical component to the professional look of a research report. Remember the recipients of the research report will likely be quite varied. It's possible one of the readers will be a statistician whose primary interest is in the quality of the data analysis and not the panache factor of its presentation. However, suppose researchers are distributing the marketing research report to a larger audience such as stockholders or otherwise interested parties. This audience is presumably diverse requiring that the report speak to their interests as well. Marketing research reports with inconsistent fonts, bullets, color schemes, layout, formatting, paragraph indenture, and word/language use convey a lack of detail to the professional appearance of the report. Also, avoid the temptation to overdo the visual display of data by using too many different types of data output. A variety of data displays will add more interest to the report but too many different data display types will impede the researcher's ability to maintain a consistent look and feel to the report. If the reader senses the report appearance is sloppy, he might look askance at the entirety of the work which he might not have otherwise have done. The research report should read as though one person wrote it even when multiple contributors prepared various parts of the report. A master editor can ensure disparate parts of the report written by different people are woven into prose seemingly written by one person.

The Marketing Research Report is the Culmination of the Marketing Research Process

In many cases the marketing researcher might include an accompanying Microsoft PowerPoint presentation for executive leadership briefing purposes. In fact, savvy marketing researchers prepare two presentations — a short and a long version in order to be prepared for any presentation contingency. There are a number of conventions when creating PowerPoint presentations that are useful. Excessive wordiness on each slide, too many moving parts, and an inability to read the slides from a certain distance, are PowerPoint presentation pitfalls to avoid. In fact, once the PowerPoint slides are created, take the printout and place the slides on the floor. If you cannot read the slides from the floor while you are standing, generally they will not be readable from the rear of an average room. Again, when using the charts and graphs discussed in this book, marketing researchers should avoid using too many types lest the report lose some of its branding edge. Once the reader gets used to one type of data output, it might be best to use that format to provide consistency. Use different data output formats if those formats add value to the research report by displaying the data in a way that demonstrates to the reader something more about the data than the previously used tools.

Generally researchers should start with broad data results and then delve more deeply into the details of the findings. For example, displaying detailed employee data such as when people were hired, how long they have worked with the company, and their position with the company *before* framing the issue that simply recaps the total number of employees by department, provides too much detail about the employees before establishing the scope of the employee issue.

Finally, use of color, heavy parchment, expensive binding, and a variety of data display types can add panache to your presentation. However, a flashy research report short on substance will not compare well to a research report that is thorough and rigorous in substance.

Common Mistakes in the Research Report

The Internet and statistical software have enabled researchers to collect and analyze data quickly. Even report writing has been affected by technology. Marketing researchers can use the Internet to see sample reports or to find report writing tips and templates of varying quality levels. Despite the flood of technology, which has been an invaluable resource and asset to the marketing research profession, marketing research reports still require researcher insight. Ultimately the marketing researcher has to make the decision as to what analysis to provide in a report and how to frame the secondary and primary findings in a meaningful way. With this challenge in mind, let's review some common mistakes *(not a comprehensive list)* that marketing researchers sometimes make in the report writing and presentation phase of the marketing research project life cycle (Figure 13.15).

Incorrect Statistics

- A research client would presume the marketing researcher providing the research knows the right statistics tool to use for a given data level. When researchers use the term *"right"* they are not referring to *appropriate* or *best* analysis tool as that's a judgment call. Researchers are referring to using the wrong data analysis tools or technique altogether. For example, suppose the marketing researcher used a *Pearson Correlation* on nominal data when it is only to be used on interval or ratio data. These types of errors might well occur

Common Report Mistakes

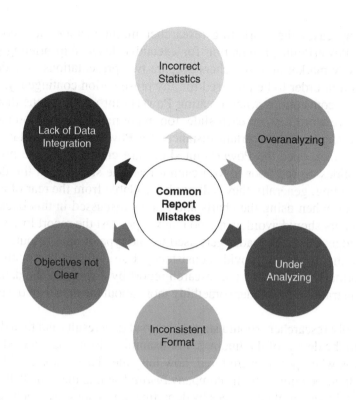

when using ANOVA, hypothesis testing, regression, and the like. Although the research client receiving the report might not know enough about statistics to catch those errors initially, they likely will eventually be spotted.

Overanalyzing

- With the ease and access to data analysis tools and techniques, marketing researchers need to resist the temptation to provide data analysis overkill with unnecessary statistics in the report or the appendix. Remember there is a research client receiving this work in most cases. The research report should have meaningful and useful data analysis without an unnecessary overreliance on elaborate statistics. However, usually research projects do require a certain level of statistical rigor. The key distinction is that the researcher should not provide statistics just to provide statistics perhaps hoping that such an approach would convey rigor or analytic gravitas.

Under Analyzing

- Suppose we have a questionnaire with 35 questions. It is not practical or fruitful to analyze every question every way *(overanalyzing)*. However taking too many short cuts or providing a too cursory analysis leaves the research recipient feeling underwhelmed as to the quality and thoroughness of the research report. Under analysis also refers to a failure to fully analyze a particular data finding which the researcher highlighted as important. For example, perhaps researchers are studying a day spa and the research reveals that 80 percent of women will *not* recommend the facility. Failure to explore further this finding represents an under analysis of a key finding the researcher identified. The researcher essentially raised a key issue only to shortchange its analysis. A summary of all questions *(marginals)* is a good first step in the analysis process but should be followed by a more detailed analysis of the significant results. Also focusing too much on descriptive analysis only, as opposed to a more analytic, inferential, approach, inhibits insightful analysis.

Inconsistent Format

- A thoroughly analyzed report will lose impact if it is poorly written or is presented with an inconsistent look and feel. The research report should use consistent style throughout its presentation. Marketing research reports that appear cobbled together from a several member research team will lack impact. When including a Microsoft PowerPoint presentation ensure that its look and feel are consistent with the research report thus creating a branded pair of research products.

Objectives Not Clear

- Before launching into the research methods and data analysis sections of the research report, take time to explain and reinforce the research objectives as not everyone hearing the presentation or reading the report is necessarily current on the nature of the research project. The research objectives help frame the reason for the research and the significance of the findings. The research approach should mirror the objectives it is intended to support.

Lack of Data Integration

- Marketing research reports that are data laden risk becoming too complicated particularly if the data analyses are not integrated. For example, suppose there is a significant amount of secondary data relevant to the research project and the research report fails to integrate the secondary data into the primary research findings. Linking the research process steps and critical findings in a manner that paints a comprehensive analytic picture will greatly increase the usefulness of the report. It is important to show how the secondary data *led* to the primary data and how the various methods of primary data *taken* together tell the story of the research project. Avoid too many data analysis outputs that are simply stand alone data observations.

Research in Practice

Case:
- After six months of research, you present your research report to the CEO of a national amusement park company. The company commissioned a study to determine why attendance at its 20 amusement parks has declined over the past 10 years. These amusement parks are considered to be of average to good quality and whose typical demographic includes couples with children under 12 and groups of teenagers.

Assignment:
- Write a three page report explaining the key components of the marketing research report and what value they bring. What are ways the researcher can instill confidence in the reader that the research report is credible and its results should be trusted? What types of data *(key questions that should be asked of customers)* might you collect for this amusement park study and in what ways, and why, do you recommend the data be displayed?

Chapter Summary

The research report is the culmination of the marketing research process. Usually the reporting includes a written document accompanied by a presentation (typically PowerPoint or Prezi) for use at executive briefings. Marketing researchers need to show value in the research report by demonstrating some acceptable level of Return on the Investment — or an accounting of how the benefits of the research outweighed the costs of that research. The marketing research report has a number of important sections that provide the framework for how the research was done. These reports are given to the research sponsor upon completion of the research study. The major sections of these reports include the title page, letter of transmittal, table of contents, executive summary, research purpose, research methods, reliability and validity accountancy, secondary findings, primary findings, conclusions & recommendations, limitations, acknowledgements, and appendices. Establishing a branded "look and feel" is an effective way to convey a professional appearance. Marketing research reports should be consistent in their use of fonts, spacing, bullets, color schemes, chart layouts, paragraph indenture, and word/language use. Most marketing reports are compiled based on data, input, and information from a number of research staff. This collaboration, while quite effective can produce a report that appears to have been written by multiple people. The marketing research report should be streamlined in a way that the reader of the report cannot detect that it was written by more than one person. The presentation, perhaps PowerPoint, part of the research report should be developed carefully and should convey succinctly the most important points of the research report. There are several types of data output that are commonly used in marketing research reports. These outputs *(by no means a complete list of options)* include column, bar, and pie charts depicting various cross tabulations, line graphs, descriptive statistics, ANOVA, chi square, histograms, correlations, and rank and percentile outputs. Using a variety of data outputs in the marketing research report will add value and interest to the report package. The marketing research report is the permanent record of the marketing research project.

ISSUE IN THE SPOTLIGHT: Presenting and Packaging Political Candidates

David Helfert, Adjunct Professor
Johns Hopkins University &
American University
Former Senior Advisor
Governor Neil Abercrombie (HI)

Political campaigns are marketing; intensely competitive, squeezed into a tight time period, usually with finite resources and always with an absolute need to capture more than half the market. There are no mulligans in politics. You rarely get a chance to go back to tweak the message or the advertising. In today's environment, public policy dialog on major national issues is also conducted like a political campaign, on the floor of the U.S. House or Senate, in dueling news conferences, on television talk shows, in newspaper op-eds or online blogs. It manifests the same highly specialized form of marketing and utilizes most of the same tools.

One of the most important tools is research. Author Lewis Carroll said, "If you don't know where you are going, any road will get you there." A typical campaign for U.S. Senate or governor today costs $5 million and up (way up in California!), depending on the state's population, the number and size of media markets and the competitiveness of the particular race. A congressional race in an urban district averages more than $1 million; state legislative races nearly as much. Even a local campaign for city council or mayor can cost hundreds of thousands of dollars. Why would any candidate or campaign even consider embarking on such an expensive journey without knowing as much as possible about the environment, the competition, the target audience and how to reach them, what issues couched in what words and phrases might best get their attention and persuade them, or without an objective means to track and evaluate the success of the campaign. This information, critical to effective and strategic decision making, is gathered using the same basic tools as any other marketing campaign. The most common are quantitative: benchmark surveys, tracking polls and media audience research.

Benchmark surveys, usually conducted through 1,000 to 1,200 interviews of likely voters, provide information to develop the campaign's strategic blueprint. Generally, they're fairly long about 20 minutes or so — and conducted months before election day. Benchmarks use objective questions to probe the current standing of the race, such as name identification and positive or negative perceptions of announced or potential candidates. They're also key in setting a campaign's platform by probing salient issues and public attitudes about issues.

Tracking polls are another commonly used form of objective research with a much smaller sample — just a few hundred — conducted over several successive evenings to measure the progress of the campaign through two or three trial heat questions: "Are you aware that there's an election for _____ coming up? If the election were held today, would you be more likely to vote for_____ or_____?" They can also be used to probe briefly for issues that emerge or evolve over the course of a campaign.

Media research, usually based on surveys conducted regularly market by market by specialized firms, determines which media the public listens to, watches, reads or accesses online. The audience data is broken down by age, gender, income and other demographic characteristics to tell an advertiser how and when to best reach a particular target audience with an advertising message. Larger campaigns requiring larger expenditures in media frequently use various forms of qualitative research to test advertising messages, even the spots themselves, before they air. This technique can be done through mall testing or online, and in more structured focus groups. The results are not statistically projectable, but allow the campaign to ask subjective questions: "Which statement/image/TV spot

do you feel has more impact? Why? Which of these words/images/TV spots do think better conveys. . . .? Would you be more likely to support a candidate who says. . . .?"

These same techniques are also used to develop and sharpen political rhetoric in public policy debates, looking for the most persuasive words and phrases about an issue. Political media writers and producers have long known intuitively that adding an emotional context or moral imperative to a political message lends impact and makes the message more memorable. Now, communication scholars are finding that such messages are actually received and processed by the human brain in different ways and through different neural pathways than messages aimed at the reason-centered lobes. This kind of research helps identify the most effective buttons to push.

Part of former House Speaker Newt Gingrich's success in building a Republican majority in the U.S. for the first time in 40 years in 1994 is credited to the effective use of message testing. It continues to be used and refined. Dr. Frank Luntz, part of the Gingrich message machine, convenes focus groups and uses a dial technology on which people record their instant reaction to speeches and other political events. Luntz also uses the dial technology to test persuasive messages, and based on his findings, advises Congressional Republicans on issue framing and effective arguments. You've heard the results, even if you weren't aware of it: partial birth abortion, War on Terror, Social Security individual accounts, Wall Street bailouts and "Obamacare" are all phrases that were audience tested to make sure they persuaded the public.

Market research has long provided the eyes and ears of political campaigns, helping them determine where they're starting from, where the need to go and how well they were progressing. In contemporary campaigns — and in public dialog over issues — market research is also helping campaigns, political organizations and interest groups find their voice.

14

International Marketing Research

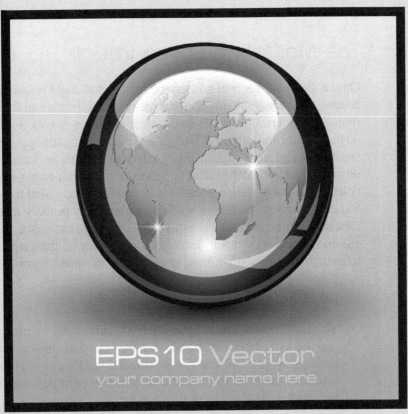

Image © Adrian Grosu, 2011. Used under license from Shutterstock, Inc.

Learning Objectives:

- Appreciate the importance of understanding an international audience
- Understand how the international marketing environment affects research
- Learn about legal, cultural, government, infrastructure, and economic environments

- Learn about the six cultural dimensions and their use in marketing research
- Appreciate the impact of international research on key research methods
- Understand measures of equivalence - item, construct, measurement, sample, and scalar

- Learn about the key people needed to execute a questionnaire in another language
- Appreciate language mapping and body language issues in international research

Chapter Fourteen

ortunate in the study of international marketing research is that there is an every expanding list of marketing research blunders from which students can learn the value of doing marketing research before entering into an international market. A simple Google search will reveal a long list of avoidable marketing missteps from Gerber's baby food selling in India without changing its labeling *(culturally in India what's on the label represents what's in the package)*, or Chevrolet selling the Nova in Spanish-speaking countries where Nova means "no go", or when Schweppes sold tonic water in Italy under the translated name of *"toilet water."* Not all mistakes are avoidable, however understanding international and culturally different environments will increase the probability that these types of errors will not result in an embarrassing blunder and potentially costly business mistake.

The Marketing Environment

One of the first aspects of understanding the challenges researchers face when conducting business in the international arena is an appreciation for the marketing environment. Understanding this environment involves conducting marketing research on the country and culture of interest and then making the appropriate price, product, promotion, and place adjustments. Understanding this environment entails extensive secondary and primary research. Secondary research might include reviewing articles, government statistics, case studies, or reports on what to expect in the country and culture where the research will take place. Key primary methods include interviewing country and cultural experts, interviewing nationals, and conducting focus groups of local residents to learn about their way of thinking. These factors often intersect and are usually related to each other in some fashion (Figure 14.1).

Legal

- The legal environment includes laws, rules, and regulations. Marketing researchers need to be aware of what they can and cannot do in a given country. Perhaps in a certain country unsolicited random digit phone calls are not allowed, or there are forms and a process that must be followed before conducting certain kinds of marketing research, or perhaps observation research or

■ **FIGURE 14.1**

The Marketing
Environment

tastes tests are not allowed without meeting certain guidelines. Laws, rules, and regulations vary greatly from country to country. A business trying to expand to an international market by implementing the marketing four Ps overseas — price, product, promotion, and place needs to know what the laws and regulations are in their targeted international market. Key considerations in each of these four areas include:

- **Pricing:** *competition, resale price maintenance, price discrimination*
- **Promotion:** *who researchers can target, decency standards, making claims*
- **Product:** *labeling and safety issues*
- **Place:** *where products can or cannot be sold — tobacco, alcohol, clothing, movies, food, etc. products*

Cultural

- Marketing researchers will benefit from understanding the cultural norms, values, and traditions of the country where the research is performed. Learning about a given country though secondary research and by interviewing experts on the country and culture of interest, will likely result in fewer mistakes during the execution of the marketing research study.
- A major part of understanding a cultural environment is an appreciation for cultural dimensions. A framework for this study was created by Dutch sociologist Geert Hofstede — www.geert-hofstede.com. Although critics have said that his six cultural dimensions are too static for diverse cultures and contain stereotypical elements, the framework does provide a useful backdrop to begin the study, discussion, and understanding of the international context business leaders face when marketing overseas (Figure 14.2).

Power Distance:
- Power distance refers to the extent to which there are gaps or distance between those in a position of power/influence and those not in such a position. Countries with high power distances are typically more structured and rule oriented where lines of authority and hierarchical expectations are

■ FIGURE 14.2
Elements of Cultural
Understanding

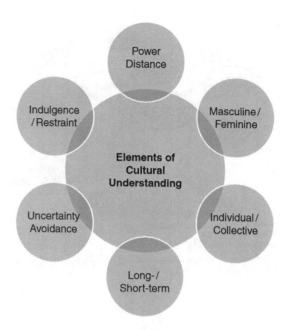

clear and not typically questioned. Low power distance cultures often have more opportunities for social mobility and a sense of equality in business and social relationships.

Masculine vs. Feminine:
• These types of cultures have relatively clear gender roles. However, this dimension is not only based on gender roles. Masculine concepts such as aggression, assertiveness, competitiveness, and ambition are hallmarks of cultures demonstrating masculine qualities. Feminine cultures often have a higher prevalence of social programs, a focus on relationships, and a sense of justice. Marketing researchers conducting a survey and interviews where these roles are clear, might not want a male interviewing a female for example.

Individual vs. Collective:
• This dimension addresses how people identify themselves in society. Highly individualistic countries focus more on the needs of individuals as opposed to collective societies where people feel more a part of a group than they do as individuals making up that group. People in collective cultures tend to identify themselves as a member of a group (church, civic group, age group, club member, etc.) as opposed to highlighting their individuality. Marketing researchers conducting surveys in highly collective cultures should ensure the research design accounts for this characteristic. For example, surveys with large attitudinal scales (such as 1 to 10) might best not be given in highly collective cultures because respondents in those cultures tend to respond more towards the middle of the scale to avoid being too "individual" by firmly expressing an opinion as represented by the top and bottom ends of a large scale.

Long- vs. Short-term:
• Determining the long- or short-term mindset of a culture is complicated. However, this dimension aims to frame the issue to address the idea that some cultures think about events and actions in the short-term and other cultures have decades or longer as their time horizon. How a culture

positions itself based on future opportunities or historic achievements plays a role in how people from those cultures view themselves in the world. Adherence to traditions and a particular way of life is an important concept when assessing this dimension. Marketing researchers should be sensitive to how a culture views itself before launching a research study featuring the people from that country or culture.

Uncertainty Avoidance:

- This concept refers to the extent to which societies, and the people from those cultures, like or do not like uncertainty. Highly litigious cultures or countries with lots of laws, rules, and regulations — or a highly centralized authority — are typically high uncertainty avoidance cultures that tend to like structure and predictability. Low uncertainty avoidance cultures don't mind ambiguity or the "unknown" and are thus prone to being less structured in their approach to living, governance, and social norms as well as being more open to new ways of doing things.

Indulgent vs. Restraint:

- The focal point of this dimension is the level of material gratification people in those cultures seek or the sense of boundaries limiting what people can have or in the actions they can take. Materialistic societies demonstrate more indulgence than cultures less focused on material goods. More austere countries are considered to show more restraint in material acquisitions — whether by choice or economic circumstances.

Government

- The government environment, of course, drives the legal requirements under which marketing researchers must operate. Governments have very different views on democracy, freedom of expression, competition, acceptable means of contact with citizenry, and the list goes on. Marketing researchers should not assume that they can operate unfettered around the world. In countries with totalitarian or otherwise strong central authority governments, marketing researchers must take great pains to ensure that all laws and acceptable conduct of behavior are being met. Gaining respondents' trust is a critical aspect of the pre survey execution plan. The notion that a government would want to see the results for the purpose of tracking the opinions of its citizen seems outdated and indeed quite preposterous for many people. Conversely, people unfamiliar with unobtrusive and less centralized governments will likely find it difficult to relate to the notion of free expression particularly when a foreigner is conducting the research. Marketing researchers can benefit from using local staff as the face of the researcher.

Infrastructure/Logistics

- Marketing researchers in western and various Asian countries enjoy reliable telephone lines, good mail distribution, access to trained staff, good focus group facilities, and easy access to many parts of the country and people. Trying to conduct a research project in Africa, for example, presents a host of infrastructure related challenges. These challenges might well escalate to problems that can affect the possibility the research project will fail. Suppose a marketing researcher needs to arrange for surveys to be shipped and distributed in a country with poor infrastructure, or needs to hire local talent to help in executing the survey in a country where trained staff is elusive, or is making 2,000 telephone calls in a country with poor phone lines and unreliable electricity. Or imagine collecting data through the Internet where the service is limited or where respondents are not permitted to view certain websites that are part of the survey. These types of challenges are real and must be addressed. A major research company like Gallup (www.gallup.com) that conducts data collection in more than 100 countries uses data collection methods and processes that vary widely depending on the countries involved in the study.

Economic

- Economic considerations play a role in the execution of a marketing research project as well. Countries with weak economies might not be fertile ground for marketing researchers to find clients who need or can afford marketing research studies. When budgets are tight, many business practices change. Advertising, training, marketing research, and travel budgets often are affected negatively. Selling marketing research services in a down economy is difficult given that many potential clients might not clearly see the immediacy of the return on investment. In countries where the economy is doing well, marketing researchers often find that the business climate for marketing research is good.

Impact of International Research on Research Methods

Not all marketing research methods are substantively affected by the international environment. However, when conducting marketing research internationally, several major techniques are affected by the conditions that arise in the international arena.

Understanding International Contexts Helps Business Leaders Expand to New Markets

Image © Janos Levente, 2011. Used under license from Shutterstock, Inc.

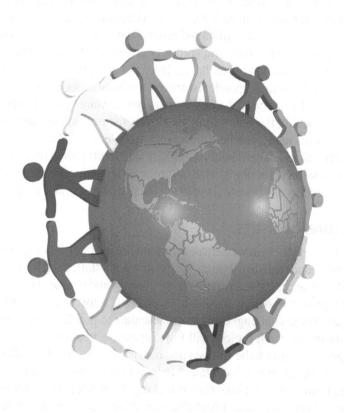

Telephone:

- Not all countries have the level of telephone penetration that the United States has. In addition, because of cell phones, the penetration rate has become more volatile worldwide. Before assuming that a telephone survey will work overseas, marketing researchers should do some homework to determine what percent of households have telephones and whether people who have a telephone are in the researcher's target population. Also, if the calls are made from a local phone, their system has to support execution of random digit dialing. Once the researcher gets through to the right person, there is a key question to ask: is the right interviewer making the calls? In some countries, a man interviewing a woman and vice versa is not acceptable. Finally, the length and complexity of the survey should be tailored to the cultural expectations of the country under study.

In-Person Interviews:

- Depending on the culture, conducting in-person interviews can be tricky. The interviewer gender and subject matter are important considerations. Also, safety is a concern. It simply might not be safe for an interviewer to approach a stranger to conduct a mall intercept interview. In many cultures, interviewees will not reveal much about themselves (perhaps they are highly collective or have high uncertainty avoidance) unless they know the interviewer. And generally it's not a good idea for the interviewer to be well acquainted with the interviewee lest various biases arise.

Focus Groups:

- Issues in conducting focus groups internationally mirror many of the same pitfalls of in-person interviewing. An additional concern is the selection of the focus group participants. Other issues that arise are recording the session, the types of incentives that are allowable and culturally acceptable, locating a qualified moderator, and finding a professional focus group facility (in many countries they don't really exist — or are not ideally suited for a focus group session).

Observation:

- Not all societies and cultures permit certain forms of observation. For example, recording people in public places is usually allowable in the United States because the law generally states that there is no expectation of privacy in public. Marketing researchers should research the rules governing observation techniques for the country where they propose to conduct an observation study. Additionally, it's not clear how observing people in public, and taking notes, would be received in certain cultures particularly with gender and religious issues that arise as they relate to decorum and privacy.

Internet and Mail/Postal Surveys:

- The key with these types of surveys is getting a good name list with correct addresses. In many underdeveloped countries the mailing list data are incomplete and incorrect. Perhaps researchers are only able to get a list of 5,000 names in the target population when they need 20,000. And of the 5,000 perhaps over half have bad e-mail or postal addresses. And perhaps Internet access is limited or restricted thus impeding researchers' ability to reach the target population. The infrastructure hurdles with postal surveys should not be underestimated. Additionally, fully controlling the sample, who answers the survey, is not possible thus casting doubt on the integrity of the

Although Data Collection Methods Vary, Turning Data into Information is Still the Focus of International Marketing Research

Image © Bruce Roiff, 2011. Used under license from Shutterstock, Inc.

sample. Finally, countries lacking freedoms foster populations ill-equipped and not predisposed to openly expressing opinions. Sending that opinion in writing through the mail or online is of special concern in these circumstances.

Measures of Equivalence

The notion of **equivalence** is critical when doing international research. Obviously words are different from language to language but even in the same language many differences prevail. There are differences in British and American English or even with word usage within a country with the same language. Differences in usage, pronunciation, and meaning are common in the same language and are magnified when translating from one language to another. There are usage nuances and cultural references that make it challenging to be fully current on all the meanings, implicit and explicit, from language to language.

- **Data Equivalence in International Research:**
  - *The extent to which data, and the way they are measured are interpreted, are understood the same way by all respondents.*

In marketing research there are several measures of equivalency that affect the quality of the marketing research study. These methods are, **item, construct, measurement, sample, and scalar (Figure 14.3).**

- **Item equivalence** refers to whether respondents understand the *words* themselves. Perhaps a questionnaire has vocabulary beyond the respondents' ability to understand. Maybe the researcher is using technical terms that the respondent does not understand. Or perhaps the survey is being translated into multiple languages and, for example, there is no good translation for

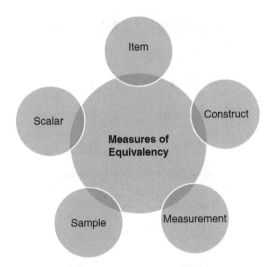

the color *"burgundy."* Perhaps in the particular language the questionnaire is being translated to — *"dark red"* is the closest equivalent word to burgundy. The more different the languages are, the more difficult it is to get an accurate translation. Even in cases of "the same" language — such as American vs. British English, the translations are not always clear. The same words might mean different things depending on the language. Figure 14.4 lists some common differences in American and British English that can make conducting a survey difficult even in the same language.

- **Construct or concept equivalence** is broader than item equivalence because it relates to how respondents view, see, or understand the content of a question. Perhaps respondents understand all the words *(item equivalence)* but they don't fully understand what is being conveyed. On standardized college entrance exams, reading comprehension is a main method of assessing students' ability to understand what was read. Examiners have little doubt that college applicants can read the words — and probably know what all the words mean. However, do students fully comprehend the totality and nuances of what they read? Have you ever read instructions for something that do not seem to make sense although you know what all the words mean? You understand the words, but not the entire content of what the instructions are trying to convey. Construct equivalencies come into play when dealing with respondents from different backgrounds, education, experiences, and cultures. Construct equivalences address whether respondents understand the frame of reference of the questions themselves. Suppose researchers were doing a survey in an authoritarian country on the process of open elections and on freedom of political dissent. In some countries, respondents would have a hard time relating to the issue and might not fully understand the meaning of the questions. They might well understand the words *(item equivalence)* but they might not have enough of an understanding of the underpinnings of democracy to feel connected enough to answer the questions. When respondents do not have an appropriate frame of reference, they might not interpret the questions the same way as respondents who *"get it"*.

■ FIGURE 14.4
American
vs.
British English

American English	British English
Apartment	Flat
Argument	Row
Baby Carriage	Pram
Band-aid	Plaster
Bathroom	Loo or WC
Flashlight	Torch
Elevator	Lift
Eraser	Rubber
Jello	Jelly
Jelly	Jam
Truck	Lorry
Sweater	Jumper
Fries	Chips

- **Measurement equivalence** refers to whether people of different countries and cultures understand the measurement or scale being used in a given question. For example, suppose people from a certain country were asked to rate their satisfaction on the service they received at a department store from A to F. Respondents in the United States would clearly understand such a scale based on the American grading system. However, it's not a given that everyone will be able to relate to such a scale. If American students received 15 out of 20 on a test they would probably feel as though they did not do very well. In their mind, that score would be 75 percent out of 100 — converting the grade to a percent out of 100 is natural to American students. However in France, 15 out of 20 would be considered quite good and in fact in some universities a 12 is considered to be an average score with perhaps only a few scores above 17. The *scale itself* is interpreted differently across various groups. This differing interpretation is the essence of measurement equivalence.
- **Sample equivalence** occurs when researchers have the right sample in both cultures. Suppose marketing researchers are studying 2,000 women who like to cook grand meals — 1,000 women from Spain and 1,000 women from Japan. Although these cultures are quite different, the study is essentially assuming one sample of 2.000 respondents who like to cook. If only half of the Spanish women actually like cooking, then the samples are not fully comparable and thus researchers have sample in-equivalence. The samples across cultures must meet the same criteria if they are to be considered one sample.
- **Scalar equivalence,** akin to *measurement equivalence,* measures whether respondents who have the same opinions record those opinions the same way on a given scale. Let's revisit the cooking example from above. If researchers

interview 10 Spanish women and 10 Japanese women separately and all 20 express a strikingly similar opinion about their level of interest in cooking, the researcher might assume that these women would *also* record their opinions similarly on a scaled question. However, when researchers give those 20 women a 1 to 10 rating scale with 10 being the highest level of interest, the average responses might be quite different. Let's say that the Spanish women's average score was 8 and the Japanese average score was 6. It appears the scale did not fully capture their opinions accurately because based on this result researchers would assume their opinions varied by 20 percent when, but based on the interviews, their opinions are actually the same. In this case, the way the scale is interpreted caused variances to occur when those variances did not really exist.

Questionnaire Execution

For international research, questionnaires are written in one language and then translated into the language where the survey will be executed. When the final questionnaire is ready for translation, marketing researchers need to have a variety of people with different skill sets to correctly translate the questionnaire into the new language and prepare it for administration. These key people are:

- **Translators:**
  - People who are fluent in both languages and can translate the survey into the new language while maintaining the meaning and intent of the original survey.
- **Reviewers:**
  - Reviewers ensure the format and structure of the survey are appropriate for the culture of interest. Reviewers determine if the questionnaire is the right length, that its appearance will speak to the audience, and that the right questions are being asked and being asked in the best way.
- **Logisticians:**
  - This group determines the best way to administer the questionnaire based on the country and culture where the research will be conducted. These people assess the efficacy of conducting a telephone, mail, Internet, or in-person survey based on what the culture expects and what the infrastructure will support. Logisticians develop the execution plan that includes the timetable and milestones for administering the survey.

Question Sequence

Sequence biases and sequencing issues are important concepts to understand when conducting international surveys. Generally, more complicated and invasive questions should be positioned towards the end of the questionnaire or interview in most surveys — including international surveys. As for the other questions, the formality with which the questions are written can have an impact on how respondents perceive those questions. When questions are translated, there can be a tendency to translate the questions literally and formally as oppose to translating the questions in a more conversational tone. The tone shift in the questionnaire makes the position in the survey more complicated because more formal questions are generally better at the end of the questionnaire. Clearly all questions can't be at the end of the questionnaire thus researchers must take special care in the sequence of the questions to avoid non-response, refusals, or cutoffs.

Language Mapping

Language mapping and flow, as studied by professor Lars Perner at the University of Southen California, is important to international research. Although not a precise or definitive measure, and prone to stereotypical biases, language mapping provides a useful visual understanding, and framework, on contextual language patterns. Writing and speaking styles in Germanic languages, such as German and English, tend to be more direct and to the point with a focus on organized and predicable sentence construction. Romance languages such as French, Spanish, and Portuguese often focus on taking a more circuitous route to the point. An emphasis on flare and expressiveness are features of these language types. Many Asian languages often rely on more circular phraseology with a more cautious road to a definitive opinion. Marketing researchers can benefit from understanding these general rules as guidance and not necessarily as definitive data, on ways to approach questionnaire writing and interviewing respondents from varying cultures. This process works both ways in that researchers should interpret questionnaire and interview results with these concepts in mind. Suppose a researcher is interviewing someone from an Asian culture and the language they use in response to the questions is not direct. A researcher might believe, perhaps falsely, that the respondent is being evasive or untruthful when in fact the respondent is simply responding in a culturally familiar way. None of these approaches is right or wrong — researchers should just be aware of the environment in which they are operating and make adjustments accordingly (Figure 14.5).

■ **FIGURE 14.5**

Language Flows

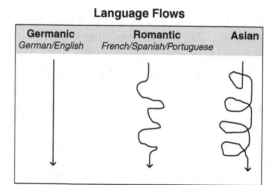

Language Flows

Germanic	Romantic	Asian
German/English	French/Spanish/Portuguese	

Body Language

Reading body language is important when doing focus groups, observation, and interviews in an international context. Imagine conducting a focus group without knowing that nodding in some cultures means "yes" and in other cultures it means "no." Also, issues of personal space, eye contact, and sitting vs. standing play roles in how comfortable international respondents are in a given situation. If a researcher is interviewing someone who needs personal space, the researcher should know the appropriate distance to ensure the respondent is comfortable. A focus group moderator should be alert to the body language of participants as it relates to attitudes, emotions, or prejudices. The body language one culture exhibits might well be different from another culture's. Suppose a researcher gives a gift to an interviewee and the interviewee's body language betrays him by revealing that he, while not verbalizing it, takes offense at the gesture. Failure to recognize body language clues limits the researcher's ability to gain insight into the mindset of research participants.

Research in Practice

Case:

- Kevin Smith, the CEO of Smith Hotels has decided the company should expand its presence in China. The company has had success in many of its international locations but the CEO is not certain where the next five hotels in China should be located. After having opened a few hotels in South America, the company found its failure to understand the South American environment and market led to several of the hotels closing despite a good general business climate in the region. Smith Hotels wants to avoid the mistakes it made in South America when it opens its new hotels in China.

Assignment:

- Create a marketing research design that accounts for the special challenges of entering an international market in general and in China specifically. What types of marketing research are you recommending be conducted — and how and why will you conduct this type of research. How will you approach the sampling plan? What is the best way to design and test a questionnaire to determine local support for a new hotel and to measure potential clients' needs and wants related to the property? Where should these hotels be located and why? Finally, what are the legal, economic, regulatory, cultural, and financial challenges that must be addressed?

Chapter Summary

Marketing internationally brings special challenges to marketing researchers. A study of the environmental factors affecting international marketing is critical to understanding the best marketing research approach. The environmental factors that require close study include: legal, cultural, government, infrastructure, and economic. Key parts of the cultural environment are the six cultural dimensions identified by Geert Hofstede. These dimensions, which provide a cultural framework as opposed to a definitive characterization are: Power distance *(the extent to which there is a gap between those with and those without power and a sense of a power hierarchy)*, masculine/feminine *(where gender roles are relatively clear and whereby masculine attributes such as assertiveness and ambition and feminine attributes such as a greater sense of social Justice, prevail)*, Long-short-term orientation *(the cultural approach to time horizons)*, individual/collective *(the sense of self vs. community or corporate needs)*, uncertainty avoidance *(the extent to which societies like structure and organization)*, indulgence/restraint *(how much societies spend on material goods or are otherwise indulgent)*. There is an effect on several key research methods resulting from the international marketing environment. Focus groups, interviews, observation, and survey construction and collection are all affected by cultural influences. Issues of body language, personal space, and appropriateness of gender roles in data collection must be considered. Measures of equivalence have an impact on the extent to which respondents interpret and understand the research questions and approach in the same way. There are five major measures of equivalence: Item *(the actual understanding of the word translation and its meaning)*, construct *(are the concepts in the questions understood equally)*, measurement *(are the data collection scales understood equally)*, sample *(is the sample correct in that they have the right experience and frame of reference to understand the meanings of the questions)*, and scalar *(do respondents who have the same opinion record their responses in the same way on a scaled question)*. Translators, reviewers, and logisticians help to ensure the interview or survey questions are written correctly and clearly, answer the research objectives, and are interpreted the same way by respondents. Language mapping is a concept of the flow and structure of language patterns across cultures. Generally Germanic languages are more linear and to the point, Romance languages often involve a less direct route to the point, and Asian languages can be more guarded in expressing strong opinions and are sometimes seen as more circular. Language mapping is a general framework for how cultures approach language and should not be taken as necessarily factual but should be considered when writing survey questions and conducting interviews. Marketing researchers will benefit from understanding the cultural and infrastructure environments of the country of study before executing a marketing research project.

Conducting a Case Analysis

Unlike the quantitative nature of surveys, a case analysis involves making both descriptive and analytic qualitative observations. Descriptive analysis involves discussing what was found in the case, whereas analytic observations include opinions on how the data should be interpreted and what the data mean. Analyzing a case study also involves making substantive judgments on the methods used and quality of the case being analyzed. Addressing the overall quality issue is valuable in a case study analysis. The writing style depends on the target audience of the readers. If peers are the recipient of the case study, the writing style should be at their level. However, if the audience is more general, it is best to write the case study assuming that the reader is intelligent but not necessarily informed on the issues relevant to the case study. A case analysis should begin by clearly defining the objective, scope, and approach of the review in order to explain the purpose of the analysis.

When conducting a case analysis, there are three key approaches, or a combination of these approaches, that the evaluator might choose; *factual, results,* and *method.* The factual approach involves the reviewer analyzing the case for factual correctness. A results analysis focuses more on the case study findings and the reviewer's opinions as to the quality and insightfulness of those findings. A method analysis addresses the reviewer's assessment as to the rigor of the process used to collect and analyze the data in the case.

The case analysis should be written in paragraph form and in a way that clearly conveys the key points of the case. It should include an analysis of the quality of the case and its applicability to the given research situation.

Sample Case Analysis Outline

1. **Define the Purpose, Scope, and Target of the Case Analysis**
   a. Purpose—why is the case analysis being conducted?
   b. Scope—what aspects of the case will be analyzed and what will not be analyzed?
   c. Target—who is the intended audience of the case analysis?
2. **Case Analysis Approach(s)**
   a. Factual
      i. Correctness of facts
      ii. How the facts were collected
      iii. How the facts were used in the case
      iv. Timeliness, relevance, and completeness of the facts
   b. Results
      i. Reasonable case conclusions
      ii. Analysis supported by the facts with limited editorial comment
      iii. Results answer the research question(s) or raise other questions
      iv. The seven "Cs"—results are complete, creditability, comprehensive, clear, compelling, concise, and correct
   c. Method
      i. How the case data was collected *(primary and/or secondary)*
      ii. Case used a logical progression of data collection steps
      iii. Balance between qualitative and quantitative collection methods
      iv. The person who collected the facts and whether that person was an honest broker in the process
3. **Analytic Method(s)**
   a. Descriptive
      i. Describe the who, what, where, when, and how issues are addressed in the case
      ii. Focus is on describing the key facts of the case
   b. Analytic
      i. Answers the why and "what do the data mean" questions
      ii. How the data elements are tied together to tell the story of the case
      iii. Reading between the lines and connecting the information in the case are keys
   c. Combination
      i. The case covers both descriptive and analytic methods
      ii. How those methods were used in tandem

4. **Dissect the Issue or Problem of the Case Focus**
   a. The issue or problem under study is stated
   b. Discuss the difference between an issue and problem
   c. How well the case addresses these issues or problems
   d. The issue or problem is comprehensive or only a part of a larger issue or problem
   e. How the key facts and issues were tied together
   f. The conclusion clearly incorporates the key case findings

APPENDIX 2

Three Cases for Analysis

Included below are three case summaries from the *Journal of Marketing Research* (JMR) for analysis and discussion. Use the outline from **Appendix 1** as a guide to analyzing these cases. The full cases follow.

1. **Mapping Online Consumer Search**

   Extrapolated from the JMR Executive Summary

   - This article examines how consumers search among competing products using an Amazon.com dataset. The resulting product search map reveals a comprehensive and detailed picture of how products compete for inclusion in the consumer search. These maps have three main benefits. First, the manufacturers obtain a detailed product-centric visualization of the competitive structure in their industry, revealing typical search patterns that involve their products. This visualization helps manufacturers identify which competing products are most frequently searched alongside their own products in a typical browsing session. Second, the proposed model is simple and can be broadly applied to numerous product categories. The case study authors' method can also be applied to product search or site navigation data from other large online retailers such as Target or Kohl's. Lastly, whereas getting frequent product-level search data or sales data using surveys is prohibitively expensive for firms selling durable goods in multiple categories, each involving a large number of alternatives, a benefit of the authors' method is that it only uses publicly available and free-of-charge summaries of search data.

2. **What Makes Consumers Willing to Pay a Price Premium for National Brands over Private Labels?**

   Extrapolated from the JMR Executive Summary

   - An increasing number of businesses are using private labels as a marketing tool. This strategic decision poses major challenges for national brands around the world as they see an encroachment on their market presence. A major marketing question is whether consumers will continue to pay a price premium for national brands over private labels. This article examines how marketing and manufacturing factors affect the price premium a consumer is willing to pay for a national brand over and above a private label. These effects are tempered by consumer perceptions of national brands' quality in relation to private labels. The model is tested on consumer survey data from 22,623 respondents from 23 countries in Asia, Europe, and the Americas across on an average of 63 consumer packaged goods categories per country.

3. **Determining Influential Users in Internet Social Networks**

   Extrapolated from the JMR Executive Summary

   - At social networking (SN) sites, content is almost entirely user-generated. To attract traffic, a SN firm itself cannot do much to drive the message beyond periodic updates of site features and design elements. The bulk of digital content—the driving force of the site's vitality and attractiveness—is produced by its users. However, users are not all created equal in the quality or quantity of their input. Community members differ widely in terms of the frequency, volume, type, and quality of digital content they generate and consume. From a managerial perspective, understanding who keeps the SN site attractive—specifically, identifying users who influence the site activity of others—is a critical piece of the marketing puzzle. A clear understanding of what drives users to SN provides marketers valuable insight when developing precise advertising targets as well as retention efforts aimed at sustaining and/or increasing the activity of influential existing users (and therefore future ad revenue). Firms operating SN sites observe an "overt" network of friends, defined according to who added whom as a friend. Most of the links in this network are "weak" in the sense that the relationships do not significantly affect behavior in the network. It is of interest to identify the "strong" links (i.e., the links corresponding to friends who affect the user's behavior). Distinguishing weak links from strong links is a complicated problem for two reasons. First, the number of overt links is large and varied. Second, the firm wants to distinguish the links fairly quickly (e.g., fewer than three months), so the number of "observations" available is fairly small. This situation sets up a challenging statistical problem explored in this case.

JUN B. KIM, PAULO ALBUQUERQUE, and BART J. BRONNENBERG*

The authors propose a new method to visualize browsing behavior in so-called product search maps. Manufacturers can use these maps to understand how consumers search for competing products before choice, including how information acquisition and product search are organized along brands, product attributes, and price-related search strategies. The product search maps also inform manufacturers about the competitive structure in the industry and the contents of consumer consideration sets. The proposed method defines a product search network, consisting of the products and links that designate whether a product is searched conditional on searching other products. The authors model this network using a stochastic, hierarchical, and asymmetric multidimensional scaling framework and decompose the product locations as well as the product-level influences using product attributes. The advantages of the approach are twofold. First, the authors simultaneously visualize the positions of products and the direction of consumer search over products in a perceptual map of search proximity. Second, they explain the formation of the map using observed product attributes. The authors empirically apply their approach to consumer search of digital camcorders at Amazon.com and provide several managerial implications.

Keywords: brand networks, asymmetric multidimensional scaling, product search, hierarchical Bayes estimation

Mapping Online Consumer Search

The marketing literature has long recognized the importance of understanding the search phase of the consumer choice process for several reasons. First, prechoice consumer activities, such as search, reveal limits on consumer consideration sets (Roberts and Lattin 1991; Siddarth, Bucklin, and Morrison 1995; Urban, Hulland, and Weinberg 1993). Second, prepurchase product search reflects consumer strategies of information acquisition, including how search is organized, which may be informative about substitution patterns and potential choices. Third, knowledge of consumer information acquisition is fundamental to planning marketing communications and retail distribution (Newman and Staelin 1972). Finally, the introduction and widespread adoption of the Internet has greatly facilitated consumer information acquisition, and online consumer search has become ubiquitous. In this context, the goals of this article are to propose a practical and exploratory method that manufacturers can use to analyze and visualize rich consumer search patterns and obtain insights into the competitive structure of online markets in their industry.

Our modeling approach begins by defining a network representation of product search data. This network expresses the topology of search across products, such as whether a given product is searched conditional on another product being searched. Then, we analyze this network using asymmetric multidimensional scaling (MDS). In particular, we propose a hierarchical MDS model that estimates product positions in a latent attribute space and direction of search along pairs of products. In addition, we implement a property fitting regression (DeSarbo and Hoffman 1987) as a hierarchical regression step in a Bayesian estimation framework to interpret the dimensions of our latent attribute space. Our complete approach to describing the product search data yields a visualization that we refer to as a "prod-

*Jun B. Kim is Assistant Professor of Marketing, College of Management, Georgia Institute of Technology (e-mail: jun.kim@mgt.gatech.edu). Paulo Albuquerque is Assistant Professor of Marketing, Simon Graduate School of Business, University of Rochester (e-mail: paulo.albuquerque@simon.rochester.edu). Bart J. Bronnenberg is Professor of Marketing and CentER Fellow at CentER, Tilburg University (e-mail: bart.bronnenberg@uvt.nl). The authors thank Andrew Ainslie, Lee Cooper, Minha Hwang, Raphael Thomadsen, and Michel Wedel for discussion and advice during this project. The third author gratefully acknowledges support from the European Commission under Marie Curie Grant, IRG 230962. Michel Wedel served as associate editor for this article.

Journal of Marketing Research
Vol. XLVIII (February 2011), 13–27

uct search map." In this map, products likely to be searched together are located close to each other, and products unlikely to be searched together are placed at distant positions. The map also depicts the relative search attractiveness of each product and identifies the direction and asymmetry of consumer search among the products. Finally, the map can be used to shed some light on substitution patterns. Local subsets of products on the map can be interpreted as stereotypical products or consideration sets that are searched together and, presumably, compete more intensely. We also argue that the product search maps are an efficient and practical way to organize the massive number of possible consideration sets.

From a managerial perspective, this article offers three important and practical features to consumer durable goods manufacturers.[1] First, it provides a descriptive model of how products are searched online. From this model, manufacturers can obtain a detailed product-centric visualization of the competitive structure in their industry, revealing typical search patterns that involve their products. This visualization also helps them identify the set of competing products that are most frequently searched alongside their own products in the same session. Second, our proposed model has broad applicability. We apply our model to online search data from the largest online retailer in the world, Amazon. com. Although we illustrate the model with data from one product category, the method applies to many product categories sold at Amazon.com—notably, to durable goods sectors, for which useful data on search and sales are often difficult to find. Our method can also be applied to product search or site navigation data from several other large online retailers (e.g., Walmart.com). Third, although obtaining frequent product-level search or sales data using surveys is prohibitively expensive for firms selling durable goods in multiple categories, each involving a large number of alternatives, a benefit of our method is that it only uses publicly available summaries of search data. This makes our proposed descriptive method for studying consumer search cost effective. In addition to being free of charge, the data we use are not survey based but rather revealed measures of consumer search, which are viewed as more reliable (Newman and Lockeman 1975).

We empirically apply our method to the study of consumer search for digital camcorders at Amazon.com. From the analysis of our product search maps, we find that consumers predominantly organize their search for a camcorder by media format (e.g., DVD, hard disk, MiniDV); that is, consumers are more likely to search multiple products that share the same media format and less likely to search across media formats. Within each media format, consumer search is price driven, with similarly priced products more likely to be searched together and, thus, to be perceived as closer substitutes. Surprisingly, the brand attribute plays a less critical role than price or media format during the consumer search process in the camcorder category.

Finally, we demonstrate that manufacturers and product managers can use our estimated product search maps to con-

duct an in-depth, product-level analysis of consumer search. For each focal product, our results indicate the comprehensive set of comparison candidates, as well as the intensity of customer traffic to and from each of these candidates.

We organize the rest of the article as follows: In the next section, we discuss the relevant literature and subsequently describe the data used in this study. Then, we put forth our model, followed by a section on estimation. Next, we discuss the results of a numerical data experiment that verifies parameter recovery of the proposed stochastic MDS model. Following this, we discuss the results of the proposed model. Finally, we conclude with managerial implications and directions for further research.

RELEVANT LITERATURE

We discuss the two research streams most relevant to this study: (1) consideration set formation and information processing and (2) asymmetric MDS. In marketing, the consideration set literature follows the footsteps of economic theory of information search (Stigler 1961) because the concept of consideration is a logical outcome of information search (Hauser and Wernerfelt 1990; Roberts and Lattin 1991). In many previous two-stage choice models, researchers have inferred consideration sets from individual-level choice data (Bronnenberg and Vanhonacker 1996; Mehta, Rajiv, and Srinivasan 2003; Siddarth, Bucklin, and Morrison 1995; Swait and Erdem 2007), with the exception of Moe (2006), who uses individual-level clickstream data for browsed products. Common to these studies is that consideration sets are latent constructs inferred from the individual panel data in consumer packaged goods and that they improve the statistical fit of the empirical model (Chiang, Chibb, and Narasimhan 1998). This approach is not applicable to studying consumer durable goods, because repeat purchases are often too infrequently observed, making the empirical investigation of product substitution in durable goods challenging. We aim to overcome this challenge by exploiting information contents in product search by a large number of consumers.

In behavioral research, Payne (1976) and Bettman and Park (1980) report that the formation of consideration sets is associated with a subset of product attributes. Furthermore, Shugan (1980) shows that selective search can be a result of rational strategies of consumer search. Most relevant to a substantive contribution of the current study is Gilbride and Allenby's (2004) work, which investigates consumer use of attribute-based screening rules in a choice-based conjoint study. They infer the screening attributes and their importance from choice decisions and report that price and body style are the two most frequently used screening attributes in the camera category. Therefore, these are the attributes that camera manufacturers should primarily consider for new product development and planning marketing communications. However, it is reasonable to assume that screening attributes are category dependent. In this study, we propose a simple and cost-effective way to identify such patterns that emerge during consumer search in durable goods, using publicly available data for a large number of categories.

We also aim to add to the literature on brand mapping (e.g., Bijmolt and Wedel 1999; Elrod 1988; Erdem 1996).

---

[1]We emphasize that our target audience is not online retailers, which have access to more detailed data, but the manufacturers that would not have access to such data.

One aspect of our contribution is to visualize products in a latent attribute space, according to whether consumers tend to search for them together. This means that instead of estimating brand maps from choices or similarity ratings used in the past, we estimate such maps from search patterns. Moreover, our data on online search patterns are generally directional (i.e., search of product A given search of product B does not generally occur with equal incidence as in the opposite direction). For our modeling purpose, we adopt an MDS framework. Multidimensional scaling is a set of mathematical techniques that are suitable to uncover the latent structure among objects in a network by exploring similarities and dissimilarities in the data. Asymmetric MDS allows the similarity between two objects to be direction dependent. A few asymmetric MDS studies have previously appeared in the marketing literature. DeSarbo and Manrai (1992) operationalize Krumhansl's (1978) conceptual model of distance density and construct a visualization of the competitive automobile segments using switching data. DeSarbo, Grewal, and Wind (2006) propose a stochastic MDS model and analyze the asymmetric competitive market structure in luxury automobile and portable phone markets using consumer consideration and choice sets. Asymmetric MDS models have also been researched and used outside marketing (e.g., Okada and Imaizumi 1987; Saburi and Chino 2008). In these models, the symmetric part of the data is typically modeled with measures of interobject distance, such as Euclidean distance between product positions, and asymmetry is allowed by increasing distance in one direction but not the other. In the modeling section, we introduce a representation of the symmetric and asymmetric components adapted from Okada and Imaizumi (1987).

SEARCH DATA

Amazon.com summarizes and posts information from consumer prepurchase browsing activities in most durable goods categories. For each available product, the data show a list of products in the same product category that were frequently viewed by shoppers in one browsing session. For example, if a large number of consumers who viewed product j also viewed product k, k appears on the viewed product list (hereinafter view list) of j. Furthermore, products in j's view list are presented in descending order of frequency, with products that appear higher having a stronger relationship to product j than products appearing further down in the view list. Collected across all J products, we refer to these data as "product search data."

The product search data are an outcome of an item-to-item, collaborative filtering mechanism, in which the relationship between two products is determined by how frequently users jointly view the products (Linden, Smith, and Zada 2005). Appendix A, Part 1, presents details on Amazon.com's data generation. The product search data constitute a collection of directional relationships or links that exist between products. When considered together, these links lead to an associative network of choice alternatives, in which a node represents a product and an edge a relationship between two products. We represent the product search data using a $J \times J$ product search matrix Y, in which an entry y_{jk} represents a presence or absence of a relationship from

product j to product k (i.e., $y_{jk} = 1$ if k appears on j's view list and $y_{jk} = 0$ if otherwise).[2] As Appendix A, Part 1, indicates, Amazon.com provides the top M most relevant products for a focal product in the view list. This means that $y_{jk} = 1$ if k is one of the top M most relevant products for focal j and $y_{jk} = 0$ if otherwise. These data are asymmetric because product j may be among the most relevant products for k, but not necessarily vice versa. Appendix A, Part 2, provides an illustrative example of the source of asymmetry in the product search data. The observed asymmetry in the product search data provides information to managers on how consumers navigate over choice options, thus allowing for a more comprehensive analysis of the relationships among the products. Therefore, it is our goal to incorporate such asymmetry explicitly in the proposed model.

For the empirical analysis, we used data from the digital camcorder category. Currently the dominant type in the camcorder category, digital camcorders store images and audio on a digital storage medium and offer good picture and sound qualities. In brief, our data collection process is as follows: We first downloaded Web pages for more than 250 camcorder products, each containing product-related data. For each product, two Web pages were downloaded. The first Web page contained information about product search data (i.e., which products consumers searched in the same online session as the chosen product). The second Web page contained detailed product information (e.g., list price, brand, media format, number of pixels, screen size, sales rankings, customer reviews), which we denote by product characteristics data. After we downloaded the Web pages, we parsed relevant information and assembled it into daily data sets. We repeated this process on a regular basis for a year beginning in June 2006 and constructed a longitudinal database.

Although our approach is scalable to the full set of products, for practical illustration, we narrowed down the number of products in the empirical study using the following criteria. First, we used products from the top four manufacturers (Sony, Canon, JVC, and Panasonic) and the three most common media formats (DVD, hard drive, and MiniDV). These four brands and three formats encompassed the large majority of digital camcorders available at Amazon.com during our data collection period. Second, we excluded professional grade digital camcorders because industry reports classify them as a separate category. Last, we excluded any product that does not appear in the view list of other products because consumer search of such product is not identified. Applying these criteria narrowed the number of products down to 62. All the top selling products are included in this subset.

In our empirical analysis, we used product search and characteristics data for August 2006. For these data, we define product j as being related to product k if j appears at least once on the daily view list of k during the month. We checked robustness of our analysis against alternative definitions of product relations. Specifically, we replicated our

---

[2]We do not have customer count data (i.e., the number of times two products are viewed together). Availability of such data would allow for a more detailed modeling approach, such as that of Wedel and DeSarbo (1996).

analysis with weighted relations between pairs of products, where the weights were based on the strength of product links over time. We operationalized this by converting the daily ranking into daily percentile rankings and then averaging them for August.[3] Our results are not sensitive to this alternative definition, and we do not include the details of this robustness check here to avoid repetition.

Table 1 shows the breakdown of these products by brand and storage media format. The table indicates that Sony has the most models sold at Amazon.com and that MiniDV is by far the most popular media storage format, constituting about half the products in our sample.

Table 2 presents a percentage breakdown of the relationships among the different brands. The first row shows the links of Sony products to products of other brands. For example, note that among all the relationships in the product search data, 18.51% are from Sony products to other Sony products and 5.17% are from Sony products to Panasonic products. For the reverse relationship, 6.25% of the links are from Panasonic to Sony.

We now discuss the relational information among the products in the product search data. Among the 62 products, the total number of existing relationships is 832, or 22% of all entries in the product search matrix Y, excluding the diagonal elements. The number of other products that appear on the view list of a given product ranges from 6 to 20, with a mean of 13.4 and a standard deviation of 3.2. The frequency with which a product appears on the view lists of other products ranges from 1 to 31, with a standard deviation of 7.5. The disparity between these two sets of summary statistics indicates that there are products that have short view lists but appear frequently on the view lists of other products (and vice versa), which provides evidence of asymmetry in the data.

Finally, we discuss a potential concern with the data available at Amazon.com. It is possible that Amazon.com could use the product search data to achieve its business goals (e.g., direct consumers to higher-margin products or clearance items). However, this is unlikely for several reasons. First, provision of truly similar products is strongly aligned with Amazon.com's commercial interests. By offering more relevant selections at lower search cost, Amazon. com is helping consumers choose products that best fit their needs, enhancing consumer shopping experience, and reducing price sensitivity (Lynch and Ariely 2000). Amazon.com's heavy investment in personalization and recommendation

---

[3] We first encode the ranking of product r_{jt}, such that the most popular product at time t is encoded as J_t and not as 1. We then compute the percentile ranking of product j at time t as (Bajari, Fox, and Ryan 2008) $\tilde{r}_{jt} = [r_{jt}/\max_k(r_{kt})] = (r_{jt}/J_t)$, where r_{jt} is j's ranking at t and J_t is the number of products at time t.

Table 1

NUMBER OF PRODUCTS BROKEN DOWN BY BRANDS AND MEDIA FORMATS

Formats	Sony	Panasonic	Canon	JVC	Total
MiniDV	8	8	11	6	33
Hard drive	4	0	0	7	11
DVD	9	5	4	0	18
Total	21	13	15	13	62

Table 2

PERCENTAGE BREAKDOWN OF PRODUCT SEARCH DATA AMONG BRANDS

Formats	Sony	Panasonic	Canon	JVC	Total (%)
Sony	18.51	5.17	6.13	3.85	33.66
Panasonic	6.25	8.53	5.05	1.44	21.27
Canon	6.49	5.53	13.34	1.80	27.16
JVC	4.45	2.88	3.00	7.57	17.90
Total (%)	35.70	22.11	27.52	14.66	100.00

Notes: For example, the cell (Panasonic, Sony) with a value of 6.25 indicates that 6.25% of all the relationships among the products are from Panasonic products to Sony products.

technologies reflects such interests. Second, the product search data are stable over time and do not show a sudden inclusion or radical movement of products at the top of the list, which would be expected if Amazon.com were to manipulate this list. Last, we verified through communications with a knowledgeable former manager at Amazon.com that the product summary data solely represent consumer browsing behavior.[4]

MODEL

The Asymmetric Distance Model

We chose to use an MDS approach, mainly driven by our interest in visualizing the similarity between product options that are searched online. Given the nature of our data, for which the tendency to search choice option k from option j is not the same as the tendency in the opposite direction, it is necessary to model similarity between a product pair asymmetrically. Therefore, our starting point in modeling is asymmetric MDS (DeSarbo and Manrai 1992; Holman 1979; Krumhansl 1978; Saburi and Chino 2008). This form of MDS generalizes symmetric MDS by using additional object-specific quantities that represent the skewness in otherwise symmetric distance. Specifically, following Saburi and Chino (2008), we define the asymmetric distance from product j to product k by

$$(1) \qquad g_{jk} = d_{jk} - r_j + r_k,$$

where d_{jk} is the distance between product j and k and r_j and r_k are quantities to be estimated, which allow for $g_{jk} \neq g_{kj}$. We define d_{jk} as the Euclidean distance between two products j and k located at coordinates z_j and z_k in a derived latent attribute space of P dimension, as follows:

$$(2) \qquad d_{jk} = \sqrt{\sum_{p=1}^{P}(z_{jp} - z_{kp})^2} = \left\| z_j - z_k \right\|.$$

The products $j = 1, \ldots, J$ can be represented graphically in maps by plotting their coordinates z_j in the latent attribute space. In this graph, r_j and r_k in Equation 1 can be depicted as the radii of circles centered at product j's and k's positions, respectively. This "position-circle" model is a

---

[4] Amazon.com chooses consumer trust and long-term relationship over short-term gains. Senior Amazon.com executives have also made this point to the press in the past. For example, the shareholder letter for the first quarter of 2009, as well as an earlier letter in 1997 available at Amazon. com's Web page, emphasizes the importance of long-term relationship with customers.

parsimonious way of representing the asymmetric similarities between brands. Thus, we model the symmetry in the data with the distance term, d_{jk}, whereas the asymmetry is captured by the difference in the radii, r_j and r_k. With this formulation, a product with a small radius will be searched more frequently and draw more search from large-radius products than vice versa.[5] A simple example illustrates this concept: Assume that for two hypothetical products, $d_{jk} = 5$, $r_j = 1$, and $r_k = 3$, where product k has a larger radius than product j. Computing distances using Equation 1, we obtain $g_{jk} = 7$ and $g_{kj} = 3$; that is, the distance from j to k is larger than that from k to j. We used this distance to express a greater likelihood (modeled next) of observing a link from the larger-radius product k to the smaller-radius product j than vice versa. To the extent that more search and more frequent consideration lead to higher sales, it is likely that a product with a small radius has higher demand than a large-radius product. To facilitate the analysis and interpretation of the map, we enforce strict positivity on the distance (d_{jk}) and radii (r_j and r_k) in Equation 1. In contrast, the resulting combined term of g_{jk} is not subject to such a restriction because our interpretation is not based on this term.

An implicit assumption in our approach is that the data are mainly driven by consumer search activities, and thus the searched products are informative about consumer desire to view the product pages. However, it is possible that Amazon.com's product recommendations and other online navigational tools influence consumer search. Among the many online features, we focus on product recommendations because research suggests that they affect consumer behavior the most (Bodapati 2008; Garfinkel et al. 2006). To infer a product search map net of the effects of Amazon.com's recommendations, we need to explicitly account for their effects. Our proposed approach is to control for such effects by adding observable recommendation features to Equation 1:

$$(3) \qquad g_{jk} = d_{jk} - r_j + r_k - \beta X_{jk}^{rec},$$

where X_{jk}^{rec} contains the online recommendations that relate options j and k and the coefficient β measures how much they affect the effective distance from j to k. In the presence of the last term, the effective distance g_{jk} is associated with the latent product positions, the radii, and Amazon.com's recommendations. Therefore, the estimated product locations z_j and radii r_j can be interpreted as net of the influence of recommendations. In the "Empirical Analysis" section, we provide details on how we operationalize the recommendations X_{jk}^{rec}.

To complete our model, we added stochasticity to the asymmetric distance variable g_{jk}. Stochastic MDS assumes that the effective distance between objects is obtained by the perturbation of the distance g_{jk}, which includes unexplained factors that may influence the relationship between j and k (DeSarbo and Cho 1989; Jedidi and DeSarbo 1991; Saburi and Chino 2008):

$$(4) \qquad s_{jk} = g_{jk} + e_{jk} = d_{jk} - r_j + r_k - \beta X_{jk}^{rec} + e_{jk},$$

where e_{jk} is a stochastic disturbance term. A feature of stochastic MDS models is that they allow for statistical inference of model parameters—in this case, the z_{jp}, r_j, and β, for all j = 1, ..., J and p = 1, ..., P.

In addition to plotting the product positions and accounting for asymmetry in product search, we aimed to interpret the dimensions of the derived space. To this end, we used property fitting, in which product characteristics such as brand and price are regressed on the estimated product positions, identifying for each characteristic a vector of directions in the map that represents the best-fitting relation to map positions. Intuitively, the obtained fitted vector points in the direction in which products with a given characteristic are located on the map.

Similar to property fitting, we interpreted the dimensions of the derived space using a hierarchical model, for which, at the upper level of the hierarchy, we estimated product positions and radii and, at the lower level of the hierarchy, we regressed the product positions and radii on product attributes. Property fitting involves regressing product attributes on map positions, whereas the hierarchical model proposed herein regresses map positions on product attributes (see also DeSarbo and Hoffman 1987). Specifically, the hierarchical model's purpose is to explain product positions z_{jp} as a linear model of product characteristics X_j:

$$(5) \qquad z_{jp} = X_j \beta_p + \varepsilon_{jp}, \; \varepsilon_{jp} \sim N(0, \sigma_p^2), \text{ for } \forall j, p,$$

where z_{jp} is the location of product j in dimension p, X_j is a $[1 \times K]$ vector of product j's attribute values, and β_p is a $[K \times 1]$ vector, where K is the number of product attributes. To be precise, Equation 5 represents the inverse of a property fitting regression. The regression coefficients $\beta_p = [\beta_{p,1}, ..., \beta_{p,K}]$ capture how the product attributes explain the product positions in the derived space. More specifically, β_p measures how well the product attributes X_j explain the pth dimension of the derived space. In a similar manner, we also explain product radii as a function of product attributes:

$$(6) \qquad r_j = X_j \beta_r + \varepsilon_j, \; \varepsilon_j \sim N(0, \sigma_r^2), \text{ for } \forall j,$$

where β_r is a $[K \times 1]$ vector that measures the effects of product attributes on the magnitude of the radii.[6]

Likelihood Function

In our modeling strategy, we aim to explain the search patterns as represented by the product search matrix, Y, an

---

[5]There are alternative ways to implement the asymmetry. For example, DeSarbo and Manrai (1992) use a distance density model, in which r_j is modeled as the density of products around j. We allow the r_j to vary independently of density. We chose this proposed model for two reasons: First, the formulation is parsimonious and flexible enough to fully capture the asymmetry among the products, and second, we are interested in explaining the radii using observable product attributes.

[6]Instead of modeling the remaining product characteristics as explicitly affecting g_{jk} in Equation 4, we chose a hierarchical model in which the product characteristics implicitly affect g_{jk} through z_j and r_j. If we include the product characteristics in Equation 4 explicitly, the resulting map would only capture the residual relationship after accounting for the product characteristics. Therefore, the map would only reflect residual search behavior among the products. We believe that the proposed product search map, which captures all relevant product information, is much more managerially useful (as in DeSarbo and Jedidi 1995; DeSarbo and Rao 1986). In addition, there are two major differences between the proposed model and that of Hoff, Raftery, and Handcock (2002). First, our model explicitly addresses the asymmetry in the data. Second, we explain the latent positions and radii using the underlying product characteristics. Thus, our hyperparameters can be potentially used in policy simulations such as positioning and repositioning (DeSarbo and Hoffman 1987; DeSarbo and Jedidi 1995). This would be a challenge using Hoff, Raftery, and Handcock's (2002) approach.

unweighted and asymmetric matrix. An entry $y_{jk} = 1$ indicates a presence of a relationship from j to k, whereas $y_{jk} = 0$ indicates an absence of a relationship. The probability of observing a relationship from j to k using the effective distance from Equation 4 is expressed as follows:

$$(7) \quad \Pr(y_{jk} = 1) = \Pr(d_{jk} - r_j + r_k - \beta X_{jk}^{rec} + e_{jk} < \beta_0 + e_{jk0}),$$

where $\beta_0 + e_{jk0}$ is a random threshold for a link to be realized. Assuming that the error terms e_{jk} and e_{jk0} are i.i.d. random variables with an extreme value distribution, we can quantify the probability of observing a link between j and k as follows:

$$(8) \quad L(y_{jk} = 1 | X^{rec}, z_j, z_k, r_j, r_k, \beta_0, \beta)$$

$$= \Pr(e_{jk} - e_{jk0} < \beta_0 - \|z_j - z_k\| + r_j - r_k + \beta X_{jk}^{rec})$$

$$= [1 + \exp(\|z_j - z_k\| - r_j + r_k - \beta X_{jk}^{rec} - \beta_0)]^{-1}.$$

Assuming conditional independence among relationships y_{jk} (see Hoff, Raftery, and Handcock 2002), the likelihood of the hierarchical model is given as follows:

$$(9) \quad L(Y | Z, R, \theta, X, X_{rec}) = \prod_{\forall j} \prod_{\forall k \neq j} \Pr(y_{jk} | X_{jk}^{rec}, z_j, z_k, r_j, r_k, \beta_0, \beta)$$

$$\times \Pr(z_j, z_k | \beta_p, \sigma_p^2, X)$$

$$\times \Pr(r_j, r_k | \beta_r, \sigma_r^2, X),$$

where $X = \{X_j\}$, $X^{rec} = \{X_{jk}^{rec}\}$, $Z = \{z_j\}$, $R = \{r_j\}$, and $\theta =$ the set of parameters. The conditional independence assumption means that after interproduct distances and asymmetries are accounted for, the relationships y_{jk} are independent. This model parsimoniously handles complex dependencies among the y_{jk} such as transitivity (i.e., in general, elevated search activity between products j and k and between products k and m implies elevated search activity between j and m) and reciprocity (i.e., elevated search activity from j to k is statistically associated with elevated search activity from k to j).[7]

ESTIMATION

Markov Chain Monte Carlo Estimation

We used Bayesian estimation to obtain the posterior distributions of the parameters of the proposed hierarchical model. Specifically, we used Markov chain Monte Carlo (MCMC) methods to simultaneously estimate the product positions z_j and radii r_j, as well as parameters β_p, β_r, and β. In Equation 3, we need to set one $r_j = 0$ for identification purposes (for additional details, see Appendix A, Part 3). Other identification conditions with respect to product positions are well documented by Abe (1998), Elrod (1988), and Erdem (1996). To initialize the MCMC, we estimated the product positions z_j and radii r_j using maximum likelihood estimation. After estimating positions z_j and radii r_j, we regressed them on the product characteristics and obtained the hyperparameter estimates of β_p and β_r. By using the maximum likelihood estimation values as the starting val-

---

[7]Recall that in addition to modeling the links y_{jk}, we also modeled the strength of the link. We did this by modeling, for each product m, whether product j or product k appears higher on m's view list. This leads to a different model than the one in Equation 8 and a different likelihood function. Because the results from the two approaches are similar, we chose to use the parsimonious model described previously. The alternative formulation and results are available from on request.

ues in the MCMC, we aimed to reduce the number of burn-in iterations in the chain (Hoff, Raftery, and Handcock 2002). We used the Metropolis–Hastings algorithm and tuned the variances of the jumping distributions that generated candidate draws. To do so, we dynamically adjusted the variances of the jumping distributions during the burn-in period to achieve an acceptance ratio of approximately 20%–25%. We performed visual inspections of the chain to verify convergence. We drew 32,000 samples from the joint posterior distribution, using 27,000 iterations for burn-in and the final 5000 iterations to compute the posterior means and standard errors of the model parameters. Appendix B gives the detailed sampling sequence of the MCMC method and the prior distributions.

Data Experiment

To verify that the proposed model is well recovered, we designed and conducted a numerical data experiment. Our data experiment is based on the parameter estimates from the actual empirical data. That is, we first estimated the hypermodel parameters from the full product search model using the actual empirical data, treated them as the true model parameters, and then used them to generate the data for the experiment. We believe the proposed approach is more realistic than that based on a randomly chosen set of true parameters.

We generated the data as follows: With values of β_p, we stochastically determined the positions z_{jp} in a two-dimensional space (p = 1, 2) as a linear combination of the seven product attribute values (K = 7) in Equation 5. We also stochastically generated the radii r_j using β_r in Equation 6.

Given the product positions, radii, and other model parameters, we computed the asymmetric distance among all product pairs using Equation 3 and the corresponding link probability $\{p_{jk}\}$ of a product pair using Equation 8. Next, we created a binary matrix Y by performing Bernoulli trials using the computed probabilities $\{p_{jk}\}$, where Y is a realization from the underlying link probabilities.

Next, using Y as our dependent variable, we estimated the hierarchical model using the steps outlined in the preceding section. The total number of parameters for location and radii is 186 because we estimate two coordinates and a radius for all J = 62 products. Only 182 parameters are identified because we needed to fix the location of one product, the radius of a product, and the first coordinate of another product. At every sweep of the sampler, in addition to sampling the locations and radii, we also drew from the posterior distributions of the hyperparameters.

The four subplots in Figure 1 facilitate a visual comparison of the true and recovered positions and radii for 62 products as well as the hyperparameters of the hierarchical model. We present the true parameter values on the x-axis and their recovered counterparts on the y-axis. In all subplots, we observed that the recovered parameters lie tightly centered on the 45-degree lines. Consistently, we find high correlations between the true and the mean of the recovered parameters, shown at the top of each subplot, ranging from .87 to .99. The 95% credibility interval of the posterior parameter distributions covers the majority of true parameter values. We conclude that the parameters of the proposed model are well recovered.

Mapping Online Consumer Search

Figure 1
DATA EXPERIMENT SCATTERPLOTS OF TRUE AND RECOVERED PRODUCT COORDINATES, RADII, AND HYPERPARAMETERS

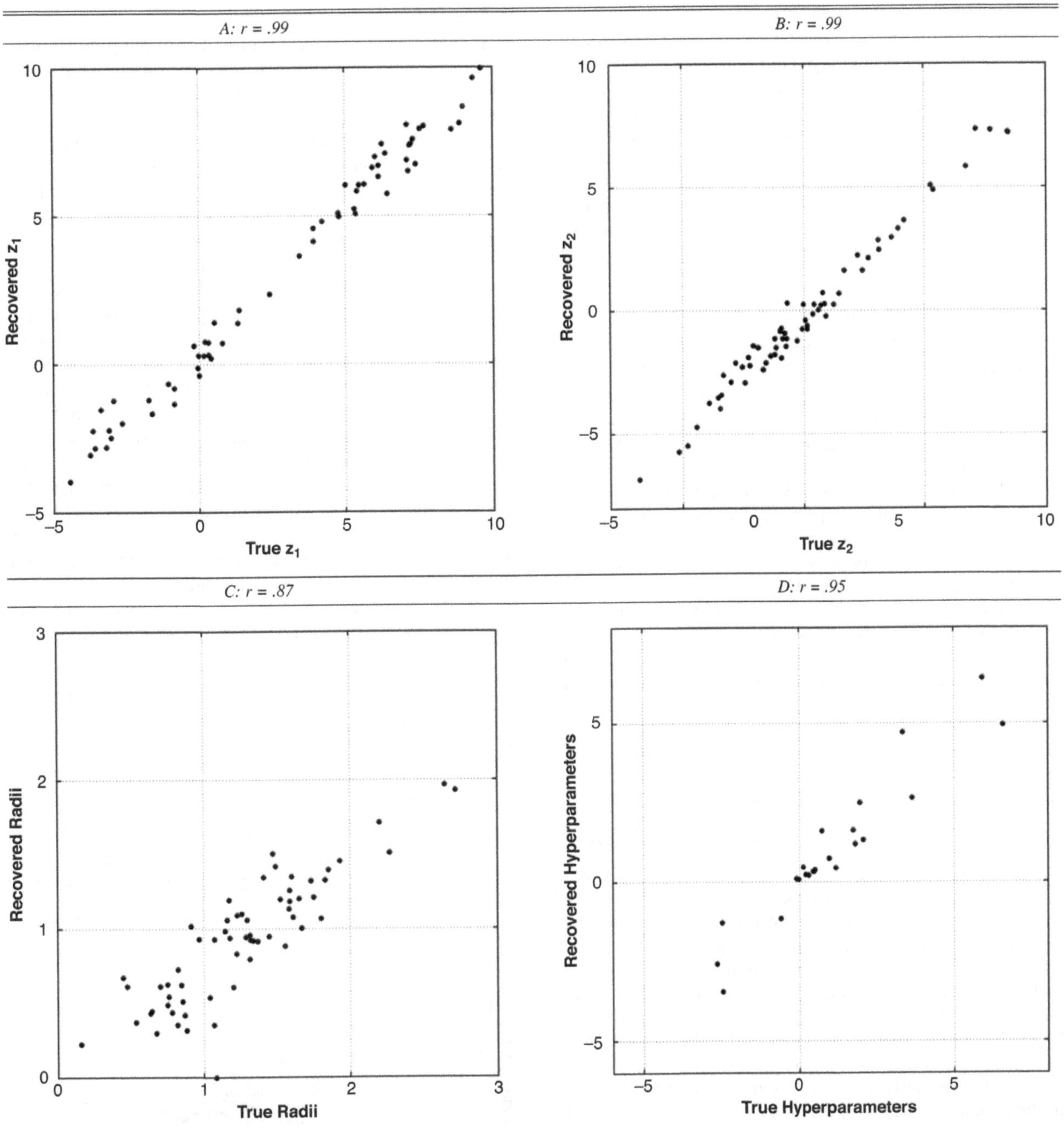

Notes: Panels A, B, C, and D show first coordinates (z_1), second coordinates (z_2), radii (r), and other model parameters ($\{\beta_0, \beta, \beta_{rec}, \beta_{list}\}$), respectively. Correlations between the true and estimated parameters are shown at the top of each plot.

EMPIRICAL ANALYSIS

Model Selection

We used the deviance information criterion for model selection.[8] We estimated four models in a 2 × 2 selection design, varying the number of dimensions of the latent product space (two dimensions versus three dimensions) and the directionality of search (symmetric, with all radii equal to 0, versus asymmetric, with product-specific radii). The results are as follows:

	Two Dimensions	Three Dimensions
Symmetric	2005	1756
Asymmetric	1919	1598

[8]We also used Bayes factors (Kass and Raftery 1995) for model selection, computed from the log marginal density. This resulted in the same model selection.

For both the two- and three-dimensional models, the inclusion of radii improves the model fit significantly. Therefore, we conclude that the product search data warrant the explicit modeling of the asymmetry.

Comparing the specifications with two and three dimensions, we observe an improvement in the deviance information criterion with the additional dimension. Many MDS applications also report a similar statistical model fit improvement with the additional dimension to the derived space (DeSarbo and Manrai 1992). As previous literature has pointed out, the decision about which dimensionality to use for a given data set is as much substantive as statistical (Kruskal and Wish 1983). Following this convention, we chose the three-dimensional model over higher-dimensional models.

Effect of Online Recommendations

We now discuss how we operationalized Amazon.com's online recommendations X_{jk}^{rec} in Equation 3 and their influence on search. There are several forms of product recommendations at Amazon.com. Because our aggregate-level data summarize within-category consumer search activities, we are mainly concerned with recommendations for products within the same category. We identified two such features. First, Amazon.com provides recommendations to other same-category products based on purchases by past consumers conditional on viewing a product. These product recommendations provide easier access to relevant products, influence consumer search behavior, and may be responsible for the formation of interproduct relationships. Second, the default category page at Amazon.com provides a list of products sorted in terms of their popularity. Product proximity in this list may affect consumer behavior (Brynjolfsson, Dick, and Smith 2004), especially during the search initiation process, inducing consumers to conduct joint search among the options and creating interproduct relationships. We parameterized X_{jk}^{rec} in Equation 3 accordingly:

$$(10) \quad g_{jk} = d_{jk} - r_j + r_k - \beta X_{jk}^{rec} = d_{jk} - r_j + r_k - \beta_{rec}N_{jk} - \beta_{list}I_{jk},$$

where N_{jk} is the fraction of days k is recommended from j, I_{jk} is an indicator variable that takes the value of 1 if j and k are located in the same page of the sorted product list, and the coefficients β_{rec} and β_{list} measure their respective effects on the effective distance g_{jk}. For example, $N_{jk} = .5$ means that k appears as a recommended product on j's product page 50% of the time during the data collection period. A larger N_{jk} and a positive β_{rec} imply a smaller g_{jk} because easy access from j to k may induce more consumer search of k from j. Similarly, if products j and k are located closer in the product list, $I_{jk} = 1$, they may lead to more frequent joint search of j and k, yielding a smaller distance g_{jk}.

In terms of results, we found that the posterior means of the recommendation coefficients, β_{rec} and β_{list}, are 10.96 and .38, with standard errors of 1.85 and .21, respectively. For products with recommendations (i.e., $\{j, k|N_{jk} > 0\}$ and $\{j, k|I_{jk} > 0\}$), these results imply that the Amazon.com recommendations increase link probabilities of $Pr(y_{jk} = 1)$ by, respectively, .14 and .007 on average. We infer that both product recommendations and colocation in the sorted list have small but significant effects on the interproduct relationship. These findings are consistent with prior research (Garfinkel et al. 2006). The estimated latent product positions as well as

the radii reported in the following section describe consumer search activities net of the effects of recommendations.[9]

Category-Level Consumer Product Search

Figure 2 shows the posterior means of the product positions and radii. This figure depicts several pieces of information about search. First, consumers are more likely to search together products that are located closer to each other during online browsing sessions. The location of products in the derived space is not uniform, and Figure 2 suggests the existence of clusters of products. These clusters have managerial relevance to manufacturers, as we discuss subsequently, and our approach readily identifies cluster membership from the product search data.

Second, a small radius means that a product will be searched more frequently in relative terms because it is more likely to become a search destination from other products than a source for search to other products. Therefore, the radii depict the directions or flows of consumer search, which is from large- to small-radii products, and identify the "absorbing" products in consumer search (small-radii products). This implies that though consumers may initiate their searches in the area in which large-radii products are located, they tend to move toward and terminate search around the location of products with small radii. For better interpretation, we display sales ranks of the products in the figure as well, with darker circles indicating products with high sales. We find that the correlation between the sales ranks and the radii is .78, confirming that search and even-

---

[9]We also estimated Equation 10 without Amazon.com's recommendations. The correlation of pairwise effective distances (g_{jk}) between the models with and without the recommendations is .99. This high correlation implies that the recommendations have only marginal effect on the overall formation of the product search map because their occurrence is quite sparse.

Figure 2
POSTERIOR MEANS OF THE ESTIMATED PRODUCT LOCATIONS AND RADII IN THE PRODUCT SEARCH MAP

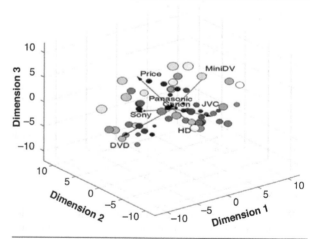

Notes: Circles represent product locations, circle radii represent the relative attractiveness of search, circle colors (darker) represent more sales, arrows represent the direction in which products with a given attribute can be found in the map, and the length of the arrows represents the degree of fit.

tually sales tend to be positively related to small-radii products. In addition, we observe that there are one or two products with small radii (and with higher sales) in each major cluster, which implies the existence of a small set of products that dominate search in the category (see also Figures 3 and 4).

Third, the arrows in the graph help interpret the latent attributes and represent the direction in which products with the corresponding attributes are likely to be found. For example, DVD-based products are more frequently found along the negative quadrant of the first dimension of the product search map. Technically, these arrows are constructed using property fitting regression coefficients. The arrow length is proportional to the R-square of each regression; in other words, a longer arrow means that the physical attribute is well explained by the latent dimensions. The arrow direction is computed as a ratio of the regression coefficients among the dimensions. Appendix A, Part 4, presents details on how to construct the arrows.

Consumer Search Patterns

We now analyze the resulting search patterns using Figures 3 and 4, the projections of the three-dimensional map onto two-dimensional spaces. First, we infer that media formats, which form three major segments in both maps, heavily guide consumer product search. This finding is confirmed by the property fitted arrows; the top three longest arrows, along with the price arrow in Figure 4, are all associated with the media formats. The three media format arrows are separated by angles of approximately 120 degrees in Figure 3, which is the maximum possible separa-

tion in a two-dimensional space. Their separations are also close to 120 degrees in Figure 4.

Second, from Figure 4, we note that the price explains the third (and also to some extent the first) dimension of the search map well. In this map, darker circles represent more expensive products (not higher sales, as in the previous two maps). The figure shows the transition of price from the lower-right-hand corner of the map (less expensive products) to the upper-left-hand corner (more expensive options). It strongly supports the view that the aggregate-level consumer search data contain information that identifies different segments in terms of price and that, in general, consumers search for products of similar price ranges.

Third, comparing the length of property fitted arrows for brand names with those of formats and price, we find that the effects of brand name on search are less important. More specifically, arrows for brand names such as Sony, JVC, and Canon are about half the size of the camcorder format arrows, and Panasonic's arrows are almost of zero length. Closer inspection reveals that Panasonic has products scattered all over the attribute space. In summary, the graph suggests that search takes place along media format first and, within media format, is based on price. In contrast, search is organized by brand to a lesser degree. We discuss the managerial implications of this search organization in the following sections.

Table 3 shows the values for the hyperparameters from our hierarchical regressions. They convey the same information as the regression coefficients from property fitting. In the hierarchical regression, one media format (DVD) and one brand (Panasonic) serve as the base, captured by the regression constant. Consistent with our findings from the

Figure 3
PROJECTION OF THREE-DIMENSIONAL PRODUCT SEARCH MAP ON DIMENSIONS 1 AND 2

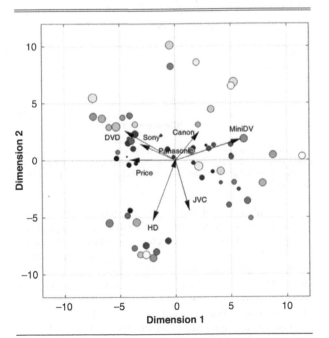

Notes: The darker circles represent products of higher sales.

Figure 4
PROJECTION OF THREE-DIMENSIONAL PRODUCT SEARCH MAP ON DIMENSIONS 1 AND 3

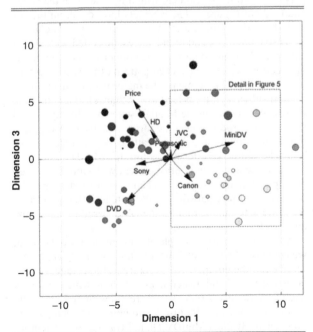

Notes: The darker circles represent more expensive products.

Table 3

REGRESSION OF PRODUCT POSITIONS AND RADII ON PRODUCT ATTRIBUTES

	Dimension 1	Dimension 2	Dimension 3	Radius
Constant	3.54 (2.53)	−1.64 (−.92)	−9.43 (−8.73)	.49 (.85)
Sony	−.67 (−1.19)	1.70 (2.45)	−2.47 (−4.00)	−.08 (−.19)
Canon	1.18 (2.07)	2.71 (4.12)	−1.52 (−2.39)	.24 (.59)
JVC	2.21 (3.34)	−1.37 (−1.93)	−.57 (−.94)	.47 (.96)
MiniDV	6.95 (12.59)	−.50 (−.52)	3.86 (4.29)	−.01 (−.03)
Hard drive	.85 (.94)	−7.75 (−9.05)	3.17 (2.75)	−.07 (−.13)
Price	−6.97 (−4.07)	3.96 (1.98)	14.19 (10.48)	1.46 (1.71)
σ^2	2.88 (.56)	5.83 (1.12)	3.12 (.82)	.61 (.12)
R^2	.89	.71	.79	.20

Notes: t-statistics are in parentheses.

product search map, the most significant and important coefficients correspond to the two media formats and price.

Last, it is important to note that the inferred consumer search strategies are similar to those in recent empirical literature, even though we do not impose a priori restrictions on the nature of consumer search. When facing a large number of options, consumers adopt heuristics-based approaches, such as noncompensatory processes (Gilbride and Allenby 2004) and lexicographic strategies (Yee et al. 2007), using observed product attributes. Prior behavioral research has reported consumers' adoption of such rules (e.g., Bettman and Park 1980; Payne 1976). Our map shows that consumers use media formats and price to direct their search in the digital camcorder category.

Product-Level Competitive Analysis

In the preceding section, we focused our discussion on consumer search patterns and competitive product structure at the category level. In this section, we demonstrate how manufacturers can use the product search map to identify neighboring products of each alternative in great detail.

As an illustration, Figure 5 focuses on an area with products in the MiniDV segment, which is located on the right-hand side of Figure 4. The products have different brands and show different prices. Darker colors indicate more expensive products, and brand names are coded with different symbols. Consistent with the conclusions of the previous section, we observe a clear pattern of increasing prices within the MiniDV segment. The majority of products at the bottom subcluster are priced lower than $300 and include the cheaper options in the MiniDV segment. Moving toward the top left, products become more expensive. Along this direction, different brands are scattered without a clear pattern. Therefore, we infer that within the MiniDV products, consumer search is more price driven, with similarly priced products more likely to be searched together and, thus, to be perceived as close substitutes. We note a similar pattern in the lower-left-hand corner for the DVD-based product cluster as well.

As a more specific example of how this map can be used, we now take the view of a manufacturer studying consumer search and the competitive structure in the category. Suppose that Sony is interested in establishing which products one of its models is regularly searched with and, thus, the products with which it closely competes. We focus on the Sony DCR-HC26, a MiniDV Digital Handycam Camcorder with 20× Optical Zoom priced at $307. Using Figure 5,

Figure 5

DETAIL OF THE PRODUCT SEARCH MAP IN THE MINIDV AREA

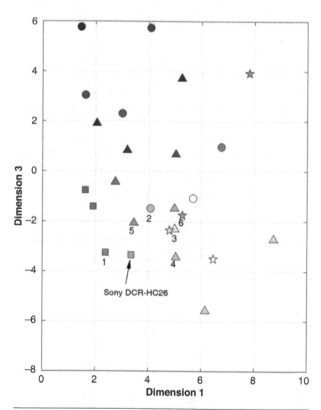

Notes: Plot symbols are as follows: Sony (square), Panasonic (circle), Canon (triangle), and JVC (star); darker colors indicate higher retail prices; and the numbered products constitute the six closest products to the Sony DCR-HC26.

Sony can identify and monitor the products located closest to this product. Table 4 lists the closest six competitors, along with some of their characteristics. These products are all MiniDVs and in a narrow price range. The average price of the cluster of numbered brands (including the Sony DCR-HC26) is $300. These products are the ones that Sony should monitor most closely because they often occur in the same set of searched products as the Sony DCR-HC26. In contrast, the average price of the cluster in the top left of the graph, containing two other Sony products, is $522. From

Table 4
PRODUCTS MOST CLOSELY SEARCHED JOINTLY WITH THE SONY DCR-HC26 RETAILING AT $307

Product Number	Brand	Price ($)	Media
1	Sony	333	MiniDV
2	Panasonic	292	MiniDV
3	Canon	262	MiniDV
4	Canon	285	MiniDV
5	Canon	313	MiniDV
6	JVC	310	MiniDV

Notes: For correspondence between product numbers and product positions, see Figure 5.

the distance between the expensive and cheaper product clusters, the Sony DCR-HC26 is not often searched together with the more expensive products, suggesting that cannibalization of higher-priced and potentially higher-margin products is not a concern in this case.

Extending the preceding example, Table 5 lists the search sets (i.e., the most commonly searched alternatives) for the three best-selling products, two Sony and one Canon. First, we note that the search is aligned with the same media formats, with each product being searched often with the same format products. Second, price seems to play an important role as well, especially for the Canon Elura-100, because prices of the five closest search substitutes fall in a tight range of −$99 to +$69. In contrast, we observe a wider price range for products that closely compete with Sony DCR-SR100. Therefore, we can conclude that cannibalization is a concern for the relatively expensive Sony DCR-SR100 because the top three most jointly searched alternatives are other less expensive Sony products. Although we are not able to measure the level of cannibalization using our approach, we believe that this information is essential for Sony managers regarding its product line management.

In general, we conclude that the maps in Figures 2–5 are useful tools for manufacturers to gauge search patterns at one of the largest online retailers, including search proximity, direction of search, and organization of search. Moreover, given any focal product, the maps are an efficient medium for manufacturers to review the competitive structure among the products and identify likely consideration sets in which their products compete. In addition, the maps are based purely on publicly available data and are relatively easy to compute.

MANAGERIAL IMPLICATIONS AND CONCLUSIONS

To the best of our knowledge, no study has previously analyzed the structure of consumer information acquisition in a product category with many choice options. In the camcorder category, the set of searched products is typically a small subset of all options, and therefore knowledge about the contents of this subset is essential to understanding consumer preferences. Online browsing behavior forms a natural environment to study product search among durable goods. Our study is also the first to use site navigation data at the world's largest online retailer, Amazon.com, that are publicly available across many product categories to investigate prepurchase search patterns.

We model product search data using a hierarchical, stochastic, and asymmetric MDS model. Using hierarchical

Table 5
MOST FREQUENTLY SEARCHED ALTERNATIVES FOR EACH TOP-SELLING PRODUCT

Focal Product/ Ranking of Conditional Search	Brand	Price ($)	Media
Sony DCR-DVD405/Retail price: $601			
1	Sony	743	DVD
2	Panasonic	699	DVD
3	Canon	647	DVD
4	Sony	522	DVD
5	Sony	639	MiniDV
Canon Elura 100/Retail price: $361			
1	Canon	313	MiniDV
2	Sony	394	MiniDV
3	Canon	293	MiniDV
4	Canon	262	MiniDV
5	Panasonic	430	MiniDV
Sony DCR-SR100/Retail price: $900			
1	Sony	600	Hard drive
2	Sony	700	Hard drive
3	Sony	800	Hard drive
4	JVC	596	Hard drive
5	JVC	697	Hard drive

Bayesian estimation, we jointly estimate product positions and product-specific influence (i.e., radius), as well as hyperparameters that measure the contributions of product attributes on the formation of the dimensions of the product search map.

From a substantive perspective, the analysis of product search data in this article provides the following findings: First, using product search maps, managers can monitor in detail each product's neighboring competitors during consumer search stages (illustrated in Figure 5). This map enables managers to scrutinize the local relationships among products and, thus, to better understand substitution patterns for their own products during consumer search activities. Unlike many brand maps in previous marketing literature, which visualize competition among a few brands, this intuitive and informative map provides detailed information on whether a product is likely to be searched more often and if it is likely to be the end of the search process.

Second, a category-level analysis helps managers understand which and to what extent product attributes influence the contents of consumer product search. We provide several category-level insights, including the competitive product structure from the product positions, direction of consumer search from the product radii, and the effects of product attributes on the formation of the search map. In addition, the arrows in the product search map, resulting from the property fitting approach, depict the degree and direction of the influence of brands, media formats, and prices on the formation of consumer product search. Useful to marketing managers in the digital camcorder category is the finding that the intensity of consumer information search within the same media format is far greater than across media formats. We find that within the same media format, consumer search is more price driven than brand driven. Overall, we find that the role of brand is less significant. This finding is consistent with a recent, large-scale industry survey that reports the wavering power of brands in consumer electronics categories (Stewart-Allen/GMI Brand Barometer). This seems to be a finding with substantial implications in, for example, advertising content decisions. *Financial Times* recently quoted a Sony executive saying, "We cannot just rely on the brand to sell the product" in an article that reports Sony's planned attempt to shift its advertising strategy (Harding 2009). Our analysis using public data from 2006 shows signs that lead to a similar conclusion in the consumer electronics market.

Third, manufacturers can use the product search map to diagnose the performance of their product lines. For example, JVC has a MiniDV-based product offered at the retail price of $424 located at (17, 0, 0) in Figure 2. Judging from its isolated position on the map, JVC managers should infer that it is not searched frequently with other products and does not compete very effectively. The relative isolation of this JVC product is confirmed by the observation that the average distance between this specific JVC product and all other MiniDV-based products is 9.5, whereas the average distance among MiniDV-based products is 7.7. In turn, this information might cause JVC management to review its product to judge the efficacy of its positioning and viability. Last, we point out that as more online data are becoming available to practitioners and the marketing research community, well-tailored MDS techniques may prove to be useful exploratory tools to analyze and enhance understanding of brand search and consideration.

This study also has limitations, which may serve as further research opportunities. First, the collected data reflect the prepurchase browsing behavior of consumers, and thus the findings only apply to prepurchase stages of shopping behavior. However, given that subsets of searched products constitute consideration sets, from which final choices are made, our findings can be used with caution to infer mechanisms responsible for choice set generation in the digital camcorder category. Second, the nature of our data and model does not allow us to model consumer heterogeneity fully. Combining the current data with other sources, such as search frequency or choice data, may make such an investigation possible. We leave this for further research.

APPENDIX A

Part 1: Amazon.com's Aggregate-Level Product Search Data

According to Amazon.com's patent (Linden, Smith, and Zada 2005), the sequence of operations generating the product search data is as follows:

1. User clickstream or query log data that reflect products each user views during an ordinary browsing session are stored for a certain period. A product is shown to a shopper only if the corresponding product detail page is requested.
2. The normalized degree of relationship between two products is measured according to how frequently consumers view them together using $r_{jk} = (n_{jk}/\sqrt{n_j}\sqrt{n_k})$, where n_j is the number of consumers who searched product j and n_{jk} is the number of consumers who searched j and k.
3. The preceding measurement is repeated on all pairs of products.
4. For each focal product, related products are sorted in the order of a descending relationship.
5. Among the sorted products, products outside the focal product's category are removed from the list. Note that a category can be defined in several different ways at Amazon.com. We only collected search data in the camcorder industry for choice options for digital camcorders and analog camcorders based on the Hi8 medium.

6. The top M related products are extracted for each focal product.

Part 2: Illustration for Asymmetric Product Search Data

We illustrate the asymmetry in the product search data. Assume three products, A, B, and C, and the following numbers of consumers who viewed each product and pairs of products: $n_A = 20$, $n_B = 10$, $n_C = 10$, $n_{AB} = 5$, $n_{BC} = 3$, and $n_{AC} = 4$.

The relationships among the three products are computed as follows:

$$r_{AB} = \frac{n_{AB}}{\sqrt{n_A}\sqrt{n_B}} = .35, r_{BC} = \frac{n_{BC}}{\sqrt{n_B}\sqrt{n_C}} = .30, r_{AC} = \frac{n_{AC}}{\sqrt{n_A}\sqrt{n_C}} = .28.$$

Table A1 lists the related products for each product using the preceding computed quantities. The first column represents the focal products and the first row represents the related products. The number in parentheses is the order in which the products appear in the view list.

Now, we focus on the one product in each row that is most closely related to each focal product. Products A's, B's, and C's closest relationships are to products B, A, and B, respectively. Table A1 shows that the product pair (A, B) is symmetric because they have the closest relationship to each other. The pair (A, C) is also symmetric because B is the closest to both products. However, the pair (B, C) is asymmetric because A is closest to B but B is closest to C; they are not mutually closest. For product search data involving a large number of products, there will be symmetric as well as asymmetric pairs of products, reflecting complex consumer product search behaviors.

Table A1
ILLUSTRATION FOR ASYMMETRIC PRODUCT SEARCH DATA

Focal Products	A	B	C
A		.35 (1)	.28 (2)
B	.35 (1)		.30 (2)
C	.28 (2)	.30 (1)	

Part 3: Identification Restrictions

The identification restrictions for our three-dimensional model are as follows: We adopt the identification restrictions in MDS that Abe (1998), Elrod (1988), Erdem (1996), and Okada and Imaizumi (1987) outline. The main goal is to prevent translation, rotation, and refection of positions during the estimation process. The conditions are as follows:

1. One product located at (0, 0, 0).
2. One product located at (0, 0, R+).
3. One product located at (0, R+, R+).

Note that in a T-dimensional space, there are T degrees of freedom for translation, $T(T - 1)/2$ degrees of freedom for rotation, and T degrees of freedom for reflection. Therefore, for T = 3, we must apply nine constraints in total. In addition, to identify the radii, we set the radius of one product to a constant (Okada and Imaizumi 1987).

Part 4: Property Fitting

In this section, we discuss how we obtain the property fitting arrows in the product search maps in Figures 2, 3, and

4. After we estimate the product positions $\mathbf{Z}$, we regress each product attribute on the product positions,

$$X_k = \mathbf{Z}\beta_k + E,$$

where X_k is a $[J \times 1]$ vector for the kth attribute values (k = 1, ..., K) for J products; $\mathbf{Z}$ is a $[J \times P]$ matrix, with each product j's coordinates $[z_{j1}, ..., z_{jP}]$ on row j; β_k is a $[P \times 1]$ vector that measures the contribution of $\mathbf{Z}$ to X_k; and E is a $[J \times 1]$ vector of errors. In our empirical analysis, J = 62, P = 3, and K = 7. For each regression for k, we obtain R_k^2 and $\hat{\beta} = [\beta_{k,1}, \beta_{k,2}, \beta_{k,3}]$, which jointly determine the arrow in Figure 2. If the kth attribute values are well explained by $\mathbf{Z}$, we obtain a high R_k^2. To represent this scenario with a long arrow, we compute the arrow vector for the kth attribute as follows:

$$\left(R_k^2 \frac{\beta_{k,1}}{\sqrt{\beta_{k,1}^2 + \beta_{k,2}^2 + \beta_{k,3}^2}}, R_k^2 \frac{\beta_{k,2}}{\sqrt{\beta_{k,1}^2 + \beta_{k,2}^2 + \beta_{k,3}^2}}, \right.$$
$$\left. R_k^2 \frac{\beta_{k,3}}{\sqrt{\beta_{k,1}^2 + \beta_{k,2}^2 + \beta_{k,3}^2}} \right).$$

Note that the total length of this arrow is R_k^2 (as desired). We repeat this process for all k to construct the arrows shown in the map.

APPENDIX B

The following are the priors for the hypermodel parameters:

$$\beta_p \sim N\left(\beta_p^0, V_{\beta_p}^0\right), \sigma_p^2 \sim IG\left(\upsilon_p^0, s_p^0\right), V_z = \begin{bmatrix} \ddots & 0 & 0 \\ 0 & \sigma_p^2 & 0 \\ 0 & 0 & \ddots \end{bmatrix}, \text{ and}$$

$$\beta_r \sim N\left(\beta_r^0, V_{\beta_r}^0\right), \sigma_r^2 \sim IG\left(\upsilon_r^0, s_r^0\right).$$

Furthermore, we assume the following parameters for the priors K = 7; p = 1, ..., P; and P = 3:

$$\beta_p^0 = 0_K, V_{\beta_p}^0 = 10^6 I_K, \upsilon_p^0 = 4, s_p^0 = 1, \beta_r^0 = 0_K, V_{\beta_r}^0 = 10^6 I_K,$$

$$\upsilon_r^0 = 4, s_r^0 = 1.$$

Here, I_K represents an identity matrix of size $[K \times K]$, and 0_K is a vector $[K \times 1]$ of zeros. The following is the sequence for the Gibbs sampler:

Step 1. Draw β_p, p = 1, ..., P.

$$\beta_p | X, Z_p, \sigma_p^2, \beta_p^0, V_{\beta_p}^0$$

$$\sim N\left\{\left[\left(V_{\beta_p}^0\right)^{-1} + X'X\right]^{-1}\left[\left(V_{\beta_p}^0\right)^{-1}\beta_p^0 + X'Z_p\right], \left[\left(V_{\beta_p}^0\right)^{-1} + X'X\right]^{-1}\right\},$$

where $Z_p = [z_{1p}, ..., z_{Jp}]$ and X is a $[J \times K]$ matrix with each product j's attributes $X_j = [X_{j1}, ..., X_{jK}]$ on row j.

Step 2. Draw σ_p^2, p = 1, ..., P.

$$\sigma_p^2 | X, Z_p, \beta_p, \upsilon_p^0, s_p^0 \sim IG\left(\upsilon_p^0 + J, \frac{\upsilon_p^0 s_p^0 + J\bar{s}_p}{\upsilon_p^0 + J}\right),$$

where $Z_p = [z_{1p}, ..., z_{Jp}]'$ and $\bar{s}_p = (1/J)\Sigma_j(z_{jp} - X_j\beta_p)^2$.

Step 3. Draw β_r.

$$\beta_r | X, R, \sigma_r^2, \beta_r^0, V_{\beta_r}^0$$

$$\sim N\left\{\left[\left(V_{\beta_r}^0\right)^{-1} + X'X\right]^{-1}\left[\left(V_{\beta_r}^0\right)^{-1}\beta_r^0 + X'R\right], \left[\left(V_{\beta_r}^0\right)^{-1} + X'X\right]^{-1}\right\},$$

where $R = [r_1, ..., r_J]$.

Step 4. Draw σ_r^2.

$$\sigma_r^2 | X, R, \beta_r, \upsilon_r^0, s_r^0 \sim IG\left(\upsilon_r^0 + J, \frac{\upsilon_r^0 s_r^0 + J\bar{s}_r}{\upsilon_r^0 + J}\right),$$

where $\bar{s}_r = (1/J)\Sigma_j(r_j - X_j\beta_r)^2$.

Step 5. Draw z_j.

Product j's position is $z_j = [z_{j1}, ..., z_{jp}]$. The conditional posterior, K, for z_{jp} is

$$K\left(z_{jp} | Y, N_{rec}, I_{list}, Z_{-jp}, \{r_j\}, X_j, \beta_p, \sigma_p^2, \beta_{rec}, \beta_{list}\right)$$
$$\propto L\left(Y | N_{rec}, I_{list}, \{z_j\}, \{r_j\}, \beta_{rec}, \beta_{list}\right) \times p\left(z_{jp} | X_j, \beta_p, \sigma_p^2\right),$$

where $Z_{-jp} = \{z_j\} \backslash z_{jp}$, $Y = \{y_{jk}\}$, $N_{rec} = \{N_{jk}\}$, $I_{list} = \{I_{jk}\}$, and

$$L\left(Y | N_{rec}, I_{list}, \{z_j\}, \{r_j\}, \beta_{rec}, \beta_{list}\right)$$

$$= \prod_{j=1}^{J}\prod_{k \neq j}^{J} \Pr\left(y_{jk} = 1 | N_{rec}, I_{list}, z_j, z_k, r_j, r_k, \beta_{rec}, \beta_{list}\right),$$

$$p\left(z_{jp} | X_j, \beta_p, \sigma_p^2\right) = \phi\left(X_j\beta_p, \sigma_p^2\right),$$

where ϕ is the probability density function of the normal distribution. We draw from the posterior using a Metropolis–Hastings algorithm. We use a normal distribution as the proposal distribution, $p(z_{jp}'|z_{jp}) = \phi(z_{jp}, \sigma_z^2)$. We accept the candidate, z_{jp}', with the following acceptance probability:

$$\min\left[1, \frac{L\left(Y | N_{rec}, I_{list}, Z_{-jp}, z_{jp}', \{r_j\}, \beta_{rec}, \beta_{list}\right)}{L\left(Y | N_{rec}, I_{list}, Z_{-jp}, z_{jp}, \{r_j\}, \beta_{rec}, \beta_{list}\right)}\right.$$
$$\left. \times \frac{p\left(z_{jp}'|X_j, \beta_p, \sigma_p^2\right)}{p\left(z_{jp}|X_j, \beta_p, \sigma_p^2\right)} \times \frac{p\left(z_{jp}'|z_{jp}\right)}{p\left(z_{jp}|z_{jp}'\right)}\right].$$

Because ϕ is symmetric, the ratio $p(z_{jp}'|z_{jp})/p(z_{jp}|z_{jp}')$ is unity. Therefore, we can simplify the preceding acceptance probability as follows:

$$\min\left[1, \frac{L\left(Y | N_{rec}, I_{list}, Z_{-jp}, z_{jp}', \{r_j\}, \beta_{rec}, \beta_{list}\right)}{L\left(Y | N_{rec}, I_{list}, Z_{-jp}, z_{jp}, \{r_j\}, \beta_{rec}, \beta_{list}\right)}\right.$$
$$\left. \times \frac{p\left(z_{jp}'|X_j, \beta_p, \sigma_p^2\right)}{p\left(z_{jp}|X_j, \beta_p, \sigma_p^2\right)}\right].$$

Step 6. Draw r_j.

The conditional posterior for r_j is as follows:

$$K\left(r_j | Y, N_{rec}, I_{list}, \{z_j\}, R_{-j}, X_j, \beta_r, \sigma_r^2, \beta_{rec}, \beta_{list}\right)$$

$$\propto L\left(Y | N_{rec}, I_{list}, \{z_j\}, \{r_j\}, \beta_{rec}, \beta_{list}\right) \times p\left(r_j | X_j, \beta_r, \sigma_r^2\right),$$

where $R_{-j} = \{r_k\} \backslash r_j$ and $p(r_j | X_j, \beta_r, \sigma_r^2) = \phi(X_j \beta_r, \sigma_r^2)$.

We accept the candidate r_j' with the following acceptance probability:

$$\min\left[1, \frac{L\left(Y | N_{rec}, I_{list}, \{z_j\}, R_{-j}, r_j', \beta_{rec}, \beta_{list}\right)}{L\left(Y | N_{rec}, I_{list}, \{z_j\}, R_{-j}, r_j, \beta_{rec}, \beta_{list}\right)}\right.$$

$$\left. \times \frac{p\left(r_j' | X_j, \beta_r, \sigma_p^2\right)}{p\left(r_j | X_j, \beta_r, \sigma_p^2\right)} \times \frac{p\left(r_j' | r_j\right)}{p\left(r_j | r_j'\right)}\right],$$

where we use the normal distribution as the proposal distribution $p(r_j' | r_j) = \phi(r_j, \sigma_R^2)$. Because ϕ is symmetric, the ratio $p(r_j' | r_j)/p(r_j | r_j')$ is unity. Therefore, we can further simplify the acceptance probability as follows:

$$\min\left[1, \frac{L\left(Y | N_{rec}, I_{list}, \{z_j\}, R_{-j}, r_j', \beta_{rec}, \beta_{list}\right)}{L\left(Y | N_{rec}, I_{list}, \{z_j\}, R_{-j}, r_j, \beta_{rec}, \beta_{list}\right)} \times \frac{p\left(r_j' | X_j, \beta_r, \sigma_p^2\right)}{p\left(r_j | X_j, \beta_r, \sigma_p^2\right)}\right],$$

Step 7. Draw β_{rec}.

The conditional posterior for β_{rec} is as follows:

$$K\left(\beta_{rec} | Y, N_{rec}, I_{list}, \{z_j\}, \{r_j\}, \beta_{list}\right)$$

$$\propto L\left(Y | N_{rec}, I_{list}, \{z_j\}, \{r_j\}, \beta_{rec}, \beta_{list}\right) \times p\left(\beta_{rec}\right),$$

where $p(\beta_{rec})$ is the prior distribution for β_{rec}. We accept the candidate β_{rec}' with the following acceptance probability:

$$\min\left[1, \frac{L\left(Y | N_{rec}, I_{list}, \{z_j\}, \{r_j\}, \beta_{rec}', \beta_{list}\right)}{L\left(Y | N_{rec}, I_{list}, \{z_j\}, \{r_j\}, \beta_{rec}, \beta_{list}\right)}\right.$$

$$\left. \times \frac{p\left(\beta_{rec}'\right)}{p\left(\beta_{rec}\right)} \times \frac{p\left(\beta_{rec}' | \beta_{rec}\right)}{p\left(\beta_{rec} | \beta_{rec}'\right)}\right].$$

Because we assume a diffuse prior for $p(\beta_{rec})$ and the normal probability density function for the proposal distribution of $p(\beta_{rec}' | \beta_{rec})$, both ratios of $p(\beta_{rec}')/p(\beta_{rec})$ and $p(\beta_{rec}' | \beta_{rec})/ p(\beta_{rec} | \beta_{rec}')$ are unity. Therefore, we can simplify the preceding acceptance probability as follows:

$$\min\left[1, \frac{L\left(Y | N_{rec}, I_{list}, \{z_j\}, \{r_j\}, \beta_{rec}', \beta_{list}\right)}{L\left(Y | N_{rec}, I_{list}, \{z_j\}, \{r_j\}, \beta_{rec}, \beta_{list}\right)}\right].$$

Step 8. Draw β_{list}.

The conditional posterior for β_{list} is as follows:

$$K\left(\beta_{list} | Y, N_{rec}, I_{list}, \{z_j\}, \{r_j\}, \beta_{rec}\right)$$

$$\propto L\left(Y | N_{rec}, I_{list}, \{z_j\}, \{r_j\}, \beta_{rec}, \beta_{list}\right) \times p\left(\beta_{list}\right),$$

where $p(\beta_{list})$ is the prior distribution for β_{list}. We accept the candidate β_{list}' with the following acceptance probability:

$$\min\left[1, \frac{L\left(Y | N_{rec}, I_{list}, \{z_j\}, \{r_j\}, \beta_{rec}, \beta_{list}'\right)}{L\left(Y | N_{rec}, I_{list}, \{z_j\}, \{r_j\}, \beta_{rec}, \beta_{list}\right)}\right.$$

$$\left. \times \frac{p\left(\beta_{list}'\right)}{p\left(\beta_{list}\right)} \times \frac{p\left(\beta_{list}' | \beta_{list}\right)}{p\left(\beta_{list} | \beta_{list}'\right)}\right].$$

Because we assume a diffuse prior for $p(\beta_{list})$ and the normal probability density function for the proposal distribution of $p(\beta_{list}' | \beta_{list})$, both ratios of $p(\beta_{list}')/p(\beta_{list})$ and $p(\beta_{list}' | \beta_{list})/ p(\beta_{list} | \beta_{list}')$ are unity. Therefore, we can simplify the preceding acceptance probability as follows:

$$\min\left[1, \frac{L\left(Y | N_{rec}, I_{list}, \{z_j\}, \{r_j\}, \beta_{rec}, \beta_{list}'\right)}{L\left(Y | N_{rec}, I_{list}, \{z_j\}, \{r_j\}, \beta_{rec}, \beta_{list}\right)}\right].$$

REFERENCES

Abe, Makoto (1998), "Error Structure and Identification Condition in Maximum Likelihood Nonmetric Multidimensional Scaling," *European Journal of Operational Research*, 111 (2), 216–27.

Bajari, Patrick, Jeremy T. Fox, and Stephen P. Ryan (2008), "Evaluating Wireless Carrier Consolidation Using Semiparametric Demand Estimation," *Quantitative Marketing and Economics*, 6 (4), 299–338.

Bettman, James R. and C. Whan Park (1980), "Effects of Prior Knowledge and Experience and Phase of the Choice Process on Consumer Decision Analysis: A Protocol Analysis," *Journal of Consumer Behavior*, 7 (3), 234–48.

Bijmolt, Tammo and Michel Wedel (1999), "A Comparison of Multidimensional Scaling Methods for Perceptual Mapping," *Journal of Marketing Research*, 36 (May), 277–85.

Bodapati, Anand (2008), "Recommendation Systems with Purchase Data," *Journal of Marketing Research*, 45 (February), 77–93.

Bronnenberg, Bart J. and Wilfried R. Vanhonacker (1996), "Limited Choice Sets, Local Price Response, and Implied Measures of Price Competition," *Journal of Marketing Research*, 33 (May), 163–73.

Brynjolfsson, Erik, Astrid A. Dick, and Michael D. Smith (2004), "Search and Product Differentiation at an Internet Shopbot," working paper, Sloan School of Management, Massachusetts Institute of Technology.

Chiang, Jeongwen, Siddhartha Chibb, and Chakravarthi Narasimhan (1998), "Markov Chain Monte Carlo and Models of Consideration Set and Parameter Heterogeneity," *Journal of Econometrics*, 89 (1–2), 223–48.

DeSarbo, Wayne S. and Jaewun Cho (1989), "A Stochastic Multidimensional Scaling Vector Threshold Model for the Spatial Representation of 'Pick Any/n' Data," *Psychometrika*, 54 (1), 105–129.

———, Rajdeep Grewal, and Jerry Wind (2006), "Who Competes with Whom? A Demand-Based Perspective for Identifying and Representing Asymmetric Competition," *Strategic Management Journal*, 27 (2), 101–129.

——— and Donna L. Hoffman (1987), "Constructing MDS Joint Spaces from Binary Choice Data: A Multidimensional Unfolding Threshold Model for Marketing Research," *Journal of Marketing Research*, 24 (February), 40–54.

——— and K. Jedidi (1995), "The Spatial Representation of Heterogeneous Consideration Sets," *Marketing Science*, 14 (3), 326–42.

——— and Ajay K. Manrai (1992), "A New Multidimensional Scaling Methodology for the Analysis of Asymmetric Proximity Data in Marketing Research," *Marketing Science*, 11 (1), 1–20.

——— and V.R. Rao (1986), "A Constrained Unfolding Methodology for Product Positioning," *Marketing Science*, 5 (1), 1–19.

Elrod, Terry (1988), "Choice Map: Inferring a Product-Market Map from Panel Data," *Marketing Science*, 7 (1), 21–40.

Erdem, Tülin (1996), "A Dynamic Analysis of Market Structure Based on Panel Data," *Marketing Science*, 15 (4), 359–78.

Garfinkel, Robert, R.D. Gopal, Bhavik K. Pathak, Rajkumar Venkatesan, and Fang Yin (2006), "Empirical Analysis of the Business Value of Recommender Systems," working paper, School of Business, University of Connecticut.

Gilbride, Timothy J. and Greg M. Allenby (2004), "A Choice Model with Conjunctive, Disjunctive, and Compensatory Screening Rules," *Marketing Science*, 23 (3), 391–406.

Harding, Robin (2009), "Sony Retunes $5bn Ad Budget," *Financial Times*, (November 17), (accessed October 8, 2010), [available at http://www.ft.com/cms/s/2/0315c95c-d3a9-11de-8caf-00144feabdc0.html].

Hauser, John R. and Birger Wernerfelt (1990), "An Evaluation Cost Model of Consideration Sets," *Journal of Consumer Research*, 16 (4), 393–408.

Hoff, Peter D., Adrian E. Raftery, and Mark S. Handcock (2002), "Latent Space Approaches to Social Network Analysis," *Journal of the American Statistical Association*, 97 (Winter), 1090–1098.

Holman, E.W. (1979), "Monotonic Models for Asymmetric Proximities," *Journal of Mathematical Psychology*, 20 (1), 1–15.

Jedidi, Kamel and Wayne S. DeSarbo (1991), "A Stochastic Multidimensional Scaling Procedure for the Spatial Representation of Three-Mode, Three-Way Pick Any/J Data," *Psychometrika*, 56 (3), 471–94.

Kass, Robert E. and Adrian E. Raftery (1995), "Bayes Factors," *Journal of the American Statistical Association*, 90 (430), 773–95.

Krumhansl, Carol D. (1978), "Concerning the Applicability of Geometric Models to Similarity Data: The Interrelationship Between Similarity and Spatial Density," *Psychological Review*, 85 (5), 445–63.

Kruskal, Joseph B. and Myron Wish (1983), *Multidimensional Scaling*. Newbury Park, CA: Sage Publications.

Linden, Greg D., Brent R. Smith, and Nida K. Zada (2005), "Use of Product Viewing Histories of Users to Identify Related Products," U.S. Patent Number: 6,912,505 B2, filed March 29, 2001, and issued June 28, 2005.

Lynch, John G., Jr., and Dan Ariely (2000), "Wine Online: Search Costs Affect Competition on Price, Quality, and Distribution," *Marketing Science*, 19 (1), 83–103.

Mehta, Nitin, Surendra Rajiv, and Kannan Srinivasan (2003), "Price Uncertainty and Consumer Search: A Structural Model of Consideration Set Formation," *Marketing Science*, 22 (1), 58–84.

Moe, Wendy (2006), "An Empirical Two-Stage Choice Model with Varying Decision Rules Applied to Internet Clickstream Data," *Journal of Marketing Research*, 43 (November), 680–92.

Newman, Joseph W. and Bradley D. Lockeman (1975), "Measuring Prepurchase Information Seeking," *Journal of Consumer Research*, 2 (3), 216–22.

——— and Richard Staelin (1972), "Prepurchase Information Seeking for New Cars and Major Household Appliances," *Journal of Marketing Research*, 9 (August), 249–57.

Okada, Akinori and Tadashi Imaizumi (1987), "Nonmetric Multidimensional Scaling of Asymmetric Proximities," *Behaviormetrika*, 14 (21), 87–96.

Payne, John W. (1976), "Task Complexity and Contingent Processing in Decision Making: An Information Search and Protocol Analysis," *Organizational Behavior and Human Performance*, 16 (August), 366–87.

Roberts, John H. and James M. Lattin (1991), "Development and Testing of a Model of Consideration Set Composition," *Journal of Marketing Research*, 28 (November), 429–40.

Saburi, S. and N. Chino (2008), "A Maximum Likelihood Method for an Asymmetric MDS Model," *Computational Statistics and Data Analysis*, 52 (10), 4673–84.

Siddarth, S., Randolph E. Bucklin, and Donald G. Morrison (1995), "Making the Cut: Modeling and Analyzing Choice Set Restriction in Scanner Panel Data," *Journal of Marketing Research*, 32 (August), 255–66.

Shugan, Steven M. (1980), "The Cost of Thinking," *Journal of Consumer Research*, 7 (September), 99–111.

Stigler, George (1961), "The Economics of Information," *Journal of Political Economy*, 69 (3), 213–25.

Swait, Joffre and Tülin Erdem (2007), "Brand Effects on Choice and Choice Set Formation Under Uncertainty," *Marketing Science*, 26 (5), 666–78.

Urban, Glen L., John S. Hulland, and Bruce D. Weinberg (1993), "Premarket Forecasting for New Consumer Durable Goods: Modeling Categorization, Elimination, and Consideration Phenomena," *Journal of Marketing*, 57 (April), 47–63.

Wedel, Michel, and Wayne S. DeSarbo (1996), "An Exponential-Family Multidimensional Scaling Mixture Methodology," *Journal of Business & Economic Statistics*, 14 (4), 447–59.

Yee, Michael, Ely Dahan, John R. Hauser, and James Orlin (2007), "Greedoid-Based Noncompensatory Inference," *Marketing Science*, 26 (4), 532–49.

JAN-BENEDICT E.M. STEENKAMP, HARALD J. VAN HEERDE, and INGE GEYSKENS*

The growing sales of private labels (PLs) pose significant challenges for national brands (NBs) around the world. A major question is whether consumers continue to be willing to pay a price premium for NBs over PLs. Using consumer survey data from 22,623 respondents from 23 countries in Asia, Europe, and the Americas across, on average, 63 consumer packaged goods categories per country, this article studies how marketing and manufacturing factors affect the price premium a consumer is willing to pay for an NB over a PL. These effects are mediated by consumer perceptions of the quality of NBs in relation to PLs. Although the results do not bode well for NBs in the sense that willingness to pay decreases as PLs mature, the authors offer several managerial recommendations to counter this trend. In countries in which PLs are more mature, the route to success is to go back to manufacturing basics. In PL development countries, there is a stronger role for marketing to enhance the willingness to pay for NBs.

Keywords: willingness to pay, private labels, cross-continent survey, consumer packaged goods, marketing-mix effects

What Makes Consumers Willing to Pay a Price Premium for National Brands over Private Labels?

The growing sales of private labels (PLs) pose significant challenges for national brands (NBs) around the world. A global study conducted by ACNielsen (2005) reveals that the growth in PL market share outpaced that of NBs in three-quarters of the consumer packaged goods (CPG) categories studied. In the United States alone, in each year of the last decade (1998–2008), PLs grew faster than NBs. In light of the recent economic recession, the future looks even bleaker. Lamey and colleagues (2007) show that PL share increases when the economy is suffering and shrinks when the economy is flourishing. However, consumers switch more extensively to PLs during an economic downturn than they switch back to NBs in a subsequent recovery, permanently boosting PL share over a succession of business cycles.

To offset their sliding sales volumes, many NB manufacturers have begun to increase their price premiums over PLs. For example, Unilever has recently been increasing prices at record rates to compensate for a 2.4% drop in European sales volumes (*The Financial Times* 2009). Similarly, Kellogg, General Mills, and Heinz have implemented strong pricing increases in an attempt to retain or grow their profits despite drops in sales volumes attributable to PLs (Facenda 2008). Unfortunately, the pricing window that opened for many CPG firms before the recent "Great Recession" seems to be closing, leaving companies in a bind. Instead of compensating for falling sales volumes, "boosting prices further could drive consumers to buy even more private-label goods; reducing the companies' sales volume and squeezing their profit margins at the factory level by

*Jan-Benedict E.M. Steenkamp is C. Knox Massey Distinguished Professor of Marketing and Marketing Area Chair, Kenan-Flagler Business School, University of North Carolina at Chapel Hill (e-mail: JBS@unc. edu). Harald J. van Heerde is Professor of Marketing, Waikato Management School, University of Waikato, and Extramural Fellow at CentER, Tilburg University, the Netherlands (e-mail: heerde@waikato.ac. nz). Inge Geyskens is Professor of Marketing, Tilborg School of Economics and Management, Tilburg University (e-mail: I.Geyskens@uvt.nl). Order of authorship is arbitrary. The authors gratefully acknowledge AiMark for providing the data. They thank the Netherlands Organization for Scientific Research for financial assistance. They greatly appreciate the constructive comments of the anonymous *JMR* reviewers. They are also grateful for the excellent feedback from participants at the Marketing Science Conference (Vancouver, Canada), London Business School, INSEAD (France), Tilburg University (the Netherlands), Goethe University (Germany), Monash University (Australia), University of Sydney (Australia), and University of Technology Sydney (Australia). Pradeep Chintagunta served as associate editor for this article.

raising the cost of production per unit" (*The Wall Street Journal* 2009, p. B1).

Although academic research has provided useful insights to combat increasing PL sales, several gaps in our understanding have yet to be addressed. First, there is a dearth of research on whether and when consumers continue to be willing to pay a price premium for NBs over PLs (for an exception, see Sethuraman and Cole 1999). This is remarkable because the ability of NBs to charge a price premium has a strong impact on profitability (Marn, Roegner, and Zawada 2003). Second, although there has been a lot of research into the consumer-side factors that drive PL success (e.g., Ailawadi, Neslin, and Gedenk 2001; Erdem, Zhao, and Valenzuela 2004), supply-side factors, in particular marketing and manufacturing, have received far less attention (for two exceptions, see Dhar and Hoch 1997; Hoch 1996). Third, almost all the existing research has been conducted in countries in which PLs are highly developed. Although it is reasonable that researchers first focus on these markets to understand how NBs can fight PLs, it is paramount that we conduct research in countries with a more recent PL history. Because the economic and marketing environments of these countries are different from those of more developed PL countries, the best ways to fight PLs may also differ.

The purpose of this study is to advance the understanding of what drives consumers to pay a price premium for NBs over PLs. We accomplish this in two ways. First, we specify effects of marketing and manufacturing factors on consumers' willingness to pay (WTP) and posit that these effects are mediated by consumer perceptions of the quality of NBs in relation to PLs. Second, we explore the possibility that the efficacy of these marketing and manufacturing factors in fostering WTP depends on a country's stage of PL development. We estimate our model with dedicated consumer survey data from 22,623 respondents from 23 countries in Asia, Europe, and the Americas across, on average, 63 CPG categories per country.

CONCEPTUAL MODERATED-MEDIATION FRAMEWORK OF DRIVERS OF WTP

Our conceptual moderated-mediation framework considers the effects of marketing and manufacturing factors on the price premium a consumer is willing to pay for an NB over a PL. We posit that the effect of these factors on WTP is mediated by consumer perceptions of the quality of NBs in relation to PLs. We expect that the effect of the quality gap on WTP is systematically moderated by two consumer factors: the consumer's involvement with the category and the consumer's beliefs about the extent to which quality and price are related (price–quality schema). Involvement is a major general moderator of consumer decision processes (Assael 1998; Celsi and Olson 1988), while price–quality schema is a key price context–specific moderator, only implicated in price judgments related to perceived quality (Lichtenstein, Bloch, and Black 1988).

Our model also includes the stage a country is in with respect to the PL life cycle. The PL environment in several countries can be considered mature in that PLs have had a major presence for many decades. In other countries, PLs are in the development stage, with PLs being a much more recent phenomenon. Because PLs require extensive learning, by both retailers and consumers, we may expect systematic differences between countries that are in the PL development versus the PL maturity stage.

Figure 1 presents our moderated-mediation framework of the drivers of WTP. Subsequently, we discuss the conceptual rationale for the direction of the expected effects.

Marketing Drivers of Perceived Quality Gap

Product innovation. Introducing new and improved products underpins the quality gap between NBs and PLs. Retailers must manage many product categories and conse-

Figure 1
CONCEPTUAL FRAMEWORK

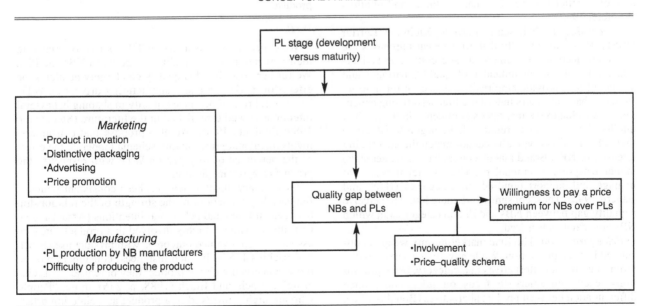

quently lack the technical and financial resources to be innovation leaders. Private labels overwhelmingly play a catch-up game, trying to copy the innovations that NBs introduce (Kumar and Steenkamp 2007). In some categories, the catch-up game is difficult to pull off because NBs actively compete by way of continuous and expensive investments in technical innovation. This puts PLs continuously at a distance, and consequently, comparative quality of PLs in these categories is lower. Conversely, if NBs fail to innovate, they lose the quality edge they typically have because it allows PLs to catch up.

Distinctive packaging. National brands try to increase the perceived quality gap not only through product innovation but also by distinctive packaging, a second essential element of an NB manufacturer's product strategy. Packaging plays a crucial role in consumers' perceptions of NBs and PLs because of (1) the large number of stockkeeping units (SKUs) in any retail store; (2) shelf layout, where competing SKUs are positioned next to each other; and (3) the limited amount of time consumers spend on each purchase decision (Kapferer 1995).

To understand the important role of packaging in shaping the perceived quality gap, we turn to perception theory. Two consumer characteristics are important in determining consumers' perceptions of stimuli: the propensity to generalize from one stimulus to another (i.e., to generalize from NBs to PLs) and the ability to discriminate between stimuli (i.e., to discriminate between NBs and PLs) (Assael 1998, pp. 211–17). If the packaging of the PL is similar to that of an NB, stimulus generalization is likely. The consumer will put the NB and the PL in the same perceptual category and will be prone to generalize perceived quality from the NB to the PL. Conversely, if the packaging of NBs is distinctive from the packaging of PLs, stimulus discrimination is more likely. In this case, the consumer is more likely to perceive a quality gap between NBs and PLs. Realizing the importance of these perceptual processes, NBs make a consistent effort to render their products' look and feel as distinct as possible from PLs, while PLs try to copy the packaging of NBs. Thus, it is not surprising that copycatting is an important area of conflict between NB manufacturers and retailers (Kapferer 1995).

Advertising. In their seminal article, Klein and Leffler (1981) derive analytically that after repeat purchases are taken into account, consumers can successfully use advertising intensity as an indicator of quality. Kirmani and Wright (1989) provide empirical evidence for this notion, showing that consumers indeed use high advertising expenditure as a clue to the marketer's confidence in the product quality. Although some retailers have begun to advertise their PLs, retailers typically cannot match the advertising intensity of NBs. Brand manufacturers have a greater stake in their categories than retailers do because retailers need to manage and support hundreds of categories (Hoch and Banerji 1993). Thus, consumers are more likely to perceive a quality gap between NBs and PLs in categories in which NBs are heavily advertised.

Price promotion. The final marketing-mix weapon considered is price promotion. While advertising serves to differentiate product alternatives in a category, price promotions teach consumers to focus on price and reduce differentiation between product alternatives (Boulding, Lee,

and Staelin 1994). Heavy price promotions cause product alternatives to be increasingly viewed as commodities purchased on the basis of price, with their distinctiveness subsequently diminished (Mela, Gupta, and Jedidi 1998). Thus, we expect that heavy price promotions in a category are associated with smaller perceived quality differences between NBs and PLs.

Manufacturing Drivers of Perceived Quality Gap

PL production by NB manufacturers. Despite the progress in PL quality over the last decades, there is still considerably more uncertainty about PL quality than there is about NB quality. Consumers realize that retailers usually do not manufacture their own PLs. In the United States alone, it has been estimated that more than half the NB manufacturers also engage in PL production. Consumer magazines and anecdotal wisdom regularly suggest that "all products come from the same factory." For example, consider a recent statement in *Consumer Reports* (2009, p. 16) that "[m]any big-name companies make their usual types of products for the stores." Indeed, well-known companies, such Alcoa, Bausch & Lomb, Del Monte, McCormick, and Heinz, engage in PL manufacturing (Kumar and Steenkamp 2007). To the extent that consumers believe that NB manufacturers produce PLs, the perceived quality gap between NBs and PLs is reduced.

Difficulty of producing the product. Conversely, consumers have no guarantee that the PL is indeed produced by a reputable NB manufacturer, because NB manufacturers are typically secretive about PL manufacturing, lest it reduces the equity of their own brands. This is an important issue for categories in which manufacturing sophistication is high. If consumers perceive that the product is difficult to make, this calls PL quality into question because consumers will not know whether the purveyor of the PL has mastered these difficulties. However, this matters less if the consumer believes that the product is easy to manufacture because, in this case, almost any manufacturer can deliver a PL of good quality. Thus, we expect that the perceived quality gap is greater in categories that are perceived as more difficult to produce.

WTP

We expect that consumers' WTP is strongly related to their perceptions of the quality gap between NBs and PLs. We further posit that this quality gap largely mediates the effects of marketing and manufacturing drivers on WTP. The central role of perceived quality in shaping behavioral intentions is well established in the literature (Steenkamp 1989; Zeithaml 1988). We also propose that consumers' involvement and price–quality schema moderate the effect of the perceived quality gap on WTP with respect to the product category in question.

Involvement. Involvement has been consistently identified as a key moderator of the strength of the relationship between attitudes and behavioral intentions (Assael 1998). Consumers who are highly involved in a product category associate highly valued outcomes with product use (Bloch and Richins 1983). In such instances, consumers will be more concerned with the product they purchase. As Lichtenstein, Bloch, and Black (1988, p. 246) argue, "People who are highly involved in a product associate important functional, social, and psychological outcomes with the product. Therefore, highly involved consumers care more about product quality." We expect that consumers who are more involved with a product category are more quality sensitive, and thus the quality gap has a larger effect on their WTP.

Price–quality schema. Consumers encounter vast amounts of quality information. Because of limited cognitive processing abilities, over time consumers develop a repertoire of abstract ideas or "schemas" about the working of the marketplace to process incoming information efficiently (Lichtenstein and Burton 1989). If consumers come to believe that quality is strongly associated with price, they may look for shortcuts in decision making and will be more likely to evoke what Peterson and Wilson (1985) call a "price–quality schema." Some consumers have a generalized price–reliance schema in that they equate higher quality with higher price, regardless of category. However, for most people, such schemas are product category specific (Peterson and Wilson 1985). People who have a stronger price–quality schema for a category will associate quality with price in that category, and thus their WTP is likely to be more strongly dependent on the perceived quality gap (Lichtenstein, Bloch, and Black 1988).

PL Life Cycle

Using the number of years PLs have been available in a country, we distinguish between two stages in the PL life cycle: development and maturity. There is no firm theory to guide us as to the likely differences between countries in the PL development versus the PL maturity stages on (interrelationships between) our constructs, but several plausible propositions can be developed. Our propositions draw on organizational learning theory (Vera and Crossan 2004) and consumer learning theory (Assael 1998). Learning theory posits that retailers (consumers) learn over time as they accumulate experiences with PLs, adjusting their strategies (perceptions) while absorbing feedback about past decisions. Moreover, for our propositions, we draw on the notion that PLs were introduced much earlier in mature economies in North America and Western Europe than in developing economies in Latin America, Eastern Europe, and the Asia-Pacific region. Because the economic and marketing environment of emerging countries is still different from that of mature economies (Burgess and Steenkamp 2006), this will also contribute to systematic differences in our model constructs. Comparing model results between PL development and PL maturity stages is of interest in its own right but also enables us to peer into the future. International product life-cycle theory (Kotabe and Helsen 2004) suggests that by comparing countries cross-sectionally on key model parameters along this implicit time dimension, we can make informed estimates about the future of PLs in countries with a more recent PL history.

Differences in levels of constructs across PL stages. Developing high-quality PLs takes time, and it takes even longer before consumers perceive changes in quality (Mitra and Golder 2006). Therefore, we expect the perceived quality gap between NBs and PLs to be smaller in countries in which PLs are in the maturity stage than in countries in which PLs are still in the development stage. Furthermore, while detailed product information from external sources is not easily available in PL development countries, in (highly developed) PL maturity countries, such information is readily available from several sources, such as *Consumer Reports* (Zhou, Su, and Bao 2002). Few things undermine price–quality schemas more than press reports stating that "private label beats national brand," "switching to store brands can be a painless way to cut your grocery bill," "good products do not have to be expensive," and "the leading national brands are losing their focus on quality" (all taken from various consumer test magazines; e.g., *Consumer Reports* 2009). Formalizing this anecdotal evidence, Apelbaum, Gerstner, and Naik (2003) study the objective quality of NBs and PLs as published in *Consumer Reports*. They find that in more than one of four CPG categories, the average PL was actually higher in objective quality than the average NB. Because these findings are likely to undermine consumers' beliefs about price–quality associations, we propose that consumers in PL maturity countries possess a weaker price–quality schema than consumers in PL development countries.

Private label maturity countries have a longer history of PL success in many categories, which can undermine consumer beliefs about the manufacturing edge of NBs. After all, how can PLs be successful over such a long period unless the category is easy to make (Aaker and Keller 1990) or unless NB manufacturers engage in PL manufacturing (Kumar and Steenkamp 2007)? These beliefs are also undermined by consumer magazine reports that PLs beat NBs on quality and that PLs are produced by NB manufacturers. Thus, we expect that consumers in PL maturity countries have weaker beliefs about the difficulty of making a category and have stronger beliefs that PLs are produced by NB manufacturers.

Differences in structural relationships between constructs across PL stages. We theorize that marketing efforts by NBs will be more important in shaping the perceived quality gap and WTP in PL development countries. This expectation is informed by the notion that the effectiveness of marketing investments will be larger in emerging markets because these countries have a much shorter history of heavy marketing, and consequently, there is more scope to build awareness and cognitions (Burgess and Steenkamp 2006). Moreover, the PL maturity countries of North America and Western Europe are postmodern societies (Inglehart and Welzel 2005) in which marketing is increasingly viewed with skepticism (Ritzer 2004). In PL maturity countries, the route to success might be going back to manufacturing basics (Slater 1997): Who produces the PL, and how difficult is that process?

METHOD

Data Collection

We calibrate our model on a data set that is unique in size and scope. We collected survey data in close collaboration with the global market research agencies TNS and GfK. Respondents in 23 countries from four continents completed the questionnaires: the United States (North America), Argentina and Brazil (Latin America), Austria, Belgium, Denmark, France, Germany, Italy, the Netherlands, Norway, Portugal, Spain, Sweden, Switzerland, the United Kingdom (Western Europe), Croatia, the Czech Republic, Hungary, Poland, Slovakia (Eastern Europe), Taiwan, and

Thailand (Asia). For countries with a high penetration of the Internet, we used a Web survey. In other countries, we used mall intercepts, using the same questionnaire layout. The questionnaire was developed in English and was translated into all local languages using the back-translation method. Modifications were made based on discussions among back-translators, authors, and headquarters of the market research agencies to maintain consistency across all countries.

Respondents were people who were primarily responsible for grocery purchases in their households and who at least occasionally patronized stores that sell NBs and PLs. They indicated how often they made a purchase in each of ten randomly drawn product categories. Respondents evaluated up to four product categories that were randomly drawn from a subset of the selected ten categories in which the respondents bought at least once every six months. We provided the respondents with definitions and examples of leading PLs and NBs to ensure consistency among respondents about what these terms mean (Ailawadi, Neslin, and Gedenk 2001). These examples were provided by the local subsidiaries of TNS and GfK and were checked by their headquarters. The final section recorded sociodemographics. The samples in each country were drawn to be broadly representative of the total population in terms of region, age, education, and gender.

A total of 22,623 respondents completed questionnaires. The number of product categories evaluated per country varied between 28 (Taiwan) and 100 (the United Kingdom), averaging 63 categories. The product categories were selected to cover a wide range of CPGs. On average, 52 respondents supplied data on each product category in each country, resulting in 74,314 observations.

Measurement

Table 1 provides the measures and sources for all variables and the mean reliability across countries, wherever applicable. We use the percentage price premium as a measure of the price premium consumers are willing to pay for NBs over PLs. This measure is comparable across consumers, categories, and countries and is easily interpretable for the respondents. Palmatier, Scheer, and Steenkamp (2007) also successfully use this measure. The assumption underlying this measure is that consumers consider percentage price differences rather than absolute differences (Monroe 1973). We obtained quality gap scores by subtracting the PLs' quality scores from the NBs' quality scores (Erdem, Swait, and Valenzuela 2006). The perceived quality gap ranges from –4 ("PLs much better than NBs") to +4 ("NBs much better than PLs").

Note that we include four sociodemographic variables (gender, household size, education, and social class), three product category dummies (beverages, household care, and personal care, with food as the baseline category), and gross domestic product (GDP) per capita to control for differences across consumers, categories, and countries. These covariates are not the focus of our study, but controlling for their effects provides a stronger test of our hypotheses (Greene 2000).

Validation

WTP. TNS and GfK conducted pretests in Germany and the United Kingdom to assess the validity of our WTP measure. Data were collected among approximately 1000

consumers per country, for 57 (Germany) and 52 (United Kingdom) CPG categories. Respondents evaluated up to 4 CPG categories on WTP. TNS and GfK also provided the actual price premium NBs command in the marketplace, based on their household scanner panels. The actual price premium is unlikely to correspond closely to the price premium consumers are on average willing to pay. After all, the actual price gap in a category is set by retailers that have multiple goals in mind, including generating store traffic, maintaining store image, building loyalty, stimulating PL sales, and maximizing profitability (Ailawadi and Keller 2004). Nevertheless, our survey measure showed significant convergent validity with the actual price premium in the market, the correlation being .50 ($p < .01$) in Germany and .42 ($p < .01$) in the United Kingdom.

Covariates. To allow for a stringent test of convergent and discriminant validity, we included all category-level constructs in a single confirmatory factor model, pooling data across countries and product categories. Although the chi-square was highly significant ($\chi^2(57) = 8208.3$, $p < .001$), other indicators suggested good fit: comparative fit index = .98, Tucker–Lewis index = .95, and root mean square error of approximation = .04. All indicators loaded significantly ($p < .001$) and substantively (standardized factor loadings exceeded .60) on their hypothesized factors. Moreover, all correlations between constructs were significantly below unity. These findings provide evidence of the convergent and discriminant validity of the measures.

We measured product innovation, advertising, and price promotion using consumer perceptions (Table 1). This enables us to differentiate the intensity of these marketing instruments experienced by individual consumers. Some consumers may be exposed to more advertising messages, promotions, or product innovations for a category than others, depending on their media and shopping behavior. To validate consumer perceptions, GfK and TNS provided market data for several categories and four countries (France, Germany, Spain, and the United Kingdom). Data were provided for the year before the survey on (1) the number of new SKUs introduced into a category relative to the total number of SKUs in that category, (2) advertising expenditures in the category, and (3) the proportion of volume sold on promotion in the category. We correlated aggregate category perceptions with these objective category data. The results appear in Table 2. All correlations were significant at $p < .05$ or better, attesting to the validity of our perceptual measures.

Estimation

Our conceptual model involves variables at three levels of aggregation: the individual level (all focal constructs), the category level (the three category dummies), and the country level (GDP per capita). The levels are hierarchical in that $i = 1, ..., n_{jk}$ individuals are nested within $j = 1, ..., J_k$ categories, which in turn are nested within each of $k = 1, ..., K$ countries. To calibrate our conceptual model, we estimate a hierarchical linear model using maximum likelihood.

Following Raudenbush and Bryk's (2002) recommendations, we centered the continuous Level 1 predictors within categories and countries, and we grand-mean-centered the Level 3 predictor (GDP per capita). Our hierarchical linear model assumes that the Level 1 error term u_{ijk} is normally distributed with zero mean and variance σ^2, the Level 2

Table 1

VARIABLES AND DATA SOURCES

Construct	Operationalization[a]	Data Source
WTP	"In the category X, how much more are you willing to pay for a brand compared to a shop's own label?" 0% (nothing), 10% more, 20% more, 30% more, 40% more, 50% more, 75% more, 100% more (twice as much), more than 100% (more than twice as much). The latter category was recoded to 125%.	Adapted from Palmatier, Scheer, and Steenkamp (2007)
Perceived quality gap	"In the category X, the quality of brands is very high." "In the category X, the quality of shops' own labels is very high." We obtained quality gap scores by subtracting the PLs' quality scores from the NBs' quality scores.	Erdem, Swait, and Valenzuela (2006)
Marketing Factors		
Product innovation ($\bar{\alpha} = .84$)	"In the category X, new products are frequently introduced." "There are many new product introductions in category X."	Own development
Distinctive packaging ($\bar{\alpha} = .60$)	"On the shelf of category X, I cannot tell a shop's own label from a brand as packages are very similar." (R) "In the category X, shops' own labels and brands look very similar." (R)	Own development
Advertising ($\bar{\alpha} = .86$)	"Brands in the category X are heavily advertised in magazines, radio, or TV." "There is a lot of advertising for brands in the category X."	Yoo, Donthu, and Lee (2000)
Price promotion ($\bar{\alpha} = .74$)	"There is always a special offer in category X." "It is easy to find a special offer in category X."	Yoo, Donthu, and Lee (2000)
Manufacturing Factors		
PL production by NB manufacturers	"In the category X, shops' own labels are produced by brand manufacturers."	Own development
Difficulty of producing the product	"In the category X, making good quality products is difficult."	Adapted from Aaker and Keller (1990)
Moderators		
Involvement ($\bar{\alpha} = .83$)	"The category X is very important to me." "The category X interests me a lot."	Zaichkowsky (1985)
Price–quality schema ($\bar{\alpha} = .76$)	"In the category X, higher priced products provide better quality than lower priced products." "In the category X, the higher the price for a product, the higher the quality of the product."	Lichtenstein and Burton (1989)
PL life-cycle stage	Dummy: 1 = PL maturity stage (countries in which PLs were introduced before 1980), and 0 = PL development stage (countries in which PLs were introduced after 1985). Countries classified in the PL maturity stage include Austria, Belgium, Brazil, Denmark, France, Germany, Italy, the Netherlands, Norway, Spain, Sweden, Switzerland, the United Kingdom, and the United States. Countries classified in the PL development stage include Argentina, Croatia, the Czech Republic, Hungary, Poland, Portugal, Slovakia, Taiwan, and Thailand.	GfK/TNS
Control Variables		
Gender	"What is your gender?" Dummy: 1 = men, and 0 = women.	GfK/TNS
Household size	"What is the size of your household? Please count all persons (adults as well as children) that live in your household at least four days per week, including yourself."	GfK/TNS
Education	"Which of these best describes your highest level of education?" 1 = "no formal education," 2 = "education up to age 12," 3 = "up to age 14," 4 = "up to age 16," 5 = "up to age 18," 6 = "higher education," and 7 = "university."	GfK/TNS
Social class	"If people in our society are divided into upper, upper-middle, middle, lower-middle, working, and lower classes, which class do you think you belong to?" (1 = "lower class," 2 = "working class," 3 = "lower-middle class," 4 = "middle class," 5 = "upper-middle class," and 6 = "upper class"). Operationalized as a dummy variable, which equals 1 if a consumer's social class is higher than the country median and 0 if otherwise.	GfK/TNS
GDP per capita	GDP per capita in thousands of U.S. dollars.	World Bank

[a]With the exception of WTP, PL life-cycle stage, and the control variables, we scored all items using a five-point scale with the following categories: "strongly disagree," "disagree," "neither agree nor disagree," "agree," and "strongly agree."

Notes: (R) = reverse coded.

Table 2

VALIDATION OF MARKETING MEASURES

	Product Innovation		Advertising		Price Promotion	
	Correlation (Perceptions, Objective Data)[a]	Number of Categories	Correlation (Perceptions, Objective Data)	Number of Categories	Correlation (Perceptions, Objective Data)	Number of Categories
France	.55***	51	.59***	53	.43**	51
Germany	.34**	59	.55**	31	.59***	59
Spain	.47**	41	.53***	41	.47**	41
United Kingdom	.31*	52	.46***	51	.74***	52

*$p < .05$.
**$p < .01$.
***$p < .001$.
[a]Perceptions are averaged across consumers within a category.

error terms u_{pjk} (for coefficient p) are multivariate normally distributed over categories with zero mean and variance–covariance matrix T_2 (with $var[u_{pjk}] = \tau_{pp}$ and $cov[u_{pjk}, u_{p'jk}] = \tau_{p,p'}$), and the Level 3 error terms u_{pk} are multivariate normally distributed with zero mean and variance–covariance matrix T_3. We allowed the effects of the predictor variables involved to vary across categories and countries. We constrained the effects of the control variables to be constant across countries (no random-error terms included at Levels 2 and 3 for these coefficients). Although all coefficients could be specified as random effects, Raudenbush and Bryk caution against such practice because it negatively affects model convergence and stability of the parameter estimates.

RESULTS

Overall Descriptive Findings

Figure 2 reports WTP averaged across categories within countries expressed as an index (United States = 100;

Figure 2

WTP AND PL SHARE AROUND THE WORLD

adjusted for differences in sociodemographic makeup and categories included in the country samples) versus the market share of PLs in that country. Willingness to pay is higher in the United States than in most other developed markets. This reflects the historically strong position of NB manufacturers in the United States compared with retailers. While most U.S. retailers operate at a regional level, brand manufacturers operate at a national level. This creates a relative disadvantage for U.S. retailers because brand manufacturers benefit from "greater national brand economies of scale in both production and advertising" (Hoch 1996, p. 94).

We expect that, in general, PLs command higher market shares in countries and categories in which WTP for NBs is lower. Figure 2 reveals that, indeed, PL share and WTP are negatively related at the country level. We also correlated PL share and WTP at the category level, by pooling across categories and countries; this yielded N = 1335 observations. The resultant correlation is −.36 (p < .001). Without suggesting a causal relation, both country- and category-level analyses show that WTP is inversely related to PL share.

The average quality gap (on a scale from −4 to +4) is only .34, with only 39% of the observations showing a quality advantage for NBs. In 43% of the cases, consumers see no quality gap between NBs and PLs, while in 18%, consumers perceive PLs to be of better quality than NBs. This provides evidence for the remarkable strides PLs have made in reducing the perceived quality gap with NBs. Although there is a lack of a generalized substantial quality advantage for NBs, there is large heterogeneity among consumers: The standard deviation in quality gap perceptions is a high 1.13, with a coefficient of variation of 3.32.

Perceived Quality Gap

Turning first to the analysis pooled across PL life-cycle stages, we show the effects of the marketing and manufacturing drivers on the perceived quality gap between NBs and PLs in Table 3. We report unstandardized parameter estimates. In multilevel analysis, standardized coefficients are not used because the variance is partitioned across different levels.

As we expected, product innovation ($\beta = .04$, $p < .001$), distinctive packaging ($\beta = .23$, $p < .001$), and advertising ($\beta = .09$, $p < .001$) increase the perceived quality gap, while price promotions reduce it ($\beta = -.05$, $p < .001$). Our expectations pertaining to the manufacturing drivers are also confirmed by the data. When consumers believe that NB manufacturers produce PLs, the perceived quality gap with NBs is reduced ($\beta = -.15$, $p < .001$). Conversely, when consumers believe that the product category is difficult to manufacture, the perceived quality gap is higher ($\beta = .05$, $p < .01$). Thus, we find strong evidence that marketing and manufacturing factors systematically affect the perceived quality gap between NBs and PLs.

WTP

Table 3 also shows the effect of the perceived quality gap on WTP, which we hypothesized to be moderated by involvement and price–quality schema. The perceived quality gap is positively related to WTP ($\beta = 2.43$, $p < .001$). As we expected, consumers who are more involved with a category ($\beta = .37$, $p < .001$) and posses a stronger price–quality schema for a particular category ($\beta = .97$, $p < .001$) draw more heavily on the quality gap in forming their WTP.

Table 3
OVERALL MODEL ESTIMATION RESULTS

	Quality Gap		WTP	
	Estimate	t-Value	Estimate	t-Value
Intercept	.30	6.44***	10.07	22.22***
Product innovation	.04	4.42***		
Distinctive packaging	.23	12.78***		
Advertising	.09	7.73***		
Price promotion	−.05	−4.61***		
PL production by NB manufacturers	−.15	−9.26***		
Difficulty of producing the product	.05	3.34**		
Quality gap			2.43	13.72***
Involvement			1.76	12.36***
Quality gap × involvement			.37	4.88***
Price–quality schema			3.47	19.97***
Quality gap × price–quality schema			.97	6.64***
Control Variables				
Gender	−.01	−.66	.12	.99
Household size	−.01	−4.05***	.10	2.50*
Education	−.01	−2.44*	.87	16.97***
Social class	.05	11.63***	.32	5.35***
Beverages	.14	8.12***	2.66	11.73***
Personal care	.17	11.00***	2.41	11.38***
Household care	−.01	−.69	−.37	−1.54
GDP per capita	−.00	−.68	−.13	−6.18***
2 × log-likelihood	−110,151.1		−306,128.6	

*p < .05.
**p < .01.
***p < .001.

In addition to their interactive effect with the quality gap, involvement and price–quality schema also have a positive main effect on WTP (involvement: $\beta = 1.76$, $p < .001$; price–quality schema: $\beta = 3.47$, $p < .001$). In conditions of high involvement, consumers are willing to pay more for NBs over PLs. Similarly, when consumers believe that paying more brings them greater quality in return, they view price in a more favorable light and are willing to pay more for NBs.

Test of Mediation

The model depicted in Figure 1 suggests that the perceived quality gap mediates the effects of marketing and manufacturing drivers on WTP. We use Baron and Kenny's (1986) sequential procedure to test the mediating effect of perceived quality gap. In the first stage, we regress WTP on all the antecedent variables (marketing and manufacturing factors) with the proposed mediator (perceived quality gap) excluded from the model. In the second stage, we include the quality gap in the model to assess whether its insertion reduces the effects of the antecedents on WTP. Mediation occurs if the effects of the antecedents on WTP are reduced in the presence of the mediator and overall fit is improved. Both conditions are met, as we show in Table 4. When we add the quality gap to the model, the effects of all marketing and manufacturing drivers are significantly reduced (all Sobel test statistics are significant at the .05 level or better). Moreover, model fit improves significantly ($\Delta\chi^2(5) = 5002.2$, $p < .001$).

The mediating role of the perceived quality gap can be further examined by evaluating the relative magnitude of the indirect effect of an antecedent to its total effect.[1] The right-hand side of Table 4 shows that the ratio of the mediated effect to the total effect ranges between 27.1% (distinctive packaging) and 72.3% (PL production by NB manufacturers) for consumers with average involvement and price–quality schema scores. On average, the perceived quality gap mediates 57.2% of the effects of the marketing and manufacturing drivers on WTP. Collectively, we find strong support for the mediating role of the perceived quality gap.

PL Life Cycle

Differences in levels of constructs across PL stages. Table 5 compares the construct means (adjusted for differences in sociodemographic makeup and categories included in the country samples) across the PL development and PL maturity stages. As we expected, the quality gap between NBs and PLs is smaller in countries in the PL maturity versus PL development stage (.26 versus .53, $p < .05$). Furthermore, consumers in PL maturity countries have weaker price–quality schemas (2.88 versus 3.22, $p < .05$) and weaker beliefs about the difficulty of making the product (2.59 versus 2.86, $p < .05$) than consumers in PL development countries. Surprisingly, the perception that PLs are produced by NB manufacturers is equally strong in both stages ($p > .05$).

Examining the differences for which we had no specific expectations, we find that consumers in countries in the PL development stage are more involved with CPG product

---

[1]A problem arises when direct and indirect effects differ in sign because the proportion can be greater than one or even negative. A solution that Alwin and Hauser (1975) propose is to take the absolute values of the quantities when computing the percentage mediated.

Table 4

MODEL ESTIMATION RESULTS: THE MEDIATING ROLE OF THE PERCEIVED QUALITY GAP

	Total Effect on WTP		Direct Effect on WTP		Indirect Effect on WTP
	Estimate	t-Value	Estimate	t-Value	% Mediation[a]
Intercept	10.10	23.28***	9.83	22.38***	
Product innovation	.95	6.73***	.29	2.67*	69.5%
Distinctive packaging	3.17	10.50***	2.31	9.14***	27.1%
Advertising	1.13	10.49***	.50	4.90***	55.8%
Price promotion	.30	1.35	−.16	−1.09	46.7%
PL production by NB manufacturers	−.94	−4.72***	−.26	−2.26*	72.3%
Difficulty of producing the product	1.07	5.41***	.30	2.37*	72.0%
Quality gap			2.05	12.72***	
Involvement			1.59	10.97***	
Quality gap × involvement			.33	4.09***	
Price–quality schema			3.46	17.24***	
Quality gap × price–quality schema			.81	5.64***	
Control Variables					
Gender	.16	1.19	.27	2.19*	
Household size	.04	1.06	.11	2.89**	
Education	.72	13.33***	.78	15.46***	
Social class	.72	11.39***	.35	5.94***	
Beverages	2.80	11.70***	2.50	11.17***	
Personal care	2.73	12.24***	2.41	11.56***	
Household care	−.57	−2.25*	−.45	−1.89	
GDP per capita	−.08	−3.09**	−.13	−6.66***	
2 × log-likelihood	−310,232.7		−305,230.5		

*$p < .05$.
**$p < .01$.
***$p < .001$.
[a]The mediated effect as a proportion of the total effect, for consumers with average involvement and price–quality schema scores.

Table 5

DESCRIPTIVE STATISTICS: CONSTRUCT MEANS ACROSS PL STAGES

| | | Mean Score | | |
	Expectation Relative to PL Maturity Stage	PL Development Stage	PL Maturity Stage	Significantly Different? (p < .05)
Quality gap	Larger in the PL development stage	.53	.26	Yes
Price–quality schema	Larger in the PL development stage	3.22	2.88	Yes
PL production by NB manufacturers	Smaller in the PL development stage	3.13	3.24	No
Difficulty of producing the product	Larger in the PL development stage	2.86	2.59	Yes
Involvement		3.40	3.20	Yes
Product innovation		3.36	3.25	Yes
Distinctive packaging		3.21	3.37	Yes
Advertising		3.53	3.46	No
Price promotion		3.26	3.22	No
WTP		12.79	10.56	Yes

categories than consumers in the PL maturity stage (3.40 versus 3.20, $p < .05$). In terms of the marketing drivers, consumers do not perceive differences in the level of advertising and price promotion across the two stages ($p > .05$). However, consumers in countries in the PL development stage perceive more product innovations in the category than consumers in countries in the PL maturity stage (3.36 versus 3.25, $p < .05$). Conversely, in PL maturity countries, consumers rate NBs higher on distinctive packaging (3.37 versus 3.21, $p < .05$). Finally, WTP is higher in the PL development stage than in the PL maturity stage (12.79 versus 10.56, $p < .05$). Thus, the more mature PLs are, the less consumers are willing to pay a price premium for NBs over PLs. To understand why this is the case, we now turn to an analysis in which we test whether the effects of the

antecedents of WTP differ for countries in the PL development stage compared with countries in the PL maturity stage.

Differences in structural relationships between constructs across PL stages. We first estimated a model in which we let PL stage interact with each of the focal independent variables. In a second step, we retained only the significant interaction effects with PL stage.[2] The results are intriguing (see Table 6).

The effects of the drivers of the perceived quality gap differ substantially across the two PL stages. More specifically,

---

[2]No substantive differences occurred between the model that included all interaction effects and the model in which we retained only the significant interactions. For ease of interpretation, we only report the latter.

Table 6

MODEL ESTIMATION RESULTS ACROSS PL STAGES

| | Quality Gap | | WTP | |
	PL Development Stage	PL Maturity Stage	PL Development Stage	PL Maturity Stage
Intercept	.29***		9.80***	
Product innovation	.04***			
Distinctive packaging	.29***	.09***		
Advertising	.11***	.07***		
Price promotion	−.05***			
PL production by NB manufacturers	−.12***	−.17***		
Difficulty of producing the product	.05***			
Quality gap			2.42***	
Involvement			1.77***	
Quality gap × involvement			.36***	
Price–quality schema			3.05***	3.73***
Quality gap × price–quality schema			.98***	
Control Variables				
Gender	−.01		.12	
Household size	−.01***		.10*	
Education	−.01*		.87***	
Social class	.05***		.32***	
Beverages	.14***		2.66***	
Personal care	.17***		2.42***	
Household care	−.01		−.37	
GDP per capita	.01**		−.10***	
2 × log-likelihood	−110,144.9		−306,124.6	

*$p < .05$.
**$p < .01$.
***$p < .001$.
Notes: Coefficients that differ between the two stages are significantly different at $p = .05$.

we find that the effects of distinctive packaging and advertising on the perceived quality gap between NBs and PLs are significantly larger in the PL development stage than in the PL maturity stage ($p < .05$). We found no significantly different effects on the perceived quality gap for the other two marketing drivers (product innovation and price promotion), though the effects were in the same direction (stronger effects in the PL development stage). Thus, there is evidence that marketing efforts (in particular, distinctive packaging and advertising) play a larger role in enhancing quality gap perceptions in countries with a more recent PL history than in countries with a longer PL history.

With respect to the manufacturing factors, the findings reverse. The belief that PLs are produced by NB manufacturers plays a significantly larger role in reducing the perceived quality gap in the PL maturity stage than in the PL development stage ($p < .05$). Thus, although there is no difference in the mean levels of the extent to which consumers in the different PL stages believe that PLs are produced by NB manufacturers, the detrimental effect of this belief on WTP is much stronger in countries with a longer PL history. Although the belief that producing good-quality products is difficult had a larger detrimental effect on the perceived quality gap in the PL maturity stage than in the PL development stage, the difference was not significant ($p > .05$).

Collectively, the manufacturing factors explain about twice as much of the Level 1 variance in the quality gap in the PL maturity stage than in the PL development stage (4.2% compared with 2.2%), whereas the Level 1 variance explained by the marketing drivers is approximately 25% lower in the PL maturity stage than in the PL development stage (5.6% compared with 7.4%). Thus, "marketing" matters more when PLs are a relatively recent phenomenon, whereas "manufacturing" matters more when PLs are more established.

If we turn to the WTP regression, we find that the perceived quality gap affects WTP equally strongly in the PL development and the PL maturity stage. However, the average perceived quality gap is larger in the PL development stage (Table 5). Thus, as far as the main effect is concerned, the larger perceived quality gap (rather than a difference in quality sensitivity) represents the reason for the higher WTP in the PL development stage. Involvement and price–quality schema enhance the effect of the quality gap to the same extent across stages.

The direct effect of price–quality schema on WTP differs significantly across the two stages: Its effect is larger in PL maturity countries ($\beta = 3.73$, $p < .001$) than in PL development countries ($\beta = 3.05$, $p < .001$). However, the net effect on WTP is counterbalanced by the lower average levels of price–quality schema in PL maturity countries. Thus, in PL maturity countries, on average, consumers have weaker beliefs about price–quality associations, but when these beliefs strengthen, the effect on WTP is stronger than for consumers in PL development countries.

For both PL stages, the perceived quality gap significantly mediates the effect of marketing and manufacturing factors on WTP. The mediational role of the quality gap works out differently in the two PL stages because the marketing and manufacturing drivers differentially affect the quality gap across the stages. In summary, marketing is more effective to increase consumers' WTP for NBs in PL

development than in PL maturity countries. In contrast, manufacturing beliefs about PLs play a larger role in PL maturity than in PL development countries.

DISCUSSION

We develop a model of the price premium consumers are willing to pay for NBs over PLs. We estimate our WTP model on a unique data set, collected among 22,623 respondents from 23 countries on four continents. In general, WTP is inversely related to PL success across categories and countries. We find systematic effects of marketing and manufacturing factors on the perceived quality gap and WTP and document the pivotal moderating role of price–quality schema and involvement. We compare the model components along two stages of the PL life cycle. Whereas the perceived quality gap exerts an equally strong influence in countries in both stages of the PL life cycle, the antecedents of the perceived quality gap differ significantly across the two stages. In countries in the PL development stage—the engine of future growth of NBs—marketing (especially advertising and distinctive packaging) is more effective in increasing the perceived quality gap between NBs and PLs than in countries in the PL maturity stage. In contrast, in countries in the PL maturity stage, there is a need to go back to manufacturing basics. In particular, the belief that PLs are produced by NB manufacturers exerts a stronger (negative) influence on the perceived quality gap than in PL development countries.

Managerial Implications

As we discussed previously, to compensate for falling sales volumes, many NB manufacturers have begun increasing their prices. Can brand managers uphold their price premiums in relation to PLs, despite sliding sales volumes and recessionary markets? We believe that they can, but the challenges are somewhat different in different regions of the world, depending on their stage of PL development.

Marketing factors. The starting point of any turnaround strategy is to embark on a program of significant quality improvement, in both PL development and PL maturity countries. It is worrisome that objective tests reveal that there is often little, if any, quality difference between PLs and NBs (Apelbaum, Gerstner, and Naik 2003), and we find that, on average, the perceived quality gap is small too. We show that product innovation significantly increases the perceived quality gap (regardless of the country's PL life-cycle stage), which in turn leads to a higher WTP. Consumer packaged goods companies need not only rely on major new product innovations; even minor innovations can contribute to NB success (Gielens and Steenkamp 2007).

We further document the key role of advertising in enhancing the perceived quality gap and WTP, both in PL maturity countries and even more so in PL development countries. It is well known that advertising is especially effective in combination with new product launches. Thus, it is worrisome that in recessionary times, when NBs are already under pressure, companies cut back on advertising and innovation activity (Axarloglou 2003; Deleersnyder et al. 2009). A cost-effective option is to run a collective advertising campaign, such as the campaign run by the Austrian Association of Brand Manufacturers (which includes companies such as Mars and Procter & Gamble as members) with the slogan "*Die Marke Garantiert den Unterschied*" ["The Brand Guarantees the Difference"]. The motivation for this campaign was that "many consumers think that PLs and NBs are actually the same product, only in different packaging" (Österreichischer Verband der Markenartikelindustrie 2004). The campaign has since been adopted by several other national associations of brand manufacturers in Europe.

Distinctive packaging is the strongest driver of the perceived quality gap and has a strong direct effect on WTP. Unfortunately, copycatting of NBs is rampant. At the 2009 Benelux Branding Congress, Sara Lee's vice president of legal affairs sharply criticized copycatting practices by PLs (Kist 2009). However, criticism is not enough. Historically, NB manufacturers have been reluctant to vigorously challenge PL copycatting for two reasons: First, how do they sue their own customers? Second, will an aggressive stance result in products being removed from the shelves of the retailer in question? Our results indicate that a timid response is no longer tenable—the effect of distinctive packaging is too strong to ignore. Brand manufacturers need to develop a reputation for aggressively pursuing retail copycat violators. The experience of companies such as Coca-Cola, Unilever, Procter & Gamble, and Kraft shows that actively pursuing any trademark and package infringement can be effective in the fight against copycatting (Kumar and Steenkamp 2007).

Heavy price promotions condition consumers to focus primarily on price and dilute the perceived quality gap between PLs and NBs, regardless of the PL stage. Thus, we document a third jeopardy of price promotions: Not only do price promotions make consumers more price sensitive (e.g., Mela, Gupta, and Lehmann 1997) and lower baseline sales (e.g., Jedidi, Mela, and Gupta 1999), but they also decrease the WTP for NBs over PLs (this study). Thus, another managerial lever to increase the perceived quality gap and, therefore, WTP is to decrease the intensity of price promotions. Our contrasting findings for advertising and price promotions show that a shift in promotion budgets from price promotions to advertising is necessary. This is exactly the opposite of current NB practice.

Manufacturing factors. Our study shows that for countries in the PL maturity stage, the marketing mix is still effective in increasing the perceived quality gap, but it is less effective than in PL development countries. This attests to the notion that marketing is increasingly viewed with skepticism in these countries. If this trend continues, marketers will have a difficult time fighting PLs with the traditional marketing instruments. Instead, our results suggest that they should pay more attention to the manufacturing side of the story.

National brand managers in PL maturity countries should counter consumer belief that PLs are produced by NB manufacturers. This belief is likely to become more widespread as consumers become more connected to each other through online networks. As a case in point, German consumers share their production beliefs and knowledge on sites such as http://www.discounter-archive.de. The most straightforward way to counter this belief is to not embark on producing PLs or to stop producing PLs. Several NBs, such as Tylenol and Pledge, have chosen to stay away from manufacturing PLs and have communicated this to consumers. Tylenol runs television advertisements in which

employees make the following promise: "We don't make store brand pain relievers. We make Tylenol." Pledge announces on its packaging in red bold capital letters that "This formula is not sold to any retailer as a store brand." However, these are exceptions rather than the rule. Most NBs that do not engage in PL production provide this information in fine print, if at all. However, NBs need to be much more explicit if they want to fight consumer perceptions that PLs are produced by NB manufacturers.

Another manufacturing factor that enhances the quality gap and WTP is consumer belief that the production of the product category is difficult, regardless of the PL life-cycle stage. Advertisements that stress the amount of knowledge that goes into producing good quality products may enhance this belief and create the basis to charge a price premium. The Dutch beer manufacturer Grolsch used to run television advertisements that showed the craftsmanship required in many different professions (e.g., making musical instruments) and, by projection, in brewing good beer. Product harm crises might also be used to NBs' advantage. Recently, several PL products containing acetaminophen were recalled. In response, Tylenol ran advertisements to reassure consumers that it was not involved in the recall and that "Tylenol products are safe and manufactured with the highest quality standards."

Consumer factors. For countries in either PL stage, strengthening consumers' price–quality schema and involvement renders the quality gap much more effective in terms of WTP. Continuous quality improvement is a prerequisite for consumers to maintain their price–quality schema for the category. Advertising messages may reinforce the idea that good quality is worth a higher price. For example, television commercials for Procter & Gamble's Dreft (a detergent for washing dishes by hand) show that though the product costs more than its unbranded rival, it also lasts much longer.

Increasing the personal relevance of the category (involvement) can also make a difference. Although relevance resides in consumers' minds, companies can work to create emotional bonds with consumers, even in mundane categories such as breadcrumbs and canned beans (Fournier 1998). Traditional advertising plays an important role in increasing the personal relevance of the category, but new forms of communication, such as buzz marketing, can also be fruitfully employed, as shown, for example, by Red Bull in the energy drink market.

Further Research

Our study has several limitations that offer opportunities for further research. We measured product innovation, advertising, and price promotion using survey data because we were unable to acquire advertising and promotion expenditures and numbers of new product introductions for all countries and categories. Further research should replicate our findings using objective measures.

Another data limitation is that countries in the PL development stage also tend to be countries in which Western NBs were introduced later than in countries in the PL maturity stage. As such, this reduces our ability to disentangle the effect of the number of years PLs have been available in a country and the number of years Western NBs have been available. In addition, we measure PL stage at the country level. TNS and GfK considered it infeasible to collect reliable and valid data on the exact start date of PLs across 1454 country–category pairs. As a result, our PL stage variable may contain some measurement error. The results for error-in-variable models (Greene 2000, p. 378) suggest that our significant effects of PL stage represent a conservative test of the true effects. Further research could attempt to collect information on PL introduction dates in specific categories for perhaps one country with a long PL presence. We focus on the generic battle between NBs and PLs rather than on specific NBs or particular PLs. It would be worthwhile to study the drivers of WTP for individual NBs and contrast them with specific PLs.

Consumers may engage in trading up in one category and trading down in another (Silverstein and Fiske 2003). Our study design does not lend itself well to study this aspect of WTP, because each consumer rated four categories at most. Further research might be able to develop an advanced imputation scheme to combine the information across all consumers to understand how trading up and down actually works out.

In summary, although our results do not bode well for NBs in the sense that WTP decreases as PLs mature, we offer several managerial recommendations to counter this trend. In PL maturity countries, the route to success is to go back to manufacturing basics. In PL development countries, marketing has a stronger role. We hope that this study will be useful to managers across the globe and will spark additional research on the epic battle between NBs and PLs.

REFERENCES

Aaker, David A. and Kevin L. Keller (1990), "Consumer Evaluations of Brand Extensions," *Journal of Marketing*, 54 (January), 27–41.

ACNielsen (2005), *The Power of Private Label 2005: A Review of Growth Trends Around the World.* New York: ACNielsen.

Ailawadi, Kusum L. and Kevin L. Keller (2004), "Understanding Retail Branding: Conceptual Insights and Research Priorities," *Journal of Retailing*, 80 (Winter), 331–42.

———, Scott A. Neslin, and Karen Gedenk (2001), "Pursuing the Value-Conscious Consumer: Store Brands Versus National Brand Promotions," *Journal of Marketing*, 65 (January), 71–89.

Alwin, Duane F. and Robert M. Hauser (1975), "The Decomposition of Effects in Path Analysis," *American Sociological Review*, 40 (1), 37–47.

Apelbaum, Eidan, Eitan Gerstner, and Prasad A. Naik (2003), "The Effects of Expert Quality Evaluations Versus Brand Name on Price Premiums," *Journal of Product and Brand Management*, 12 (2–3), 154–65.

Assael, Henry (1998), *Consumer Behavior and Marketing Action*, 5th ed. Cincinnati: South-Western College Publishing.

Axarloglou, Kostas (2003), "The Cyclicality of New Product Introductions," *Journal of Business*, 76 (January), 29–48.

Baron, Reuben M. and David A. Kenny (1986), "The Moderator-Mediator Variable Distinction in Social Psychological Research: Conceptual, Strategic, and Statistical Considerations," *Journal of Personality and Social Psychology*, 51 (6), 1173–82.

Bloch, Peter H. and Marsha L. Richins (1983), "A Theoretical Model for the Study of Product Importance Perceptions," *Journal of Marketing*, 47 (Summer), 69–81.

Boulding, William, Eunkyu Lee, and Richard Staelin (1994), "Mastering the Mix: Do Advertising, Promotion, and Sales Force Activities Lead to Differentiation," *Journal of Marketing Research*, 31 (May), 159–72.

Burgess, Steven M. and Jan-Benedict E.M. Steenkamp (2006), "Marketing Renaissance: How Research in Emerging Consumer Markets Advances Marketing Science and Practice," *International Journal of Research in Marketing*, 23 (December), 337–56.

Celsi, Richard L. and Jerry C. Olson (1988), "The Role of Involvement in Attention and Comprehension Processes," *Journal of Consumer Research*, 15 (September), 210–24.

Consumer Reports (2009), "It Pays to Buy Store Brands," (October), 16–20.

Deleersnyder, Barbara, Marnik G. Dekimpe, Jan-Benedict E.M. Steenkamp, and Peter S.H. Leeflang (2009), "The Role of National Culture in Advertising's Sensitivity to Business Cycles: An Investigation Across Continents," *Journal of Marketing Research*, 46 (October), 623–36.

Dhar, Sanjay and Stephen Hoch (1997), "Why Store Brand Penetration Varies by Retailer," *Marketing Science*, 16 (3), 208–227.

Erdem, Tülin, Joffre Swait, and Ana Valenzuela (2006), "Brands as Signals: A Cross-Country Validation Study," *Journal of Marketing*, 70 (January), 34–49.

———, Ying Zhao, and Ana Valenzuela (2004), "Performance of Store Brands: A Cross-Country Analysis of Consumer Store-Brand Preferences, Perceptions, and Risk," *Journal of Marketing Research*, 41 (February), 86–100.

Facenda, Vanessa (2008), "Why Commodity Inflation Helps CPGs," *Brandweek*, (February 25), 4.

The Financial Times (2009), "Unilever Faces Removal from Delhaize Shelves," (February 10), [available at http://www.ft.com/home/us].

Fournier, Susan (1998), "Consumers and Their Brands: Developing Relationship Theory in Consumer Research," *Journal of Consumer Research*, 24 (March), 343–73.

Gielens, Katrijn and Jan-Benedict E.M. Steenkamp (2007), "Drivers of Consumer Acceptance of New Packaged Goods: An Investigation Across Products and Countries," *International Journal of Research in Marketing*, 24 (June), 97–111.

Greene, William (2000), *Econometric Analysis.* Upper Saddle River, NJ: Prentice Hall.

Hoch, Stephen J. (1996), "How Should National Brands Think About Private Labels?" *Sloan Management Review*, 37 (Winter), 89–102.

——— and Shumeet Banerji (1993), "When Do Private Labels Succeed?" *Sloan Management Review*, 34 (Summer), 57–67.

Inglehart, Ronald and Christian Welzel (2005), *Modernization, Cultural Change, and Democracy.* New York: Cambridge University Press.

Jedidi, Kamel, Carl F. Mela, and Sunil Gupta (1999), "Managing Advertising and Promotion for Long-Run Profitability," *Marketing Science*, 18 (1), 1–22.

Kapferer, Jean-Noel (1995), "Stealing Brand Equity: Measuring Perceptual Confusion Between National Brands and 'Copycat' Own-Label Products," *Marketing and Research Today*, 23 (May), 96–103.

Kirmani, Amna and Peter Wright (1989), "Money Talks: Perceived Advertising Expense and Expected Product Quality," *Journal of Consumer Research*, 16 (December), 344–53.

Kist, Bas (2009), "Echt, Net Echt of Bijna Namaak" ["Real, Apparently Real or Nearly Fake"], *NRC Handelsblad*, (May 12), 18.

Klein, Benjamin and Keith B. Leffler (1981), "The Role of Market Forces in Assuring Contractual Performance," *Journal of Political Economy*, 89 (4), 615–41.

Kotabe, Masaaki and Kristiaan Helsen (2004), *Global Marketing Management*, 3d ed. New York: John Wiley & Sons.

Kumar, Nirmalya and Jan-Benedict E.M. Steenkamp (2007), *Private Label Strategy.* Cambridge, MA: Harvard Business School Press.

Lamey, Lien, Barbara Deleersnyder, Marnik G. Dekimpe, and Jan-Benedict E.M. Steenkamp (2007), "How Business Cycles Contribute to Private Label Success: Evidence from the United States and Europe," *Journal of Marketing*, 71 (January), 1–15.

Lichtenstein, Donald R., Peter H. Bloch, and William C. Black (1988), "Correlates of Price Acceptability," *Journal of Consumer Research*, 15 (September), 243–52.

——— and Scot Burton (1989), "The Relationship Between Perceived and Objective Price–Quality," *Journal of Marketing Research*, 26 (November), 429–43.

Marn, Michael V., Eric V. Roegner, and Craig C. Zawada (2003), "The Power of Pricing," *McKinsey Quarterly*, 1, 27–36.

Mela, Carl F., Sunil Gupta, and Kamel Jedidi (1998), "Assessing Long-Term Promotional Influences on Market Structure," *International Journal of Research in Marketing*, 15 (2), 89–107.

———, ———, and Donald R. Lehmann (1997), "The Long-Term Impact of Promotion and Advertising on Consumer Brand Choice," *Journal of Marketing Research*, 34 (May), 248–61.

Mitra, Debanjan and Peter N. Golder (2006), "How Does Objective Quality Affect Perceived Quality? Short-Term Effects, Long-Term Effects, and Asymmetries," *Marketing Science*, 25 (3), 230–47.

Monroe, Kent B. (1973), "Buyers' Subjective Perceptions of Price," *Journal of Marketing Research*, 10 (February), 70–80.

Österreichischer Verband der Markenartikelindustrie (2004), "Die Marke Garantiert den Unterschied," memo, Vienna, Austria.

Palmatier, Rob, Lisa K. Scheer, and Jan-Benedict E.M. Steenkamp (2007), "Customer Loyalty to Whom? Managing the Benefits and Risks of Salesperson-Owned Loyalty," *Journal of Marketing Research*, 44 (May), 185–99.

Peterson, Robert A. and William R. Wilson (1985), "Perceived Risk and Price-Reliance Schema," in *Perceived Quality*, Jacob Jacoby and Jerry C. Olson, eds. Lexington, MA: Heath, 247–68.

Raudenbush, Stephen W. and Anthony S. Bryk (2002), *Hierarchical Linear Models: Applications and Data Analysis Methods*, 2d ed. Newbury Park, CA: Sage Publications.

Ritzer, George (2004), *The McDonaldization of Society*. Thousand Oaks, CA: Pine Forge Press.

Sethuraman, Raj and Catherine Cole (1999), "Factors Influencing the Price Premiums that Consumers Pay for National Brands over Store Brands," *Journal of Product and Brand Management*, 8 (August), 340–51.

Silverstein, Michael J. and Neil Fiske (2003), "Luxury for the Masses," *Harvard Business Review*, 81 (4), 47–57.

Slater, Don (1997), *Consumer Culture and Modernity*. Cambridge, UK: Polity Press.

Steenkamp, Jan-Benedict E.M. (1989), *Product Quality*. Assen, the Netherlands: Van Gorcum.

Vera, Dusya and Mary Crossan (2004), "Strategic Leadership and Organizational Learning," *Academy of Management Journal*, 29 (2), 222–40.

The Wall Street Journal (2009), "Store Brands Squeeze Big Food Firms: After Profiting From Higher Prices, ConAgra and Other Makers Are Rethinking Strategy as Volume Falls," (March 27), B1.

Yoo, Boonghee, Naveen Donthu, and Sungho Lee (2000), "An Examination of Selected Marketing Mix Elements and Brand Equity," *Journal of the Academy of Marketing Science*, 28 (2), 195–211.

Zaichkowsky, Judith L. (1985), "Measuring the Involvement Construct," *Journal of Consumer Research*, 12 (December), 341–52.

Zeithaml, Valarie A. (1988), "Consumer Perceptions of Price, Quality, and Value: A Means–End Model and Synthesis of Evidence," *Journal of Marketing*, 52 (July), 2–22.

Zhou, Kevin Zheng, Chenting Su, and Yeqing Bao (2002), "A Paradox of Price-Quality and Market Efficiency: A Comparative Study of the U.S. and China Markets," *International Journal of Research in Marketing*, 19 (4), 349–65.

MICHAEL TRUSOV, ANAND V. BODAPATI, and RANDOLPH E. BUCKLIN*

The success of Internet social networking sites depends on the number and activity levels of their user members. Although users typically have numerous connections to other site members (i.e., "friends"), only a fraction of those so-called friends may actually influence a member's site usage. Because the influence of potentially hundreds of friends needs to be evaluated for each user, inferring precisely who is influential—and, therefore, of managerial interest for advertising targeting and retention efforts—is difficult. The authors develop an approach to determine which users have significant effects on the activities of others using the longitudinal records of members' log-in activity. They propose a nonstandard form of Bayesian shrinkage implemented in a Poisson regression. Instead of shrinking across panelists, strength is pooled across variables within the model for each user. The approach identifies the specific users who most influence others' activity and does so considerably better than simpler alternatives. For the social networking site data, the authors find that, on average, approximately one-fifth of a user's friends actually influence his or her activity level on the site.

Keywords: Internet, social networking, Bayesian methods

Determining Influential Users in Internet Social Networks

In 1995, when the first notable social networking (SN) Web site, Classmates.com, was launched, few might have guessed that 15 years later, SN sites would have tens of millions of users and would be valued at billions of dollars. Currently, SN sites attract more than 90% of all teenagers and young adults in the United States and have a market of approximately 80 million members. The cover of *Business-Week* magazine's issue dated December 12, 2005, suggests that the next generation of Americans could be called the MySpace generation. Emphasizing the importance of SN to marketing, the Marketing Science Institute (2006) designated "The Connected Customer" as its top research priority.

The core of an SN site is a collection of user profiles (Figure 1) where registered members can place information that they want to share with others. For the most part, users are involved in two kinds of activities on the site: Either they create new content by editing their profiles (e.g., adding pictures, uploading music, writing blogs and messages), or they consume content that others create (e.g., looking at pictures, downloading music, reading blogs and messages). On most SN sites, users can add other users to their networks of "friends." Usually, one user initiates the invitation, and the other user accepts or rejects it. When accepted, the two profiles become linked.

The most popular SN site business model is based on advertising. As users surf through a site, advertisements are displayed on the Web pages delivered to the users. Social networking firms earn revenue from either showing advertisements to site visitors (impressions) or being paid for each click/action taken by site visitors in response to an advertisement. Consequently, user involvement with a site (e.g., time spent on the site, number of pages viewed, amount of personal information revealed) directly translates into firm revenue. Social networking firms have commonly used members' profile information for ad targeting purposes.

*Michael Trusov is Assistant Professor of Marketing, Robert H. Smith School of Business, University of Maryland (e-mail: mtrusov@rhsmith. umd.edu). Anand V. Bodapati is Associate Professor of Marketing (e-mail: anand.bodapati@anderson.ucla.edu), and Randolph E. Bucklin is Peter W. Mullin Professor (e-mail: rbucklin@anderson.ucla.edu), Anderson School of Management, University of California, Los Angeles. The authors are grateful to Christophe Van den Bulte and Dawn Iacobucci for their insightful and thoughtful comments on this work. John Hauser served as associate editor for this article.

© 2010, American Marketing Association
ISSN: 0022-2437 (print), 1547-7193 (electronic)

Journal of Marketing Research
Vol. XLVII (August 2010), 643–658

THE ROLE OF USERS IN USER-GENERATED CONTENT ENVIRONMENTS

At SN sites, the content is almost entirely user generated. To attract traffic, an SN firm itself cannot do much beyond periodic updates of site features and design elements. The bulk of digital content—the driving force of the site's vitality and attractiveness—is produced by its users. However, users are not all created equal. Community members differ widely in terms of the frequency, volume, type, and quality of digital content generated and consumed. From a managerial perspective, understanding who keeps the SN site attractive—specifically, identifying users who influence the site activity of others—is vital. Such understanding permits more precise ad targeting as well as retention efforts aimed at sustaining and/or increasing the activity of influential existing users (and, therefore, future ad revenue).

The importance of identifying influential users on an SN site has been recently highlighted by Google's efforts to improve ad targeting at MySpace.com. Apparently disappointed with the returns from its recent deal to place advertising on MySpace.com, Google is developing algorithms to improve the identification of influential users (Green 2008). The idea is to target advertisements at site members who get the most attention, not simply those with certain characteristics in their profiles. Ad buyers have indicated that they would pay premium rates for this type of influence-based targeting. Google has filed a patent application, having apparently adapted its PageRank algorithm to the problem (Green 2008). The financial implications of improved ad targeting are significant because display ad pricing varies widely with audience attractiveness. For example, Walsh (2008) reports cost per thousand impressions varying from \$.05 to \$.80 or more.

Our objective is to develop and test a methodology to identify influential users in online social networks on the basis of a simple metric of their activity level. In this article, we consider a user "influential" in a social network if his or her activity level, as captured by site log-ins over time, has a significant effect on others' activity levels and, consequently, on the site's overall page view volume. An example of this type of influence is given by Holmes (2006), who reports that when a popular blogger left his blogging site for a two-week vacation, the site's visitor tally fell, and content produced by three invited substitute bloggers could not stem the decline.

EMPIRICAL INFERENCE OF SITE USAGE INFLUENCE

Most existing studies on social influence adopt a survey approach. Although questionnaires may work well for small groups, for an online community with millions of members, surveys are problematic. Fortunately, in computer-mediated environments, users' online activities can be tracked and recorded. The model we develop infers site usage influence from secondary data on member log-in activity. It can be easily extended to other online activity measures that are potentially available to SN site managers, such as the amount of time spent on the Web site and the number of messages sent. In this study, we use the number of log-ins per day as an effective correlate for these other measures.

Our approach is based on the following logic: Users log in to the site to consume new digital content that other users produce. From the traces others leave (e.g., the last log-in date and time, time-stamped content updates), users can infer how active a specific person has been on the site and update their expectations for future activity. Logging in is more attractive when a user expects that there is likely to be new content to view. Accordingly, we propose that a member's site usage level at each point is driven by his or her expectation about the volume and update frequency of relevant new content created by others. User expectations are formed from recent experiences. For example, if, for the past few log-in occasions, the user observed an increase in volume and/or update frequency of new content, he or she might choose to wait less time before logging in again.

In our data set, which comes from a major SN site, we tracked daily log-in activities of anonymous community members, treating the frequency of log-ins as a proxy for usage. A higher number of log-ins per day is taken to be a sign of higher usage, while a lower number of log-ins implies lower usage. In addition, because both processes—content consumption and content creation—constitute site usage, we assume that during high-usage days, the user has more opportunities to produce more content than during low-usage days. We can use the data to ascertain the effect of any change in a user's behavior (either increasing or decreasing usage) on the behavior of those linked to him or her. If a member increases his or her usage and the people connected also increase their usage (possibly because of their interest in what this person is creating), we propose that this identifies this person as influential. Conversely, if a member's usage goes up or down and usage does not change among the people connected to him or her, we propose that this person is not influential.

With the data and this notion of influence, we attempt to identify users whose behavior on the site has the most significant impact on the behavior of others in the network. Note that this formalization of "influence" fits well with the firm's business objectives. Managers need to know who stimulates activity levels among other members of the network. As expected, our empirical results show significant heterogeneity among users on two dimensions: susceptibility to influence from other users and the extent of influence on others in the network. The findings indicate that social influence in an online community is similar to what, according to studies in sociology, is experienced offline. The average user is influenced by relatively few other network members and, in turn, influences few people. In addition, having many friends (i.e., linked profiles) does not make users influential per se.

The problem of identifying influential users with site activity data is difficult because the data are typically sparse relative to the number of effects that need to be evaluated. Thus, simple approaches to effects estimation do not do well (as we demonstrate subsequently). A common way to address the sparse number of individual-level observations in, for example, UPC (Universal Product Code) scanner panel data is to use Bayesian shrinkage, in which strength is pooled across panelists. This approach is grounded on the

assumption that the effect of a certain variable (e.g., price) for a given panelist is related to the effect of the same variable on other panelists. Unfortunately, we cannot use this type of Bayesian shrinkage here because the variable set differs across users. At an SN site, each user has a unique set of friends, potentially hundreds, and it is the friends' activity levels that make up the variable set. To accommodate this, we propose to use a different type of Bayesian shrinkage in which strength is pooled across variables within an individual rather than across individuals.

We organize the rest of this article as follows: In the next section, we provide a brief overview of the study context and introduce key terminology. Then, we touch on two streams of related literature: social influence and online communities. We continue with a description of the proposed method, model formulation, and empirical estimation on field data from an SN site. Next, using simulated data, we assess the ability of our model to recover true levels of user influence. We then discuss managerial implications and illustrate the potential financial benefits of applying the approach versus some naive methods. We conclude with a summary, limitations, and directions for further research.

THE STUDY CONTEXT AND KEY TERMINOLOGY

A profile holder at an SN site can acquire new friends by browsing and searching the site and sending requests to be added as a friend. The resulting "friendship" network can be represented by a connected, undirected graph with binary edges. As an example, we focus on a specific person in a hypothetical network, Allison (Figure 2). Allison's ego-centered network is a network of her friends. In Figure 2, Panel A, the friends (the people with whom Allison has exchanged invitations) are Kate, Alberto, Rene, John, Stan, Bret, Ana, and Gert. Among these friends, there are just a few who actually make the site attractive to Allison. From Allison's perspective, these are "important" friends. She comes back to the site looking for new content produced by them, while tending to ignore updates in other connected profiles. She also updates her profile and posts new content motivated by the expectation that her important friends will view these updates. In turn, from the perspective of some of her friends, Allison also might be important. It is possible that some of Allison's friends are regularly checking for content she produces or are motivated to contribute new content in the hope that Allison will view it. In this sense, Allison's online activity influences their behavior. The goal in this study is to develop a method to estimate the extent and the direction of the influence associated with each edge in the graph.

The study of relationships among interacting units is a cornerstone of social network analysis (SNA)—a set of theories and methods that enable the analysis of social structures; these methods are specifically geared toward an investigation of the relational aspects of these structures (Scott 1992).[1] Usually, the importance of an individual actor (in this case, a community member) can be inferred from his or her location in the network (e.g., Iacobucci 1990, 1998; Iacobucci and Hopkins 1992). On most SN sites, the network is based on friendship, or links established through exchange of electronic invitations. Because these links are easily observable by the firm, it might be tempting to apply SNA to infer a person's importance. This would likely

---

[1]For a broad overview of SNA applications in marketing, see Iacobucci (1996) and Van Den Bulte and Wuyts (2007).

Figure 2
INFERRING A USER'S INFLUENCE

A: Allison's Ego-Centered Network of Friends

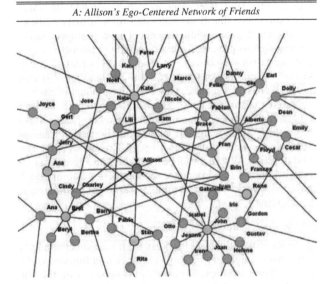

B: Allison's Network of Influence

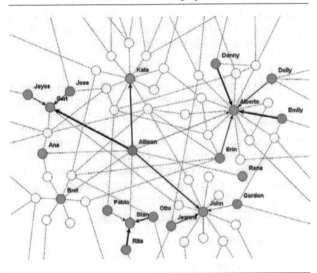

on site usage. Therefore, a better input for SNA techniques would be a network in which the link from Actor A to Actor B has a weight proportional to User A's influence on User B's site usage. Our approach is intended to infer such a network. We can then use SNA tools to evaluate a person's importance in this influence-based network, in addition to, or in place of, a person's importance based on, for example, network connections and nonconnections alone.

LITERATURE

Social influence occurs when a person adapts his or her behavior, attitudes, or beliefs to the behavior, attitudes, or beliefs of others in the social system (Leenders 2002). Social influence has been the subject of more than 70 marketing studies since the 1960s. Overall, scholarly research on social and communication networks, opinion leadership, source credibility, and diffusion of innovations has long demonstrated that consumers influence other consumers (Phelps et al. 2004). Influence does not necessarily require face-to-face interaction but rather is based on information about other people (Robins, Pattison, and Elliott 2001). In an online community, information is passed among individual users in the form of digital content. Here, we consider a particular type of social influence that takes place in an online community—namely, when members change their site usage in response to changes in the behavior of other members.

Though a relatively new area in marketing research, online communities have attracted the attention of many scholars. Dholakia, Bagozzi, and Pearo (2004) study two key group-level determinants of virtual community participation—group norms and social identity—and test the proposed model using a survey-based study across several virtual communities. Kozinets (2002) develops a new approach to collecting and interpreting data obtained from consumers' discussions in online forums. Godes and Mayzlin (2004) and Chevalier and Mayzlin (2006) examine the effect of online word-of-mouth communications. Dellarocas (2005) analyzes how the strategic manipulation of Internet opinion forums affects the payoffs to consumers and firms in markets of vertically differentiated experience goods. Narayan and Yang (2006) study a popular online provider of comparison-shopping services, Epinions.com, and model the formation of relationships of "trust" that consumers develop with other consumers whose online product reviews they consistently find to be valuable. Finally, Stephen and Toubia (2010) examine a large online social commerce marketplace and study economic value implications of link formation among sellers.

The current research's contribution lies at the intersection of social influence and online communities. First, we believe that online SN sites are a unique type of online community. Some aspects of socializing in the virtual worlds of MySpace and Facebook are similar to the online bulletin board type of interactions found on movie or consumer product review sites (the most common type of online communities studied in the marketing literature). However, the dissimilarities (e.g., the number of people involved, the motives for and nature of interactions, the revenue-generating models) are too numerous to treat them the same way. Second, previous research has not examined peer influence on individual-level site usage, the focus of our study. Finally,

imply that a person who has more linked profiles is more important than someone with fewer links.[2]

However, analyzing the network of friendship links might not be the best alternative when a firm wants to know who is important in terms of influencing site usage. A link between two profiles on an SN site does not necessarily imply influence.[3] To study a user's influence, we need to use a network in which the relationships represent influence

---

[2]Social network analysis can also use other structural measures to flag possibly "important" network players.

[3]Numerous anecdotal examples from press and personal interviews with SN site participants suggest that for many members, having their profiles linked to a large number of other users is a matter of prestige or competition rather than a sign of importance or popularity. In addition, people often accept invitations from others just to avoid seeming impolite. Thus, a network of friends might consist of a network of total strangers with whom almost no interaction takes place.

from a methodological perspective, none of the aforementioned empirical studies simultaneously model individual-level influence within a group of users. They either focus on interaction within a dyad (e.g., Narayan and Yang 2006) or consider aggregated group-level measures (e.g., Dholakia, Bagozzi, and Pearo 2004; Godes and Mayzlin 2004).

MODELING AND ESTIMATION

Our objective is to estimate the influence of each SN site member on the site usage of other members. For an online community with N members, we would need to evaluate $N \times (N-1)/2$ possible pairs of users on two dimensions: direction and strength. For a real-world network with millions of members, this task is both infeasible and unnecessary. In a typical large online community, most members never interact and are not even aware of one another's existence. To take advantage of this sparseness, we used a prefiltering condition that significantly reduces the number of potential connections to be evaluated. We argue that a good candidate for a prefiltering condition is the existence of an explicit connection between profiles established through an invitation mechanism.[4] Accordingly, we estimate the direction and strength of an influence only for profiles linked by a friendship connection.

A person is part of a user's "first-level network" of friends if the person has a friendship connection with the user in the sense we described previously. The person is taken to be in the user's "second-level network" of friends if he or she is not part of the user's first-level network but is in the first-level network of someone else who is in the user's first-level network. Higher-level networks are defined in a similar way. In our modeling approach, we consider a user's activity independent of the activity of second-level friends conditional on the activity of first-level friends. This does not imply that a second-level friend has no effect on a user. Rather, it means that a second-level friend has an effect only through a first-level friend. Formally, this means that first-level friends' activities represent sufficient statistics for other users' activities. For example, in Figure 2, Panel A, Allison may have an effect on Emily, but Alberto's activities are sufficient for characterizing this effect. This is a natural assumption to make, given the nature of the network; a closely analogous assumption is typically made in spatial statistics models. (Note that this assumption would be flawed if the network structure was misspecified, as when Allison and Emily know each other directly outside the online social network and there are interactions other than those through Alberto.)

The assumption of conditional independence from second- and higher-level friends enables us to adopt an ego-centered approach to the analysis. Taking one user of an online community at a time, we search for influential friends within the user's ego-centered network. This

answers the question, Who is influencing a given user? For example, in Figure 2, Panel A, we treat Allison as an ego and evaluate the impact of her friends—Kate, Alberto, Rene, John, Stan, Bret, Ana, and Gert—on her site usage. The outcome is that Bret, Kate, and John influence Allison to different degrees, while the others have no impact on her. Repeating this process for every person in the network, we treat each user as an ego once and as a potential "influencer" the number of times equal to the number of friends he or she has. In Figure 2, Panel B, a by-product of the ego-centered analysis for Kate, Alberto, Rene, John, Stan, Bret, Ana, and Gert is Allison's influence on them. Here, Allison has a strong impact on Gert, a moderate impact on Kate and John, and a weak impact on Alberto. This answers the second question, Who is influenced by the same given user? In network terms, the procedure reconstructs a full influence-based network by performing a series of ego-centered estimations.

Model Specification

To identify influential friends within an ego-centered network, we model a user's log-in activity as a function of the user's characteristics, the user's past behavior on the site, and the log-in activity of the user's friends. We suggest that the count of individual daily log-ins follows a Poisson distribution with rate parameter λ_{ut}, which may vary across users (u) and time (t). Accordingly, we model the number of daily log-ins y_{ut} as a Poisson regression:

$$(1) \qquad y_{ut} \sim \text{Poisson}(\lambda_{ut}).$$

We derive the Poisson regression model from the Poisson distribution by specifying the relationship between the rate parameter λ_{ut} and predictors (e.g., Cameron and Trivedi 1998). We group the predictors into two sets: self effects and friend effects. Self effects include covariates such as user-specific intercepts, day of the week, and past log-ins. Friend effects consist of friends' lagged log-in activity. It is customary to use exponential rate parameterization, giving the logarithm of the rate parameter as follows:

$$(2) \qquad \log(\lambda_{ut}) = \text{Self Effects}_{ut} + \text{Friend Effects}_{ut}.$$

More specifically, we have

$$(3) \qquad \log(\lambda_{ut}) = \alpha_{u1}x_{u1t} + \alpha_{u2}x_{u2t} + ... + \alpha_{uK}x_{uKt}$$
$$+ \beta_{u1}z_{u1t} + \beta_{u2}z_{u2t} + ... + \beta_{uF_u}z_{uF_ut},$$

where

x_{ukt} = user-specific covariate k (e.g., intercept, day-of-the-week effect, log-ins at $t-1$),

z_{uft} = weighted average of lagged log-in activities of friend f of user u at time t,

F_u = number of friends of user u,

α_{uk} = coefficient of user-specific covariate k, and

β_{uf} = coefficient of friend f for user u.

Equation 3 specifies that a user's site usage at any given time depends, among other things, on the site usage of this person's friends. The proposed model captures this process through the friend-specific coefficients β_{uf}. If friend k is among the user's "important" friends (i.e., his or her activity level has an impact on the site attractiveness for the user), the corresponding coefficient β_{uk} will be significantly

---

[4]Some other alternatives, such as cross-profile visitations and message exchanges, might also be considered candidates for the prefiltering condition, but unfortunately, these are not available to us in the data set. However, this limitation of the data set does not present a serious problem in this research, because the bulk of the interaction on a typical SN site occurs among profiles that have been connected through invitations. Moreover, an absence of invitation-based connections between two profiles often imposes serious limitations on a level of interaction (e.g., ability to consume and/or exchange digital content).

different from zero. We note that learning about the activity levels among a user's friends is likely to take time. Thus, for each friend f of user u, we construct a covariate z_{uft} as a weighted average [$w_u(d)$] of friend f's log-in activities over the past D days. This is given in Equation 4:

$$(4) \qquad z_{uft} = \sum_{d=1}^{D} w_u(d) \times y_{f(t-d)}, \text{ where } \sum_{d=1}^{D} w_u(d) = 1,$$

where $y_{f(t-d)}$ is the number of log-ins for friend f at time t − d.

We also adopt an exponential smoothing expression for $w_u(d)$, following the spirit of Guadagni and Little (1983). We define $w_u(d)$ (Equation 5) as a function of lag d and a smoothing parameter ρ_u:

$$(5) \qquad w_u(d) = \frac{\exp(-d \times \rho_u)}{\displaystyle\sum_{k=1}^{D} \exp(-k \times \rho_u)}.$$

We believe that the past actions of friend f are likely to have a diminishing-in-time impact on user u's activity level at time t. So, we expect $w_u(d)$ to be a decreasing function in d. We allow for full heterogeneity in the smoothing parameter across users. The flexibility of this approach allows the weight distribution over the past D days to vary from being equal for all lags when $\rho_u \to 0$ to the entire mass concentrating on the first lag for larger ρ_u (e.g., when ρ_u equals 5 the first lag receives 99.3% of the weight). Figure 3 plots a few examples of $w_u(d)$ for different values of ρ_u. We preset D to be seven days.[5]

Among several alternative specifications for count data models, we chose the Poisson regression because it integrates well with the variable selection algorithm (described subsequently) and results in a parsimonious and scalable solution, which is critical in real-world applications. We

---

[5]Although we can also estimate D as part of the model, the results are not sensitive to changes in D for values greater than 5. We also acknowledge that D could be made user specific; however, this is impractical because it slows down the estimation procedure without providing any significant benefits.

Figure 3
EXAMPLES OF WEIGHTS w(d) DISTRIBUTION ACROSS D LAGS FOR DIFFERENT ρ_u

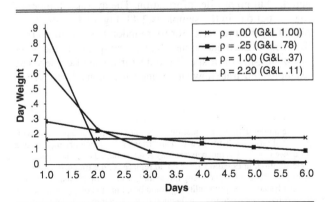

Notes: G&L = Guadagni and Little (1983).

benchmarked the performance of the Poisson model against the more flexible negative binomial distribution specification (sometimes preferred to the Poisson because of the equidispersion assumption) and did not find any significant difference in the estimation results.

A limitation of the model is that explosion is a theoretical possibility. For example, consider a situation in which one user amplifies another user's future activity and, in turn, this other user amplifies the first user's activity. This situation can create a positive feedback loop that causes each user's activity level to increase indefinitely.[6] We believe that the characteristics of the data and the estimation results make the risks of this relatively small. First, we observe that user activity levels are roughly equivalent at the start and end of the 12-week observation period. This suggests that explosion, if any, is slow. Second, the estimated directions of influence between users are primarily unidirectional; that is, when user u influences user u', user u' does not influence user u. This also greatly diminishes the likelihood of explosion.

Estimation Challenges

In the data, the typical user has approximately 90 friends, and many have hundreds of friends. The panel has approximately 80 observations for each user. Thus, we encounter the "large p, small n" situation in which the number of parameters to be estimated is large relative to the number of observations. This means that these parameters cannot be reliably estimated in a fixed-effects framework. One way to address this is to estimate the model specified in Equation 3 but only for each user–friend pair at a time (controlling for other user-specific covariates x_{uk}). A problem with this approach is that the activity levels of a user's friends are often correlated. The bias from omitting the effects of the user's other friends is likely to produce inflated estimates for the influence of each friend. (We actually observe this effect in the simulation results described subsequently.)

An alternative approach is to use a random-effects framework in which we pool strength across parameter estimates from multiple samples through Bayesian shrinkage. This has been widely done in the analysis of scanner panel data when estimating a given household's response coefficients for marketing variables (e.g., price and advertising). The modeling assumption is that the response coefficients for the various households are drawn from a distribution so that the coefficient values for other households reveal something about the coefficient values for the given household.

In our setting, however, we cannot apply the usual type of Bayesian shrinkage. In the scanner panel situation, the variable set (e.g., price and advertising), whose effects we are trying to determine, is constant across households. In the social network situation, the variables correspond to friends, and different users have different sets of friends. This means that the variable set differs, often completely, across users.

To address this challenge, we propose to shrink not across users but across friends within a user. To do this, we need to choose the across-friends distribution of the β_{uf} terms in Equation 3. A key consideration is that the average user probably tracks just a few other friends. Thus, for a given

---

[6]We thank an anonymous reviewer for making this important point.

user, most of the β_{uf} coefficients in Equation 3 are likely to be zero. This makes it prudent to choose the across-friends distribution of the β_{uf} terms to have a point mass at zero. For example, we could consider a mixture density in which one component has a point mass at zero and another component is a Gaussian distribution with a mean and variance to be estimated. Alternatively, we could consider a latent class model in which the mixture density consists of multiple point-mass densities with one point located at zero. We elect to pursue the latent class approach here primarily because the estimation algorithm is of high computational efficiency. This also is important for scalability in the applied use of our approach.

To implement a latent class model, the analyst needs to select the number of mass points. Fortunately, this selection can be based on several well-known criteria, including the deviance information criterion (DIC) (Spiegelhalter et al. 2002), the Bayes factor, and cross-validation. In the empirical application, models with two or three point masses perform about the same (as we detail subsequently). Thus, we focus the following discussion on the two-class case—that is, we assume that the across-friends distribution of influence coefficients β_{uf} has a mass point at zero and another somewhere else. We need to estimate the location of this other mass point and its weight. We then use this generating distribution to pool strength across friends to estimate the values of the influence coefficients for each specific friend. (In the Appendix, we describe the algorithm for the general case with more than two point masses.)

We can decompose each friend-specific coefficient from Equation 3 into a user's susceptibility to friends' influence, denoted by β_u, and a binary parameter γ_{uf}:

$$(6) \qquad \beta_{uf} = \beta_u \times \gamma_{uf}.$$

The binary parameter, γ_{uf}, is 1 if friend f is influential and 0 if otherwise. This approach enables us to parsimoniously capture two phenomena: (1) A friend is either influential or not, so β_{uf} becomes either zero or not, and (2) the susceptibility to friends' influence, β_u, can vary from user to user. All the model parameters can be drawn from the conditional posterior densities given the other parameters' values, and we detail these in the Appendix.

We now describe how γ_{uf} is drawn because it is an unconventional part of our Gibbs sampler:

$$(7) \qquad \gamma_{uf, \forall f} \mid \bullet \propto \mathrm{Bin}\left(\gamma_{uf} \Big| \frac{c_{uf}}{c_{uf} + d_{uf}}\right),$$

where

> $c_{uf} = p_u \times L_u(\bullet, \gamma_{uf} = 1)$,
> $d_{uf} = (1 - p_u) \times L_u(\bullet, \gamma_{uf} = 0)$,
> L_u = the Poisson likelihood function for user u, and
> p_u = prior probability of friend f being influential for user u (estimated in the sampler).

In each iteration of the Gibbs sampler, a friend-specific γ_{uf} is drawn as a Bernoulli random variable, with the success probability based on the ratio of the likelihood with friend f's effect included (i.e., with $\gamma_{uf} = 1$) to model likelihood without friend f (i.e., with $\gamma_{uf} = 0$). From the perspective of variable selection, the posterior mean of γ_{uf} is a probability that the corresponding covariate z_{uf} should be included in

the model. The behavioral interpretation is that friend f has a nonzero influence on user u. Let IF_u denote the sum of all the γ_{uf} terms for any particular user u. The IF_u can be interpreted as the number of influential friends. The p_u term is updated by drawing from the beta distribution $\mathrm{Beta}(1 + IF_u, 1 + F_u - IF_u)$, which has a mean that is approximately equal to the empirical fraction of influential friends.[7]

To apply the approach at an SN site, we might need to estimate millions of ego-centered networks. The proposed decomposition in Equation 6 results in a very scalable solution. Updating β coefficients collapses to a simple Poisson regression with a small number of parameters. Indeed, conditional on γ_u, sufficient statistics for β_{uf} become an inner product of vector $z_{ut} = [z_{u1t}, z_{u2t}, ..., z_{uFt}]$ and vector $\gamma_u = [\gamma_{u1}, \gamma_{u2}, ..., \gamma_{uF}]$. Accordingly, we can rewrite Equation 3 as follows:

$$(8) \qquad \log(\lambda_{ut}) = \alpha_{u1}x_{u1t} + \alpha_{u2}x_{u2t} + ... + \alpha_{uK}x_{uKt} + \beta_u \sum_{f=1}^{F_u} \gamma_{uf} z_{uft}.$$

To draw α_{uk} and β_u, we use the Metropolis–Hastings algorithm within Gibbs sampling steps. Instead of the usual random walk, we use an independence chain sampler, in which the proposal density is a normal approximation to the posterior density from the Poisson likelihood. The likelihood considered is conditional on the realizations of γ_u on that iteration. This means that the proposal density is adaptive in that it varies from iteration to iteration as a function of the γ_u values. The proposal density for α_{uk} and β_u is a normal distribution centered at the maximum likelihood estimate for Equation 8, with the variance equal to the inverse Fisher information matrix.

ILLUSTRATING THE METHODOLOGY WITH FIELD DATA

We apply the model to data obtained from a major SN site, which wants to remain anonymous. In the 12-week data set, we track daily log-in activities for a random sample of 330 users, their 29,478 friends, and their 2,298,779 friends' friends. We refer to these groups as Level 1, Level 2, and Level 3 networks. For Level 1 and Level 2 network members, we observe full profile information (e.g., networking goals, number of friends, number of profile views) as well as self-reported demographics (e.g., age, education, income, zip code). For Level 3 users, we have information on log-in activity but no profile information. The average number of log-ins per day in the sample is 2.48. Figure 4 gives examples of log-in time series for four randomly selected users in the sample. Each bar on the graphs corresponds to the number of log-ins on a specific date for a specific user. The examples illustrate how site usage varies considerably from

---

[7]The model defined in Equation 7 does not control for a possible reciprocity of influence between user u and friend f. We recognize that treating influence in a dyad as independent may result in biased estimates. As a possible solution, in Equation 7, we could replace p_u, the friend-independent prior probability of friend being influential, with a term p_{uf} that is specific to each friend f. The probability p_{uf} could be a function of γ_{fu}, thus making the stochastic realizations γ_{uf} a function of γ_{fu}, accommodating reciprocity. We plan to address this issue in further research.

Figure 4

LOG-IN TIME-SERIES EXAMPLES FOR FOUR USERS

A: Daily Log-In Activity, User 97, Mean = 3.25, Mode = 5

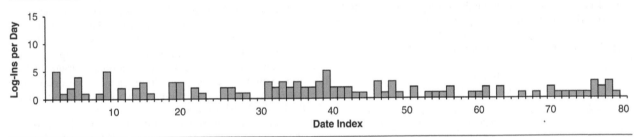

B: Daily Log-In Activity, User 12, Mean = 1.43, Mode = 1

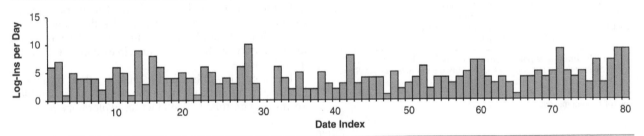

C: Daily Log-In Activity, User 118, Mean = 4.31, Mode = 4

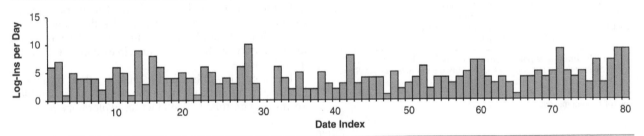

D: Daily Log-In Activity, User 26, Mean = 2.67, Mode = 2

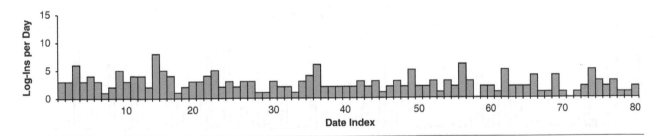

one user to another (e.g., User 118 logs in an average of 4.3 times per day, and User 12 logs in an average of 1.4 times per day).

Model Estimation

We estimate the model using the previously described Bayesian approach, implemented with Markov chain Monte Carlo (MCMC) methods. To complete the model specification, we introduce priors over the parameters common to all users (see the Appendix). We monitor chains for convergence, and after convergence, we allow long chains to run. We burn 50,000 draws and simulate an additional 50,000.

Estimation Results

Using the model in Equation 3, we perform ego-centered estimations for all users in the Level 1 and Level 2 networks. Because of the limited information on the Level 3 network, we present the findings in the following sequence: First, we focus on the 330 Level 1 network users. The objectives are to highlight the importance of peer effects in predicting individual user behavior, to demonstrate variations in the probability of influence across friends, and to show how profile information can be used to explain these variations. Second, we perform ego-centered analyses for Level 2 network users. Note that by construction, members of the

Level 1 network are (1) friends of Level 2 network users and (2) members of the Level 3 network. As a by-product of this analysis, we obtain estimates for the influence of Level 1 users on Level 2 users.

Level 1 network estimation results. In addition to Equation 3, we estimate two benchmark models. Model 1 incorporates self effects only. Model 2 includes the effect of all the user's friends (i.e., all the γ_{uf} are set equal to 1). Model 3 is the proposed model of Equation 3. For model fit and comparisons, we use the DIC. As Table 1 shows, the proposed model provides a significantly better fit to the data than the two benchmarks.

On an individual level, we observe the anticipated heterogeneity among users in terms of the number of influential friends. In Figure 5, we show two users with a similar number of friends, approximately 100 each, but distinct patterns for influential friends. Bars on these graphs correspond to the posterior probability that a particular friend influences the user. For the first user, we observe a few influential friends, and for the second, there are none. Figure 6 shows

Table 1
MODEL FITS

Model	Description	Fit (DIC)
Model 1	User self effects only (none of friends are influential)	76,613.66
Model 2	Self plus all friends' effects (all friends are influential)	76,010.93
Model 3	Self and friends effects with variable selection (some friends are influential)[a]	72,863.45

[a]The DIC for a three point masses model is 72,294.40, which is only slightly better than a DIC of 72,863.45 in a two point masses case. Thus, for expositional ease, we focus the discussion on the two-class case. The Appendix describes the algorithm for two point masses and for the general case of K point masses.

the empirical distribution of the posterior mean γ_{uf} for the entire sample. The distribution is considerably skewed to the left, which indicates that most of the posterior means γ_{uf} are relatively small. In other words, friends corresponding to these small γ_{uf} have a low probability of influencing site usage.

A key construct of interest is $\Sigma_{f=1}^{F_u} \gamma_{uf}$, the total number of influential friends for user u. A good point estimate for this construct is given by computing its expected value over $f(\gamma)$, the posterior joint density of all the gamma terms across friends. The expression for this expected value is as follows:

$$(9) \qquad \mathrm{Infl}_u = \int_{\gamma_u} \sum_{f=1}^{F_u} \gamma_{uf} \times f(\gamma) d\gamma_u.$$

This integral is estimated by Monte Carlo using the draws of γ_{uf} over the MCMC iterations. To aid interpretability, we also compute $S_u = \mathrm{Infl}_u/F_u$, which is a point estimate for the fraction of friends who influence user u. A sample average S_u is approximately 22%, and a sample average Infl_u is approximately ten people. On average, about one of five friends within an ego-centered network significantly affects the log-in decisions of ego.

If a user has no friends influencing him or her, Model 2 should be better than Model 3. The DIC (calculated individually for each ego-centered network) shows no decrement in fit for 32% of people in the Level 1 network as we go from Model 3 to Model 2. Behaviorally, this suggests that 32% of users do not have any "influential" friends whose log-in activity on the site would help explain variations in their site usage.

The probability of being influential in a dyad (γ_{uf}) might be explained by static measures available from user profiles. To investigate this, we conduct an exploratory posterior

Figure 5
ESTIMATION RESULTS FOR TWO USERS

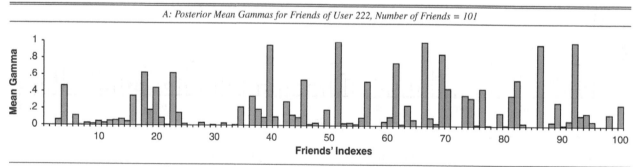

A: Posterior Mean Gammas for Friends of User 222, Number of Friends = 101

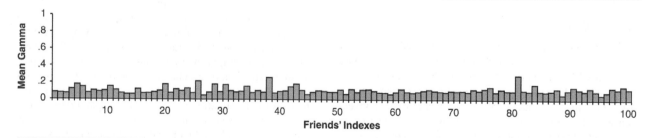

B: Posterior Mean Gammas for Friends of User 98, Number of Friends = 105

Figure 6
DISTRIBUTION OF POSTERIOR MEAN γ_{uf}

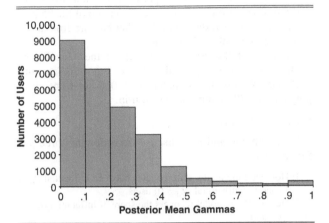

analysis.[8] We regress the logit-transformed posterior values for γ_{uf} on several covariates extracted from the user profiles: gender combination for the dyad (in this case, we chose male user, female friend), months the friend has been a member, same ethnicity for user and friend, user's dating objective, and relative age.

Table 2 gives the results from the regression. We find that female friends tend to influence the site usage of male users more than other gender combinations. Users who have been members of the site longer have more influential member friends. A user is more influenced by a member friend of the same ethnicity. Users with dating objectives have fewer friends who are influential. Finally, friends who are older than the user have less influence.

These exploratory results suggest that posterior analysis based on profile information could help the firm predict the probability of influence for any dyad in the network (because all members provide profile data at sign-up). However, note that the profile data we analyze here explains relatively little of the total variation in influence—the R-square for the regression is .11, and it does not improve with the addition of other profile variables. This indicates that there may be serious limitations to using profile information alone for advertising and retention targeting, as some practitioners have indicated (Green 2008).

---

[8]We can modify the model defined in Equations 1–4 to incorporate profile data in a hierarchical way by adding priors on γ_{uf}. We leave this extension for further research.

Table 2
EXPLAINING VARIATION IN THE POSTERIOR MEAN VALUES FOR γ_{uf}: THE PROBABILITY OF BEING INFLUENTIAL IN A DYAD

Covariate	Coefficient[a]	t-Statistic
Gender combination (female friend/male user)	.26	4.72
Months user has been a member	.36	18.02
Friend is of the same ethnicity as user	.25	6.34
User is looking for a date	−.66	−15.82
Friend is older than user	−.08	−2.04
R^2		11%

[a]Left-hand side: $\log[\hat{\gamma}_{uf}/(1 - \hat{\gamma}_{uf})]$.

We also examined the distribution of the smoothing parameter ρ_u across users (Figure 7). The empirical distribution has a bimodal shape, with one mass point at approximately 2.2 (corresponding to 90% of weight assigned to lag 1) and the second mass point at approximately .25 (weights slowly decrease with lag).

Variation in ρ_u may be explained, in part, by the log-in pattern of a corresponding user. To investigate this, we regressed ρ_u on the mean and the variance of daily log-ins (calculated on a holdout sample). We find that for users with high (higher means) and stable (lower variances) log-in activities, more weight is assigned to the recent activity.[9] Conversely, less active or irregular users have weights more evenly distributed across lags. Behaviorally, this implies that it may take less time for "regular" users to learn about changes in friends' behavior and to form new expectations regarding content updates.

Level 2 network estimation results. In discussing Google's patent application for ranking influence, Green (2008) raises the notion of computing a user's "Google number"—the sum total of a person's influence on others. In a similar spirit, to estimate a person's influence in an online community, we need to evaluate his or her impact on egos within each ego-centered network of which he or she is a member. Therefore, we first estimate ego-centered networks of all Level 2 users. Then, for each user (u) of a Level 1 network, we calculate the network influence (I_u) as a sum of the marginal impacts he or she has on egos (e) in the Level 2 network (Equation 10):[10]

$$(10) \quad I_u = \sum_{e=1}^{F_u} \int_{\gamma_{ue}} \int_{\beta_{ue}} \overline{y}_e \times \beta_{ue} \times \gamma_{ue} \times f(\gamma_{ue}, \beta_{ue}) d\gamma_{ue} d\beta_{ue},$$

---

[9]The regression coefficient for the mean of daily log-ins is .05 (t = 5.05), and the coefficient for the variance of daily log-ins is .18 (t = 8.67).

[10]For the Poisson regression, the average response effect to a one-unit change in regressor can be calculated as follows:

$$\frac{1}{n}\sum_{i=1}^{n}\frac{\partial E[y_i|x_i]}{\partial x_i} = \hat{\beta}_j \times \frac{1}{n}\sum_{i=1}^{n}\exp(x_i'\hat{\beta}).$$

For the Poisson regression model with intercept included, this can be shown to simplify to $\overline{y} \times \hat{\beta}$ (Cameron and Trivedi 1998).

Figure 7
DISTRIBUTION OF SMOOTHING PARAMETER ρ_u

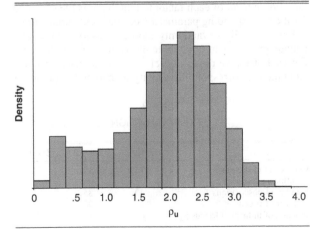

where

$\bar{y}_e$ = the average number of daily log-ins of user e,
F_u = the number of ego-centered networks user u enters as a friend (i.e., the number of friends of user u), and
$f(\gamma_{ue}, \beta_{ue})$ = the posterior distribution of γ_{ue} and β_{ue}.

The findings indicate that the majority of users have little impact on the behavior of others. However, some show a significant influence. As we expected, the extent of this influence also varies considerably across users. For example, some users with similar numbers of friends have total network impacts that differ by a factor of eight. These results reflect the ability of our method to identify influential users in the network and to quantify the likely extent of this influence.

ILLUSTRATING THE METHODOLOGY WITH SIMULATED DATA

We also used simulated data to examine the performance of the proposed Bayesian shrinkage approach. Specifically, we are interested in assessing how well the procedure recovers the identity of influential users under varying conditions. We designed the simulated data sets to be in the stochastic neighborhood of the data used in the field application.

The variable set for the simulation consists of two parts: the predictor variables and the response variable. The predictor variables correspond to the lagged activity levels of a user's friends, and the response variable corresponds to the activity level of a specific focal user. The predictor variables in the simulation take values corresponding to the empirically observed lagged activity levels of a user's set of friends. The response variable's values are then simulated from the Poisson model on the basis of the predictor variables and the assumed values for the parameters of the model. The model parameters are γ_{uf}, which represents whether friend f is influential on the focal user u, and β_u, which represents the influence strength of a friend who is influential. The term p_u represents the fraction of friends who are influential on user u. We vary these model parameters over multiple replications. We also vary T, the number of periods observed, and F_u, the number of friends (both influential and noninfluential) that user u has.

The simulation data sets are drawn according to a $3 \times 3 \times 3 \times 3$ design (81 simulation settings in total) produced by manipulating the four factors specified in Table 3. We chose the middle level of each factor to match the value obtained for the corresponding parameter from the field application.

For each cell, we randomly choose 20 users with several friends greater than or equal to the value of F_u in that cell. For each user, we randomly select F_u of that user's friends and take the corresponding activity data to be the predictor

variables. The value of T, the number of periods observed, is 85 in the empirical data set. If T in a cell is 40, we randomly subselect 40 of the 85 periods. If T in a cell is 170, half the observations are an exact replication of the 85 periods in the empirical data, and the other half are from a random sampling with replacement.

For each of the 20 users in each of the 81 cells, we applied the estimation procedure to the corresponding simulated data. We ran the samplers for 10,000 iterations, dropping the first 8000 iterations as burn-in.

Simulation Results

We computed and now discuss the following three performance measures:

1. How well the model differentiates between influential ($\gamma_{uf} = 1$) and noninfluential ($\gamma_{uf} = 0$) users,
2. How well the model recovers the share of influential friends (p_u), and
3. How well the model recovers the strength of an influential friend's influence β_u.

Measure 1: identifying the influentials. We assess how well the model predicts whether a certain friend is influential. The prediction is based on the posterior mean $\hat{\gamma}_{uf}$. Specifically, we predict that friend f is influential if $\hat{\gamma}_{uf}$ exceeds a threshold C. We consider two ways of setting C. The first is to set C to 1/2; we label this the $C_{.5}$ threshold. The other is to set C to minimize the total misclassification error in predicting influentials on a certain holdout sample for that cell; we label this the C_{opt} threshold. In actual practice, we would not be able to set the value of C in the latter way, because we would not observe the true value of γ_{uf}. We considered this threshold only to understand how much worse the simple $C_{.5}$ threshold would be relative to the best possible choice.

Across all 81 cells, the fraction of correctly classified friends varies between 68% and 100% for the $C_{.5}$ threshold and between 77% and 100% for the C_{opt} threshold. The average fraction is 90% for the $C_{.5}$ threshold and 92% for the C_{opt} threshold. Thus, the optimal threshold yields only slightly better performance than the simple threshold of 1/2, and therefore we drop C_{opt} from further discussion.

We also conducted an analysis of variance to explore the differences in the correct classification rate across the 81 cells. The main effects for the first two factors, β_u and T, were not statistically significant (at least for the cells considered in our design). For the other two factors (F_u and p_u), we found strong effects, each significant well beyond the .01 level. For the main effect F_u, number of friends, the mean for the correct classification rate was 95.4% for $F_u = 45$, 90.8% for $F_u = 90$, and 84.9% for $F_u = 180$. Thus, as the number of friends increases, it becomes more difficult to distinguish influential from noninfluential friends. For the fraction of influential friends, p_u, the mean correct classification rate was 96.9% for $p_u = .05$, 92.3% for $p_u = .1$, and 82% for $p_u = .2$. As the proportion of influential friends rises, it becomes somewhat more difficult to distinguish them from noninfluential ones. We chose the specific experiment design to match the field data's structure, and it is important to keep in mind that these patterns may not extend to different designs.

Table 3
SIMULATION DESIGN

	Level 1	Level 2	Level 3
Coefficient of friend's f influence on user uβ_u	.12	.14	.16
Number of observations T	40	85	170
Number of friends F_u	45	90	160
Fraction of influential friends p_u	.05	.1	.2

Measure 2: estimating the share of influential friends. We now report how well the methodology recovers the fraction of influential friends. As we discussed previously (see Equation 9), this fraction is estimated as $S_u = Infl_u/F_u$, where $Infl_u = \int_{\gamma_u} \Sigma_{f=1}^{F_u} \gamma_{uf} \times f(\gamma) d\gamma_u$ and the integration is over the posterior density of the γ_{uf} terms. Across all users in all 81 cells, the correlation between the true fraction and the estimated fraction is .88. The mean absolute value of the difference (MAD) between the actual and the estimated fraction is .05. An analysis of variance shows that the main effects for the four factors are not strongly significant.

Measure 3: estimating the influence strength of influential friends. The β_u parameter represents the influence strength of influential friends. Table 4 summarizes the recovery results for the β_u parameter at each level in the simulation design. We report the mean value of β_u for each of the three factor levels averaged over all the 27 cells with a particular (true) value for β_u. Table 4 also reports the absolute error over the 27 cells. Dividing the absolute error by the true value gives the relative error; this is 21% on average, a figure we consider reasonably low given the difficulty of the problem. The error is strongly affected by the number of observations, T. The relative error is approximately 29% for T = 40 days, 20% for T = 85 days, and 14% for T = 170 days. This suggests that accuracy in estimating a user's β_u goes up moderately quickly as additional days of activity are recorded and available for analysis.

Comparison with an Alternative Method

We used the simulation to compare the performance of our proposed Bayesian shrinkage approach with a simpler, non-Bayesian alternative. Specifically, we estimate the Poisson regression for each user–friend pair, controlling for other user-specific covariates; we label this the "univariate friend model." In this simpler approach, we use t-statistics to identify the subset of friends whose log-ins significantly explain the focal user's site activity. Using the simulated data, we estimate $3 \times 3 \times 3 \times 3 \times 20 \times F_u$ Poisson regressions by maximum likelihood and calculate t-statistics ($t_{\beta_{uf}}$) for each β_{uf}. We classify friends with $t_{\beta_{uf}} \geq 1.96$ as influential.

Across the 81 simulation designs, the univariate friend model correctly classified the influential friends between 46% and 92% of the time, with an average of 65%. This is substantially worse than the performance of the proposed Bayesian approach, for which the average correct recovery rate is 90% (using the 1/2 threshold). Thus, the simulation results support the use of the more elaborate Bayesian modeling procedure for the purposes of identifying influential users. Taken together, the simulation studies provide encouraging evidence for the performance of the proposed method for estimating influence levels for users in an online social network.

We also compared the performance of the proposed model with a non-Bayesian alternative, assuming that data simulation follows the latter.[11] Under such a scenario, the "true" model is a fixed-effects model in which each friend is associated with an individual β_{uf} coefficient. Note that, in practice, a full fixed-effects model can be estimated only for network members who have more log-in observations than friends. In the data set, only 60% of users satisfy this condition.

We use the following simulation procedure to generate data from the non-Bayesian alternative model. For all users in the Level 1 network, we estimate a univariate (in number of friends) Poisson regression model (controlling for self effects). We set all β_{uf} with $t_{\beta_{uf}} \geq 1.96$ equal to zero. Next, using these β_{uf} and assuming a full fixed-effects model (multivariate in number of friends Poisson regression), we generate the dependent variable for 85 observations in the actual sample. We simulated another 20 observations from the same empirical distribution to generate a holdout sample. The procedure ensures that the simulated data are in the stochastic neighborhood of the field application but generated according to a non-Bayesian alternative model. Finally, we estimate two models (a univariate non-Bayesian model whose parameters are indicated by superscript NB and the proposed Bayesian model indicated by superscript B) using the first 85 observations and compare in- and out-of-sample performance. The results show that in-sample recovery of β_{uf} is better with the proposed Bayesian model. Initially, this result was surprising because theory predicts that the data-generating model should perform no worse than alternative models, but the theoretical prediction is only an asymptotic result. In small samples, the Bayesian can do better because it is a shrinkage estimator and therefore has a variance advantage, which can offset the "bias" disadvantage that comes from the generating process being different from what is implicitly assumed by the Bayesian model.

The correlation between β_{uf} and $\hat{\beta}_{uf}^{NB}$ is .59, and for β_{uf} and $\hat{\beta}_{uf}^{B}$, it is .70. The MAD between β_{uf} and $\hat{\beta}_{uf}^{NB}$ is .066, and for β_{uf} and $\hat{\beta}_{uf}^{B}$, it is .014. Finally, the MAD calculated on the out-of-sample predictions of y is approximately 7% lower for the Bayesian approach (3.78 versus 4.08). In summary, the simulation shows that the proposed Bayesian model is robust under a data-generation process that assumes heterogeneity in friend effects within a user.

MANAGERIAL IMPLICATIONS FROM THE FIELD DATA ANALYSIS

In this section, we discuss implications for managers of applying the model in practice. First, we ask how well the univariate friend model and some simple descriptors of user activity, such as friend count and profile views, capture the influence levels of the site's most important users. Second, we evaluate scenarios to quantify the financial value of retaining the site's most influential users. Both analyses show that the proposed Bayesian approach offers significant potential benefits to managers concerned with targeting users for advertising and retention.

A practical consideration is whether the Bayesian approach is likely to offer meaningful gains in the identifi-

Table 4
RECOVERY OF β_u

	Level 1	Level 2	Level 3
Actual value of β_u	.12	.14	.16
Mean of $\hat{\beta}_u$ across the 27 corresponding cells	.11	.13	.14
Mean absolute error $|\hat{\beta}_u - \beta_u|$ across the 27 corresponding cells	.024	.029	.035

---

[11]We thank the associate editor for this suggestion.

Influential Users in Internet Social Networks

cation of the most influential users compared with simple metrics. To address this, we evaluate how well other plausible measures of user importance do in capturing influence. Specifically, we examine the number of friends and the number of profile views ("hits") for each user. For a sample of 330, the correlation between a person's total marginal impact (the estimate of influence as revealed by the model and Equation 10) and his or her total number of friends is .72. The correlation between total marginal impact and profile views is .34. Although the number of friends and profile views both predict influence, considerable variance remains unexplained.

We also note that focusing on correlations alone could be potentially misleading in a practical sense. This stems from the likelihood that managerial interest is focused on members with the highest levels of influence (e.g., the top 5% or 10% of users). Because of their social influence and impact on the site activity of others, these top users are likely to be the most valuable to advertisers and most important for the site to retain as members (Green 2008). We compared how well the univariate friend model and the simple metrics of friend count and profile views predict influence at the top of the list. In Table 5, we present data for the top 10% (33 users) of the sample and show the cumulative impact obtained by proceeding further down the list. We place the values for the top 5% (corresponding to the cumulative impact at User 16) in boldface for discussion purposes. At this point, ranking by friend count yields a substantially lower network impact (43.49 versus 82.53).[12] The ratio is worse for profile views, at 24.37/82.53. Finally, the non-Bayesian alternative produces the best result of three naive rankings, which is still substantially lower than the proposed model (61.15 versus 82.53).[13] According to the foregoing analysis, simpler metrics, such as friend count and profile views, are likely to be inadequate proxies for user influence. As we noted previously, practitioners have been disappointed with the ability of simple metrics to capture influence on SN sites (Green 2008).

The relative payoffs from targeting based on estimated network influence are greatest at the top of the site's member list, but they continue to reach below the top 10%. For example, if we were to extend Table 5 to the entire sample of 330 users, we would find that the top 33% of influencers are responsible for 66% of the total impact. In practice, even narrowly focused targets (e.g., 5% of users) would involve addressing millions of user members at the major SN sites.

We now turn to implications of the model for managing retention efforts. In network settings, customer value to the

Table 5

COMPARISON OF CUMULATIVE INFLUENCE CAPTURED

Top k	Centile	Cumulative Network Impact of Top k People When Ranked by			
		Proposed Model	Univariate Friend Model	Number of Friends	Number of Profile Views
1	.3%	10.44	4.41	4.41	2.60
2	.6%	17.89	8.24	6.63	4.88
3	.9%	24.53	11.57	9.35	6.67
4	1.2%	30.47	13.40	11.09	10.44
5	1.5%	35.87	17.17	15.68	10.47
6	1.8%	40.85	22.56	18.25	11.95
7	2.1%	45.57	25.80	19.72	14.27
8	2.4%	50.16	32.44	24.44	14.84
9	2.7%	54.58	39.89	26.98	15.91
10	3.0%	58.99	43.50	29.82	16.94
11	3.3%	63.16	45.68	32.60	18.48
12	3.6%	67.19	49.85	35.32	20.22
13	3.9%	71.12	52.70	37.01	20.65
14	4.2%	74.95	56.73	39.05	21.39
15	4.5%	78.77	59.42	40.90	23.12
16	**4.8%**	**82.53**	**61.15**	**43.49**	**24.37**[a]
17	5.2%	86.14	62.77	48.47	25.42
18	5.5%	89.47	65.50	49.93	25.56
19	5.8%	92.70	66.66	53.86	26.85
20	6.1%	95.92	68.67	56.46	37.29
21	6.4%	99.03	74.61	60.23	39.46
22	6.7%	102.04	76.09	64.26	41.09
23	7.0%	105.04	78.70	66.05	41.24
24	7.3%	107.96	81.33	70.22	43.27
25	7.6%	110.81	85.93	72.38	43.98
26	7.9%	113.64	88.53	73.97	44.18
27	8.2%	116.47	90.47	75.88	45.01
28	8.5%	119.28	92.51	78.71	46.87
29	8.8%	122.05	94.35	82.53	47.54
30	9.1%	124.78	96.94	85.75	50.14
31	9.4%	127.51	99.51	88.07	50.58
32	9.7%	130.23	101.50	90.80	50.77
33	10.0%	132.92	105.32	94.41	53.54

[a]Read as follows: Cumulative network impact of top 16 users identified by the proposed model is 1.35 times (82.53/61.15), 1.9 times (82.53/43.49), and 3.4 times (82.53/24.37) greater than the total impact of top 16 users identified by the non-Bayesian alternative model, the number of friends, and the number of profile views, respectively.

firm is not solely a function of the cash flows generated by a customer but also a function of the effect of this customer on other customers (Gupta, Mela, and Vidal-Sanz 2006). The negative impact of an influential user leaving the site is not limited to the lost revenues from, for example, ad impressions not served to this particular person. Rather, the site usage of all linked (dependent) users will be affected as well. Therefore, when determining how much a firm should be willing to spend to retain a particular customer, the user's network influence should be part of the valuation. In addition, if there is cost associated with retention efforts (e.g., an incentive for site usage stimulation, such as access to special features and monetary rewards), the firm needs to know whom to target.

A simple approach would be to choose people at random. This is actually similar to what MySpace.com did historically with its "Cool New People" feature—picking users at random and showing their profiles on the site's home page. This gives a popularity boost to the selected profiles. Alternatively, the site may focus on users who have many friends or users with a high number of profile views. Finally, the firm may consider targeting influential users identified by

---

[12]Because both rankings use the same measure of individual marginal impact to calculate the cumulative top k impact, the first list is by construction greater than the naive ranking for each value of k. Therefore, it is a given that, in Table 5, the numbers in the "Proposed Model" column are greater than the numbers in the "Number of Friends" column.

[13]The procedure closely follows the one for the Bayesian method, except the selection criterion for influential users is based on the t-statistics calculated for each β_{uf} from pairwise Poisson regressions. We classify friends with $t_{\beta_{uf}} \geq 1.96$ as influential. Ranking is based on the total marginal impact, which we calculate as follows:

$$I_u = \sum_{e=1}^{F_u} \overline{y}_e \times \beta_{ue} \times I\left(t_{\beta_{ue}} \geq 1.96\right).$$

some empirical model; for this, we compare the proposed model and a non-Bayesian alternative.[14]

To gauge returns from targeted retention, we examine the potential effects on advertising revenue from impressions. While CPM (cost per mille, or cost per thousand impressions) on some premium sites can be as high as $15, most SN sites have a CPM under $1. Price quotes from several SN sites indicate that $.40 per thousand impressions is a reasonable benchmark. According to the data provided by the anonymous SN site, the average number of pages viewed on a community site by a unique visitor per month is approximately 130. From what we have observed across multiple SN sites, the average page carries approximately two to three advertisements. Thus, the average user contributes approximately $.13 per month or $1.50 a year of revenue from this source. From the data, we observe that users visit the site an average of 2.48 times per day, so each log-in generates approximately $.00175.

We can use the data in Table 5 to develop a numerical estimate of what would happen to the network if top users drop activity levels to zero (i.e., go from 2.48 to 0 log-ins).[15] In the sample of 330 users, the loss of the top 5% of users, ranked by influence, corresponds to a drop of 209.15 log-ins in the network (2.48×84.33). This translates into approximately $.3654 per day. If the drop in network activities persists, the total loss to the firm is approximately $133 a year ($.3654 \times 365$ days). Scaling this number to match the size of the target group of an actual network (approximately ten million users in the case of MySpace.com), the annual financial impact would be $78.5 million. In addition, each user alone (ignoring network effects) contributes approximately $1.50 a year of impression-based ad revenue, which, for ten million users, is $15 million. Adding these gives the payoff from retention actions in this scenario as approximately $93.5 million, given that the firm targets the top 5% of influential users as identified by our model.[16]

We repeat this analysis for the four other targeting approaches. In the case of random selection, the cumulative impact of losing 5% of users is a drop of 57.72 daily log-ins ($2.48 \times 1.369 \times 17$), which translates into approximately $.1008 per day or $36.81 a year ($.1008 \times 365$ days).[17] Scaling up to the size of the actual network and adding users' "stand-alone" value gives $36.65 million in payoff. Targeting on the basis of the number of friends and the number of profile views results in total payoffs of $57.78 million and $38.16 million, respectively. Finally, targeting on the basis of ranking results produced by the univariate friend model yields a total payoff of $72.7 million. All these

are substantially below the $93.5 million associated with targeting from the proposed model. In summary, compared with simpler alternatives, application of the Bayesian approach might significantly improve the ability of SN sites to target their most influential members and to design and implement cost-effective retention programs.

CONCLUSION

Firms operating SN sites observe an "overt" network of friends, defined according to who added whom as a friend. Most of the links in this network are "weak" in the sense that the relationships do not significantly influence behavior in the network; thus, identifying the "strong" links (i.e., the links corresponding to friends who affect a given user's behavior) is of interest. However, distinguishing weak links from the strong links is a difficult problem for two reasons. First, the number of overt links is large. Second, the firm wants to distinguish the links fairly quickly (e.g., in less than three months), so the number of "observations" available is fairly small. This sets up a challenging P > N problem.

To address this, we develop and test a nonstandard Bayesian shrinkage approach in which the shrinkage is done across predictors within a model. Specifically, we implement a highly scalable Poisson regression model that shrinks influence estimates across friends within users. The primary intended contribution is a methodology for extracting, with limited data, the strong links from a large overt network that has mostly weak links. To the best of our knowledge, existing research, drawing from the literature on variable subset selection, has not yet done this in an application to massive right-hand-side expressions.

We tested the model on field data provided by an anonymous SN site. As expected, we found that relatively few so-called friends are actually significant influencers of a given user's behavior (22% is the sample mean), and substantial heterogeneity across users also exists. We also found that descriptors from user profiles (e.g., gender, stated dating objectives) lack the power to enable us to determine who, per se, is influential—the R-square is 11%. The spirit of this finding is corroborated by Google's recent efforts to better quantify social influence so that it might extract more revenue from targeted advertising on MySpace.com.

We also assessed the model's performance using simulated data. Specifically, we showed that the model performs well in correctly recovering the influential users and other key features of the data. Our Bayesian shrinkage approach also performs much better than a simpler, regression-based alternative model.

Our application to the field data provides a vivid illustration of the set of results that firms could obtain from applying the model in practice. We believe that these also have important implications for SN sites as businesses. In addition to the poor performance of profile descriptors in predicting influence, we showed that friend counts and profile views also fall short of being able to identify influential site members, especially for the most important 5%–10% of users. Examining a user retention scenario, we also illustrate the potential for large gaps in financial returns to the firm from using the model-based estimates of influence versus friend count, profile views, or, as MySpace.com has done, random selection.

Our approach could be readily applied to other data that might also be available to firms operating SN Web sites. For

---

[14]None of these approaches indicate how responsive the selected people are to the firm's retention efforts. We suggest that this can be determined through a series of small-scale field experiments with different target groups. We thank the associate editor for this suggestion. In addition, a more comprehensive targeting approach should take into account a person's propensity to leave the site with and without the program.

[15]Because the analysis does not reveal any significant correlation between a number of daily log-ins and strength of network influence, we use a sample average of 2.48 log-ins per day instead of individual-level daily log-in averages.

[16]We acknowledge that our approach is an oversimplification. To accurately infer the network impact caused by losing a customer, the model needs to take into consideration several other factors, which we do not discuss here. The main purpose of this example is to illustrate that different targeting approaches can lead to substantially different financial implications.

[17]The average predicted impact across users in our sample is 1.369; 17 people correspond to approximately 5% of users in the sample.

example, we could augment the data set with richer information on the overt links (e.g., with details of the interactions). With richer information of this kind, the P > N situation is exacerbated, and the primary benefits of the methodology are enhanced. In this article, we chose to illustrate the methodology with log-in data, primarily because these are the data on which the partner SN firm operated. Apart from privacy and storage cost concerns, SN firms focus on own profile page visitation and log-in data because the own profile page is the center point of the typical user's activity and interactivity in the site. To make site usage easy, sites offer ways to minimize the need for a user to explicitly navigate to a friend's page to see the friend's activities. Major sites compile the main updates of a user's friends' profiles and present this compilation directly on the user's own profile page. Nonetheless, should managers or investigators want to extend the model to include additional usage information, the modeling approach we present herein—namely, Bayesian shrinkage across the friend effects within a user—should readily extend.

We also note that our model does not incorporate the potential dynamics in a user's influence over time. To address this, heterogeneity in β_u along the time dimension can be added. In further research, this might be done by using, for example, a hidden Markov approach.

Another potential limitation to this research is shared by most Internet-related studies. It is difficult, if not impossible, for a firm to know comprehensively when and how users interact with one another through other digital media. From interviews with several users, we learned that many maintain profiles on multiple SN sites, as well as digital communications, such as instant messaging, SMS (short message service), and BlackBerry e-mails. Other researchers, such as Park and Fader (2004), note the inherent limitations of models built on behavioral data collected on a single site when users' activities go beyond it. Padmanabhan, Zheng, and Kimbrough (2001) also warn of possibly erroneous conclusions from models that are limited to such data. The offline interactions of users are also potentially relevant and, in general, not available to researchers or managers. In this article, as do many others in Internet marketing, we focus on modeling online activity tracked by a single site and must leave the potential role of other Internet and offline activities for further research.

A final limitation is that we are unable to address how responsive the top "influencers" selected by our approach are likely to be to marketing actions (e.g., targeted advertising, a firm's retention efforts). This means that the managerial implications of the modeling approach are illustrative at this stage. Going forward, we believe that the value of identifying influential users can be established through relatively straightforward (and small-scale) field experiments. The contribution of this research is to address the methodological hurdles involved in suitably identifying such users so that the process of targeting and intervention can advance. (The Web Appendix at http://www.marketingpower.com/jmraug10 includes additional figures and tables omitted from the article for space consideration.)

APPENDIX

The Prior Distributions

1. $\alpha_{uk} \sim \text{Normal}(0, 100I)$.

2. $\beta_u \sim \text{Normal}(0, 100I)$, truncated at 0 on the left.
3. γ_{uf}
   - Two point masses case:
     $\gamma_{uf} = 1$ with probability p_u, and $\gamma_{uf} = 0$, with probability $1 - p_u$.
   - K point masses case:
     $\gamma_{uf} = k$ with probability p_{uk}, where k is a class index.
4. p_u
   - Two point masses case:
     $p_u \sim \beta(a, b)$ with $a = b = 1$.
   - K point masses case:
     $p_u \sim \text{Dirichlet}(a_1, a_2, \ldots, a_K)$, where $a_1 = a_2 = \ldots = a_K = 1$.
5. $\rho_u \sim \text{Uniform}(c_1, c_2)$, where $c_1 = .01$ and $c_2 = 5$ (ρ_u at value c_1 results in weight being evenly distributed over all D lags, and c_2 is chosen to have more than 99% of weight assigned to the first lag).

The Gibbs Sampler

For each user (ego) u:

1. Generate $\alpha_u, \beta_u | \gamma_u, X_u, Z_{uf}$.

We use an independence Metropolis–Hastings sampler, where the Poisson likelihood function is approximated by a normal distribution with Metropolis correction. We generate parameter values $\alpha_u^{(n)}$ and $\beta_u^{(n)}$ using a normal distribution centered at the maximum likelihood estimate (MLE) for Equation 8 with the variance equal to the asymptotic variance (approximated by inverse of the Hessian H of the log-likelihood). The likelihood considered is conditional on the realizations of γ_u on that iteration. We reject candidates for $\beta_u \leq 0$ (note that in K point masses case, β_u is a vector of K – 1 elements because for $k = 1$, β_{u1} is set to be 0). We accept the new values of $\alpha_u^{(n)}$ and $\beta_u^{(n)}$ with the following probability:

$$\Pr(\text{accept})$$

$$= \min\left\{ L_u\left(\alpha_u^{(n)}, \beta_u^{(n)} | \gamma_u^n\right) \times f_\alpha\left(\alpha_u^{(n)}\right) \times f_\beta\left(\beta_u^{(n)}\right) \right.$$

$$\times \exp\left[-\frac{1}{2}\left(\begin{bmatrix} \alpha_u^{(o)} \\ \beta_u^{(o)} \end{bmatrix} - \begin{bmatrix} \alpha_u^{(\text{MLE})} \\ \beta_u^{(\text{MLE})} \end{bmatrix} \right)' H\left(\begin{bmatrix} \alpha_u^{(o)} \\ \beta_u^{(o)} \end{bmatrix} - \begin{bmatrix} \alpha_u^{(\text{MLE})} \\ \beta_u^{(\text{MLE})} \end{bmatrix} \right) \right] \Bigg/$$

$$L_u\left(\alpha_u^{(o)}, \beta_u^{(o)} | \gamma_u^n\right) \times f_\alpha\left(\alpha_u^{(o)}\right) \times f_\beta\left(\beta_u^{(o)}\right)$$

$$\times \exp\left[-\frac{1}{2}\left(\begin{bmatrix} \alpha_u^{(n)} \\ \beta_u^{(n)} \end{bmatrix} - \begin{bmatrix} \alpha_u^{(\text{MLE})} \\ \beta_u^{(\text{MLE})} \end{bmatrix} \right)' H\left(\begin{bmatrix} \alpha_u^{(n)} \\ \beta_u^{(n)} \end{bmatrix} - \begin{bmatrix} \alpha_u^{(\text{MLE})} \\ \beta_u^{(\text{MLE})} \end{bmatrix} \right) \right], 1 \Bigg\},$$

where L_u is an individual likelihood function and f_α and f_β are priors on α_u and β_u, respectively. Otherwise, we keep parameter values from the previous iteration $\alpha_u^{(o)}$ and $\beta_u^{(o)}$.

2. Generate $\gamma_{uf} | \alpha_u, \beta_u, X_u, Z_{uf}$ for all "friends" f of user (ego) u.

In the two point masses case, we draw γ_{uf} as a Bernoulli selecting a friend index f in a random order:

$$\Pr(\gamma_{uf} = 1)$$

$$= \left\{ \frac{L_u\left(\alpha_u, \beta_u, \gamma_{uf}^{(1)}\right) \times p_u}{L_u\left(\alpha_u, \beta_u, \gamma_{uf}^{(1)}\right) \times p_u + L_u\left(\alpha_u, \beta_u, \gamma_{uf}^{(1)}\right) \times (1 - p_u)} \right\},$$

where $L_u(\alpha_u, \beta_u, \gamma_{uf}^{(1)})$ is an individual likelihood evaluated when $\gamma_{uf} = 1$ and $L_u(\alpha_u, \beta_u, \gamma_{uf}^{(0)})$ is an individual likelihood evaluated when $\gamma_{uf} = 0$.

In the K point masses case, we draw γ_{uf} as a categorical random variable selecting a friend index f in a random order:

$$\Pr\left(\gamma_{uf} = k\right) = \left\{ \frac{L_u\left(\alpha_u, \beta_u, \gamma_{uf}^{(k)}\right) \times p_{uk}}{\sum_{j=1}^{K} L_u\left(\alpha_u, \beta_u, \gamma_{uf}^{(j)}\right) \times p_{uj}} \right\},$$

where $L_u(\alpha_u, \beta_u, \gamma_{uf}^{(k)})$ is an individual likelihood evaluated when $\gamma_{uf} = k$ (i.e., friend f is assigned to class k).

3. Generate $p_u | \gamma_{uf \text{ for } \forall f}$.

In the two point masses case, we draw $p_u \sim \beta(a + IF_u, b + F_u - IF_u)$, where $IF_u = \sum_{\forall f} \gamma_{uf}$ and F_u is the number of "friends" of user u.

In the K point masses case, we draw $p_u \sim \text{Dirichlet}(a_1 + F_{u1}, a_2 + F_{u2}, \ldots, a_K + F_{uK})$, where $F_{uk} = \sum_{\forall f} 1(\gamma_{uf} = k)$.

4. Generate $\rho_u | \alpha_u, \beta_u, \gamma_{uf}, X_u, Z_{uf}$.

We draw a smoothing parameter ρ_u using a random walk Metropolis–Hastings algorithm. A candidate $\rho_u^{(n)}$ is formed as $\rho_u^{(n)} = \rho_u^{(o)} + \zeta$, where $\zeta \sim \text{Normal}(0, \sigma_\rho)$ and σ_ρ is being adjusted dynamically during burn-in iterations to ensure acceptance rate in the 25%–45% range. It is fixed thereafter. We accept the new value of $\rho_u^{(n)}$ with the following probability:

$$\Pr\left(\text{accept}\right) = \min\left\{ \frac{L_u\left(\alpha_u, \beta_u, X_u, Z_{uf}^{(n)}\right) \times f_\rho\left(\rho_u^n\right)}{L_u\left(\alpha_u, \beta_u, X_u, Z_{uf}^{(o)}\right) \times f_\rho\left(\rho_u^o\right)}, 1 \right\},$$

where

$$z_{uft}^{(n)} = \sum_{d=1}^{D} w_{ud}^{(n)} \times y_{f(t-d)},$$

$$w_u^{(n)}(d) = \frac{\exp\left(-d \times \rho_u^{(n)}\right)}{\sum_{k=1}^{D} \exp\left(-k \times \rho_u^{(n)}\right)}, \text{ and}$$

$$f_\rho = \text{prior on } \rho_u.$$

If a candidate value $\rho_u^{(n)}$ is accepted, we use new weights w_u to calculate Z_{uf}. Otherwise, we keep parameter values from the previous iteration $\rho_u^{(o)}$ and do not update Z_{uf}.

REFERENCES

Cameron, A. Colin and Pravin K. Trivedi (1998), *Regression Analysis of Count Data*. Cambridge, UK: Cambridge University Press.

Chevalier, Judith A. and Dina Mayzlin (2006), "The Effect of Word of Mouth on Sales: Online Book Reviews," *Journal of Marketing Research*, 43 (August), 345–54.

Dellarocas, Chrysanthos N. (2005), "Strategic Manipulation of Internet Opinion Forums: Implications for Consumers and Firms," working paper, Robert H. Smith School of Business, University of Maryland.

Dholakia, Utpal M., Richard P. Bagozzi, and Lisa Klein Pearo (2004), "A Social Influence Model of Consumer Participation in Network- and Small-Group-Based Virtual Communities," *International Journal of Research in Marketing*, 21 (3), 241–63.

Godes, David and Dina Mayzlin (2004), "Using Online Conversations to Study Word-of-Mouth Communication," *Marketing Science*, 23 (4), 545–60.

Green, Heather (2008), "Google: Harnessing the Power of Cliques," *BusinessWeek*, (October 6), 50.

Guadagni, Peter M. and John D.C. Little (1983), "A Logit Model of Brand Choice Calibrated on Scanner Data," *Marketing Science*, 2 (3), 203–238.

Gupta, Sunil, Carl F. Mela, and Jose M. Vidal-Sanz (2006), "The Value of a 'Free' Customer," Working Paper No. 07-035, Harvard Business School, Harvard University.

Holmes, Elizabeth (2006), "No Day at the Beach: Bloggers Struggle with What to Do About Vacation," *The Wall Street Journal*, (August 31), B1.

Iacobucci, Dawn (1990), "Derivation of Subgroups from Dyadic Interactions," *Psychological Bulletin*, 107 (1), 114–32.

———, ed. (1996), *Networks in Marketing*. Newbury Park, CA: Sage Publications.

——— (1998), "Interactive Marketing and the Meganet: Network of Networks," *Journal of Interactive Marketing*, 12 (Winter), 5–16.

——— and Nigel Hopkins (1992), "Modeling Dyadic Interactions and Networks in Marketing," *Journal of Marketing Research*, 29 (February), 5–17.

Kozinets, Robert V. (2002), "The Field Behind the Screen: Using Netnography for Marketing Research in Online Communities," *Journal of Marketing Research*, 39 (February), 61–72.

Leenders, Roger Th.A.J. (2002), "Modeling Social Influence Through Network Autocorrelation: Constructing the Weight Matrix," *Social Networks*, 24 (1), 21–48.

Marketing Science Institute (2006), "2006–2008 Research Priorities," (accessed April 28, 2010), [available at http://www.msi.org/pdf/MSI_RP06-08.pdf].

Narayan, Vishal and Sha Yang (2006), "Trust Between Consumers in Online Communities: Modeling the Formation of Dyadic Relationships," working paper, Stern School of Business, New York University.

Padmanabhan, Balaji, Zhiqiang Zheng, and Steven O. Kimbrough (2001), "Personalization from Incomplete Data: What You Don't Know Can Hurt," in *Proceedings of the Seventh ACM SIGKDD International Conference on Knowledge Discovery and Data Mining*. New York: Association for Computing Machinery, 154–64.

Park, Young-Hoon and Peter S. Fader (2004), "Modeling Browsing Behavior at Multiple Websites," *Marketing Science*, 23 (3), 280–303.

Phelps, Joseph E., Regina Lewis, Lynne Mobilio, David Perry, and Niranjan Raman (2004), "Viral Marketing or Electronic Word-of-Mouth Advertising: Examining Consumer Responses to Pass Along Email," *Journal of Advertising Research*, 44 (4), 333–48.

Robins, Garry, Philippa Pattison, and Peter Elliott (2001), "Network Models for Social Influence Processes," *Psychometrika*, 66 (2), 161–90.

Scott, John (1992), *Social Network Analysis*. Newbury Park, CA: Sage Publications.

Spiegelhalter, D.J., N.G. Best, B.P. Carlin, and A. Van der Linde (2002), "Bayesian Measures of Model Complexity and Fit," *Journal of the Royal Statistical Society: Series B*, 64 (4), 583–39.

Stephen, Andrew T. and Olivier Toubia (2010), "Deriving Value from Social Commerce Networks," *Journal of Marketing Research*, 47 (April), 215–28.

Van den Bulte, Christophe and Stefan Wuyts (2007), *Social Networks and Marketing*. Cambridge, MA: Marketing Science Institute.

Walsh, Mark (2008), "Goldstein at IAB: Marketers Can't Ignore Social Media," *Online Media Daily*, (June 3), (accessed September 30, 2008), [available at http://www.mediapost.com/publications/index.cfm?fuseaction=Articles.san&s=83859].

Website Sources

Marketing Research Glossary:
- www.marketresearchterms.com

Statistical Terms in Sampling:
- www.socialresearchmethods.net/kb/sampstat.php

Statistical Sampling Techniques:
- www.experiment-resources.com/statistical-sampling-techniques.html

Sample Size Calculators:
- www.surveysystem.com/sscalc.htm
- www.raosoft.com/samplesize.html
- www.macorr.com/ss_calculator.htm

Distribution Tables (F, t, Z, and Chi Square):
- www.statsoft.com/textbook/distribution-tables

Experimental Design:
- www.socialresearchmethods.net/kb/desexper.php
- www.statsoft.com/textbook/experimental-design

Questionnaire Design:
- www.cc.gatech.edu/classes/cs6751_97_winter/Topics/quest-design
- www.analytictech.com/mb313/principl.htm
- www.samplequestionnaire.com/questionnaire-design-examples.html

Descriptive Statistics:
- www.socialresearchmethods.net/kb/statdesc.php
- http://mste.illinois.edu/hill/dstat/dstat.html

Inferential Statistics:
- www.socialresearchmethods.net/kb/statinf.php

Basic Statistics:
- www.statsoft.com/textbook/basic-statistics

GLOSSARY

Alternative Hypothesis Used in hypothesis testing, the notion that there is a statistical relationship between variables. When the test statistic probability is greater than a certain significance level.

Analysis of Variance (ANOVA) A statistics method that measures the level of variability between the means and variances of respective datasets and whether those differences are statistically significant.

Analytical Model A visual depiction of the cause and effect relationships amongst the dependent and independent research variables.

Applied Research Research geared towards answering a specific problem or addressing a specific issue.

Auspices Biases The tendency of biases to enter a research project based on who is conducting the research. For example: respondents might be more prone to positive responses if they like the research sponsor or more negative responses if they do not like the research sponsor. Some research sponsors remain anonymous to avoid this bias.

Availability Rate The extent to which targeted respondents are available to participate in the research.

Balanced Scale Scales with an equal number of positive and negative endpoints on the scale.

Basic Research General research designed to expand the bases of knowledge that sometimes leads to applied research.

Box Plot A visual way of presenting quantitative data that separates the data into quartile ranges which depicts the data median and data outliers.

Brand Aided Recall When a respondent recollects a brand or concept but needs cues to fully recall the brand or concept.

Brand Recognition When a respondent simply recalls or recognizes a brand, concept, etc. Marketing research is used to measure the impact of brand awareness and as a tool for determining brand equity.

Brand Unaided Recall When a respondent can recall details about a product or concept without assistance or prompting.

Bulletin Board An online place to post feedback on a particular issue. Marketing researchers conduct content analysis as a means of measuring the impact of this resource.

Case Analysis Often qualitative research whereby the researcher examines a relevant case and applies the findings to his research.

Causal Research Research that details the cause and effect relationship amongst dependent and independent variables. Causal research requires proving concomitant variation, time order of occurrence, and systematic elimination of other possible independent variable causes.

Census An exact enumeration—for example: asking *"all"* possible respondents a set of questions.

Central Limit Theorem   The statistical notion that data will become increasing normal as the sample size grows. The Central Limit Theorem is the foundational piece to the utility of samples in research. First developed by French Mathematician Abraham de Moivre.

Chi Square   A statistical probability that compares the expected value with the observed value of variables to determine whether differences *(variance)* in the data are significant.

Client Confidentiality   The notion that the marketing researcher keeps the client information internal to the research provider thus protecting the privacy of the client. Client confidentiality is a major ethical issue in marketing research.

Closed Ended Questions   Survey questions with a controlled set of responses.

Cluster Sampling   A probability sampling technique whereby elements of a population are grouped and then a census of the group is taken.

Coding   The process of assigning numerical codes to categorical data.

Comparative Scales   Ordinal scales whereby the respondent ranks choices from a list by making comparisons as to the other choices on the list.

Computer Assisted Telephone Interview (CATI)   Survey method where the respondents' answers are entered into software that can be immediately tabulated.

Concept Testing   The process of testing a concept directly with the product or service end user—who then provides valuable feedback.

Concomitant Variation   A statistical construct that measures the correlation between variables that facilitates statistical predictability. One of the three conditions of proving causation.

Confidence Interval   A statistical concept that enables researchers to presume the actual range of all data of a given data based on a sampling of that data.

Conjoint Analysis   *"Considered Jointly"* this technique measures the relative weight and thus importance of various factors in the decision making process. For example: customer satisfaction at a restaurant might be due to—50% food quality, 20% service, 15% ambiance, 10% parking, and 5% reputation.

Consent Forms   A form respondents sign consenting to participate in the research study. Usually used mainly for experimental design, focus group, and interview related methods.

Constant Sum Scale   A comparative ratio scale method that asks respondents to ascribe points to each given attribute within a prescribed point total.

Construct Equivalence   The extent to which respondents understand and interpret the underlying concepts behind a question on a questionnaire equally. This issue is of particular importance in cross cultural survey research when questionnaires are translated into other languages.

Construct Validity   The extent to which researchers measure what they intended, or think, that they measured.

Consumer Panels   A sample of respondents who provide input to a research study during set period of time.

Content Analysis   A technique whereby the researcher reviews written data *(such as a case or news articles)* and gleans patterns of information from the content of the reviewed documents.

Contrived Observation   An observation technique whereby the researcher manipulates the situation for the purpose of observing the subjects' reaction to the created situation.

Control Group   As part of experimental design, the control group is not affected by a change in the independent variables that is introduced to the experimental group.

Convenience Sampling   A non-probability sampling technique that targets respondents in high traffic *(thus "convenient" to the researcher)* locations such as a shopping mall or a university student union.

Convergent Validity   A validity testing technique that seeks to show that other research sources reached *(the convergence of other research)* similar conclusions to the conclusions reached by the researcher.

Conversation Trackers   An Internet technique that maps conversation patterns *(such as twitter, blogs, etc.)*. An Internet form of content analysis.

Cooperation Rate   The percent of qualified respondents who agree to participate in the research.

Cover Letter   A letter accompanying a survey inviting participation in the survey. It usually includes information about the researcher, the research purpose, the survey length, an indication of how they were selected to participate, the time the survey will take, whether the survey is anonymous and confidential, and a thank you for participating.

Criterion Validity   A validity testing technique that relies on applying a set of criterion to determine if the responses received are valid *(should be trusted as true)*. Suppose 80% of students *"say"* they want to be a doctor yet most answer *"no"* to criterion questions related to the requirements of becoming a doctor.

Cross Sectional Survey   A survey technique where one set of respondents are asked a set of questions once. Cross sectional surveys are a *"snapshot in time"* and do not account for changes in opinions.

Cross Tabulation   A data analysis technique that compares two *(bi variate)* or more *(multi variate)* variables. For example: 50% of our survey respondents were women *(uni variate)* but 28% were women over 30 years old *(bi variate)* and 15% were women over 30 years old and who live in the city *(multi variate)*. Cross tabulations are a staple data analysis technique in marketing research.

Cutoff   Respondents who end a survey prematurely by refusing to continue.

Data Cleaning   The post data collection process of ensuring that there are no errors or inconsistencies in the dataset. For example, suppose some respondents said they did not own a car but later in the survey indicated that they owned a Ford. This inconsistency should be identified and questioned.

Data Mining   The process of extrapolating information from a set of data.

Data Range   The highs and lows of a response set. For example, the oldest respondent was 50 and the youngest was 20, the range was 30.

Data Warehouse   A system that stores vast amounts of data used by researchers.

Decision Support System (DSS)   A system that ties together various marketing data sources which provides the organization's leadership the information from which business decisions can be made.

Degrees of Freedom   When using a sample—the process of subtracting 1 from the total number of observations to correct for overestimating the variability in the sample set of data.

Dependent Variable   Variables whose change is *"dependent"* on a change in the independent variable. For example, restaurant sales are *"dependent"* on the factors *(independent variables)* that lure customers to the restaurant.

Descriptive Research   Research that *"describes"* the data. For example, 65% like yellow, 34% are men, 82% work on weekends, and 27% watch Star

Trek—these percentages simply *"describe"* data. Descriptive statistics answers the who, what, where, how, and when questions. Causal research answers the *"why"* questions.

Design Control   A technique for controlling extraneous variables in experimental design that aims to design the experiment in a way that mitigates the impact of known extraneous variables.

Diagnostic Research   Research that answers the *"why"* related questions of causal research. This type of research is used as a basis to predict behaviors.

Direct Mail Survey   A survey collection method whereby respondents get a questionnaire in the mail and have to mail back their responses.

Disguised Observation   An observation technique when the subject does not know they are being observed. This technique might be necessary to preserve the integrity of what is really being observed.

End User   The ultimate user of marketing research. The sponsor of the research. Many companies *(end users)* hire marketing research companies to conduct research for their use.

Ethnographic Research   A form of behavioral observation research that seeks to measure respondent actions in *"real world"* settings.

Executive Interview   Individual depth interviews of thought leaders designed to capture the most current information on a research topic. The results of which are usually incorporated into other aspects of the research project.

Executive Summary   A short, usually no more than a page, summary of the most important research findings. The Top Line Report might be more in-depth than the executive summary.

Experimental Design   A marketing research technique that tests the impact on a dependent variable from a change to an independent variable. For example, measuring the change to sales *(dependent variable)* resulting from a change in price *(independent variable)*.

Experimental Treatment   The change in the independent variable in experimental design. For example, changing the product size *(independent variable)* is the *"treatment."*

Expert Survey   A survey *(often relatively short)* of experts who will provide a higher level of insight to a given topic than would the general population.

Exploratory Research   Typically qualitative, exploratory research is used to gain a general understanding of the research topic from which more detailed research can be done.

Extraneous Variable   Variables that are not under the direct or indirect control of the researcher in experimental design yet whose impact can be mitigated. Examples: weather, government regulations, competition, and road construction.

Extremity Bias Error   A survey bias that occurs when respondents choose the extreme points of a scale *(1 or 10 on a 1 to 10 scale for example)* based on a desire to stand out rather than on the reality of their opinions—which might legitimately be a 1 or 10.

Face Validity   A qualitative validity testing technique that determines whether the results of research makes sense *"on the face of it."* For example, if 80% of students think the basketball coach should be fired after losing all the games of the year—*"on the face of it"* those results seem valid.

Field Experiment   A experiment in an uncontrolled setting—or *"in the field."*

Finite Multiplier   A sampling adjustment technique that reduces a statistically calculated sample size without affecting the original error estimation.

Focus Group   A qualitative structured brainstorming technique of knowledgeable people to examine critical aspects of a given research topic. Typically held in a focus group facility—these two hour sessions have 8–12 screened participants and are run by a moderator.

Focus Group Facility   The location where focus groups are conducted—usually with an observation room and with the ability to record the session.

Focus Group Incentives   Incentives offered to focus group participants to thank them for participating. These incentives usually include money. The incentive amount should be enough to compensate participants for their time and for expressing an opinion but not be so high as to bias that opinion.

Focus Group Moderator   The person who manages the focus group session.

Focus Group Moderator Guide   A written guide *(not seen by the focus group participants)* the focus group moderator uses that identifies the major issues that need to be covered during the focus group. The guide would typically have key questions to prompt the moderator and would have timed sections of the key issue areas to keep the moderator on track.

Forced Scale   A scaled question with no neutral or middle option such as *"on a scale of 1 to 4"* or *"a scale of 1 to 6."*

Forensic Observation   An observation technique that gathers tangible observation evidence from which conclusions can be drawn. Examples: DNA, store receipts, credit card transactions, and tire skid marks.

Frequency Distribution   A distribution of data that details how many, and of what percent, each response is in a given set of data. For example: perhaps 31% like red, 21% like green, 15% like blue, and so on.

Frugging   An unethical practice of fund raising under the guise of research.

Full Service Provider   A marketing research company that provides all aspects of the marketing research process from data collection, to analysis, to report presentation.

Group Dynamics   The *"life or personality"* a focus group takes when a group of people act together. Observing body language, word usage, and tone are critical to understanding a group dynamic.

Histogram   A bar chart that shows the relative frequency distribution of the data as well as a cumulative percent of the total. For example: 10% said yellow and 5% said green thus 15% said yellow or green. The 15% represents the cumulative data.

Hypothesis Testing   A statistical method to test whether a theory is correct.

Incidence Rate   The percent of qualified *(relevant to the research at hand)* respondents in the population.

Independent Variable   A variable in experimental design that can be manipulated by the researcher to see its impact on the dependent variable. Examples: price, product color, hours of operation, store layout, membership privileges—all of these can be directly controlled.

Individual Depth Interview (IDI)   One-on-one interviews of respondents. These sessions can last an hour and are of generally expert level interviewees.

Individual vs. Collective Orientation   Geert Hofstede's cultural dimension that measures the extent to which people associate and identify themselves as part of a large group or more as individuals. This concept is important in cross cultural research. www.geert-hofstede.com

Instrument Variation   The change of the data collection technique *(the instrument)* during a research study. For example: collecting 100 respondents by telephone and 100 through in person interviews.

Interval Data   Non comparative data that demonstrates three of the four data characteristics—description, order, and distance. Interval data reveals the relative distance between responses. For example, a *"5"* on a 1 to 10 scale compared to an *"8"* on the same scale reveals a difference between the responses that can be calculated.

Interval Estimate   The estimated range of the true population mean based on the sample mean. For example suppose 65% of respondents in a survey said *"yes"* to a given question with a 3% margin error. Thus were we to ask the entire population between 62% and 68% *(interval estimation)* of the population would say *"yes."*

Interviewer Bias Error   Error caused by the interviewer. For example: suppose a respondent was intimidated by an interviewer and his responses were thusly affected.

Interviewer Instructions   A list of instructions the interviewer uses a guide during an interview that includes key questions to ask, how long to spend on various topics, natural follow-up questions, and interviewee tidbits about the person being interviewed.

Inverse Correlation   Sometimes called "negative correction"—this occurs when variables move in the opposite direction. For Example: as miles go up while driving, gas in the tank goes down.

Item Equivalence   The extent to which respondents interpret the words on a questionnaire the same way. This issue is of particular importance in cross cultural survey research when questionnaires are translated into other languages.

Itemized Rating Scale   A survey scale technique enabling the respondent to rate each item independently of the other items in the question.

Judgment Sampling   A sampling technique that relies on expert judgment to determine the sample size or respondent composition.

Laboratory Experiment   An experiment in a controlled *(or at least largely controlled)* setting.

Language Mapping   The understanding that different languages have different flows and place varying levels of importance on how questions are worded and presented. This issue is of particular importance in cross cultural survey research when questionnaires are translated into other languages.

Letter of Transmittal   The correspondence from the researcher that relinquishes the research product to the research sponsor for his use.

Likert Scale   Usually a 1 to 5 attitudinal rating scale.

Longitudinal Survey   A survey that asks questions of the same sample over a certain period of time. These surveys enable researchers to measure opinion changes over time.

Long-vs. Short-term Orientation   Geert Hofstede's cultural dimension that measures the extent to which people view the world in the short-or long-term. This concept is important in cross cultural research. www.geert-hofstede.com

Low Balling Pricing   An unethical practice by a research provider offering marketing research services below cost and then raising the costs once the work begins. This practice is a form of *"bait and switch."*

Mall Intercept Survey   A general term for convenience sampling whereby the researcher approaches respondents in high traffic locations.

Margin of Error   The percent fluctuation—or range—between the sample result and its projection to the population. For example: suppose 65% of survey respondents said *"no"* to a particular survey question with a margin of error of ±3%. Thus were we to ask the entire population the same question, between 62% and 68% of the population would say *"no"* to the question at hand. Margins of error are a function of the variance and confidence interval associated with a population. Generally the smaller the sample size the larger the error—keeping variance and confidence intervals the same.

Marginals   A summation of each question in the survey. Marginals are a good first step in the data analysis process.

Marketing Research Association (MRA)   The professional association of marketing research professionals founded in 1957—www.marketingresearch.org.

Marketing Research   The process of collecting and analyzing data that produces information useful to, for example, business leaders.

Marketing Research Institute International (MRII)   A marketing research certificate program hosted through the University of Georgia founded in 1995—www.georgiacenter.uga.edu/mrii

Marketing Research Report   The final product in a marketing research study that includes all aspects of the project including: the letter of transmittal, an executive summary, the research purpose, the research methods *(primary and secondary data collection methods)*, the primary and secondary research findings, conclusions and recommendations, the limitations, and appropriate acknowledgements.

Masculine/Feminine Orientation   Geert Hofstede's cultural dimension that measures the extent to which culturals are more masculine or feminine in their thinking and actions. This concept is important when conducting cross cultural research. www.geert-hofstede.com

Maturation   An extraneous variable in experimental design when a test subject's circumstances change over the course of the research study in a way that affects the study.

Mean   The sum of the observations divided by the number of observations.

Measure of Association   A statistical method that measures the extent to which variable A changes when variable B changes.

Measure of Dispersion   A statistical method that measures the relative spread of data. Range, standard deviation, and variability are measures of data dispersion—or how spread the data are.

Measurement Error   Error associated with the way the data were collected and not the sample itself. Also called *"non sampling error."*

Measures of Central Tendency   Mean, median, and mode are measures of the centrality of data.

Measures of Dispersion   Range, standard deviation, and variability are measures of data dispersion—or how spread the data are.

Measures of Equivalence   The umbrella concept addressing the extent to which respondents interpret the questions associated with a research project the same way. This issue is of particular importance in cross cultural survey research when questionnaires are translated into other languages.

Mechanical Observation   An observation technique that uses a mechanical means to measure the observations such as traffic counters, voice pitch analysis, and grocery store scanners.

Median The middle observation in an ordered dataset.

Mode The most frequently occurring variable.

Mortality The loss of test subjects during the course of an experiment. Mortality is an extraneous variable.

Moving Average An average that uses a pre-described set of previous observations as the basis for calculating the average.

Multidimensional Scales Scales that measure more than one aspect of an issue or topic. For example: measuring all components related to the factors comprising *"the perfect vacation."*

Multiple Choice Scale A scale that enables the respondent to check more than one response such as *"check the top three choices"* or *"check all that apply."*

Mystery Shopping A form of ethnographic research whereby a researcher poses as a *"customer"* for the purpose of observing some issue or action. Used in competitor research as well as by organizations for training purposes. Mystery shopping levels are determined by the level of involvement or interaction the mystery shopper has with the person *"being shopped."*

Natural Observation An observation technique whereby the researcher observes the test subject in a natural setting and thus without any contrived intervention.

Nominal Data The least sophisticated form of data—nominal data are categorical and descriptive only.

Non Comparative Scales Scales enabling respondents to answer independently of the other choices in the response set. Rating each choice in the answer set on a scale of 1 to X for example.

Non Forced Scale Scales with an odd number of choices thus enabling respondents to response neutrally such as a 1 to 5 or a 1 to 7 scale.

Non Probability Sampling A non-random sampling technique that uses researcher judgment in selecting who will be in the survey. Examples: judgment, convenience, snowball, and quota.

Non Response Error When someone does not respond to any questions in a survey. This error causes surveys to be non-representative of the population.

Non Sampling Error Error associated with the way the data were collected and not the sample itself. Also called *"measurement error."*

Normal Distribution A data distribution with a standard deviation (SD) of 1 where the mean, median, and mode are the same and 67% of the observations fall within 1 SD of the mean, 95% are within 2 SD of the mean, and 99%+ are 3 SD from the mean.

Null Hypothesis Used in hypothesis testing, the notion that there is no statistically significant relationship between variables.

Observation Research A form of research using observation to establish patterns of behavior.

One-dimensional Scales Questions that examine only one aspect of an issue such as the color of a car—as opposed to all the features of the car.

Open Ended Questions Qualitative nominal questions allowing the respondent to write freely his response.

Open Observation An observation technique whereby the respondent knows the purpose of the observation and is usually aware that the observation if occurring.

Ordinal Data A comparative form of data demonstrating description and order *(but not distance between the answers).* For example, *"place these soft drinks in order of preference."*

Over Sampling   The need to ask more people than required to compensate for those people who are contacted and refuse to participate in the research study. Much like when airlines overbook seats—few people get bumped on over-booked flights due to a calculated percentage of *"no shows."*

Pearson Correlation   A measure of association that demonstrates the extent to which interval or ratio data move in the same or opposite direction together. For example, when prices go down, sales go up would reveal an inverse correlation between these ratio data sets.

Perceptual Mapping   The process of visually depicting consumers perceptions about a product or service. Usually using two key concepts related that issue as the anchors.

Physical Control   The process of physically controlling the parameters of an experiment to mitigate the impact of extraneous variables on the experiment.

Point Estimate   The estimated point in the population based on the sample. For example: 81% of the respondents said *"yes"* to a particular questions. The 81% represents the *"point"* which is the estimate of the whole population were a census to be done.

Population   All elements of a target segment.

Positive Correlation   When one variable goes up the other goes up—or when once variable goes down the other variable goes down. These paired variables move in the same direction. For example: when students study more, their grades increase.

Power Distance Index   Geert Hofstede's cultural dimension that measures the extent to which authority is viewed. This concept is important in cross cultural research. www.geert-hofstede.com

Pre/Post Measurement   As part of running an experiment, the process of measuring the independent variable before and after the treatment.

Predictive Research   Research in which the conclusions enable researchers to predict *(with varying levels of accuracy)* the outcome of events based on certain inputs.

Pre-Experimental Design   An experiment that has neither a control group nor a clear pre/post measurement calculation.

Primary Data   Data collected directly from the subject of interest. Examples: focus groups, interviews, surveys, observation, and experiments.

Probability Sampling   A random sampling technique whereby each respondent has a known probability of being selected into the sample. Examples: simple random, systematic, cluster, and stratified.

Projective Techniques   Moderator driven techniques used to elicit responses from focus group members. Examples: word association, sentence completion, and photo sorts.

Push Polling   An unethical practice of leading respondents towards a certain answer by virtue of biased phrased questions from a manipulative interviewer.

p-Value   A statistical significance test—when the calculated p-value is lower than the significance level—the null hypothesis is rejected.

Q-Sorting   An analysis technique that uses a progressive ranking process to continually reduce the response set to the top few *(consensus driven)* choices.

Qualitative Research   Research that focuses on categorical analysis and general observations of data leading to a more in-depth understanding of behaviors. Examples: analyzing focus groups and interviewers.

Quantitative Research   Research that uses numerical analysis to explain both simple and complex behaviors.

Quasi Experiment   An experiment whereby the researcher lacks full control over the process and variables.

Question Sequence   The impact the order of questions has on the questionnaire process. To reduce question sequence order bias, researchers can scramble the order of the questions on a questionnaire—unless the order of the questions is important to understanding the purpose of the survey.

Questionnaire   A list of questions designed to answer a research question.

Quota Sample   A non-probability sampling technique whereby the researcher decides to add or remove subjects from the sample based on some quota standard.

Random Digit Dialing   A probability form of simple random sampling used in telephone surveys whereby phone numbers are automatically dialed at random until a suitable number of respondents completes the survey.

Rank and Percentile   A data analysis technique that sorts data from the highest to the lowest observation while providing the relative percent of the total each observation lies.

Rank Order Scale   Ordinal scales whereby the data are ranked in order of preference. Usually no ties are permitted.

Ratio Data   The highest form of data—ratio scales exhibit all the characteristics of data: description, order, distance, and origin. Numeric data such as: age-35, income-$54,432, and number of students in a class-46.

Refusal   Subjects who refuse to participate in any aspect of the research.

Regression   A statistical method for analyzing the relative impact of each respective independent variable on the dependent variable of study.

Regression to the Mean   The tendency of test subjects' opinions to gravitate towards the mean, or average answer, the longer they are in the research study.

Reliability   The extent to which the survey responses are internally consistent. For example: if a respondent says they hate blue and later indicates that all the cars they have bought were blue—the researcher might be well advised to question the reliability of that respondent.

Request for Information   The process of publically asking for information on a given topic that prompts organizations and companies to submit information on that topic. Used as an initial step in determining what information is available in the marketplace on a given topic.

Request for Proposal   A request from a marketing research end user to interested marketing research parties to submit a proposal to conduct a research project.

Request for Quote   The invitation from an end user to the marketing research community to submit a pricing proposal to complete a particular research project.

Research Bias   Biases that occur that have a negative impact on the integrity of the research results. These biases can be created intentionally or unintentionally by the researcher or the respondent.

Research Design   The blueprint and method for developing, executing, analyzing, and reporting marketing research. The research design should be done before the research has started and requires input from the researcher and the research sponsor to ensure all parties agree with the purpose and scope of the marketing research project.

Research Hypothesis A research statement of purpose that makes a claim or argument that the marketing research project hopes to resolve. For example: sales are declining due to poor product quality, or customer service is lower than it has been in 10 years, or if we open a hotel in this location it will be profitable.

Research Limitations An accounting, usually at the end of a research report, of the problems or challenges faced during the research process. Researchers should include the mitigation strategy that was used to compensate for these limitations. Limitations might include: difficulty gaining access to respondents, software glitches, or lack of good secondary data.

Research Method The detailed primary and secondary sequential research steps taken to complete a research project. Often seen as *"methodology."*

Research Statement The purpose of the research—the question(s) the researcher hopes to answer in the course of the research project.

Researcher Certification A professional marketing research certification process managed through the Marketing Research Association that aims to provide credentialing to marketing research providers. The program is the Professional Researcher Certification, or PRC, process.

Response Rate The percent of solicited respondents who participate in the research. The true significance of the response rate is the non-response rate. In other words, were respondents who did not respond significantly different from those who did respond? If so, the sample is not fully representative of the population of interest.

Sample Selection Bias A bias stemming from selecting inappropriate respondents into the sample. For example: suppose researchers were conducting a survey of college students and 25% of the sample had never been to college.

Sample Size The total number of respondents, representative of the target population, needed to complete a survey within a desired margin or error.

Sampling The process of taking a small sample of a targeted population and projecting the results of that sample onto the general population of interest. Sampling can be done by non-probability means (non-random) or probability means (random). Determine the sample size is critical. Sample sizes can be determined judgmentally or statistically.

Sampling Error Error associated with the sample itself. Suppose 10% of the survey respondents did not respond truthfully to a survey. The sample itself is now inaccurate—and this error will be carried to the projection onto the generally population that the sample is supposed to represent.

Sampling Frame The subset of the target population from which the sample is drawn. For example: suppose researchers want to survey students and there are 30,000 students on campus. It might be easier to take a subset of that population (a frame) of business school students—of 2,000. This population of 2,000 students is easier to obtain than the 30,000. This process works only when the sample frame is statistically representative of the targeted population.

Scalar Equivalence The extent to which respondents understand the scales being used equally. This issue is of particular importance in cross cultural survey research when questionnaires are translated into other languages.

Scatter Plot A visual representation on two variables revealing the liner extent of their association. Often used as a visual depiction of a correlation analysis.

Screening Questions Questions used to determine the suitability of someone as a respondent in a research project. For example: if researchers are examining people's experiences of traveling to Alaska, a screening questions would determine if the respondent had been to Alaska—if not, they would not be in the research study.

Secondary Data   Data collected by a third party that the researcher is using as a foundational piece of the research project. Sources include: the Internet, newspapers, journals, magazines, and books. Assessing the quality of the secondary research is important by ensuring that the secondary data used is relevant, timely, complete, of quality, and sufficient.

Semantic Differential Scale   A scale that uses opposite concepts on either end of the scale and asks the respondent to select their answer along that continuum. For example: hot/cold, old/new, or expensive/inexpensive. These scales help researchers to gauge emotional reactions to concepts.

Sentence Completion Test   A projective technique used to solicit quick feedback or impressions about an issue. For example: complete the sentence—the president is _____.

Simple Random Sampling   A probability form of sampling whereby each element in the targeted population has a known chance, or probability, of being selected into the sample. For example: random digit dialing or the lottery.

Skip Pattern   A questionnaire design technique that has respondents skip non-applicable questions on a questionnaire.

Snowball Sampling   A non-probability sampling technique whereby respondents refer other people into the survey who then in turn refer others—and so on until the desired sample size is reached.

Spearman Correlation   A rank order correlation used as a measure of association between ordinal data.

Standard Deviation   A measure of dispersion that reveals how varied around the mean a dataset is.

Stapel Scale   A scale that places the issue of interest at the center of the scale with a certain number of positive and negative responses above and below the centered issue.

Statistical Control   Statistical adjustment technique used to correct for errors in survey research.

Statistical Significance   The notion that differences in data are statistically significant if the difference between data are due to factors other than random chance.

Stem and Leaf Plot   A visual way of displaying quantitative data that reveals the spread, shape, and distribution of the data.

Stratified Sampling   A probability sampling technique that divides skewed data into normally distributed sub groups from which probability samples can be taken. This process compensates for non-normally distributed dataset.

Structured Observation   An observation method whereby the researcher observes subjects' behaviors against a list of behaviors important to the researcher. This method enables the observation to be more focused.

Sub Group Analysis   A research technique that identifies pockets of like sub groups of data amongst the larger set of data. Sub group analysis forms the basis of market segmentation.

Sugging   An unethical practice of selling under the guise of research.

Surrogate Information Error   Error that occurs when respondents are being affected (often unbeknownst to the researcher) by something unrelated to the research at hand. For example: suppose a member of a focus group recently went through some personal trauma—this trauma might affect his responses to focus group questions even though the focus group is about an unrelated subject to the trauma.

Survey   The process of asking respondents a series of questions. Often used synonymously with "questionnaire." There are many forms of surveys including: Internet, mail, telephone, and in-person.

Survey Research Error   Error to the research caused by chance variations *(the random difference between a sample and a population)* or by systematic errors of execution caused by the respondent, the researcher, or both parties. Survey error can be either intentionally created or unintentionally occurring.

Survey Stability   The extent to which survey responses, from one survey to the next, provide statistically predicable results.

Syndicated Data Service   A customized data provider.

Systematic Elimination   The process of systematically eliminating (one by one) an independent variable as being a causal factor into the change in the dependent variable. Part of experimental design and one of the three major hurdles to proving causation.

Systematic Error   Error in marketing research associated with some flaw in the research execution. For example: perhaps the questionnaire was poorly worded, or the sample was inappropriate, or the focus group moderator was inexperienced.

Systematic Sampling   A probability sampling technique the selects samples based on some predetermined pattern. Selecting every nth person for example. Typically the skip interval is calculated by dividing the sample size into the population size.

Test and Re-Test   A reliability measure whereby the researcher will compare responses to the same question given multiple times to determine in the responses are stable—that the respondents are giving the same answers to the same questions.

Test Marketing   The process of testing a product or service in the marketplace.

Testing Effect   As part of experimental design—a result that is an effect of the testing itself.

Time Sequence   The order of occurrence involving independent and dependent variables. Time sequence is a factor contribution to proving causation.

Top Line Report   A summary of the major findings of a research report. Usually used to brief top management on the most critical research findings.

t-Test   A sampling statistic used in hypothesis testing for small samples—usually fewer than 30 respondents.

Type I Error   Rejecting the null hypothesis when in fact it is true.

Type II Error   Accepting the null hypothesis when in fact it is false.

Unbalanced Scale   Scales that are weighted with more positive or more negative endpoints. Researchers should justify their use in the method section of the research paper.

Uncertainty Avoidance Index   Geert Hofstede's cultural dimension that measures the extent to which people avoid uncertainty. This concept is important when conducting cross cultural research. www.geert-hofstede.com

Unstructured Observation   Observation whereby the researcher observes subjects without a list of specific behaviors to look for.

Validity   The extent to which the research conclusions correctly reflect the actual opinions of the target population.

Variance   The amount of variability, or difference, between data sets. Data demonstrating high levels of variability provide researchers the opportunity to identify possible sub groups.

Z-Score   A score that depicts the distance from the mean given normally distributed data.

Z-Test   A sampling statistic used in hypothesis testing for samples over 30 respondents.

WORKS CITED AND SUGGESTED READING

"An Eyeball Test for Better Ads," *Business 2.0,* March 2007.

"Dell Uses Social Media in China Market," *Society for New Communications Research,* May 2011.

"Frequently Asked Questions," *Zogby International,* February 2007.

"Guide to Test Market Selection," *Creating Marketing,* 2000.

"Mystery Shopper," *Smart Money,* December 2005.

"Phone Surveys Skewed by Cell-Only Homeowners," *Quirk's Marketing Research Review,* October 2007.

"Research Department as Bellwether?" *Quirk's Marketing Research Review,* August 2007.

"Survey Finds Acceptance of Focus Group Video Transmission." *Quirk's Marketing Research Review,* August 2006.

"The Quest for the Perfect Online Ad," *Business 2.0,* March 2007.

"Tips Offer Better Response Rates, Engaging Surveys," *Marketing News,* April 2007.

Acquadro, C., Jambon B., Ellis D., Marquis P., "Language and Translation Issues: Quality Life and Pharmacoeconimics in Clinical Trials," Philadelphia, Lippincott-Raven. 1996.

Akchin, Don, "Quick & Dirty," Non Profit World. June 2001.

Albaum, Gerald; Roster, Catherine; Yu, Julie; and Rogers, Robert, "Simple Rating Scale Formats: Exploring Extreme Responses," *International Journal of Marketing Research,* 49 no.5 . 2007.

Aldenderfer, M.S., Blashfield, R.K., Cluster Analysis. Beverly Hills, CA. Sage Publications. 1984.

Althoff, Stefan, "Does the Survey Sender's Gender Matter?" *Quirk's Marketing Research Review,* February 2007.

Alwin, D.F., "Feeling Thermometers Versus 7-point Scales: Which are Better?" *Sociological Methods and Research.* 1997.

Alwin, D.F., Krosnick, J.A., "The Reliability of Survey Attitude Measurement," *Sociological Methods and Research.* 1991.

American Marketing Association Definition of Marketing Research—www.marketingpower.com.

Andersen, R. Kasper, J., Frankel, M.R. "Total Survey Error," San Francisco Jossey-Bass. 1979.

Andrews, F.M., "Construct Validity and Error Components of Survey Measures: A Structural Modeling Approach. *Public Opinion Quarterly,*" 1984.

Artiola, I., Fortuny, L., Mullaney, H. "Neuropsychology with Spanish Speakers: Language Use and Proficiency Issues for Test Development," *Journal of Clinical and Experimental Neuropsychology.* 1997.

Ayidiya, S.A., McClendon, M.J., "Response Effects in Mail Surveys," *Public Opinion Quarterly.* 1990.

Ayres, Joe, "Are Reductions in CA an Experimental Artifact? A Solomon Four-Group Answer," *Communication Quarterly.* Winter 2000.

Backstrom, C.H., Hursh-Cesar, G. Survey Research. New York, Wiley Publications. 1981.

Becker, G., "Alternative Methods of Reporting Research Results", 1991. *American Psychologist.*

Belson, W., "The Design and Understanding of Survey Questions," London, Gower. 1981.

Benson, Barbara, "Market Researcher Wins Clients with Documentaries," *Crain's New York Busines*s, April 2001.

Berg, B.L. "Qualitative Research Methods for the Social Sciences," 1998. Boston, Allyn & Bacon.

Berry, J.W.; Poortinga, Ype, H.; Segall, Marshall H.; Dasen, Pierre R., Cross-Cultural Psychology, Research and Applications," Cambridge University Press. 2004.

Berry, J.W., Handbook on Cross Cultural Psychology. Boston, Allyn & Bacon. 1997.

Blalock, H.M., Social Statistics, New York: McGraw-Hill. 1979.

Bowers, Diane, "New Requirement for Research: Privacy Assurance and Professional Accountability," *CASRO Journal.* 2002.

Bradburn, N.M. "Response Effects. The Handbook of Survey Research," Rossi, P.H., Wright, J.D. New York. Academic Press. 1983.

Breech, Poppy, "Research Proves the Obvious," *Marketing.* March 2001.

Brehm, J., "The Phantom Respondents—Opinion Surveys and Political Representation," Ann Arbor, University of Michigan Press. 1993.

Brick, J.M., Kalton, G. "Handling Missing Data in Survey Research," *Statistical Methods in Medial Research.* 1996.

Brislin, R.W., "Back Translation for Cross Cultural Research," *Journal of Cross-Cultural Research Psychology.* 1970.

Brislin, R.W., "Translation and Content Analysis or Oral and Written Material," Handbook of Cross-Cultural Psychology. Boston. Allyn and Bacon. 1980.

Brislin, R.W., "Translation Applications and Research," New York. Gardner. 1976.

BusinessWeek, "Satisfaction not Guaranteed," June 2006.

Byron, Ellen, "A Virtual View of the Store Aisle," *The Wall Street Journal*, October 3rd, 2007.

Callegaro, Mario, "Web Questionnaires: Tested Approaches from Knowledge Networks for the Online World," Spring 2008.

Campbell, D.R. & Stanley, J.C., "Experimental and Quasi-experimental Designs for Research," New York, Rand McNally, 1966.

Carmines, E.C., and Zeller, R.A., "Reliability and Validity Assessment on Qualitative Applications in the Social Sciences," Beverly Hills, CA, Sage Publications. 1979.

Catterall, Miriam, "Using Projective Techniques in Education Research," *British Educational Research Journal.* April 2000.

Clancy, Kevin J., "Brand Confusion," *Harvard Business Review.* March 2002.

Clark, H.H., Schober, M.F., "Asking Questions and Influencing Answers-Questions about Questions: Inquiries into Cognitive Bases of Surveys," Tanur, J., New York. Springer. 1992.

Cleary, T.A., Hilton, T.L., "An Investigation of Item Bias," *Educational and Psychological Measurement.* 1968.

Cohen, J. and Cohen, P, "Applied Multiple Regression-Analysis for the Behavioral Sciences," Hillsfale, NJ: Lawrence Erlbaum. 1983.

Couper, M.P. Groves, M.N., "The Roles of the Interviewer in Survey Participation," *Survey Methodology.* 1992.

Cowan, Charles D., "Using Multiple Sample Frames to Improve Survey Coverage, Quality, and Costs," *Marketing Research*, December 1991.

Czaja, Ron, "Designing Surveys; A Guide to Decisions and Procedures," Thousand Oaks, CA. Sage Publications. 2004.

Darlington, R.B., "Regression and Linear Models," McGraw-Hill. 1990.

De Heer, W. "Survey Practices in European Countries. Measuring Adult Literacy," London: Office of National Statistics. 2000.

De Leeuw, E.D., "Reducing Missing Data in Surveys: An Overview of Methods," Quality & Quality. 2001.

De Leeuw, E.D., Collins, M. "Data Collection and Survey Quality. Survey Measurement and Process Quality," New York. Wiley. 1997.

Einot, I., & Gabriel, K.R., "A Study of the Powers of Several Methods of Multiple Comparisons," *Journal of American Statistical Association.* 1975.

Emerson, J. and Strenio, J., "Boxplots and Batch Comparisons," D. Hoaglin, F. Mosteller, and J. Tukey. Understanding Robust and Exploratory Data Analysis. New York. John Wiley Publishing. 1983.

Farris, Paul W., "Overcontrol in Advertising Experiments," *Journal of Advertising Research.* December 2000.

Fielding, "Resorts—Email Alerts Revive Flat Business on Slopes," *Marketing News*, 3/1/2005.

Fisher, R.A. "Statistical Methods for Research Workers," Edinburgh: Oliver and Boyd. 1925.

Fisher, R.A. "Statistics Methods for Research Workers," Edinburgh—Oliver and Boyd. 1925.

Frazer, L., Meredith, L., "Questionnaire Design & Administration," Brisbane, Australia. Wiley. 2000.

Frick, R.W., "The Appropriate use of Null Hypothesis Testing," *Psychological Methods,* 1996.

Garg, Rajendar, K., "The Influence of Positive and Negative Wording and Issues Involvement on Response to Likert Scales in Marketing Research," *Journal of Marketing Research Society,* 38. 1996.

Geertz, Clifford, "Interpretation of Cultures." New York Basic Books. 2000.

Gigerenzer, G. A., Handbook for Data Analysis in the Behavioral Sciences— Methodological Issues. Hillsdale, NJ. Lawrence Erlbaum. 1993.

Gillin, Donna, and Sheppard, Jane, "The Fallacy of Getting Paid for Your Opinions," *Marketing Research*, fall 2003.

Gnanedesdesikan, R., "Methods for Statistical Analysis of Multivariate Observations," New York—Wiley. 1977.

Godfrey, K., "Comparing the Means of Several Groups," *The New England Journal of Medicine.* 1985.

Goldman, Alfred E. and Schwrtz McDonald, Susan, "The Group Depth Interview: Principles and Practice. Englewood Cliffs," NJ: Prentice Hall Publishers. 1987.

Goldsmith, Ronald, E., "The Focus Group Research Handbook," *The Services Industries Journal.* July 2000.

Haaijer, Rinus, "Response Latencies in the Analysis of Conjoint Choice Experiments," *Journal of Marketing Research*. August 2000.

Hair, Joseph; Wolfinbarger, Mary; Ortinau, David; Bush, Robert, Essentials of Marketing Research, Mcgraw Hill. 2010.

Halme, Merja, "Dealing with Interval Scale Data in Data Development Analysis," *European Journal of Operational Research*. February 16, 2002.

Harris, R.J., "Significance Tests Have Their Place," *Psychological Science*. 1997.

Have, Paul, "Understanding Qualitative Research and Ethnomethodology," Thousand Oaks, CA: Sage Publications. 2004.

Hays, W., Statistics. New York: Holt, Rinehart & Winston. 1993.

Heist, Gregory S., "Beyond Brand Building," *Quirk's Marketing Research Review*, August 2007.

Henderson, Naomi, "Art and Science of Effective In-Depth Qualitative Interviews," *Quirk's Marketing Research Review*, December 1998.

Herrmann, D.J. Raybeck, D. "Similarities and Differences in Meaning in Six Cultures," *Journal of Cross-Cultural Psychology*. 1981.

Hess, Jennifer, "The Effects of Person-Level Versus Household-Level Questionnaire Design on Survey Estimates and Data Quality," *Public Opinion Quarterly*. Winter 2001.

Hutton, Tara, "My Cell Phone, My Life," *Quirk's Marketing Research Review*.

Jeffreys, H., "Random and Systematic Arrangements," *Biometrika*. 1939.

Jowell, R., "How Comparative is Comparative Research?" *American Behavioral Scientist*. 1988.

Kalehoff, M., "A Note About Tracking Cookies"—mediapost.com. 2009.

Kanji, G.K., "100 Statistical Tests," Newbury Park, CA. Sage Publications. 1993.

Katona, Zsolt; Pal Zubcsek, Peter; and Sarvary, "Network Effects and Personal Influences: The Difference of an Online Social Network," *The Journal of Marketing Research*, June 2011.

Keillor, B., Owens, D., Pettijohn., C. "A Cross-Cultural Cross-National Study of Influencing Factors and Socially Desirable Response Biases," *International Journal of Market* Research. 2001.

Kendall, M.G., "Rank Correlation Methods," London: Griffin. 1962.

Keppel, G. Design and analysis: "A Researcher's Handbook," Englewood Cliffs, NJ, Prentice Hall. 1991.

Kish, L., "Survey Sampling, "New York, John Wiley Publishing. 1995.

Kozinets, Robert V., "The Field Behind the Screen: Using Netnography for Marketing Research in Online Communities." *Journal of Marketing Research*, 39. 2002

Kurpius, Sharon, E., "Testing and Measurement," Thousand Oaks. Sage Publications. 2002.

Laurent, Gilles, "Improving the External Validity of Marketing Models: A Plea for More Qualitative Input," *International Journal of Research Marketing*. September 2000.

Lee, Eunkyu, Lee, "Are Consumer Survey Results Distorted? Systematic Impact of Behavioral Frequency and Duration on Survey Response Errors," *Journal of Marketing Research*. February 2000.

Linnett, Richard, "Reebok Re-Brands for Hip-Hop Crowd," *Advertising Age*. January 2002.

Little, R.J.A. & Rubin, D.B., "Statistical Analysis with Missing Data," New York, John Wiley Publishing, 1987.

McDaniel, Carl and Gates, Roger, Marketing Research Essentials, John Wiley Publishing. 2010.

MacDougall, Colin, "Planning and Recruiting the Sample for Focus Groups and In-Depth Interviews," *Qualitative Health Research*. January 2001.

Malhotra, Naresh K., Marketing Research, An Applied Orientation, Pearson Prentice Hall Press, Upper Saddle River, NJ. 2007.

Malhotra, Naresh K., Exploitation to Engagement: The Role of Marketing Research in Getting Close to Niche Markets," *International Journal of Market Research*. 2003.

Malhotra, Naresh K., McCort, Daniel, "A Cross-Cultural Comparison of Behavior Intent Models: Theoretical Consideration and Empirical Investigation," International Marketing Review. 2001.

Malhotra, Naresh, K.; Kim, Sung; Agarwal, James, "Internet Users' Information Privacy Concerns (IUIPC): The Construct, the Scale, and a Causal Model," *Information Systems Research*, December 2004.

Maxwell, S., Delaney, H., & Dill, C., "Another Look at ANOVA Versus Blocking," *Psychological Bulletin*, 95. 1994.

Miles, Matthew B., and Huberman, Michael A., Qualitative Data Analysis: An Expanded Source Book," Thousand Oaks, CA. Sage Publications. 1994.

Moe, Wendy W. and Trusov, Michael, "The Value of Social Dynamics in Online Product Ratings Forums," *The Journal of Marketing Research*, June 2011.

Mostellar, F. and Tukey, J.W., "Data Analysis and Regression," Reading, MA: Addison-Wesley. 1977.

Neal, William, "Getting Serious about Marketing Research," *Marketing Research,* 2002.

Newton, Rae. R and Rudestam, Kjell Erik, Your Statistical Consultant, Sage Publications. 1999.

Nielsen Online, Buzzmetrics: "The Global Measurement Standard in Consumer Related Media." 2008.

Online Focus Groups, Video Diary Qualitative Research Software, www.qualvu.com/video. 2009.

Ozer, D.J. "Correlation and the Coefficient of Determination," *Psychological Bulletin*, 97. 1985.

Payne, S.L., "The Art of Asking Questions," *Princeton University Press*, 1951.

Peter, Paul J., Olson, Jerry C., Consumer Behavior, Ninth Edition, McGraw-Hill. 2010.

Perner, Lars, "Language Mapping", The University of Southern California.

Pigott, T.D., "Methods for Handling Missing Data in Research Synthesis," E.H. Cooper and L.V. Hedges. *The Handbook of Research Synthesis*. New York: Russell Sage Foundation. 1994.

Practical Sampling, Gary T. Henry. Sage Publications, 1990.

Rapaille, Clotaire, The Culture Code: An Ingenious Way to Understand Why People Around the World Buy and Live as They Do. New York—Broadway Books. 2006.

Raymond, Joan, "Home Field Advantage," *American Demographics*, April 2001.

Richardson, Steven, "Respondents Lie and Good Ideas Die," *Quirk's Marketing Research Review*, May 2007.

Robinson, William, T., "Is the First to Market the First to Fail?" *Journal of Marketing Research.* February 2002.

Rook, Dennis, W., "The Ritual Dimension of Consumer Behavior," *Journal of Consumer Research.* 1985.

Rosenthal, R. & Rosnow, R.L., "Essentials of Behavioral Research: Methods and Data Analysis," New York, Mcgraw Hill. 1991.

Ruggless, Ron, "Boston Market Rolls Out Latest Fast Casual Rotisserie Grill Unit," *Nation's Restaurant News.* December 2003.

Rydholm, Joseph, "What do Clients Want from a Research Firm?" *Marketing Research Review.* October 1995.

Sayre, Shay, "Qualitative Methods for Marketplace Research," Thousand Oaks, CA. Sage Publications. 2001.

Schindler, Robert M., "The Real Lesson on New Coke: The Value of Focus Groups for Predicting the Effects of Social Influence." *Marketing Research: A Magazine of Management & Applications.* 1992.

Schmidt, F.L., "What do Data Really Mean? Research Findings, Meta-Analysis, and Cumulative Knowledge in Psychology," *American Psychologist.* 1992.

Schneider, K.C., "Uniformed Response Rate in Survey Research," *Journal of Marketing Research*, 12. 1985.

Serlin, R.C., "Confidence Intervals and the Scientific Method. A Case for Holm on the Range," *Journal of Experimental Education,* 61. 1993.

Shaver, J., "What Statistical Significance Testing is, and What it is Not," *Journal of Experimental Education,* 61. 1993.

Silk, Alvin J., What is Marketing?, *Harvard Business School Press,* 2006.

Sirdeshmukh, Deepak, "Consumer Trust, Value, and Loyalty in Relational Exchanges," *Journal of Marketing.* January 2002.

Sonnier, Garrett and Ainslie, Andrew, "Estimating the Value of Brand Image Associations: The Role of General and Specific Brand Image," *The Journal of Marketing Research,* June 2011.

Spiggle, Susan, "Analysis and Interpretation of Qualitative Data in Consumer Research," *Journal of Consumer Research,* 21. 1994.

Statistics in Small Doses, Winifred Mary Castle. University of Rhodesia, Longman Group Limited, 1984.

Stenbecka, Caroline, "Qualitative Research Requires Quality Concepts of its Own," *Management Decision,* 39. 2001.

Stevens, Berni, "Best Practices for Online Qualitative Research," *Quirk's Marketing Research Review,* August 2007.

Stewart, Allyson, "Do Your International Homework First," *Marketing News.* January, 1999.

Strauss, Anselm and Corbin, Juliet, "Basics of Qualitative Research—Grounded Theory Procedures and Techniques," Beverly Hills, CA, Sage Publications. 1990.

Tatsuoka, M.M., "Significance Tests," Champaign, IL Institute for Personality and Ability Testing. 1971.

The Greenbook International Directory of Marketing Research Companies and Services—www.greenbook.org.

The Marketing Research Toolbox, Edward F. McQuarriw. Santa Clara University, Sage Publications, 2006.

Thompson, B., "The Use of Statistical Significance Tests in Research: Bootstrap and Other Alternatives," *Journal of Experimental Education.* 1993.

Tukey, J.W., "Exploratory Data Analysis," MA: Addison-Wesley. 1977.

USA Today, "Customers Ditching Landline Phones," May 14th 2008.

Vinarsky, Cynthia, "Test Market for Smokeless Tobacco," *Knight Ridder Tribune Business News.* March 11, 2002.

Wade, Kenneth, R., "Focus Groups' Research Role is Shifting," *Marketing News.* March 2002.

Wainer, H., "How to Display Data Badly," *The American Statistician.* 1984.

Warschawski, David, "Effective Branding Means Sensitivity to Consumer Feelings and Experience," *Boston Business Journal.* July 2004.

Wells, William and Lo Scruto, Leonard, "Direct Observation of Purchasing Behavior," *Journal of Marketing Research*, August 2007.

Wells, William D., "Recognition, Recall, and Rating Scales," *Journal of Advertising Research.* December 2000.

Welty, Ron, "21st Century Mystery Shopping," *Quirk's Marketing Research Review*, January 2005.

Wilcox, Steve, "Sampling and Controlling a TV Audience Measurement Panel," *The Journal of Marketing Research.* January 2000.

Winer, B.J. "Statistical Principles in Experimental Design," New York: McGraw-Hill. 1971.

Woodside, Arch G., and Wilson, Elizabeth J., "Case Study Research Methods for Theory Building," *Journal of Business and Industrial Marketing*, 18. 2003.

Wright, Kevin B., "Research Internet-Based Populations: Advantages and Disadvantages of Online Survey Research," *Journal of Computer-Mediated Communication*, 10, April 2009.

Wright, R.L. Understanding Statistics: "An Informal Introduction for the Behavioral Sciences," New York, Harcourt, Brace, and Jovanovich. 1976.

Zaltman, Gerald, "How Customers Think: Essential Insights into the Mind of the Market, Boston, Harvard Business School. 2003.

www.esomar.org.

www.gallup.com.

www.marketingresearch.org.

www.nielsen.com.

INDEX